QUANT DEVELOPERS' TOOLS AND TECHNIQUES

Manfred Hindering

Jul 02, 2024

CONTENTS

Introduction

As a quant developer in the past, it was quite challenging to acquire suitable datasets for any meaningful quantitative analysis. As technological innovations such as decentralized trading platforms are emerging, more programming-savvy traders enter the scene and actively attempt to conquer and master this innovative field. This is particularly true for the crypto markets, where the trading platforms are built with the programmer in mind, therefore it has never been easier to retrieve market data and process it in an automated fashion.

As a programmer, times have never been better to make a living by trading and coding - either individually or for trading firms around the world. Technological advances in computing equipment, programming and analytical tools allow the keen programmer to "make a killing" while doing something you enjoy doing.

The crypto market, for example, represents an asset class much like the forex market. However, it is still young and presents its fair share of inefficiencies and idiosyncrasies, which translate into opportunities for the astute quant developer to exploit.

This volume introduces the tools and techniques for the programming-oriented developer to take advantage of such opportunities in an automated fashion. The bad news is, to succeed in this ever-evolving and challenging field, you will have to know a lot of mathematics, statistics, coding, financial & market theory, and so on.

About the Series

This series is intended for finance professionals, such as risk controllers, equity analysts, quantitative developers, data scientists, and everybody interested in trading and winning in the financial markets.

If you plan to become a quant developer, this volume is the prelude to a comprehensive series, presenting and demonstrating the tools and techniques required to succeed in this new data-driven world, such as:

Volume 1: Statistics, Visualization, Simple- & Multiple Linear Regression

> *...build up the basis for a solid understanding of the first parts of the QUANT body of knowledge, in a learning-by-example fashion.*

Volume 2: Multiple- & Logistic Regression, Bayes' Theorem & Forecasting, Ratios & Risk Measures & Monte Carlo Simulation, and Technical Analysis

> *...build up the basis for a solid understanding of the covered parts of the QUANT body of knowledge, in a learning-by-example fashion*

Volume 3: SQLite Database Programming, Pandas DataFrames, Time Series Analysis, and Autoregression Models

> *...further broadens your understanding of the tools and techniques required to succeed in the QUANT profession, again in a learning-by-example format.*

Volume 4: Data Management, Clustering & Forecasting Techniques, Stochastic Programming, Microstructure Analysis, Trading Strategy Development, Neural Network- & Machine Learning Techniques

> *...set up the foundation for a very lucrative career in quant development. As learning-by-example is the most effective way to learn and master this complex material essential for the QUANT profession, which is the most lucrative although challenging profession, i know of. To become a QUANT pro, certainly requires an in-depth mastery of the QUANT body of knowledge, to excel in this ever evolving and challenging profession.*

About the Author

Manfred holds a Bachelor of Arts in Software Engineering and a Bachelor of Arts in Business Administration.

As a corporate controller, he helped build a business intelligence solution for a large Silicon Valley corporation, involving financial modeling, forecasting, budgeting, and ad-hoc analytics. While working as a software developer he developed an industrial-strength ERP/MIS solution, thereby establishing a solid foundation in coding and software engineering principles.

He has 15+ years of consulting experience in the financial and trading industry, doing financial modeling, and quantitative analytics for firms at home and abroad, as well as trading system development for a mid-sized high-frequency trading firm; building quant tools in C#, C++, PHP, Python. Additionally, he created an equity analytics toolbox consisting of 50+ tools supporting equity analysts.

Sincerely Yours,
Manfred Hindering

Copyright

ISBN: 979-8-22425-053-0
qbooks Publishing

Cover by Jansen Design · Painting by Grimaldi

Installing Python

A brief overview of how to get started in setting up a suitable Python development environment for the presented examples to work properly.

The Python software can be obtained from here.
https://www.python.org/

The preferred Visual Studio Code Editor can be obtained from here.
https://code.visualstudio.com/

The PyCharm IDE provides a popular alternative and can be obtained from here.
https://www.jetbrains.com/pycharm/download/

All software examples are built with the 3.9.13 release of the Python installation. To confirm the installed Python version by issuing this command in the terminal-$ window:

```
python --version
```

Creating a virtual environment

It is highly recommended to set up a virtual environment and install the required packages there. To set up such a virtual environment, type in the terminal-$ window:

```
python -m venv venv
```

Installing Packages

The pip or pip3 package manager is used to manage and install the required packages. Check the version of the package manager, by issuing this command to the terminal-$ window.

```
pip --version
```

Issue the following commands in the terminal-$ window to install the packages.

```
pip install scipy==1.7.3
pip install scikit-learn==1.1.3
pip install pandas==1.5.2
pip install matplotlib==3.6.2
pip install statsmodels==0.13.2
pip install seaborn==0.11.2
pip install mplfinance==0.12.9b5
```

```
pip install yfinance==0.1.87
pip install pandas_datareader==0.10.0
pip install pymannkendall==1.4.2
pip install faker==4.1.1
pip install ipykernel==6.21.3
pip install openpyxl==3.1.2
```

Any dependent packages will also be installed.

A comprehensive list of all installed packages can be obtained by issuing this command to the terminal-$ window.

```
pip list
```

Caveat Emptor

All examples are intended for demonstration and education purposes only, as they do not constitute any consulting or investment advice.

The software code segments are provided as is, with no guarantee or warranty attached, as they are intended for your inspiration, and to build upon while developing your systems.

Part I

Statistics

CHAPTER 1

STANDARD NORMAL DISTRIBUTION

The standard normal distribution is one of the most famous statistical distributions. It was discovered by Carl Friedrich Gauss and is therefore often called Gaussian normal distribution or bell-shaped curve.

The Gaussian normal distribution is a continuous probability distribution and is frequently used in the statistics and data science disciplines to represent real random variables whose distributions are unknown.

1.1 Probability density function PDF

The probability density function (PDF) of the normal distribution is defined as:

$$f(x) = \frac{1}{\sigma\sqrt{2\pi}}e^{-\frac{1}{2}\left(\frac{x-\mu}{\sigma}\right)^2}$$

The random variable X described by the probability density function is a variable that follows a normal distribution with mean μ of 0 and a variance σ^2 of 1.

Normal distribution notation is:

$$X = \mathcal{N}(\mu, \sigma^2)$$

The area under the curve equals 1, which is represented by the following integral.

$$\int_{-\infty}^{+\infty} f(x) \cdot dx = 1$$

The pdf(x) function returns the probability density value for a given x. For example, we compute the probability of a value x smaller than

- $P(x < 1)$
- $P(x < 2)$

The probability of a value falling within the interval of $[1, 2]$ is given like this.

- $P(1 \leq x < 2)$

In the following Python code segment, we implement this concept:

```
from scipy.stats import norm

# cumulative density function
a = norm.cdf(x=1, loc=0, scale=1)
b = norm.cdf(x=2, loc=0, scale=1)
# inspect
print(f"P(x < 1)       = {a:.6f}")
print(f"P(x < 2)       = {b:.6f}")
print(f"P(1 < x < 2) = {b-a:.6f}")
```

```
P(x < 1)     = 0.841345
P(x < 2)     = 0.977250
P(1 < x < 2) = 0.135905
```

A graphical representation of the probability density function pdf() can be seen in the following diagram. Additionally, as described in Scipy [2023], we compute the integral $[1, 2]$ of the probability density function pdf(), and report the result.

```
area = integrate.quad(distribution_function, x1,x2)[0]
print(f'P({x1} < x < {x2}) = {area:.5f}')
```

In the following Python code section, we implement this approach.

```
import numpy as np
import matplotlib.pyplot as plt
from scipy.stats import norm
import scipy.integrate as integrate

# callback function
callback_function = lambda x: norm.pdf(x, loc=0, scale=1) # pdf()
# interval
x1 = 1
x2 = 2
# density function
step = 0.01
x = np.arange(-4, 4, step)
y = norm.pdf(x, loc=0, scale=1)
```

(continues on next page)

(continued from previous page)

```
# blue area
x_interval = np.arange(x1, x2, step)
y_interval = norm.pdf(x_interval, loc=0, scale=1)
# plot
fig = plt.figure(figsize=(6,3))
plt.plot(x, y)
plt.grid()
plt.title('Probability Density Function')
plt.fill_between(x_interval, y_interval, alpha=0.25)
plt.xlabel('x')
plt.ylabel('pdf(x)')
plt.show()
# inspect
area = integrate.quad(callback_function, x1, x2)[0]
print(f'P({x1} < x < {x2}) = {area:.5f}')
```

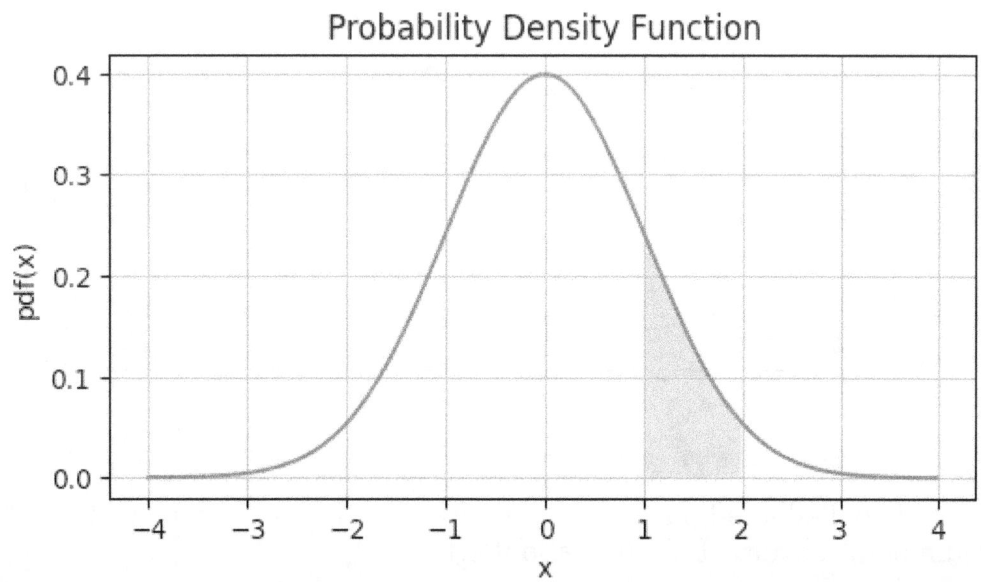


```
P(1 < x < 2) = 0.13591
```

Since the `norm.pdf()` function returns a probability density function (PDF), it can be used in conjunction with libraries such as SciPy, NumPy and `matplotlib`, to plot the PDF of the normal distribution. We use the domain: $[-4 < x \leq 4]$ and values of $\mu = 0$ and $\sigma = 1$. The plot function becomes:

```
plot(x-values, y-values)
```

and produces the following graph.

```
import numpy as np
```

(continues on next page)

(continued from previous page)

```
import matplotlib.pyplot as plt

x = np.arange(-4, 4, 0.001)
# plot
fig, ax = plt.subplots(figsize=(6,3))
ax.plot(x, norm.pdf(x)) # pdf
ax.grid(True)
ax.set_title('Probability Density Function')
ax.set_xlabel('x')
ax.set_ylabel('pdf(x)')
plt.show()
```

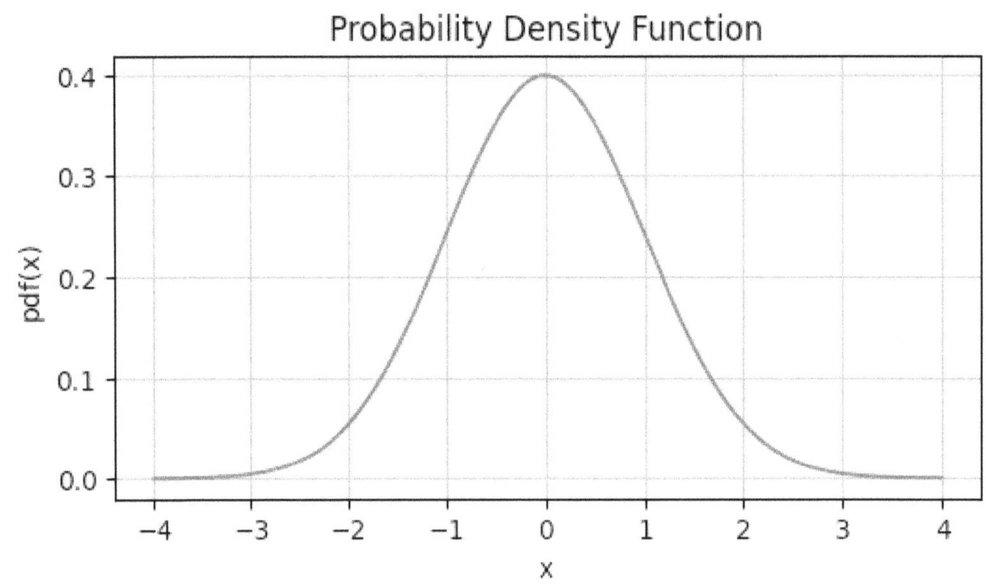

The curve is bell-shaped, and it is symmetrical around the x-axis at $\mu = 0$. Its maximum point occurs at $\mu = 0$ at about 0.4.

1.1.1 Plot density function with different standard deviations

We plot the probability density function of the standard normal distribution where the mean μ stays constant, and we apply different standard deviations like σ_1, σ_2, σ_3, σ_4.

The probability density function `norm.pdf()` method has keywords for the location `loc` which specifies the mean and the `scale` keyword which specifies the standard deviation. In Python, we implement this idea, like so:

```
import numpy as np
import matplotlib.pyplot as plt
```

(continues on next page)

(continued from previous page)

```
# plot
fig, ax = plt.subplots(figsize=(6,3))
x = np.linspace(-10,10,100)
std_list = [1.0, 2.0, 3.0, 6.0]
colors = ['red', 'green', 'maroon', 'black']
linestyles = ['dashed','solid','solid','dotted']
for i, std in enumerate(std_list):
    ax.plot(x, norm.pdf(x, scale=std),
            label=f'$\\sigma_1={std:.1f}$')
    ax.get_lines()[i].set_color(colors[i])
    ax.get_lines()[i].set_linestyle(linestyles[i])
ax.set_xlabel('x')
ax.set_ylabel('pdf(x)')
txt = "Normal distribution, variable $\\sigma_i$"
ax.set_title(txt)
ax.legend(loc='best', frameon=True)
ax.set_ylim(0,0.45)
ax.grid(True)
plt.show()
```

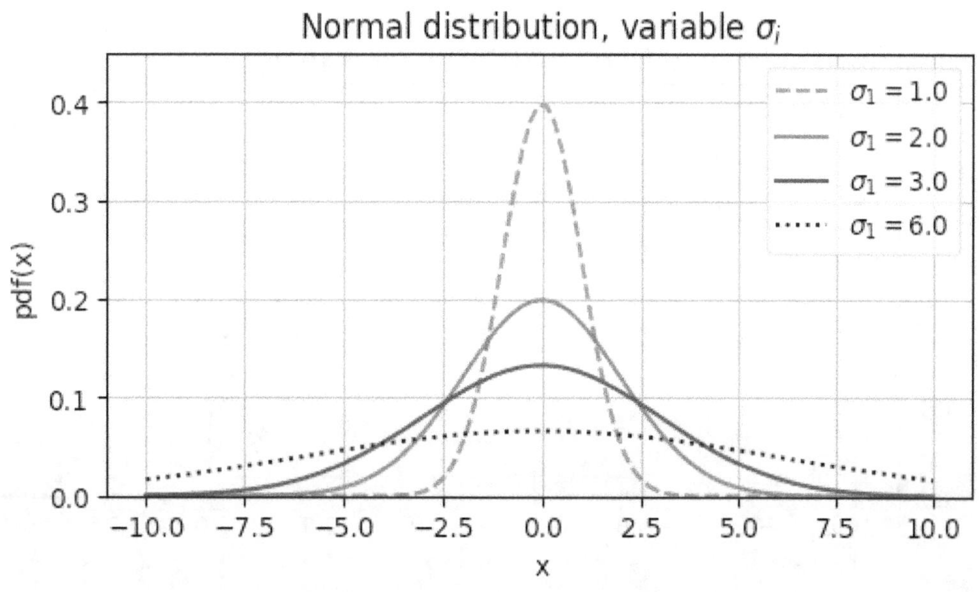

1.1.2 Plot density function with different means

We plot the probability density functions of the normal distribution where the standard deviation $\sigma = 1$ remains constant, and we vary the mean. Let $\mu_1 = -4$, $\mu_2 = -1.5$, $\mu_3 = 0$, and $\mu_4 = 6$. In Python, we write:

```
import numpy as np
import matplotlib.pyplot as plt
```

(continues on next page)

(continued from previous page)

```
# plot
fig, ax = plt.subplots(figsize=(7,3))
x = np.linspace(-10,10,100)
mean_list = [-4.0, -1.5, 0.0, 6.0]
colors = ['red', 'green', 'maroon', 'black']
linestyles = ['dashed','solid','solid','dotted']
for i,mean in enumerate(mean_list):
    ax.plot(x, norm.pdf(x,loc=mean),
            color=colors[i],
            label=f'$\\mu_{i+1}={mean:.1f}$')
    ax.get_lines()[i].set_linestyle(linestyles[i])
ax.set_xlabel('x')
ax.set_ylabel('pdf(x)')
txt = 'Normal distribution, variable $\\mu_i$'
ax.set_title(txt)
ax.legend(loc='best', frameon=True)
ax.set_ylim(0,0.45)
ax.grid(True)
plt.show()
```

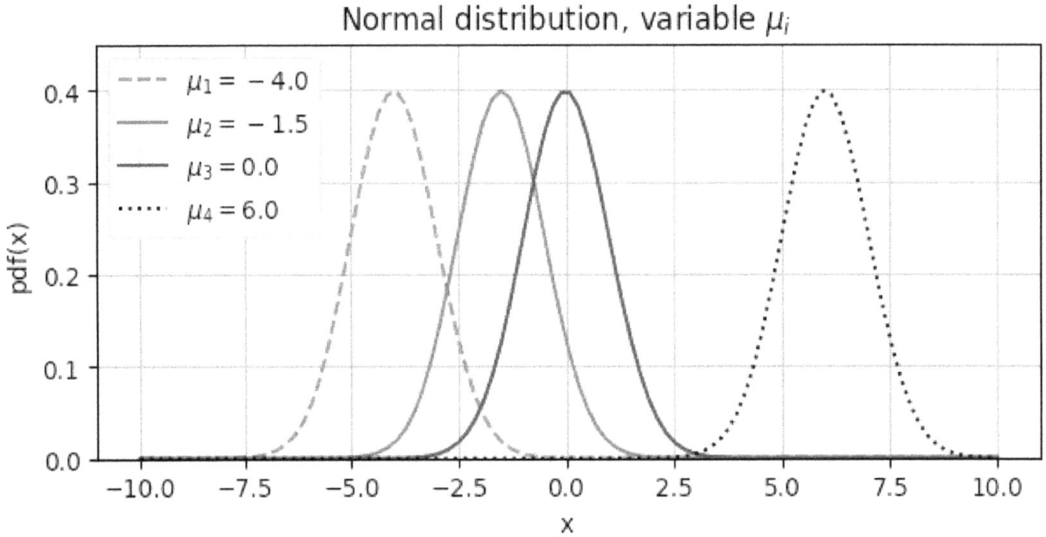

The mean of the distribution determines the location of the center of the graph.

Please observe the above graph, the shape does not change by changing the mean value μ, however, the graph is translated horizontally with changing mean values μ.

1.1.3 Random numbers drawn from the standard normal distribution

We make use of the `norm.rvs()` function to generate normally distributed random numbers. The functions signatures are:

```
xs = norm.rvs(scale=2, loc=0, size=15000)
```

where the:

- `scale`: the standard deviation
- `loc`: the mean
- `size`: the number of data points to produce

Then we create a histogram of the numbers and superimpose the probability density function onto it. In the following code section, we implement this idea.

```
import numpy as np
import matplotlib.pyplot as plt
from math import sqrt

# plot
fig, ax = plt.subplots(figsize=(6,3))
# x axis
x = np.linspace(-8,8,100)
# random normal values
xs = norm.rvs(scale=2, loc=0,
              size=150000,
              random_state=1)
m = np.mean(xs)
v = sqrt(np.var(xs))
# probability density function
p = norm.pdf(x,
            scale=2)
ax.plot(x, p, c='r',
        label='normal distribution',
        linewidth=5,
        linestyle=':')
# histogram
ax.hist(xs, bins=90, alpha=0.8,
        density=True,
        label='histogram')
ax.set_xlabel('x')
ax.set_ylabel('pdf(x)')
ax.set_title(f'Normal Distribution $\\mu={m:.0f}$, $\\sigma={v:.0f}$')
ax.grid(True)
leg = plt.legend()
plt.show()
```

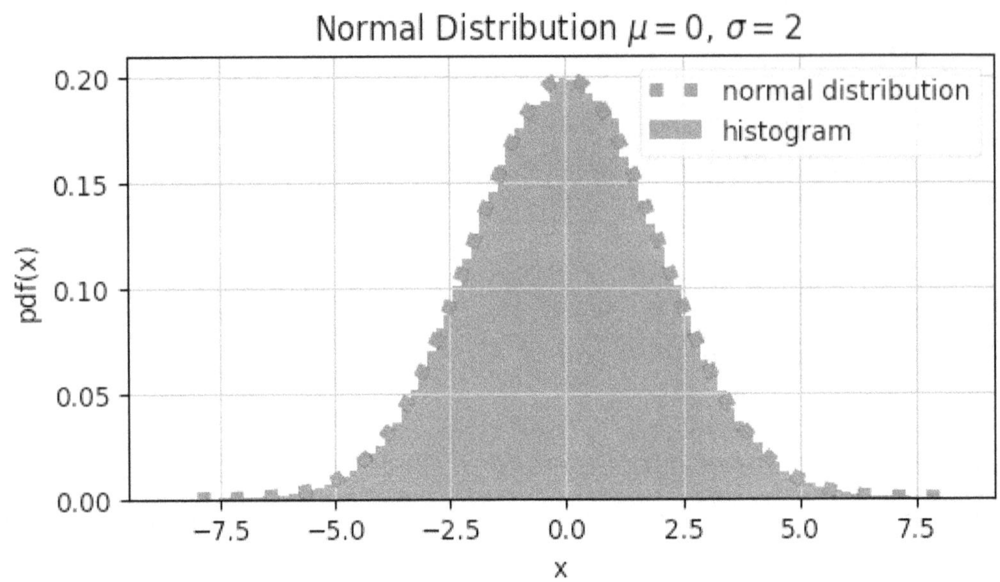

1.2 Cumulative density function CDF

The cumulative density function of a random variable X, evaluated at x, is the probability that X will take a value less than or equal to x denoted as $P(X \leq x)$. Since the normal distribution is continuous, the shaded area of the curve represents the probability that X is less or equal to x.

Integrating the probability density function:

$$P(X \leq x) = F(x) = \int_{-\infty}^{x} f(t)dt$$

with $x \in \mathbf{R}$

We make use of the `fill_between()` method, which has the following signature:

```
ax.fill_between(px, norm.pdf(px),
                alpha=0.5, color='r')
```

It shades the area between the two specified curves.

```
import numpy as np
import matplotlib.pyplot as plt

# plot
fig, ax = plt.subplots(figsize=(5,3))
# probability density function
```

(continues on next page)

(continued from previous page)

```
x= np.arange(-4,4,0.001)
ax.plot(x, norm.pdf(x))
ax.set_title('Probability Density Function')
ax.set_xlabel('x')
ax.set_ylabel('pdf(x)')
ax.grid(True)
# fill_between
px = np.arange(-4, 1, 0.01)
py = norm.pdf(px)
ax.fill_between(px, py,
                alpha=0.15, color='r')
ax.set_ylim(0,0.5)
ax.text(-1, 0.1,"$P(x < 1)$", fontsize=10)
plt.show()
```

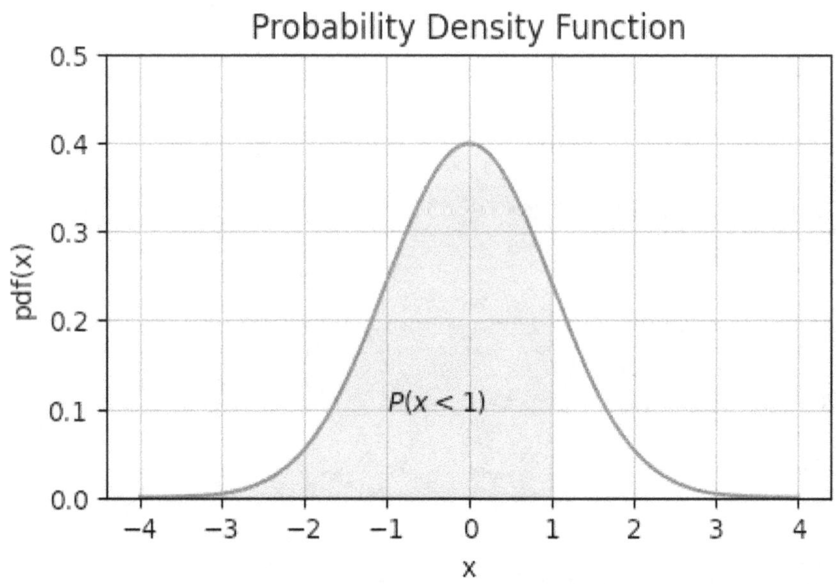

1.2.1 Calculate probabilities

Given the mean $\mu = 3$ and the standard deviation $\sigma = 2$, we can compute the probability of $P(X \leq 2)$ by applying the cumulative density function `cdf()`.

$$X = \mathcal{N}(3, 2^2)$$

In the `norm.cdf()` function, the location `loc` keyword specifies the mean and the `scale` keyword specifies the standard deviation. In Python, we implement this example:

```
from scipy.stats import norm

# compute cdf values
cdf_2 = norm.cdf(x=2, loc=3, scale=2)
print(f'P(x < 2) = {cdf_2:.5f}')
```

```
P(x < 2) = 0.30854
```

1.2.2 Visualize PDF and CDF

Now we plot the probability density function `pdf()`, and we shade the area for cdf($x \leq 2$), like so:

```
import numpy as np
import matplotlib.pyplot as plt

# prepare
cdf_2 = norm.cdf(x=2, loc=3, scale=2)
# plot
fig, ax = plt.subplots(1,2,figsize=(9,4))
x = np.arange(-4,10,0.001)
# probability density function
ax[0].plot(x, norm.pdf(x,
                       loc=3,
                       scale=2))
ax[0].set_title('Probability Density Function')
ax[0].set_xlabel('x')
ax[0].set_ylabel('pdf(x)')
ax[0].grid(True)
# fill_between
px = np.arange(-4,2,0.01)
py = norm.pdf(px, loc=3, scale=2)
ax[0].fill_between(px, py,
                   alpha=0.15, color='b')
ax[0].set_ylim(0,0.25)
ax[0].text(0.4,0.02, round(cdf_2,4), fontsize=1)
# cumulative density function
ax[1].plot(x, norm.cdf(x, loc=3, scale=2))
ax[1].set_title("Cumulative Density Function")
ax[1].set_xlabel('x')
ax[1].set_ylabel('cdf(x)')
ax[1].grid(True)
# cross hair
ax[1].axvline(2, color='r', linestyle=':', alpha=0.5)
r = norm.cdf(2, loc=3, scale=2)
ax[1].axhline(r, color='r', linestyle=':', alpha=0.5)
ax[1].text(-2,0.22, round(r,4), fontsize=10)
plt.show()
```

(continues on next page)

(continued from previous page)

```
# inspect
print(f'P(x < 2) = {r:.5f}')
```

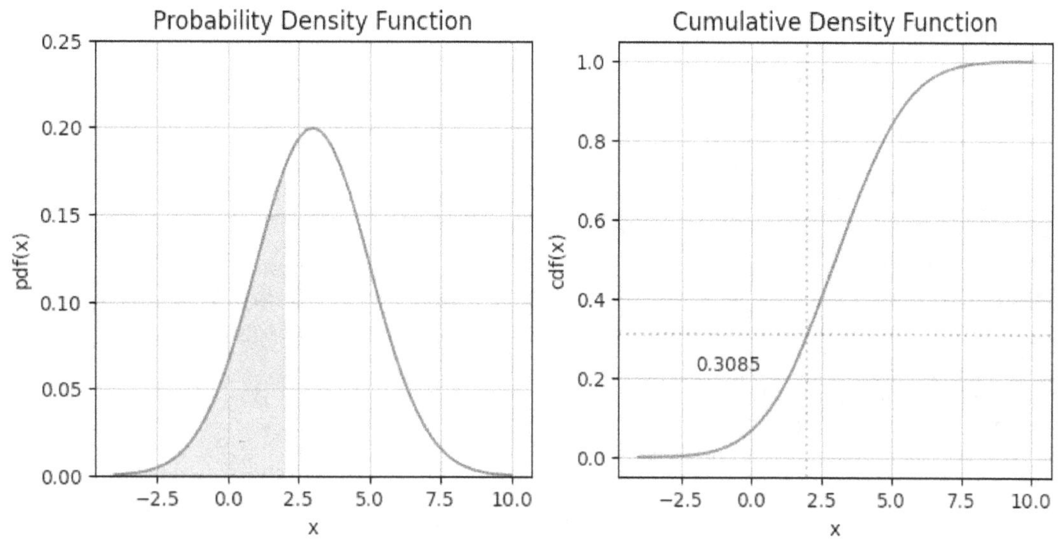


```
P(x < 2) = 0.30854
```

1.2.3 Compute the interval between values

Suppose we have a standard normal distribution with $\mu = 1$ and $\sigma = 2$, like so

$$X = \mathcal{N}(1, 2^2)$$

and to find the probability of the interval between values [a,b], we compute the `cdf(b)` and subtract the `cdf(a)` from it, to arrive at the difference. For example, to compute $P(0.5 < x \leq 2)$ with a mean of $\mu = 1$ and a standard deviation of $\sigma = 2$, we compute `cdf(2)` minus `cdf(0.5)`.

In the following Python code section, we implement this approach.

```
# cumulative density function
area = norm(3,2).cdf(2) - norm(3,2).cdf(0.5)
print(f'P(0.5 < X < 2 = {area:.5f}')
```

```
P(0.5 < X < 2 = 0.20289
```

And plot a graph to visualize the result.

$$X = \mathcal{N}(1, 2^2)$$

```
import numpy as np
import matplotlib.pyplot as plt

# x-axis
x = np.arange(-6,8,0.01)
# plot
fig, ax = plt.subplots(figsize=(6,3))
ax.plot(x,
        norm.pdf(x, loc=1, scale=2))
txt = 'Normal Distribution $\\mathcal{N}(1, 2^{2})$'
ax.set_title(txt)
ax.set_xlabel('x')
ax.set_ylabel('pdf(x)')
ax.grid(True)
# plot
px = np.arange(0.5,2,0.01)
ax.set_ylim(0,0.25)
ax.fill_between(px,
                norm.pdf(px, loc=1,
                             scale=2),
                             alpha=0.15,
                             color='b')
# difference between
pro = norm(1, 2).cdf(2) - norm(1,2).cdf(0.5)
ax.text(0.68, 0.02, '{:.5f}'.format(pro),
                                fontsize=10)
plt.show()
```

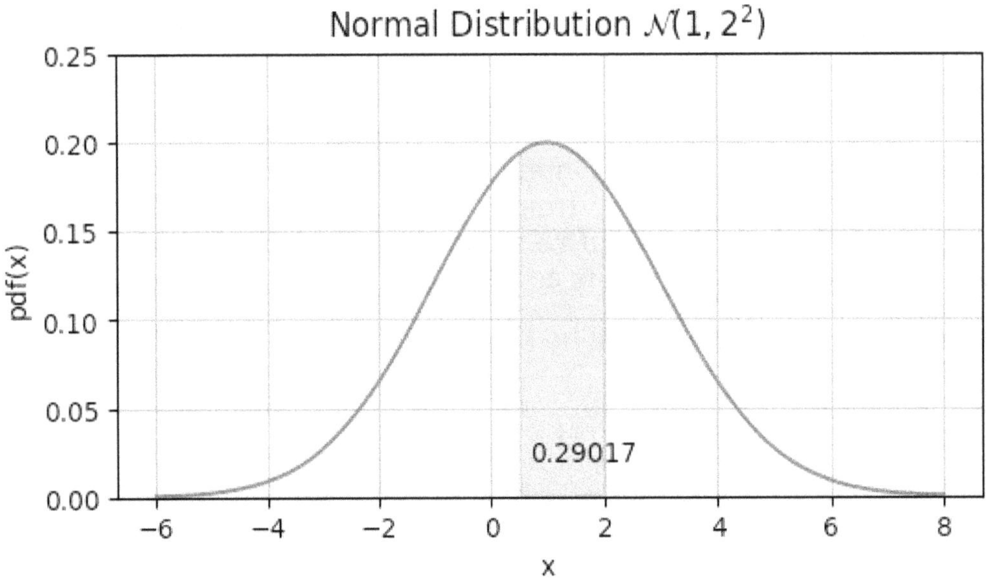

To find the probability of $P(X \geq 4)$, we can use survival function `sf()`, which returns a value of $1 - cdf$, and has the following signature:

```
norm.sf(x=4, loc=3, scale=2)
```

returns the probability for x being greater than 4, or $P(X \geq 4)$ where μ = 4, and σ = 2.

```
import numpy as np
import matplotlib.pyplot as plt
from scipy.stats import norm

x = np.arange(-6, 8, 0.01)
gr4sf = norm.sf(x=4, loc=3, scale=2)
print(f'P(X > 4) = {gr4sf:.5f}')
```

```
P(X > 4) = 0.30854
```

1.3 Survival function

We plot the survival function `sf()` along with the cumulative density function `cdf()` to enhance our understanding of this function. We observe that the survival function is the one complement to the cumulative density function, and both functions are inversely related to each other by:

$$sf = (1 - cdf)$$

In Python, we implement:

```
import matplotlib.pyplot as plt
from scipy.stats import norm

fig, ax = plt.subplots(figsize=(6,3.5))
x = np.arange(-4, 10, 0.01)
ax.plot(x, norm.sf(x, loc=3, scale=2))
ax.plot(x, norm.cdf(x, loc=3, scale=2))
ax.set_title('Survival- and Cumulative Density Function')
ax.set_xlabel('x')
ax.set_ylabel('probability')
ax.legend(('sf()','cdf()'))
ax.grid(True)
plt.show()
# inspect
print(f'sf(x < 4) = {norm.sf(x=4, loc=3, scale=2):.5f}')
print(f'1-cdf(x < 4) = {(1-norm.cdf(x=4, loc=3, scale=2)):.5f}')
```

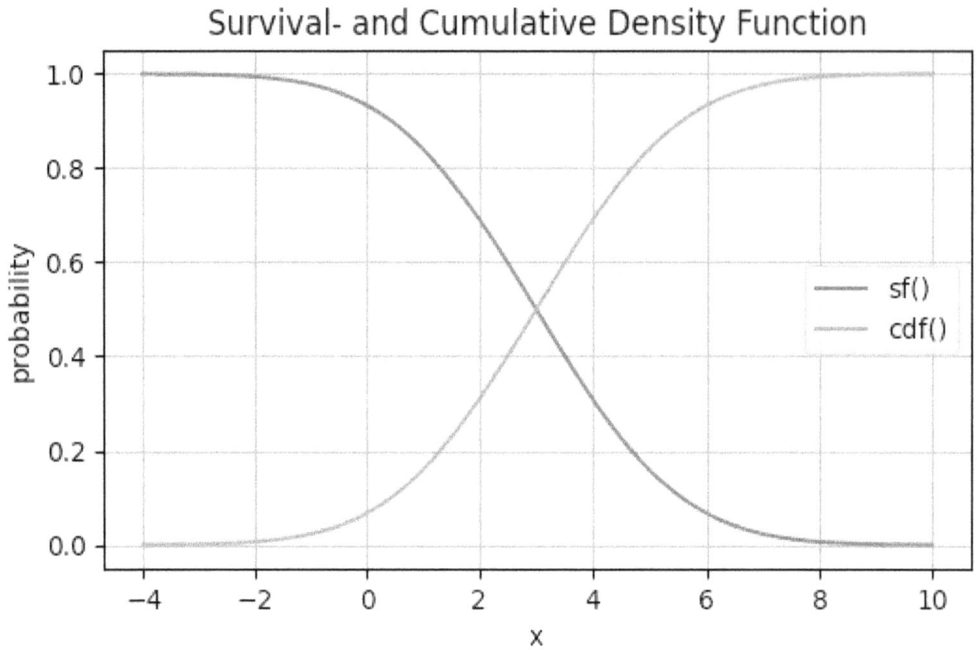


```
sf(x < 4) = 0.30854
1-cdf(x < 4) = 0.30854
```

In the following Python code segment, we plot the probability density function.

```
import numpy as np
import matplotlib.pyplot as plt
from scipy.stats import norm

# plot
fig, ax = plt.subplots(figsize=(6,3))
x = np.arange(-4,10,0.01)
ax.plot(x, norm.pdf(x, loc=3, scale=2))
txt = 'Probability Density Fkt. N(3,$2^2$)'
ax.set_title(txt)
ax.set_xlabel('x')
ax.set_ylabel('pdf(x)')
ax.grid(True)
ax.set_ylim(0,0.25)
# interval [-4 < x < 10]
x = np.arange(-4,10,0.01)
# sf(x < 4)
sf_4 = norm.sf(x=4, loc=3, scale=2)
cdf_4 = norm.cdf(x=4, loc=3, scale=2)
# fill between [ x > 4 ]
px = np.arange(4,10,0.01)
py = norm.pdf(px, loc=3, scale=2)
ax.fill_between(px, py,
                alpha=0.15, color='g')
```

(continues on next page)

(continued from previous page)

```
ax.text(4.5,0.02,"sf(x) %.4f" %(sf_4),
                                fontsize=10)
plt.show()
# inspect
print(f'sf(x < 4)      = {sf_4:.5f}')
print(f'1-cdf(x < 4) = {1-cdf_4:.5f}')
```

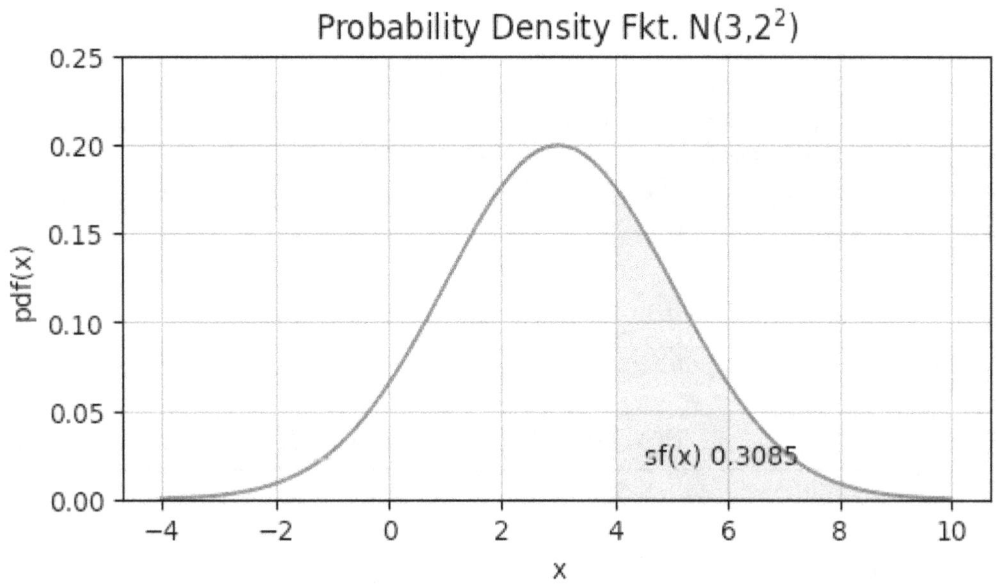


```
sf(x < 4)      = 0.30854
1-cdf(x < 4) = 0.30854
```

The above figure is the visual representation of the formula:

$$sf(x) = 1 - P(X \leq x)$$

In Python, we have:

```
import numpy as np
import matplotlib.pyplot as plt

# plot
fig, ax = plt.subplots(figsize=(6,3))
x = np.arange(-8, 10, 0.01)
ax.plot(x, norm.pdf(x, loc=2.5, scale=2))
txt = 'Probability Density Fkt. N(3,$2^2$)'
ax.set_title(txt)
ax.set_xlabel('x')
ax.set_ylabel('pdf(x)')
ax.grid(True)
ax.set_ylim(0,0.25)
```

(continues on next page)

(continued from previous page)

```
# fill between
x1 = np.arange(4, 10, 0.01)
ax.fill_between(x1,
            norm.pdf(x1,loc=2.5, scale=2),
                alpha=0.15, color='g')
# fill between
x2 = np.arange(-4, 4, 0.01)
ax.fill_between(x2,
            norm.pdf(x2,loc=2.5,scale=2),
                alpha=0.15, color='r')
# normal distribution
a1 = norm.cdf(x=4, loc=2.5, scale=2)
a2 = 1 - norm.cdf(x=4, loc=2.5, scale=2)
ax.text(4.5,0.02,round(a2,4), fontsize=10)
ax.text(1,0.02,round(a1,4), fontsize=10)
plt.show()
# inspect
print(f'P(x < 4)      = {a1:.5f}')
print(f'1 - P(x <4 ) = {a2:.5f}')
```

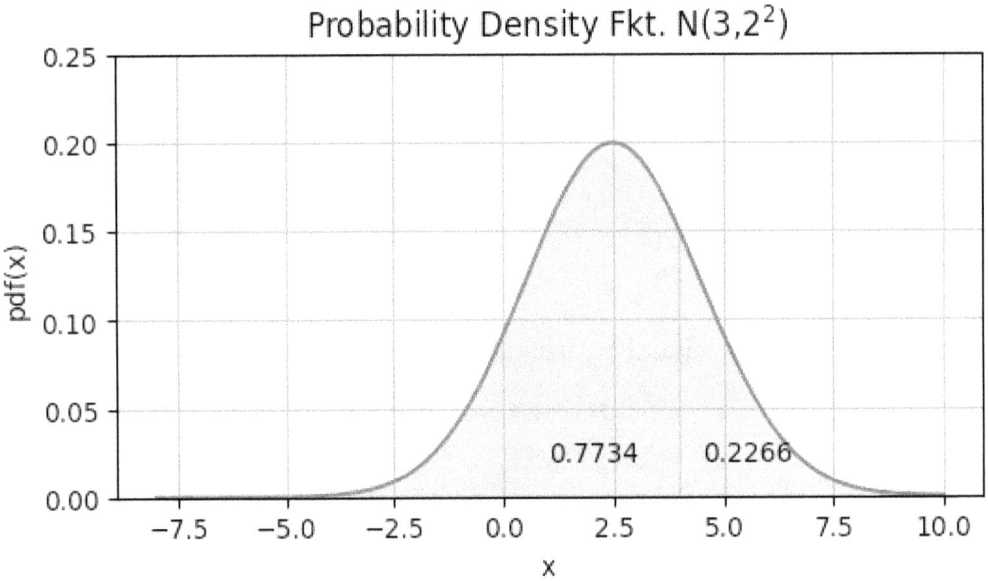


```
P(x < 4)      = 0.77337
1 - P(x <4 ) = 0.22663
```

1.4 Computing quantile

As given by Statista [2023], a quantile defines a cutoff point dividing the sorted dataset or probability distribution into continuous intervals of equal probability. Some quantiles even have specific names, such as:

- `quartile`: one quarter of the distribution
- `quintile`: one fifth of the distribution
- `percentile`: one hundreds of the distribution

To compute the quantile manually, we apply the following formula, which returns the cutoff point x_p within the dataset, associated with the desired quantile p. The x_p values are computed with the following formula:

$$x_p = \frac{1}{2}(x_{np} + x_{np+1})$$

where

- n: the number of observations
- p: the desired quantile
- $n{\cdot}p$: the product of the length of the data vector and the desired p quantile

1.4.1 Compute 20 %-quantile manually

Suppose we have a set of measurements and want to determine the 20% quantile. Meaning that we want to find the cutoff point below or equal which lies 20% of the cumulative distribution.

data = [3, 5, 5, 6, 7, 7, 8, 10, 10]

with

- n : the length of the data vector
- q : the desired quantile $q = 0.2$

The dataset is sorted in ascending order.

The nq is computed as: $nq = 9 \cdot 0.2 = 1.8$

The derivation of the $x_{0.20}$ value becomes.

$$
\begin{aligned}
x_{0.20} &= \frac{1}{2}(x_{9*0.2} + x_{9*0.2+1}) \\
x_{0.20} &= \frac{1}{2}(x_{1.8} + x_{2.8}) \\
x_{0.20} &= \frac{1}{2}(x_2 + x_3) \\
x_{0.20} &= \frac{1}{2}(5 + 5) = 5
\end{aligned}
$$

Note that the q value is supplied in decimal form (q=0.2)

1.4.2 Compute 20 %-quantile using the NumPy percentile() function

In Python, we make use of the `percentile()` function of the NumPy library, which has the following signature:

```
numpy.percentile(data, q)
```

Note that q value is applied in percentage form (q=20).

```
q = 20
print(f'{q}%-quantile = {np.percentile(x,q)}')
```

We might want to check the documentation for the `percentile()` function.

```
import numpy as np
# help(np.percentile)
```

In the following Python code segment, we implement this approach.

```
import numpy as np

x = [3, 5, 5, 6, 7, 7, 8, 10, 10]
q = 20 # 20 percentile
# results
print(f'mean              = {np.mean(x):.4f}')
print(f'n                 = {len(x):.1f}')
print(f'np                = {len(x) * q/100:.1f}')
print(f'q                 = {q:.4f}')
# quantile
print(f'{q}%-quantile   = {np.percentile(x,q):.1f}')
# 4 quartile
print('quartiles:')
print(f'100%-quantile = {np.percentile(x,100):.1f}')
print(f' 75%-quantile = {np.percentile(x,75):.1f}')
```

(continues on next page)

(continued from previous page)

```
print(f' 50%-quantile = {np.percentile(x,50):.1f}')
print(f' 25%-quantile = {np.percentile(x,25):.1f}')
```

```
mean           = 6.7778
n              = 9.0
np             = 1.8
q              = 20.0000
20%-quantile  = 5.0
quartiles:
100%-quantile = 10.0
 75%-quantile = 8.0
 50%-quantile = 7.0
 25%-quantile = 5.0
```

Interpretation

Observe that the `percentile()` function provides several options on how any interpolation is done. For illustration purposes, all available options are presented.

The computed 20%-quantile is 5 and matches the manual calculation.

1.4.3 Compute quantile using cdf() function

Since the cumulative density function `CDF` is monotonically increasing, we can assume the existence of an inverse function, which we denote as CDF^{-1}.

If CDF is the cumulative density function of X or `cdf(x)`, then $CDF^{-1}(\alpha)$ is the value of x_α such that $P(X \leq x_\alpha) = q$, this is called the q-quantile of CDF.

Some special cases have particular names, such as:

- $CDF^{-1}(0.25)$: the first quartile.
- $CDF^{-1}(0.50)$: the second quartile, and is known as the median.
- $CDF^{-1}(0.75)$: the third quartile.
- $CDF^{-1}(1.00)$: the fourth quartile.

The percentage point function `ppf()` is used to compute the q-quantile values.

$$P(X < x_q) = CDF^{-1}(q)$$

where

- q-value is the quantile.

Recall that the percentile point function `ppf()` is the inverse of the cumulative density function `cdf()`.

For example, given the μ of 1 and the standard deviation σ of 3 of the normal distribution $\mathcal{N}(1, 3^2)$ we attempt to find the quantile for q in $P(X < x_q) = q$ by using the ppf() method. Suppose we have N values drawn from the standard normal distribution $\mathcal{N}(1, 3^2)$ and try to find the 50%-quantile, 25%-quantile, 10%-quantile, and the 1%-quantile, respectively.

$$P(X < 0.5) = q$$

```
q = norm.ppf(q=0.50, loc=1, scale=3)
```

In the following Python code segment, this is implemented and the computed percentiles are presented.

```
import numpy as np
import matplotlib.pyplot as plt
import math
import scipy.stats as stats

print('using cdf():')
# median (two quantile)
q = norm.ppf(q=0.50, loc=1, scale=3)
print(f'50%-quantile (q=0.50) = {q:.5f}')
# quartiles (four quantile)
q = norm.ppf(q=0.25, loc=1, scale=3)
print(f'25%-quantile (q=0.25) = {q:.5f}')
# deciles (10 quantile)
q = norm.ppf(q=0.10, loc=1, scale=3)
print(f'10%-quantile (q=0.10) = {q:.5f}')
# percentiles (100 quantile)
q = norm.ppf(q=0.01, loc=1, scale=3)
print(f' 1%-quantile (q=0.01) = {q:.5f}')
# parameters
mu = 1
variance = 9
N = 1000000
R = 1
sigma = math.sqrt(variance)
# normal distributed values
x = np.linspace(mu-R*sigma, mu+R*sigma, N)
samples = np.random.normal(mu,sigma, N)
normal = np.array((sorted(samples)))
print()
# verify results
print('using percentile():')
print(f'50%-quantile = {np.percentile(normal,50):.5f}')
print(f'25%-quantile = {np.percentile(normal,25):.5f}')
print(f'10%-quantile = {np.percentile(normal,10):.5f}')
print(f' 1%-quantile = {np.percentile(normal,1):.5f}')
```

```
using cdf():
50%-quantile (q=0.50) = 1.00000
25%-quantile (q=0.25) = -1.02347
10%-quantile (q=0.10) = -2.84465
 1%-quantile (q=0.01) = -5.97904

using percentile():
50%-quantile = 0.99767
25%-quantile = -1.02225
10%-quantile = -2.84673
 1%-quantile = -5.98106
```

1.4.4 Compute quantile using cdf() and ppf() function with plot

The cumulative density function `cdf()` calculates the probability for a given normal distribution value, while the percent point function `ppf()` calculates the normal distribution value for which a given probability is the required value. The `cdf()` and `ppf()` are the inverse functions of each other.

We attempt to compute a set of quantiles using the `cdf()` function and verify the results using the `ppf()` function, additionally, we verify the results using the `percentile()` function. In Python, we implement:

```
import numpy as np
import matplotlib.pyplot as plt
import math
from scipy.stats import norm

# parameters
mu = 1
variance = 9
N = 1000000
R = 1
# dataset
sigma = math.sqrt(variance)
x = np.linspace(mu-R*sigma, mu+R*sigma, N)
samples = np.random.normal(mu,sigma, N)
normal = np.array((sorted(samples)))
# plot
fig, ax = plt.subplots(1, 2, figsize=(8.5,3.5))
# ppf
x1 = np.arange(0,R, 0.001) # interval
y1 = norm.ppf(x1, loc=1, scale=3)
ax[0].plot(x1, y1)
ax[0].set_title('Percentage Point Function ppf()')
ax[0].set_xlabel('x')
ax[0].set_xlim(-0.02,1.02)
```

(continues on next page)

(continued from previous page)

```
ax[0].set_ylabel('ppf(x)')
ax[0].grid(True)
# cdf
R2 = 8
x2 = np.arange(-R2, R2, 0.001) # interval
y2 = norm.cdf(x2, loc=1, scale=3)
ax[1].plot(x2, y2)
ax[1].set_title("Cumulative Density Function cdf()")
ax[1].set_xlabel('x')
ax[1].set_ylabel('cdf(x)')
ax[1].grid(True)
plt.show()
# compute cdf values
print('using cdf():')
print(f'cdf(-5)   = {norm.cdf(-5, loc=1, scale=3):.5f}')
print(f'cdf(-2.5) = {norm.cdf(-2.5, loc=1, scale=3):.5f}')
print(f'cdf(0.0)  = {norm.cdf(0.0, loc=1, scale=3):.5f}')
print(f'cdf(2.5)  = {norm.cdf(2.5, loc=1, scale=3):.5f}')
print(f'cdf(5.0)  = {norm.cdf(5.0, loc=1, scale=3):.5f}')
print(f'cdf(7.5)  = {norm.cdf(7.5, loc=1, scale=3):.5f}')
print()
# verify results using inverse ppf function
print('using ppf():')
print(f'ppf(0.0228) = {norm.ppf(0.0228, loc=1, scale=3):.5f}')
print(f'ppf(0.1217) = {norm.ppf(0.1217, loc=1, scale=3):.5f}')
print(f'ppf(0.3694) = {norm.ppf(0.3694, loc=1, scale=3):.5f}')
print(f'ppf(0.6915) = {norm.ppf(0.6915, loc=1, scale=3):.5f}')
print(f'ppf(0.9088) = {norm.ppf(0.9088, loc=1, scale=3):.5f}')
print(f'ppf(0.9849) = {norm.ppf(0.9849, loc=1, scale=3):.5f}')
print()
# verify results using percentile function
print('using percentile():')
print(f' 2.28%-percentile = {np.percentile(normal,2.28):.5f}')
print(f'12.17%-percentile = {np.percentile(normal,12.17):.5f}')
print(f'36.94%-percentile = {np.percentile(normal,36.94):.5f}')
print(f'69.15%-percentile = {np.percentile(normal,69.15):.5f}')
print(f'90.88%-percentile = {np.percentile(normal,90.88):.5f}')
print(f'98.49%-percentile = {np.percentile(normal,98.49):.5f}')
```

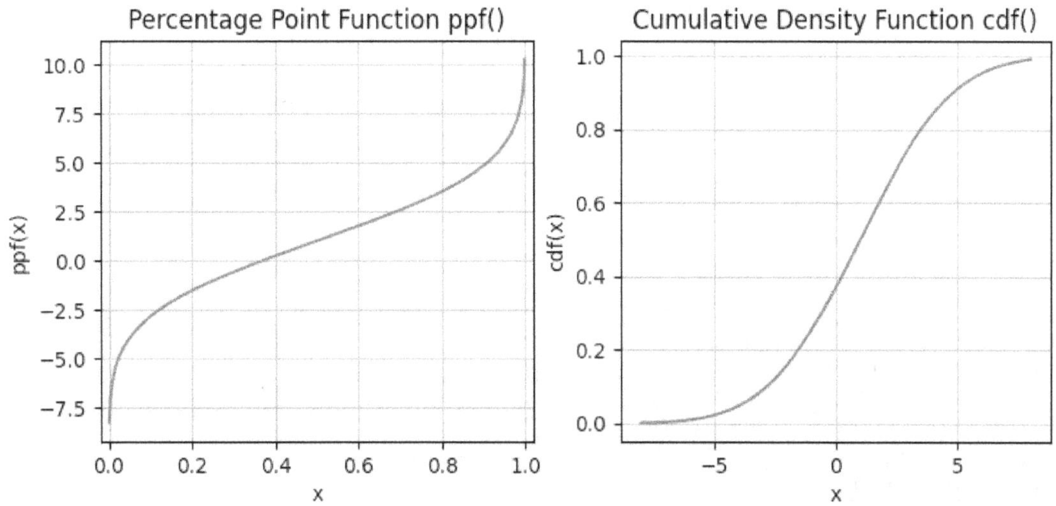


```
using cdf():
cdf(-5)   = 0.02275
cdf(-2.5) = 0.12167
cdf(0.0)  = 0.36944
cdf(2.5)  = 0.69146
cdf(5.0)  = 0.90879
cdf(7.5)  = 0.98487

using ppf():
ppf(0.0228) = -4.99723
ppf(0.1217) = -2.49959
ppf(0.3694) = -0.00033
ppf(0.6915) = 2.50032
ppf(0.9088) = 5.00021
ppf(0.9849) = 7.50237

using percentile():
 2.28%-percentile = -4.99976
12.17%-percentile = -2.50096
36.94%-percentile = 0.00379
69.15%-percentile = 2.50233
90.88%-percentile = 4.99712
98.49%-percentile = 7.49268
```

1.5 Probability density function PDF

The probability density function is presented as a graph with shaded areas.

```
import numpy as np
import matplotlib.pyplot as plt

# probability density function
fig, ax = plt.subplots(figsize=(5,3))
x = np.arange(-8, 8, 0.001)
ax.plot(x, norm.pdf(x,
                    loc=1,
                    scale=3))
ax.set_title('Probability Density Function N(1,$3^2$)')
ax.set_xlabel('x')
ax.set_ylabel('pdf(x)')
ax.grid(True)
# percentage point function
quantile = norm.ppf(q=0.494,
                    loc=1,
                    scale=3)
# fill between
px = np.arange(-8, quantile, 0.01)
py = norm.pdf(px,
              loc=1,
              scale=3)
ax.fill_between(px, py, alpha=0.15, color='b')
ax.text(.8,0.02,"x= %.2f" %quantile, fontsize=10)
ax.text(-5,0.05,"P(X)=0.494", fontsize=10)
ax.set_ylim(0,0.15)
plt.show()
# inspect
print('ppf(0.494) represents', int(quantile*100), '% quantile')
```

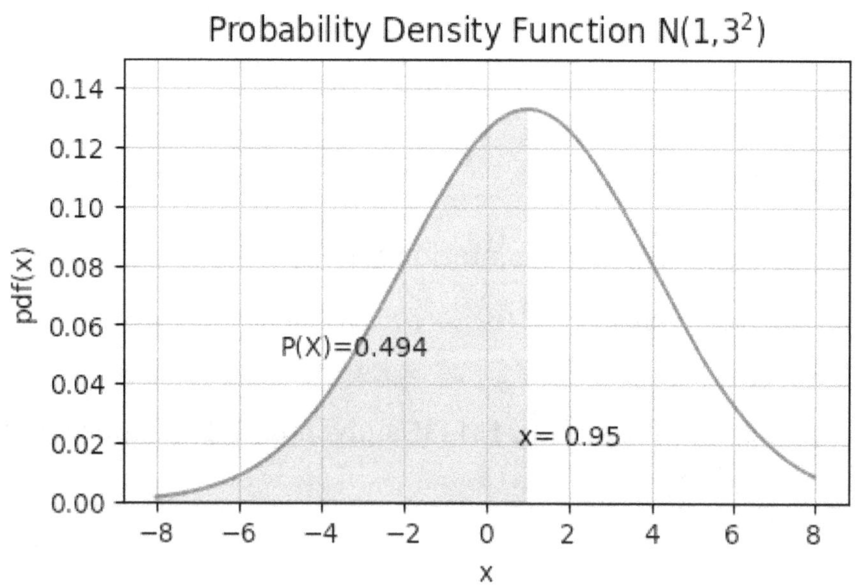


```
ppf(0.494) represents 95 % quantile
```

1.6 Inverse survival function

With the same mean and standard deviation, $X = \mathcal{N}(1, 3^2)$, we can find the quantile b in $P(X \geq b) = 0.198$ using the inverse survival function `isf()`. This is the same as using percentage point function `ppf()` with $q = (1 - 0.198)$. In the following Python code segment, we demonstrate the usage:

```
# inverse survival function
r = norm.isf(q=0.198,
             loc=1,
             scale=3)
print('P(X > 0.198) = {p1:.5f}'.format(p1=r) )
# percent point function
s = norm.ppf(q=(1-0.198),
             loc=1,
             scale=3)
print('P(X > 0.198) = {p1:.5f}'.format(p1=s) )
```

```
P(X > 0.198) = 3.54636
P(X > 0.198) = 3.54636
```

```
# percent point function
r = norm.ppf(q=(1-0.198),
             loc=1,
```

(continues on next page)

(continued from previous page)

```
scale=3)
print('quantile (1-0.198) = {p1:.5f}'.format(p1=r) )
```

```
quantile (1-0.198) = 3.54636
```

We might want to bring up the documentation for the survival function.

```
from scipy.stats import norm
# print(help(norm.isf))
```

A plot of the inverse survival function `isf()` is given and its properties in the interval $[0, 1]$ are investigated.

```
x = np.arange(0, 1, 0.001)
ax.plot(x, norm.isf(x, loc=1, scale=3))
```

Additionally, a range of `isf()` values ranging from $[0.1, 0.9]$ in steps of 0.01 is computed and the values are reported. This allows us to further our understanding of the `isf()` function and to develop an intuition about it, as documented in SciPyDocs [2023].

```
import numpy as np
import matplotlib.pyplot as plt
from scipy.stats import norm

# plot
fig, ax = plt.subplots(1, 2, figsize=(10,3))
# inverse survival function
x1 = np.arange(0, 1, 0.01) # interval
y1 = norm.isf(x1,
              loc=1,
              scale=3)
ax[0].plot(x1, y1)
ax[0].set_title('Inverse Survival Function isf()')
ax[0].set_xlabel('x')
ax[0].set_xlim(-0.02,1.02)
ax[0].set_ylabel('isf(x)')
ax[0].grid(True)
# cumulative density function
x2 = np.arange(-20, 20, 0.01) # interval
y2 = norm.cdf(x2,
              loc=1,
              scale=3)
ax[1].plot(x2, y2)
ax[1].set_title('Cumulative Density Function cdf()')
ax[1].set_xlabel('x')
ax[1].set_xlim(-7,7)
```

(continues on next page)

(continued from previous page)

```
ax[1].set_ylabel('cdf(x)')
ax[1].grid(True)
plt.show()
# inspect
print(f'isf(0.1) = {norm.isf(0.1, loc=1, scale=3):.5f}')
print(f'isf(0.2) = {norm.isf(0.2, loc=1, scale=3):.5f}')
print(f'isf(0.4) = {norm.isf(0.4, loc=1, scale=3):.5f}')
print(f'isf(0.6) = {norm.isf(0.6, loc=1, scale=3):.5f}')
print(f'isf(0.8) = {norm.isf(0.8, loc=1, scale=3):.5f}')
print(f'isf(0.9) = {norm.isf(0.9, loc=1, scale=3):.5f}')
```

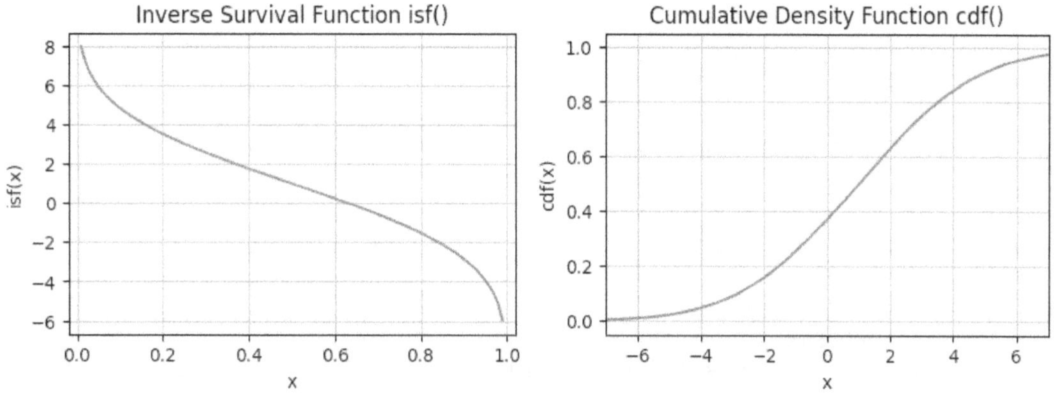


```
isf(0.1) = 4.84465
isf(0.2) = 3.52486
isf(0.4) = 1.76004
isf(0.6) = 0.23996
isf(0.8) = -1.52486
isf(0.9) = -2.84465
```

1.7 Confidence Interval around the mean

The `norm.interval()` method returns endpoints of the range that contains 95 percent of the distribution $N(0,1)$, given a level of significance of α =0.05.

```
a,b = norm.interval(confidence=0.95, loc=0, scale=1)
```

where:

- `confidence`: confidence level $(1-\alpha)$
- `loc`: the location of the distribution μ
- `scale`: the variance of the distribution σ

returns:

- a: the beginning of the range
- b: the ending of the range

Given a level of significance of $\alpha = 0.05$, the confidence interval $[a, b]$ gives the range of values, for which we have 95 % confidence, that the true value lies within.

For example, with a mean of 0 and a standard deviation of 1, we want to find 95% of the probability. The `norm.interval()` function returns a and b values around the mean, in this case, $\mu = 0$ and $\sigma^2 = 1$.

$$X = \mathcal{N}(0, 1^2)$$

```
import warnings
warnings.filterwarnings('ignore')
import scipy

# parameters
alpha=0.05
# compute interval
if scipy.__version__ == "1.7.3":
    a,b = norm.interval(alpha=(1-alpha), loc=0, scale=1)
else:
    a,b = norm.interval(confidence=(1-alpha), loc=0, scale=1)
# results
print('scipy.version:',scipy.__version__)
print('confidence interval = [{p1:.4f},{p2:.4f}]'.format(p1=a,p2=b))
```

```
scipy.version: 1.7.3
confidence interval = [-1.9600,1.9600]
```

```
import numpy as np
import matplotlib.pyplot as plt
from scipy.stats import norm

# parameters
alpha = 0.05
# compute interval
if scipy.__version__ == "1.7.3":
    a, b = norm.interval(alpha=(1-alpha), loc=0, scale=1)
else:
    a, b = norm.interval(confidence=(1-alpha), loc=0, scale=1)
# plot
fig, ax = plt.subplots(figsize=(6,3))
x = np.arange(-4,4,0.001)
ax.plot(x, norm.pdf(x))
ax.set_title(f"Confidence Interval [{a:.3f}, {b:.3f}]")
```

(continues on next page)

(continued from previous page)

```
ax.set_xlabel('x')
ax.set_ylabel('pdf(x)')
ax.grid(True)
ax.set_ylim(0,0.5)
# fill between
px = np.arange(a,b,0.01)
ax.fill_between(px, norm.pdf(px), alpha=0.15, color='r')
ax.text(-0.7,0.45, f"$\\alpha={alpha}$", fontsize=12)
plt.show()
# results
print('scipy.version:', scipy.__version__)
print(f'confidence interval = [{a:.4f} {b:.4f}]')
```

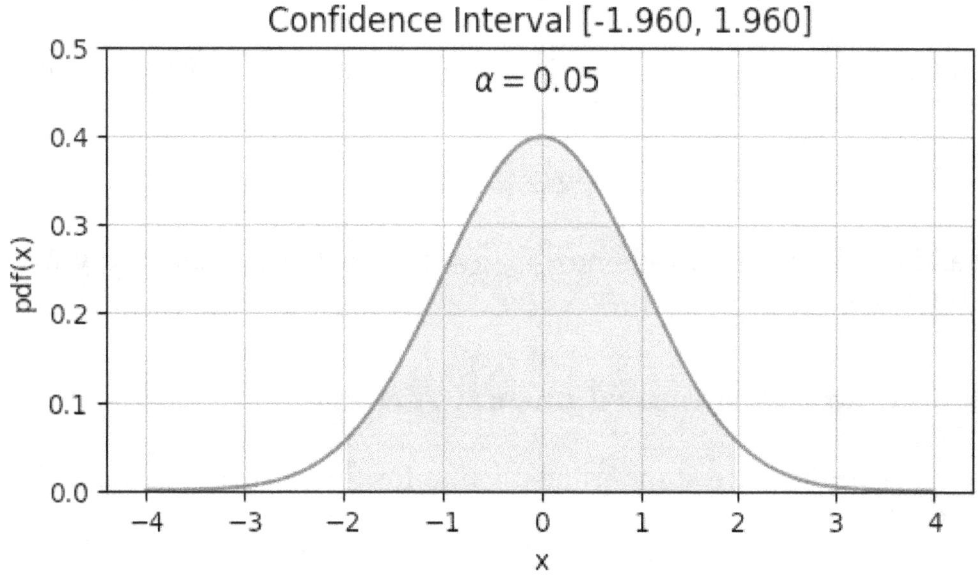


```
scipy.version: 1.7.3
confidence interval = [-1.9600 1.9600]
```

Note: Observe the usage of the version property of the scipy library, to distinguish between versions with slightly different parameter syntax. This technique might be helpful in circumstance were an library update is not desired.

1.8 Standard normal distribution

When $\mu = 0$ and $\sigma = 1$, it is called the standard normal distribution. The above probability function is simplified to:

$$X = \mathcal{N}(1, 3^2)$$

$$\Phi(x) = \frac{1}{\sqrt{2\pi}}e^{-\frac{x^2}{2}}$$

Note, that all normal curves can be related to the standard normal distribution.

1.8.1 Standardized normal variable

To standardize a random variable into the standardized normal variable $Z \sim N(0, 1)$ we use the transformation:

$$Z = \frac{(x - \mu)}{\sigma}$$

The standardized value Z tells how many standard deviations away from the mean the value is.

1.8.2 Finding the standard normal variable

For example, to find the standardized value for $x = 1$ with a mean of 2 and a standard deviation of 3.

For

$$X = \mathcal{N}(2, 3^2)$$

and

$$Z = \frac{(1 - 2)}{3}$$

We can use `norm.cdf()` function to find the probability and use `norm.ppf()` function with $\mu = 0$ and $\sigma = 1$ to find the standardized value. In Python, we implement this approach in the following code section:

```
# cumulative density function
r = norm.cdf(1, loc=2, scale=3)
print(f"cdf(x<1) = {r:.5f}")
```

```
cdf(x<1) = 0.36944
```

```
# percent point function
q1 = norm.cdf(1, loc=2, scale=3)
r = norm.ppf(q=q1)
print(f"ppf(x<1) = {r:.5f}")
```

```
ppf(x<1) = -0.33333
```

The cumulative density function `cdf()` calculates the probability for a given normal distribution value, and the percentage point function `ppf()` calculates the normal distribution value for which a given probability is the required value.

Observe, that these functions are inversely related to each other.

```
import numpy as np
import matplotlib.pyplot as plt

# plot
fig, ax = plt.subplots(figsize=(6,3))
x= np.arange(-4,4,0.001)
ax.plot(x, norm.pdf(x))
ax.set_xlabel('x')
ax.set_ylabel('pdf(x)')
ax.grid(True)
# interval
a = -4.0
b = 1.65
px = np.arange(a,b,0.01)
ax.set_ylim(0,0.5)
# fill between
ax.fill_between(px, norm.pdf(px), alpha=0.15, color='b')
ax.text(1.2,-0.08,"x=1.65", fontsize=12)
ax.text(-1, 0.15, "0.9505", fontsize=12, alpha=0.5)
ax.set_title('Probability Density Function')
plt.show()
```

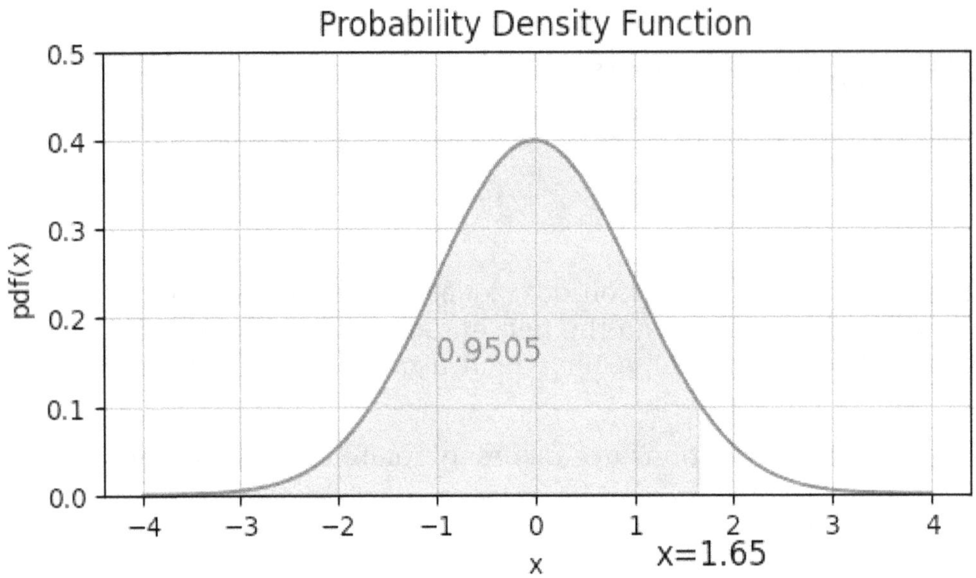

We compute the `ppf(0.95)` as 1.655 and the `cdf(1.655)` as 0.950 and in the following Python code segment, we implement this idea.

```
from scipy.stats import norm

# ppf, cdf
p = norm.ppf(0.95)
c = norm.cdf(p)
# inspect
print(f'ppf(0.95) = {p:.5f}')
print(f'cdf(1.65) = {c:.5f}')
```

```
ppf(0.95) = 1.64485
cdf(1.65) = 0.95000
```

CHAPTER 2

MAPPING TO NORMAL DISTRIBUTION

The power transform is useful as a data transformation technique in modeling, where homoscedasticity and normality are required.

We explore the usage of `PowerTransformer` with Box-Cox and Yeo-Johnson transforms, as well as the QuantileTransformer applied to different probability distributions, like:

- Log-normal
- Chi-squared
- Uniform

to make the transformed distribution conform more to the required normal distribution.

Although the transformation maps the data to the normal distribution successfully, there are certain datasets, where success is not guaranteed. This outcome emphasizes the importance of data visualizing before and after any transformation is performed, to visually confirm that the produced result is satisfactory.

We make use of the `PowerTransformer()` function from the `sklearn` library, which has the following signature:

```
bc = PowerTransformer(method='box-cox')
yj = PowerTransformer(method='yeo-johnson')
```

Note: Keep in mind that the Box-Cox transformation, does not support negative input values.

For comparison, we show the results from the `QuantileTransformer`, which can force any arbitrary distribution into a standard normal distribution, provided a sufficiently large sample.

We apply the `QuantileTransformer()`, also from the `sklearn` library, which has this signature:

```
qt = QuantileTransformer(output_distribution='normal',random_state=rng)
```

In the case of small datasets the use of the PowerTransformer is recommended instead, since the QuantileTransformer is prone to overfitting in such circumstances.

2.1 log-normal distribution to normal distribution

A sample of size N is drawn from the log-normal distribution. We attempt to apply different transformations to the data, to make it look more normally distributed $N(0,1)$.

One such transformation might help satisfy the underlying assumption of normality which many statistical or regression procedures make, to arrive at valid inferences.

We apply the Box-Cox, Yeo-Johnson, and Quantile transformations to the log-normal distributed dataset and visually inspect the transforming results.

```
import numpy as np
import matplotlib.pyplot as plt
import math
from sklearn.preprocessing import PowerTransformer
from sklearn.preprocessing import QuantileTransformer
from sklearn.model_selection import train_test_split

def power_transforms(data, meth='box-cox'):
    """ docstring """
    pt = PowerTransformer(method=meth)
    X_train, X_test = train_test_split(data, test_size=.5)
    X_trans = pt.fit(X_train).transform(X_test)
    lambdas = round(pt.lambdas_[0], 2)
    return X_train, X_trans, lambdas
```

```
# parameters
n_samples = 200000
n_bins = int(math.sqrt(n_samples/2))
colors = ['darkorange', 'goldenrod', 'seagreen', 'royalblue', 'red']
# generate log-normal data
rng = np.random.RandomState(304)
X_lognormal = rng.lognormal(size=(n_samples, 1))
# plot
fig = plt.figure(figsize=(9,6))
ax1 = fig.add_subplot(221)
X_train, X_test = train_test_split(X_lognormal, test_size=.5)
ax1.hist(X_test,
         color=colors[4],
         bins=n_bins)
# grid lines
ax1.grid(True, linestyle='--', color='black')
ax1.set_title('Log-Normal', fontsize=12, fontweight='bold')
# plot
ax2 = fig.add_subplot(222)
X_train, X_trans, BC_lambdas = power_transforms(data=X_lognormal,
                                                meth='box-cox')
ax2.hist(X_trans,
         color=colors[3],
         bins=n_bins)
ax2.grid(True, linestyle='--', color='grey') # grid lines
ax2.set_title('{} transform'.format('Box-Cox'), fontsize=12)
# plot
ax3 = fig.add_subplot(223)
X_train, X_trans, YJ_lambdas = power_transforms(data=X_lognormal,
                                            meth='yeo-johnson')
ax3.hist(X_trans,
         color=colors[0],
         bins=n_bins)
# grid lines
ax3.grid(True, linestyle='--', color='grey')
ax3.set_title('Yeo-Johnson transform', fontsize=12)
# plot
ax4 = fig.add_subplot(224)
qt = QuantileTransformer(output_distribution='normal',
                                            random_state=rng)
# Data split into train and test set
X_train, X_test = train_test_split(X_lognormal, test_size=.5)
X_trans = qt.fit(X_train).transform(X_test)
ax4.hist(X_trans,
         color=colors[1],
         bins=n_bins)
ax4.grid(True, linestyle='--', color='grey')
ax4.set_title('Quantile transform', fontsize=12)
plt.tight_layout()
plt.show()
# inspect
```

(continues on next page)

(continued from previous page)

```
print('number of bins       :', n_bins)
print('box-cox lambdas      :', BC_lambdas)
print('yeo-johnson lambdas :', YJ_lambdas)
```

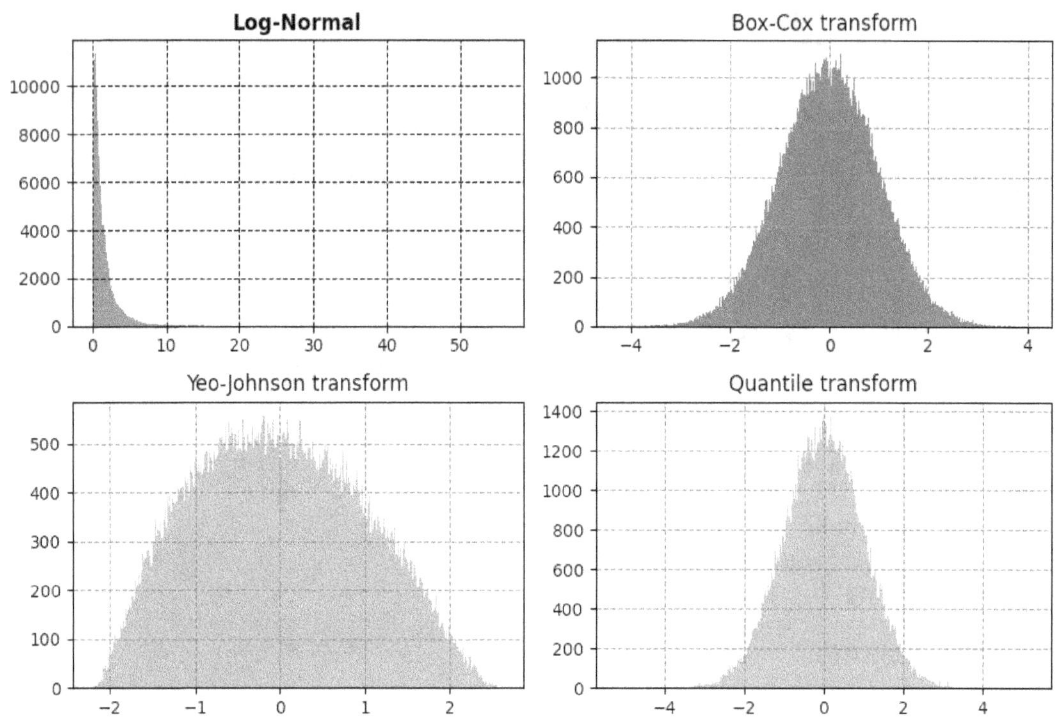


```
number of bins       : 316
box-cox lambdas      : -0.0
yeo-johnson lambdas : -0.84
```

2.2 Chi-square to normal distribution

A sample of size N is drawn from the χ^2 distribution. We attempt to apply different transformations to the data, to make it look more normally distributed $N(0,1)$.

One of those transformations might help satisfy the underlying assumption of normality which many statistical or regression procedures make, to arrive at valid inferences.

We apply the Box-Cox, Yeo-Johnson, and the Quantile transformation to the χ^2 distributed dataset and visually inspect the transforming results. In Python, we implement:

```
# parameters
n_samples = 200000
n_bins = int(math.sqrt(n_samples/2))
colors = ['darkorange', 'goldenrod',
          'seagreen', 'royalblue', 'red']
# generate chi-square distributed data
rng = np.random.RandomState(304)
X_chisquare = rng.chisquare(df=3, size=(n_samples, 1))
# plot
fig = plt.figure(figsize=(9,6))
ax1 = fig.add_subplot(221)
X_train, X_test = train_test_split(X_chisquare,
                                   test_size=.5)
ax1.hist(X_test,
         color=colors[4],
         bins=n_bins)
ax1.grid(True, linestyle='--', color='black')
ax1.set_title('Chi-square distribution',
              fontsize=12, fontweight='bold')
# plot
ax2 = fig.add_subplot(222)
X_train, X_trans, BC_lambdas = power_transforms(
    data=X_chisquare, meth='box-cox')
ax2.hist(X_trans,
         color=colors[3],
         bins=n_bins)
ax2.grid(True, linestyle='--', color='grey')
ax2.set_title('Box-Cox transform', fontsize=12)
# plot
ax3 = fig.add_subplot(223)
X_train, X_trans, YJ_lambdas = power_transforms(
    data=X_chisquare, meth='yeo-johnson')
ax3.hist(X_trans,
         color=colors[0],
         bins=n_bins)
ax3.grid(True, linestyle='--', color='grey')
ax3.set_title('Yeo-Johnson transform', fontsize=12)
# plot
ax4 = fig.add_subplot(224)
qt = QuantileTransformer(output_distribution='normal',
                         random_state=rng)
X_train, X_test = train_test_split(X_chisquare,
                                   test_size=.5)
X_trans = qt.fit(X_train).transform(X_test)
ax4.hist(X_trans,
         color=colors[1],
         bins=n_bins)
ax4.grid(True, linestyle='--', color='grey')
ax4.set_title('Quantile transform', fontsize=12)
plt.tight_layout()
plt.show()
```

(continues on next page)

(continued from previous page)

```
# inspect
print('number of bins        :', n_bins)
print('box-cox lambdas       :', BC_lambdas)
print('yeo-johnson lambdas :', YJ_lambdas)
```

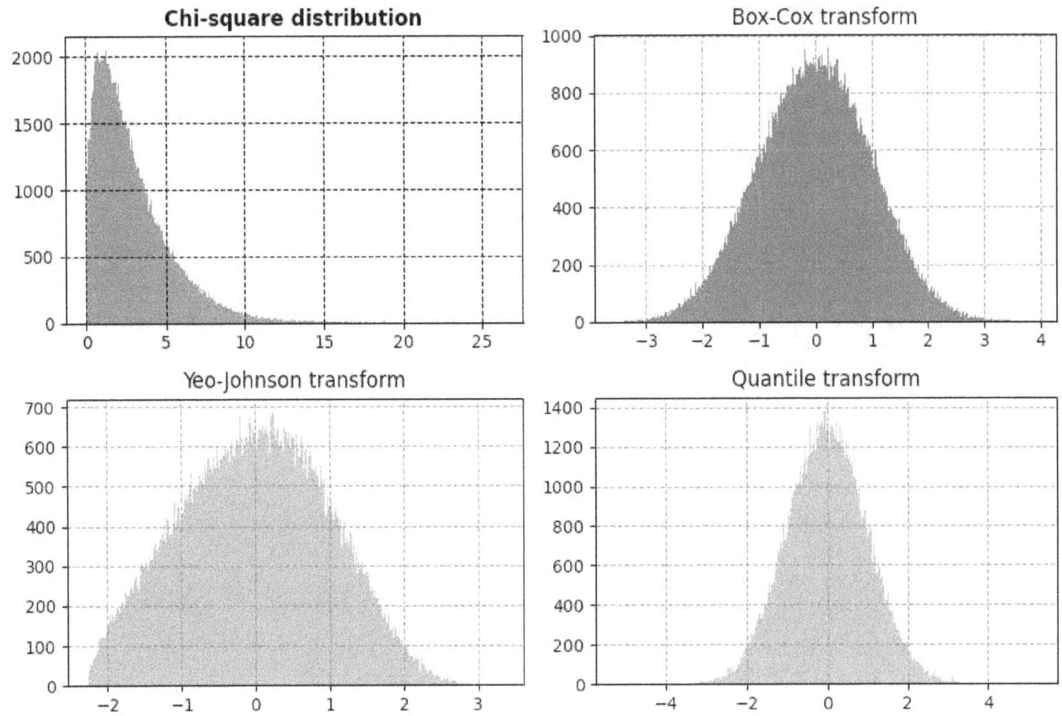


```
number of bins      : 316
box-cox lambdas     : 0.29
yeo-johnson lambdas : -0.1
```

2.3 Uniform to normal distribution

A sample of size N is drawn from the uniform distribution $U[0,1]$. We attempt to apply different transformations to the data, to make it look more normally distributed $N(0,1)$. One such transformation might help satisfy the underlying assumption of normality which many statistical or regression procedures make, to arrive at valid inferences.

We apply the Box-Cox, Yeo-Johnson, and Quantile transformations to the uniformly distributed dataset and visually inspect the transforming results. In Python, we implement:

```
# parameters
n_samples = 200000
n_bins = int(math.sqrt(n_samples/2))
colors = ['darkorange', 'goldenrod',
          'seagreen', 'royalblue', 'red']
# generate uniform distributed data
rng = np.random.RandomState(304)
X_uniform = rng.uniform(low=0, high=1, size=(n_samples, 1))
# plot
fig = plt.figure(figsize=(9,6))
ax1 = fig.add_subplot(221)
X_train, X_test = train_test_split(X_uniform,
                                   test_size=.5)
ax1.hist(X_test,
         color=colors[4],
         bins=n_bins)
ax1.grid(True, linestyle='--', color='black')
ax1.set_title('Uniform distribution', fontsize=12,
              fontweight='bold')
# plot
ax2 = fig.add_subplot(222)
X_train, X_trans, BC_lambdas = power_transforms(
                          data=X_uniform, meth='box-cox')
ax2.hist(X_trans,
        color=colors[3],
        bins=n_bins)
ax2.grid(True, linestyle='--', color='grey')
ax2.set_title('Box-Cox transform', fontsize=12)
# plot
ax3 = fig.add_subplot(223)
X_train, X_trans, YJ_lambdas = power_transforms(
        data=X_uniform, meth='yeo-johnson')
ax3.hist(X_trans,
         color=colors[0],
         bins=n_bins)
ax3.grid(True, linestyle='--', color='grey')
ax3.set_title('Yeo-Johnson transform', fontsize=12)
# plot
ax4 = fig.add_subplot(224)
qt = QuantileTransformer(output_distribution='normal',
                         random_state=rng)
X_train, X_test = train_test_split(X_uniform, test_size=.5)
X_trans = qt.fit(X_train).transform(X_test)
ax4.hist(X_trans,
         color=colors[1],
         bins=n_bins)
ax4.grid(True, linestyle='--', color='grey')
ax4.set_title('Quantile transform', fontsize=12)
plt.tight_layout()
plt.show()
# inspect
```

(continues on next page)

(continued from previous page)

```
print('number of bins       :', n_bins)
print('box-cox lambdas      :', BC_lambdas)
print('yeo-johnson lambdas :', YJ_lambdas)
```

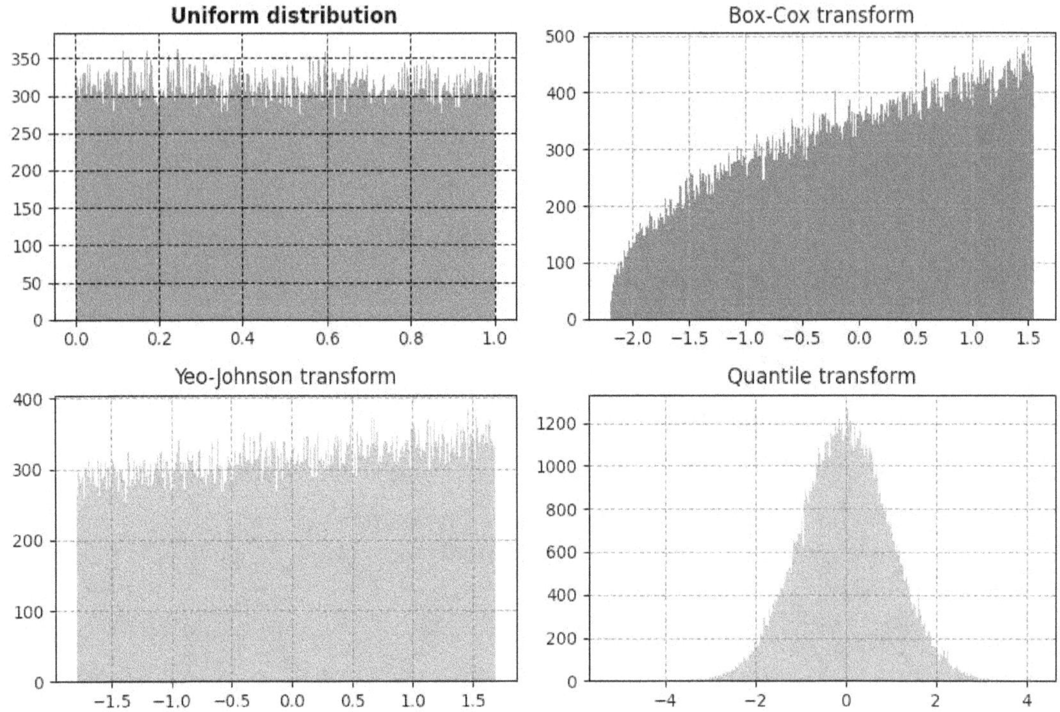


```
number of bins      : 316
box-cox lambdas     : 0.71
yeo-johnson lambdas : 0.73
```

CHAPTER 3

RANDOM NUMBERS

The random module can be used to generate random numbers. These random numbers are deterministic and therefore called pseudo-random numbers. This deterministic property of the random numbers is controlled by a seed parameter passed to the algorithm.

This deterministic property of the pseudo-random number generator makes it possible to recreate the same set of random numbers, each time, which is a very desirable property for the reproducibility of experiments. In Python, we explore this feature, by using the `seed()` method from the random package, like so:

```
np.random.seed(N)
```

where

- `N`: is a chosen integer to control the set of pseudo-random numbers created

The `normalvariate()` method is part of the random module. It is used to return a pseudo-random floating point number, drawn from the normal distribution. It has this signature:

```
random.normalvariate(mean, sigma)
```

With the parameters:

- μ: mean or expected value
- σ: sigma or standard deviation

and it returns a single random floating point number, drawn from a normal distribution.

Before we use the random module, we might want to bring up its documentation.

```
import random
# print(help(random))
# print(help(random.normalvariate))
# print(help(random.seed))
```

3.1 Random number, drawn from normal distribution

We make use of the `normvariate()` function to produce pseudo-random numbers. The function has the following signature:

```
random.normalvariate(mu=100, sigma=50)
```

where

- `mu`: is the mean or expected values
- `sigma`: is the standard deviation of the values

returning

- a single pseudo-random floating point number, which is drawn from the normal distribution $N(\mu, \sigma^2)$.

3.2 Random numbers, without seed

In the following section, we produce 5 normally distributed random numbers. Observe that all numbers are different because we did not set a seed value.

```
import random

# 5 random number
print('random normal numbers, without seed:')
for i in range(5):
    print( random.normalvariate(mu=100, sigma=50) )
```

```
random normal numbers, without seed:
113.40685519792896
87.54761395675011
147.16398636407928
172.8528401298401
192.05547977085877
```

3.3 Random numbers, with seed

The pseudo-random number algorithm is supplied with a start number N to the `seed(N)` function, which controls the sequence of generated numbers. When passing the seed value to the pseudo-random number generator algorithm, it will generate the same pseudo-random number, each time.

```
random.seed(1)
print(random.normalvariate(mu=100, sigma=50))
```

This property enables the scientist to repeat the same experiment over and over again. In Python, this approach is implemented in the following code segment.

```
import random

print('random numbers, with seed:')
for i in range(5):
    random.seed(1) # reproducibility
    print(random.normalvariate(mu=100, sigma=50))
```

```
random numbers, with seed:
130.3727928821853
130.3727928821853
130.3727928821853
130.3727928821853
130.3727928821853
```

3.4 Generate synthetic charts

To make the experiment reproducible, we provide the pseudo-random number generator algorithm with a seed value, like so:

```
random.seed(N)
```

This instructs the number generator, to produce the same sequence of random numbers each time, according the the passed-in number N. Note, that different numbers of N will result in different random sequences, however reproducible.

In the next step, we produce a sequence of returns for a fictitious equity instrument and visualize this dataset in a plot called synthetic returns.

```
rv = random.normalvariate(mu,sigma)
```

Then, we collect those synthetic returns into a Python list called "cums", and apply the cumsum() function from the NumPy library, like so:

```
plt.plot(cums[-300:])
```

Finally, by visualizing the first 300 observations, we arrive at the desired synthetic chart. We make use of the plot() function from the matplotlib library, to make the plot.

```
import matplotlib.pyplot as plt
import numpy as np
import math
import random

# parameters
time = 8760
mu = 0
sigma = 1
# random numbers
nums = []
random.seed(12) # reproducible
for i in range(time):
    rv = random.normalvariate(mu, sigma)
    nums.append(rv)
# plot
fig = plt.figure(figsize=(8, 1.5))
plt.plot(nums[-300:])
plt.grid(True)
plt.title("synthetic returns")
plt.xlabel("time steps")
plt.ylabel("returns")
plt.show()
# plot
fig = plt.figure(figsize=(8,3.5))
cums = np.cumsum(nums)
plt.plot(cums[-300:]) # cum returns
plt.grid(True)
plt.title("synthetic chart")
plt.xlabel("time steps")
plt.ylabel("close")
plt.show()
```

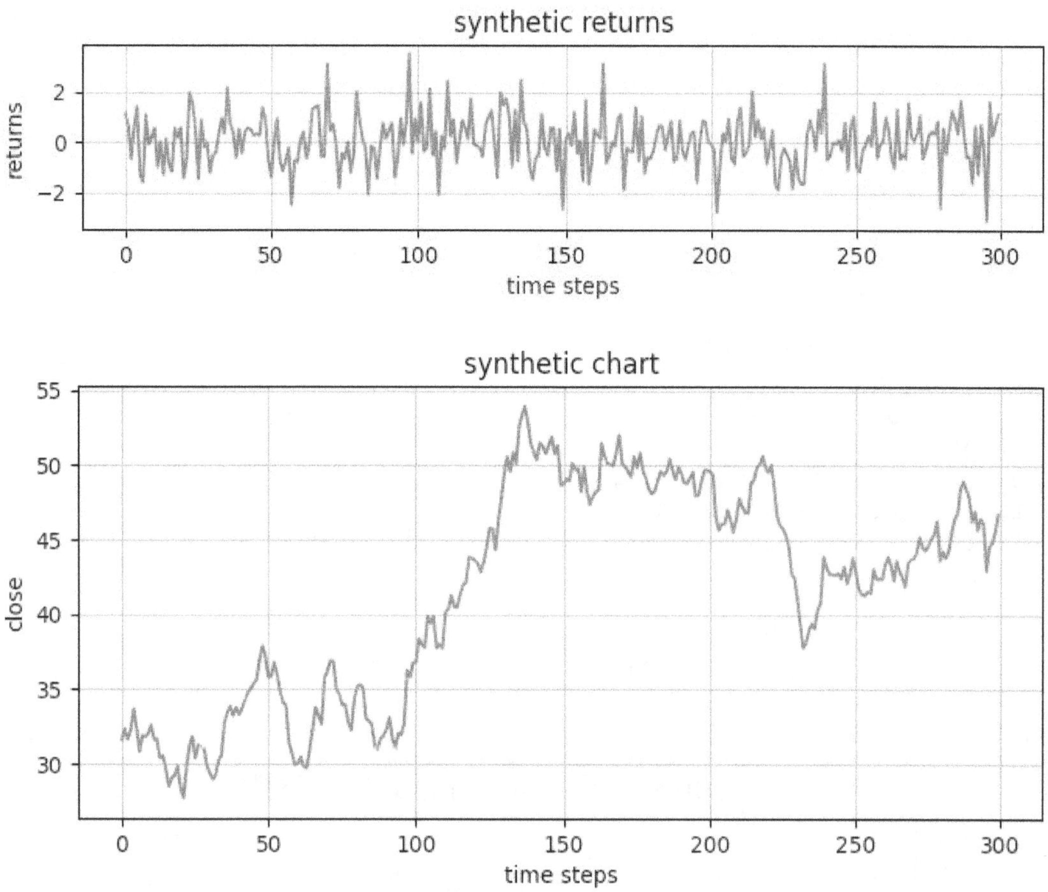

3.5 Generate a histogram, which converges to normal distribution

We observe how the histogram will converge to the density function of the normal distribution, once the number of trials increases.

According to de Mondragon [2021], Study.com [2023], the mean height of men is 178 cm with a 7 cm standard deviation.

We apply a simulation approach to verify that the mean height of men is indeed normal distributed $N(178, 7)$, and in Python code, we implement:

```
import random
import matplotlib.pyplot as plt
import statistics
import math

# parameters
trials = 20000
```

(continues on next page)

(continued from previous page)

```
nbins = int(math.sqrt(trials))
# random numbers
nums = []
m, s = 178, 7
random.seed(1)
for i in range(trials):
    temp = random.normalvariate(mu=m, sigma=s)
    nums.append(temp)
# plot
fig = plt.figure(figsize=(6,3))
plt.hist(nums,
         bins=nbins)
plt.grid(True)
mean = statistics.mean(nums)
std = statistics.stdev(nums)
plt.title(f"{trials} trials, {nbins} bins, N({mean:.0f},{std:.0f})")
plt.show()
# inspect
print(f"bins : {nbins:.0f}")
print(f"mean : {mean:.6f}")
print(f"std  : {std:.6f}")
```

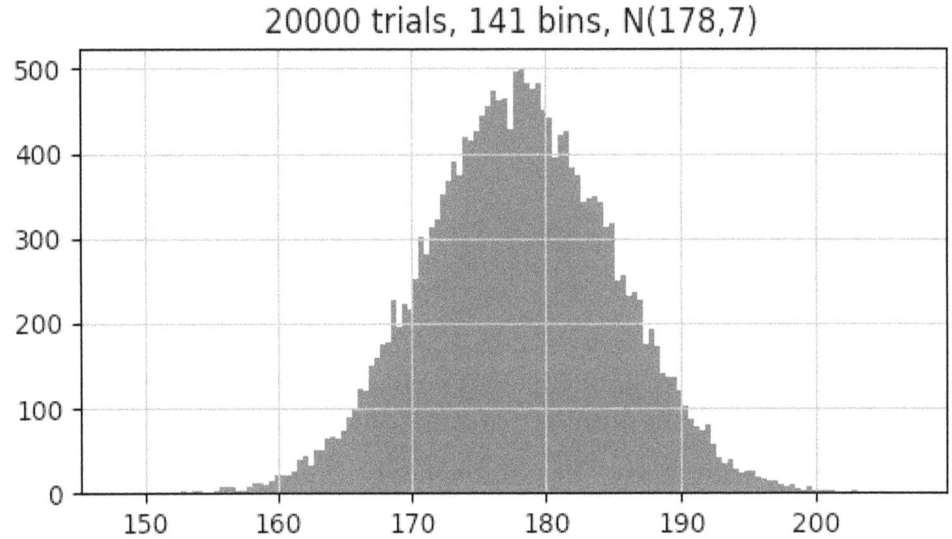


```
bins : 141
mean : 177.962758
std  : 7.022014
```

In statistics terms, kernel density estimation (KDE) is a non-parametric approach to estimating the probability density function for a given sample. According to PandasDocs [2023] this function uses a Gaussian kernel and includes automatic bandwidth determination.

The kde() method is used to compute and plot the kernel density estimate from given histogram data. It has the following signature:

```
df.plot.kde(ax=ax[1], bw_method=0.3)
```

```
import matplotlib.pyplot as plt
import pandas as pd

# DataFrame
df = pd.DataFrame({'sample': nums,})
# plot
fig, ax = plt.subplots(nrows=1, ncols=2, figsize=(9,3))
txt1 = f"{trials} trials, {nbins} bins, N({mean:.0f},{std:.0f})"
df.plot.hist(bins=nbins,
             ax=ax[0],
             title=txt1)
ax[0].grid()
txt2 = f"{trials} trials, {nbins} bins, N({mean:.0f},{std:.0f})"
df.plot.kde(ax=ax[1],
            bw_method=0.3,
            title=txt2)
ax[1].grid()
plt.show()
```

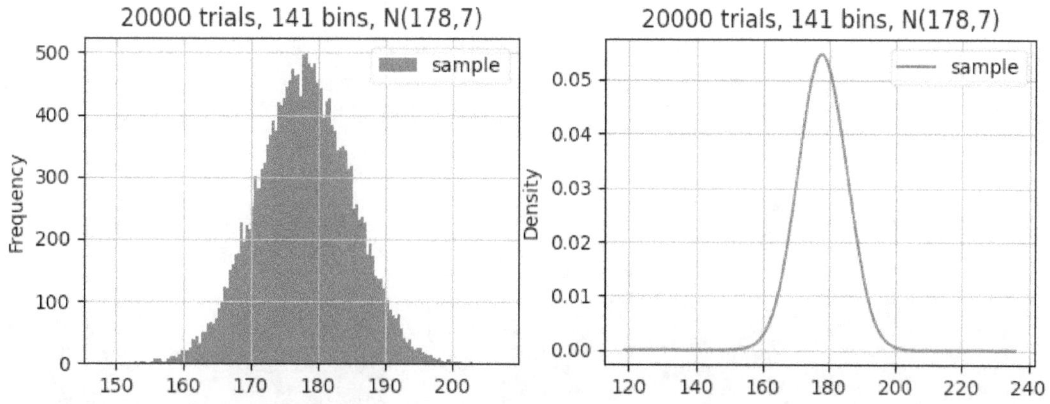

Interpretation

According to the central limit theorem, as the number of trials increases, the mean and standard deviation of the sample converge towards the normal distribution.

With a sample size of about 20000 we get close to the normal distribution $N(178, 7)$, exactly what was expected.

CHAPTER 4

TEST DISTRIBUTION FOR NORMALITY

The standard normal distribution is frequently used in probability distribution where the mean value equals 0 and the standard deviation equals 1 or $N(0, 1)$.

It has this fundamental property that is used under the central limit theorem, which states that the average of many samples of random variables is itself a random variable, whose distribution converges to the normal distribution as the number of samples increases.

Many statistical tests assume that the sample data is to be normally distributed. To confirm that this property is met, we apply tests for normality. There are four ways to check if the normality assumption is satisfied:

- Visual Method - Create a Histogram.
- Visual Method - Create a Q-Q plot.
- Formal Statistical Test - Shapiro-Wilk Test.
- Formal Statistical Test - Kolmogorov-Smirnov Test.

In the following Python code segment, each of these methods is applied and their properties are discussed.

After studying the normal distribution and understanding its characteristics, we now want to test if a given distribution conforms to the normal distribution. For that, we build two datasets of random values drawn from the standard normal distribution $N(\mu, \sigma)$ and the uniform distribution $U[1, 0]$

To further our understanding of a given distribution, we employ statistical tests as well as visualization techniques.

4.1 Visualize the data in plots

It is almost always a good idea to plot any given dataset, to gain an intuition about it. In Python, we implement this approach and show the diagrams side-by-side.

```
import numpy as np
import matplotlib.pyplot as plt

# parameters
N = 40000
# dataset
np.random.seed(1) # reproducibility
a = np.random.randn(N) # N(0,1)
b = np.random.rand(N) # U(0,1)
# plot
fig = plt.figure(figsize=(9,3))
ax1 = fig.add_subplot(1, 2, 1)
ax2 = fig.add_subplot(1, 2, 2)
ax1.hist(a,
         bins=50)
ax1.set_xlabel('x')
ax1.set_ylabel('frequency')
ax2.hist(b,
         bins=50)
ax1.grid(True)
ax2.grid(True)
ax1.set_title("Normal Distribution")
ax2.set_title("Uniform Distribution")
ax2.set_xlabel('x')
ax2.set_ylabel('frequency')
fig.tight_layout()
plt.show()
```

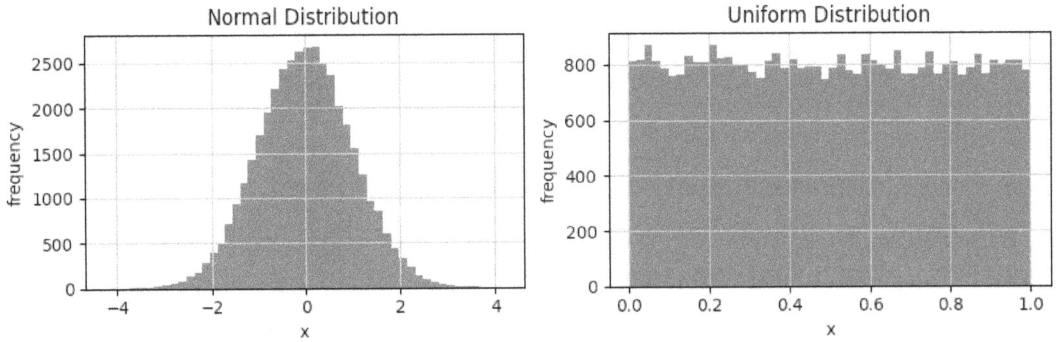

4.2 Plot theoretical versus ordered quantile

The `probplot()` method calculates the quantile for a probability plot and generates a probability plot of sample data against the quantile of a specified theoretical distribution. By default, the normal distribution is set to be the default theoretical distribution. It has the following signature:

```
stats.probplot(a, dist="norm", plot=ax1)
```

where

- `a`: the data to plot
- `dist`: set to "norm" for normal distribution to test against
- `plot`: set to "ax1", the plot area receiving the output

A probability or Q-Q (quantile-quantile) plot can be used to compare two probability distributions by plotting their quantile against each other. In this case, we use a Q-Q plot to compare the data series to a theoretical normal distribution. The function draws the theoretical distribution on the x-axis and the calculated quantile on the y-axis, indicated by the 45° red line in both figures.

If the ordered values are similar to the theoretical quantile then, the points in the Q-Q plot will lie closely to the red line. In another situation, if the data and the distribution are linearly related, the plot points will almost lie on a line, but not necessarily the red 45° line.

The left figure shows data in the y-axis was almost similar to the normal distribution. However, the right figure highlights that the random data, drawn from the uniform distribution, does not follow the normal distribution at all. Hence its Q-Q plot deviates substantially from the 45° line.

Interpreting the Q-Q plot is not an exact science, and if we look at the y-axis in the right figure the scale between $[0, 1]$ would be an indication from which distribution this quantile was drawn.

In the following code segment, we demonstrate this approach in Python and compare the resulting diagrams.

```
import scipy.stats as stats
import numpy as np

# parameters
N = 40000
# datasets
np.random.seed(1)  # reproducibility
a = np.random.randn(N) # normal distribution N(0,1)
b = np.random.rand(N) # uniform distribution U(0,1)
# plot left
```

(continues on next page)

(continued from previous page)

```
fig = plt.figure(figsize=(9,4))
ax1 = fig.add_subplot(1, 2, 1)
stats.probplot(a, dist="norm", plot=ax1)
ax1.grid()
ax1.set_title("Normal distribution", fontsize=12)
ax1.set_xlabel("Theoretical quantile")
ax1.set_ylabel("Ordered quantile")
# plot right
ax2 = fig.add_subplot(1, 2, 2)
stats.probplot(b, dist="norm", plot=ax2)
ax2.grid()
ax2.set_title("Uniform distribution", fontsize=12)
ax2.set_xlabel("Theoretical quantile")
ax2.set_ylabel(None)
fig.tight_layout()
plt.show()
```

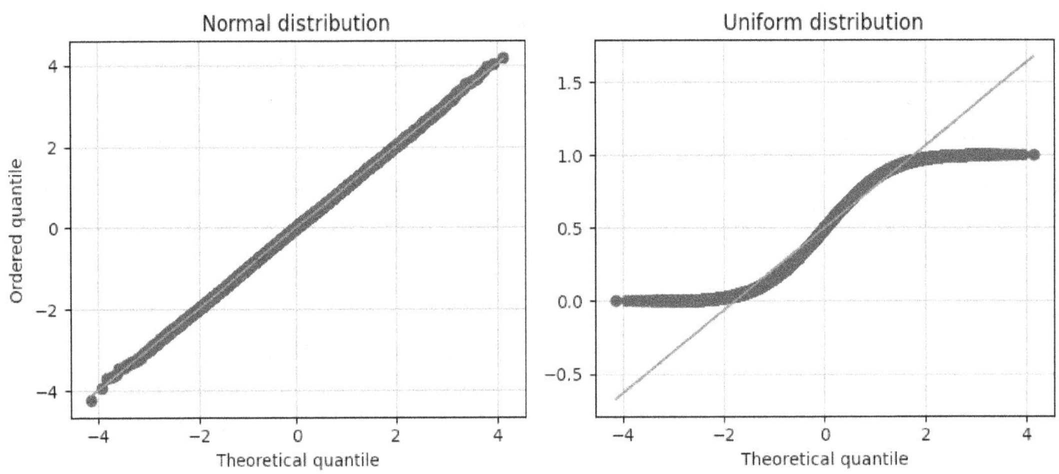

4.3 Shapiro-Wilk (SW) Test for Normality

To set up the statistical test, we formulate:

Hypothesis

- H_0 sample data was drawn from a normal distribution
- H_1 sample data was not drawn from a normal distribution

level of significance

- $\alpha = 0.05$

For N > 5000 the SW-statistic is accurate but the p_{value} may be unreliable. The chance of rejecting the null hypothesis H_0, even if it is true, is 5% regardless of sample size.

Remember, this is a two-sided test, and we allocate $\frac{\alpha}{2}$ in either tail of the distribution. This means that if the p_{value} is above $\frac{\alpha}{2}$, we fail to reject this null hypothesis and conclude that the data is normally distributed. However, if the p_{value} is below $\frac{\alpha}{2}$ then we can reject the null hypothesis, and conclude that the data series is normally distributed.

In the following code segment, we implement this test in Python and examine the results.

4.3.1 Sample drawn from normal distribution

```
from scipy import stats
import numpy as np

# parameters
N = 4000
alpha = 0.05
# dataset
np.random.seed(1)
a = np.random.randn(N) # normal distribution N(0,1)
# shapiro-wilk test
c = stats.shapiro(a)
print("Shapiro-Wilk Test:")
print("SW-statistic          : {:.4f}".format(c[0]))
print("pvalue                : {:.4f}".format(c[1]))
print("level of significance : {:.2f}".format(alpha))
print("two-sided test")
print("Hypothesis")
print("H0: sample drawn from a normal distribution")
print("H1: sample not drawn from a normal distribution")
if c[1] < alpha/2:
    print("reject H0")
    print("Not Normal")
else:
    print("fail to reject H0")
    print("Normal")
```

```
Shapiro-Wilk Test:
SW-statistic          : 0.9996
pvalue                : 0.6921
level of significance : 0.05
two-sided test
Hypothesis
H0: sample drawn from a normal distribution
H1: sample not drawn from a normal distribution
fail to reject H0
Normal
```

Interpretation

The SW-statistic is reported as 0.9996 and the associated p_{value} is 0.6921.

Since the $p_{value} \geq \frac{\alpha}{2}$ of 0.025, we fail to reject the null hypothesis H_0. It can be concluded, at the chosen level of significance α, that the sample was drawn from a normal distribution, and we can have (1-α) or 95% confidence in this assessment.

This result is hardly surprising since the sample was created from a normal distribution.

4.3.2 Sample drawn from the uniform distribution

We perform the same analysis on a data sample, drawn from a uniformly distributed population like $U[0, 1]$. In the following Python code segment, we implement this idea, like so:

```
from scipy import stats
import numpy as np

# parameters
N = 2000
alpha = 0.05
# dataset
np.random.seed(1) # reproducibility
b = np.random.rand(N) # uniform distribution U(0,1)
# shapiro-wilk test
d = stats.shapiro(b)
# results
print("Shapiro-Wilk Test:")
print("SW-statistic          : {:.4f}".format(d[0]))
print("p-value               : {:.3E}".format(d[1]))
print("level of significance : {:.2f}".format(alpha))
print("two-sided test")
print("Hypothesis")
print("H0: sample drawn from a normal distribution")
print("H1: sample not drawn from a normal distribution")
if d[1] < alpha/2:
    print("reject H0")
    print("Not Normal")
else:
    print("fail to reject H0")
    print("Normal")
```

```
Shapiro-Wilk Test:
SW-statistic          : 0.9529
p-value               : 7.033E-25
level of significance : 0.05
two-sided test
Hypothesis
```

(continues on next page)

(continued from previous page)

```
H0: sample drawn from a normal distribution
H1: sample not drawn from a normal distribution
reject H0
Not Normal
```

Interpretation

The SW-statistic is reported at 0.9529 and the associated p_{value} at 7.033E-25, almost zero.

This test is set up to be a two-tailed test, therefore we allocate $\frac{\alpha}{2}$ in either tail of the distribution.

Since the $p_{value} \leq \frac{\alpha}{2}$ of 0.025, we reject the null hypothesis H_0 in favor of the alternative hypothesis H_1. Therefore, we conclude that the sample is not drawn from a normal distribution. We can have (1-α) or 95% confidence in this assessment.

This result is hardly surprising since we created the sample from a uniform distribution and therefore our test for normality fails, which is expected.

4.4 Skewness and Kurtosis

This method computes the skewness and kurtosis statistics, which inform us about the shape of the given distribution, and we compare them to the known properties of the normal distribution. This is not a formal test for normality, however, it gives a more in-depth insight into the shape of the distribution.

Skewness is a measure of the symmetry in a distribution and the symmetrical dataset will have a skewness equal to 0. So, the normal distribution has a skewness of 0.

Kurtosis is a measure of the combined sizes of the two tails. It measures the amount of probability in the tails, and the value is often compared to the kurtosis of the normal distribution, which is equal to 3.

The methods `skew()` and `kurtosis()` are the built-in functions we use to compute these statistics. By default, the kurtosis is reported in Fisher's definition. The function signature becomes:

```
stats.kurtosis(a, fisher=True)
```

Note: If Fisher definition is used, then 3 is subtracted from the result to give 0 for a normal distribution.

We can also specify the Pearson definition, so the value 3 should appear for the data series close to the normal distribution.

Since the `describe()` method, available from the stats library, reports the kurtosis always in the Fisher definition, we set both functions, that is, the `kurtosis()`, and `describe()` to use the Fisher definition to make the reported results comparable.

4.4.1 Sample drawn from the normal distribution

```
from scipy import stats
import numpy as np

# parameters
N = 20000
# datasets
np.random.seed(1) # reproducibility
a = np.random.randn(N) # normal distribution N(0,1)
# compute
s = stats.skew(a)
k = stats.kurtosis(a, fisher=True)
d = stats.describe(a)
# inspect
print("Skewness and Kurtosis:")
print(f"Skewness            : {s:.4f}")
print(f"Kurtosis            : {k:.4f}")
print(f"nobs                : {d.nobs:.0f}")
print(f"Kurtosis Fisher  : {d.kurtosis:.4f}") # Fisher
print(f"Kurtosis Pearson : {d.kurtosis+3:.4f}") # Pearson
print(f"Skewness            : {d.skewness:.4f}")
print(f"Mean                : {d.mean:.4f}")
print(f"Variance            : {d.variance:.4f}")
```

```
Skewness and Kurtosis:
Skewness         : 0.0057
Kurtosis         : -0.0018
nobs             : 20000
Kurtosis Fisher  : -0.0018
Kurtosis Pearson : 2.9982
Skewness         : 0.0057
Mean             : 0.0096
Variance         : 1.0000
```

4.4.2 Sample drawn from the uniform distribution

```
from scipy import stats
import numpy as np

# parameters
N = 20000
# datasets
np.random.seed(1) # reproducibility
b = np.random.rand(N) # uniform distribution U(0,1)
# compute
s = stats.skew(b)
kf = stats.kurtosis(b, fisher=True)
kp = stats.kurtosis(b, fisher=False)
d = stats.describe(b)
# results b
print("Skewness and Kurtosis:")
print(f"nobs             : {d.nobs:.0f}")
print(f"Skewness         : {s:.4f}")
print(f"Kurtosis Fisher  : {kf:.4f}")
print(f"kurtosis Fisher  : {d.kurtosis:.4f}") # Fisher
print(f"Kurtosis Pearson : {kp:.4f}")
print(f"kurtosis Pearson : {d.kurtosis+3:.4f}") # Pearson
print(f"skewness         : {d.skewness:.4f}")
print(f"mean             : {d.mean:.4f}")
print(f"variance         : {d.variance:.4f}")
```

```
Skewness and Kurtosis:
nobs             : 20000
Skewness         : -0.0187
Kurtosis Fisher  : -1.2012
kurtosis Fisher  : -1.2012
Kurtosis Pearson : 1.7988
kurtosis Pearson : 1.7988
skewness         : -0.0187
mean             : 0.5013
variance         : 0.0832
```

Interpretation

If skewness is positive, it means the right-hand tail is longer and if skewness is negative, the left-hand tail tends to be longer. If it falls between -0.5 and 0.5, then the datasets are quite symmetrical.

A kurtosis is said to measure the tail heaviness of the distribution. It increases as the tails become heavier, and decreases when the tails get lighter. We can assume that a kurtosis is 3 for the normal distribution, according the the Pearson measure. Observe, that when the kurtosis is given in Fisher notation, it reports 0 for the same normal distribution; it's just an offset of 3.

Skewness and kurtosis measures are summary statistics. They are not statistical tests for normality, Nonetheless, we can compare those statistics to the well-known properties of the normal distribution and infer from the comparison.

4.5 Sample drawn from the log-normal distribution

4.5.1 Create a Histogram

If the histogram is nearly bell-shaped, then the data is assumed to be normally distributed. To demonstrate this, we create a histogram from the dataset which itself follows a log-normal distribution. Then we examine ways to visualize how the distribution is deviating from an assumed normal distribution.

In the following Python code segment, we implement this approach, like so:

```
import matplotlib.pyplot as plt
import numpy as np
import math
from scipy.stats import lognorm

# parameters
N = 300000
a = 0.5
b = 1
bins = 200
# dataset
np.random.seed(1)
lognormal_dataset = lognorm.rvs(s=a,
                                scale=math.exp(b),
                                size=N)
# plot
fig = plt.figure(figsize=(6,4))
plt.hist(lognormal_dataset,
         edgecolor=None,
         bins=bins,
         alpha=0.7)
plt.grid(color="black",
         linestyle="--",
         linewidth=1,
         alpha=0.25)
plt.title("Log-Normal distribution")
plt.xlabel('x')
plt.ylabel("frequency")
plt.show()
```

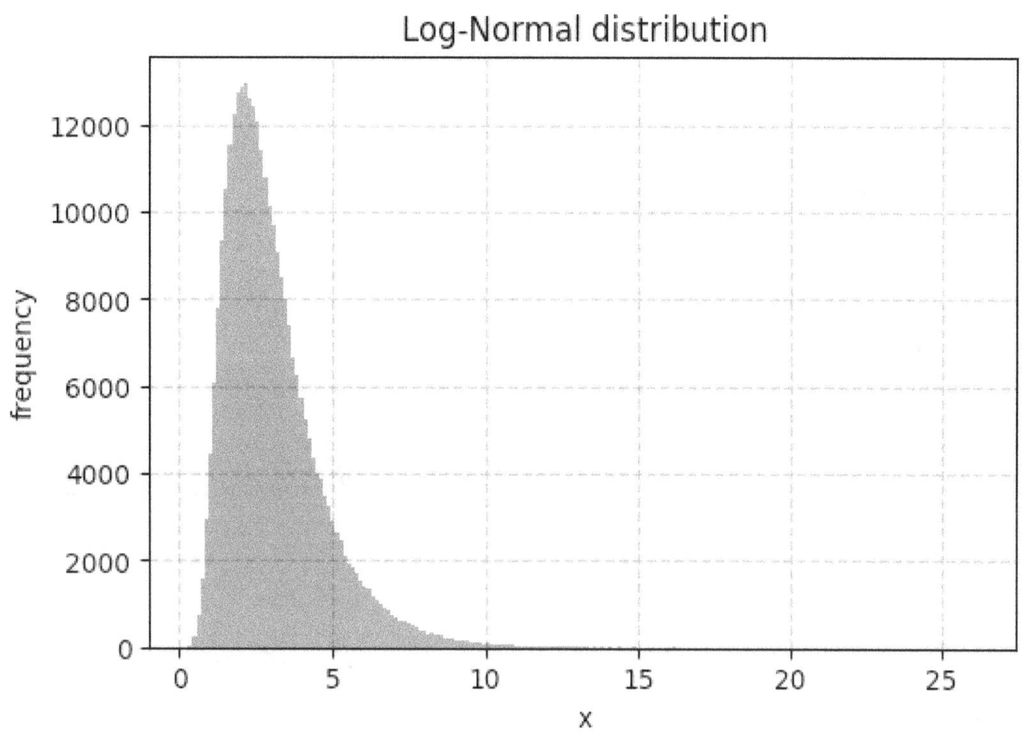

By visually inspecting this histogram, we can observe that the dataset does not even remotely look like a bell-shaped distribution, and hence it is not normally distributed. This is expected, though.

4.5.2 Visual Method - Create a Q-Q plot

If the points in the plot approximately follow the straight diagonal line, then the data is assumed to be normally distributed. This can be visualized in a so-called `Q-Q plot`, where the straight diagonal line represents a normal distribution, however, our dataset follows the log-normal distribution and deviates significantly from the 45-degree line. We conclude that the dataset is not normally distributed.

```
import math
import numpy as np
from scipy.stats import lognorm
import statsmodels.api as sm
import matplotlib.pyplot as plt

# parameters
N = 3000
# log-normal distributed values
np.random.seed(1) # reproducibility
lognormal_sample = lognorm.rvs(s=0.5,
```

(continues on next page)

(continued from previous page)

```
                                             scale=math.exp(1),
                                             size=N)
# Q-Q plot
fig = plt.figure(figsize=(6,4))
ax1 = fig.add_subplot(1, 1, 1)
sm.qqplot(lognormal_sample,
          line="45",
          ax=ax1)
plt.grid(color="grey", linestyle=":", linewidth=1)
plt.title("Log-Normal Q-Q diagram", fontsize=12)
plt.show()
```

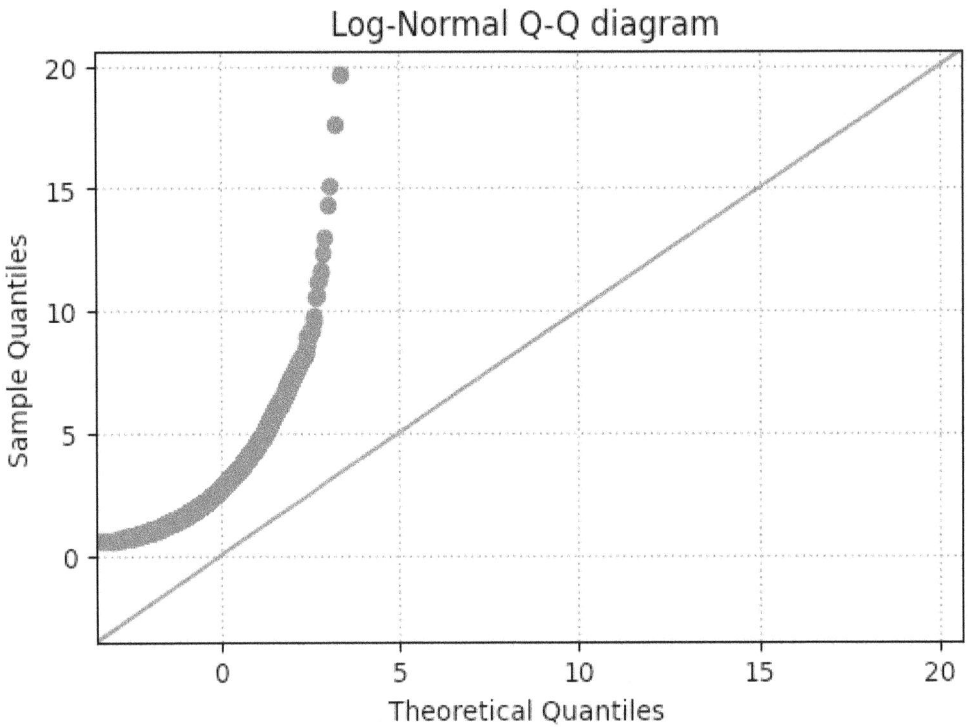

Interpretation

If the points on the plot fall along a straight diagonal line, then we assume that the dataset is normally distributed. However, if the points deviate from the diagonal line, we conclude that the dataset is not drawn from a normally distributed population.

This is hardly surprising, considering that we applied the log-normal distribution to generate the dataset used in this procedure.

4.5.3 Statistical Method - Shapiro-Wilk (SW) Test

A formal statistical test, such as the Shapiro-Wilk (SW) Test for normality can be performed. To set up the statistical procedure, we formulate.

Hypothesis

- H_0: the data series follows the normal distribution
- H_1: the data series does not follow the normal distribution

with a level of significance $\alpha = 0.05$

Remember, that our generated dataset follows the log-normal distribution, so we expect a failure to confirm that the dataset is normally distributed.

In the following Python code section, we demonstrate this test procedure and implement it. The results are reported and interpreted.

```
import math
import numpy as np
from scipy.stats import shapiro
from scipy.stats import lognorm

# parameters
N = 3000
alpha = 0.05
np.random.seed(1)
lognormal_sample = lognorm.rvs(s=0.5,
                               scale=math.exp(1),
                               size=N)
# Shapiro-Wilk test for normality
s, p = shapiro(lognormal_sample)
# results
print("Shapiro-Wilk Test:")
print("SW-statistic           : {:.4f}".format(s))
print("p-value                : {:.4E}".format(p))
print("level of significance : {:.2f}".format(alpha))
print("two-tailed test")
print("Hypothesis")
print("H0: the sample is normally distributed")
print("H1: the sample is not normally distributed")
if p < alpha/2:
    print("reject H0")
    print("Not Normal")
else:
    print("reject H1")
    print("Normal")
```

```
Shapiro-Wilk Test:
SW-statistic           : 0.8703
p-value                : 1.6816E-44
```

(continues on next page)

(continued from previous page)

```
level of significance : 0.05
two-tailed test
Hypothesis
H0: the sample is normally distributed
H1: the sample is not normally distributed
reject H0
Not Normal
```

Interpretation

From the computation output, it can be observed that the test statistic is 0.8703 and the corresponding p_{value} is 1.68E-44, almost zero. The test is set up to be a two-sided test, therefore we allocate $\frac{\alpha}{2}$ in either tail of the distribution.

Since the p_{value} is less than $\frac{\alpha}{2}$ of 0.025, we reject the null hypothesis H_0, in favor of the alternative hypothesis H_1. The data provides sufficient evidence to conclude that the sample does not come from a normal distribution. Such a claim can be made with (1-α) or 95% confidence.

4.5.4 Statistical Method - Kolmogorov-Smirnov (KS) Test

We perform a Kolmogorov-Smirnov (KS) Test for the normal distribution of the data series. To set up the statistical procedure, we formulate:

Hypothesis

- H_0: the data series follows the normal distribution
- H_1: the data series does not follow the normal distribution

with a level of significance $\alpha = 0.05$

If the p_{value} of the KS-Test is greater than $\frac{\alpha}{2}$ of 0.025, then the data is assumed to be normally distributed.

Keep in mind, that the sample is generated the way that it is following the log-normal distribution, so we know the outcome of the formal KS-Test already.

In the following Python code section, this procedure is implemented and the results are interpreted.

```
import math
import numpy as np
from scipy.stats import kstest
from scipy.stats import lognorm

# parameters
N = 3000
alpha = 0.05
```

(continues on next page)

(continued from previous page)

```
np.random.seed(1) # reproducibility
lognormal_sample = lognorm.rvs(s=0.5,
                               scale=math.exp(1),
                               size=N)
# Kolmogorov-Smirnov test
s, p = kstest(lognormal_sample, "norm")
# results
print("Kolmogorov-Smirnov Test:")
print("KS-statistic           : {:.4f}".format(s))
print("p-value                : {:.4E}".format(p))
print("level of significance : {:.2f}".format(alpha))
print("two-tailed test")
print("Hypothesis")
print("H0: the sample is normally distributed")
print("H1: the sample is not normally distributed")
if p < alpha/2:
    print("reject H0")
    print("Not Normal")
else:
    print("reject H1")
    print("Normal")
```

```
Kolmogorov-Smirnov Test:
KS-statistic          : 0.8413
p-value               : 0.0000E+00
level of significance : 0.05
two-tailed test
Hypothesis
H0: the sample is normally distributed
H1: the sample is not normally distributed
reject H0
Not Normal
```

Interpretation

The KS-statistic is reported as 0.8413 and the corresponding p_{value} is 0.0E0, almost zero.

The KS-Test is set up to be a two-tailed test, so we allocate $\frac{\alpha}{2}$ in either tail of the distribution.

Since the $p_{value} \leq \frac{\alpha}{2}$ of 0.025, we reject the null hypothesis H_0, in favor of the alternative hypothesis H_1. The data provides sufficient evidence, at the chosen level of significance (α), to conclude that the sample data does not come from a normal distribution. We can have (1-α) or 95% confidence in this assessment.

4.6 Preprocessing non-normal input data

If a given dataset is not normally distributed, we can apply one of the following transformations to make it more normally distributed:

- Square root transform : the values from x to $x^{1/2}$
- Cube root transform : the values from x to $x^{1/3}$
- Log transform : the values from x to $log(x)$

By applying one of these procedures, the transformed dataset becomes more normally distributed, and after the normality property is statistically confirmed, the aforementioned tests and procedures can be applied.

CHAPTER 5

STATISTICAL SIGNIFICANCE TEST

Statistical significance means that a produced result has a reason behind it and not by chance.

The `scipy.stats` module of the SciPy library, provides us with functions to perform such statistical significance tests. In the following section, we discuss some concepts and keywords commonly encountered when conducting statistical tests.

In the following sections, we discuss keywords and concepts often encountered while conducting statistical tests.

5.1 Hypothesis Testing

A hypothesis is an assumption about a statistical parameter for a population. The null hypothesis H_0 assumes that the observation is not statistically significant, and the alternative hypothesis H_1, on the other hand, assumes that the observations are due to some reason and therefore significant.

For example, if we have a situation where we need to distinguish between "better or worse", the hypothesis can be formed like this:

Hypothesis

- H_0 a student is worse than average
- H_1 a student is better than the average

The level of significance could be set to α = 0.05.

Other popular choices for the level of significance are α = 0.1, α = 0.05 and α = 0.01.

5.1.1 One-tailed test

A one-tailed test is appropriate if the estimated value departs from a reference value in only one direction, left or right, but not both. When our hypothesis is testing for one side of the value only, it is called a one-tailed test. Therefore, we can formulate:

Hypothesis

- H_0 "failure rate" > k
- H_1 "failure rate" < k

The level of significance could be set to α = 0.05

5.1.2 Two-tailed test

A two-tailed test is appropriate if the estimated value is greater or less than a certain value. When our hypothesis is testing for both sides of the values, we say this is a two-tailed test. To set up the test procedures, we formulate:

Hypothesis

- H_0: the mean is equal to k
- H_1: the mean is not equal to k

level of significance

- $\frac{\alpha}{2}$ = 0.025, in either tail

In this case, the mean is less than, or greater than k, and both sides of the distribution are considered.

5.1.3 Alpha (α) value

The α value denotes the level of significance.

For example, let α = 0.05, meaning that we demand a level of confidence of (1 - α) in our assessment.

Common choices for α are 0.01, 0.05, or 0.1, corresponding to a confidence of 99%, 95%, and 90%, respectively.

5.1.4 Tail probability (p_{value})

The p_{value} value indicates how close to the extreme the data is. The p_{value} is compared against the chosen level of significance α, to determine the statistical significance.

If $p < \alpha$, we reject the null hypothesis and say that the data is statistically significant. Otherwise, if $p > \alpha$, we fail to reject the null hypothesis.

5.2 Student-t Test for equality of means

The Student-t Test is used to determine if there is a significant difference between the means (μ_1, μ_2) of two samples. The test evaluates if the two samples were drawn from the same distribution. It is a two-tailed test.

We make use of the `ttest_ind()` function, provided by the `scipy.stats` library, which takes two samples of equal size and produces a tuple of Student-t statistics and p_{values}. It has the following signature:

```
res = ttest_ind(v1, v2)
```

where

- v1, v2: are the two input data series
- `res`: the return values as a tuple (t-statistic and p_{value})

This is a two-sided test assuming the two independent samples have identical expected values $\mu_1 = \mu_2$, and that the populations have identical variances $\sigma_1^2 = \sigma_2^2$.

With a Student-t test, we are trying to ascertain if the samples `v1` and `v2` both come from the same distribution, and we formulate:

Hypothesis

- H_0 the expected values $\mu_1 = \mu_2$ are similar
- H_1 the expected values $\mu_1 \neq \mu_2$ are not similar

level of significance

- $\alpha = 0.05$

In the following Python code section, two examples are implemented, to explore this function in greater detail.

Before the `ttest_ind()` function is used, we might want to bring up its documentation. And check the parameters, return values and potential limitations.

```
from scipy.stats import ttest_ind
# print(help(ttest_ind))
```

5.2.1 Samples v1 and v2 with equal means

For demonstration purposes, we generate two data series v1 and v2 of length N. The v1 sample is drawn from the normal distribution and is used as a reference, and the v2 sample is drawn from the normal distribution and is tested against the reference distribution.

The Student-t Test establishes whether the two samples are drawn from the same distribution and have similar means or expected values. We formulate the

Hypothesis

- H_0: the expected values are equal $(\mu_1 = \mu_2)$
- H_1: the expected values are not equal $(\mu_1 \neq \mu_2)$

level of significance

- $\alpha = 0.05$

The Student-t Test is set up to be a two-tailed test, so $\frac{\alpha}{2}$ is allocated in each tail of the distribution. In the following Python code segment, this approach is implemented and the results are presented.

```
import numpy as np
from scipy.stats import ttest_ind, describe

# parameters
N = 120000
alpha = 0.05
# Samples drawn from the normal distribution
np.random.seed(124) # reproducibility
v1 = np.random.normal(size=N) # normal, reference
v2 = np.random.normal(size=N) # normal
# Student-t Test
res = ttest_ind(v1, v2)
print("Student-t Test:")
print(f"t-statistic            : {res.statistic:.6f}")
print(f"p-value                : {res.pvalue:.6f}")
print(f"level of significance : {alpha:.2f}")
print("two-tailed test")
print("Hypothesis")
print("H0: the means are Equal")
print("H1: the means are Not Equal")
if res.pvalue < alpha/2:
    print("reject H0")
```

(continues on next page)

(continued from previous page)

```
    print("Not Equal")
else:
    print("fail to reject H0")
    print("Equal")
```

```
Student-t Test:
t-statistic             : -0.764297
p-value                 : 0.444691
level of significance : 0.05
two-tailed test
Hypothesis
H0: the means are Equal
H1: the means are Not Equal
fail to reject H0
Equal
```

Interpretation

The t-statistic is reported as 0.7642 and the associated p_{value} is 0.4447.

Since the $p_{value} > \frac{\alpha}{2}$ of 0.025, we cannot reject the null hypothesis H_0. The sample provides sufficient evidence to conclude that the expected values of both samples μ_1 and μ_2 are equal. At the chosen level of significance α, we can have (1-α) or 95% confidence in this assessment.

A visual inspection of the plots quite confirms this.

```
import pandas as pd
import matplotlib.pyplot as plt

# DataFrame
df = pd.DataFrame({"reference - normal distribution": v1,
                   "sample - normal distribution": v2})
# plot
fig, ax = plt.subplots(nrows=1,ncols=2, figsize=(8.5,3))
df.hist(bins=100, ax=ax)
ax[0].set_xlabel('$\mu$')
ax[0].set_ylabel('frequency')
ax[1].set_xlabel('$\mu$')
ax[1].set_ylabel('frequency')
plt.show()
```

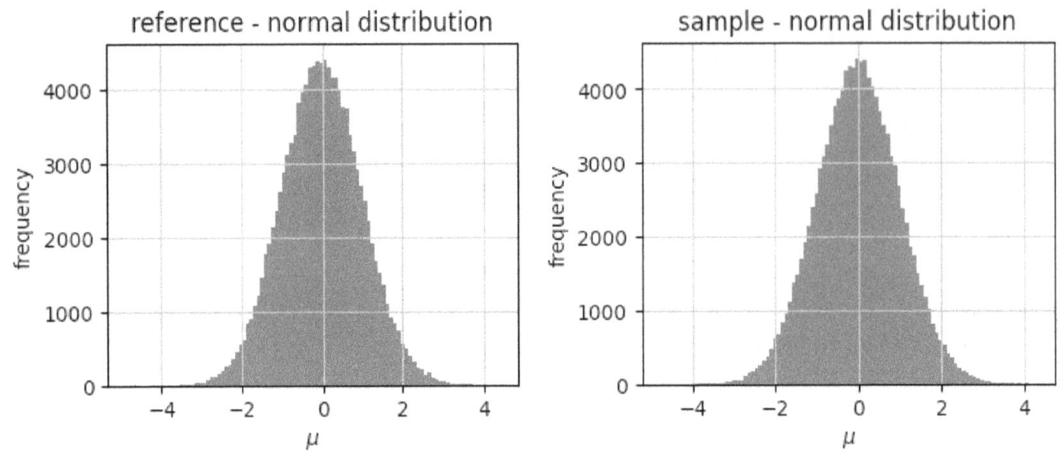

5.2.2 Samples v1 and v2 with unequal means

In this example, we generate two data series `v1` and `v2` of length `N`. The `v1` sample is drawn from the normal distribution and is used as a reference, and the `v2` sample is drawn from the log-normal distribution and tested against normal or reference distribution `v1`. The Student-t Test tries to establish whether the two samples are drawn from the same distribution and therefore have similar means or expected values. To set up the statistical procedure, we formulate the

Hypothesis

- H_0: the expected values are equal, $\mu_1 = \mu_2$
- H_1: the expected values are not equal, $\mu_1 \neq \mu_2$

level of significance

- $\alpha = 0.05$

The Student-t Test is set up as a two-tailed test, meaning that $\frac{\alpha}{2} = 0.025$ is allocated in each tail of the distribution. In the following code segment, this process is implemented and its results are presented and interpreted.

```
import numpy as np
from scipy.stats import ttest_ind, describe

# parameters
N = 20000
alpha = 0.05
# Samples drawn from normal and log-normal distribution
np.random.seed(124)
v1 = np.random.normal(size=N) # normal, reference
v2 = np.random.lognormal(size=N) # log-normal
# Student-t Test
```

(continues on next page)

(continued from previous page)

```
res = ttest_ind(v1, v2)
print('Student-t Test:')
print(f"t-statistic              : {res.statistic:.6f}")
print(f"p-value                  : {res.pvalue:.6E}")
print(f"level of significance : {alpha:.2f}")
print("two-tailed test")
print("Hypothesis")
print("H0: the means are Equal")
print("H1: the means are Not Equal")
if res.pvalue < alpha/2:
    print("reject H0")
    print("Not Equal")
else:
    print("fail to reject H0")
    print("Equal")
```

```
Student-t Test:
t-statistic           : -95.640918
p-value               : 0.000000E+00
level of significance : 0.05
two-tailed test
Hypothesis
H0: the means are Equal
H1: the means are Not Equal
reject H0
Not Equal
```

Interpretation

The t-statistic is reported as t = -95.64 and the associated p_{value} = 0.0e0, almost zero.

Since the p_{value} is smaller than the $\frac{\alpha}{2}$ = 0.025, we reject the null hypothesis H_0, in favor of the alternative hypothesis H_1. The sample data provides sufficient evidence to conclude that the expected values of both samples μ_1 and μ_2 are not equal. At the chosen level of significance α, we can have (1-α) or 95% confidence in this claim.

The visual inspection of the plots confirms this.

```
import pandas as pd
import matplotlib.pyplot as plt

df = pd.DataFrame({"normal distribution v1": v1,
                   "log-normal distribution v2": v2})
# plot
fix, ax = plt.subplots(1, 2, figsize=(8.5,3))
df.hist(bins=60,
        ax=ax)
```

(continues on next page)

(continued from previous page)

```
ax[0].set_xlabel('$\mu$')
ax[0].set_ylabel('frequency')
ax[1].set_xlabel('$\mu$')
ax[1].set_ylabel('frequency')
plt.show()
```

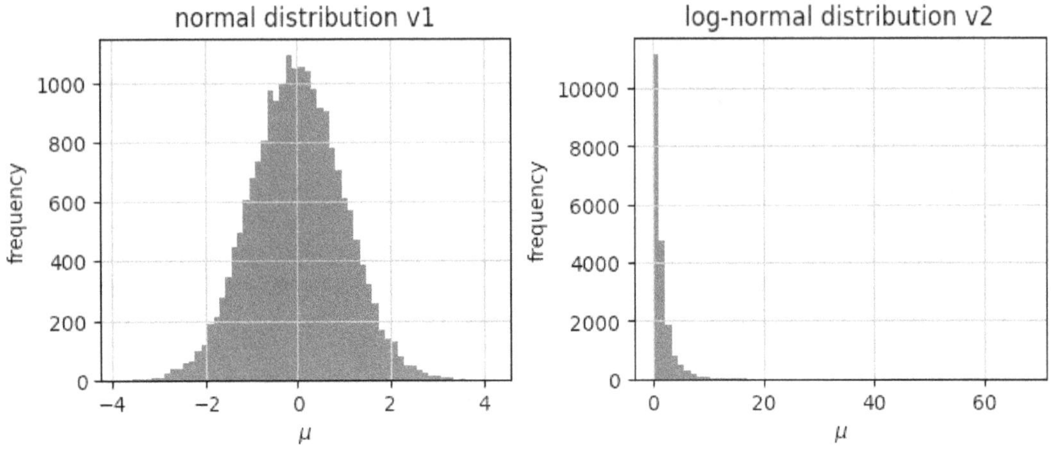

5.3 Kolmogorov-Smirnov (KS) Test for Normality

The Kolmogorov-Smirnov (KS) Test is used to statistically confirm if a given sample follows the normal distribution. We make use of the `kstest()` function from the `scipy` library. We pass in the data sample v and the cumulative density function as a second parameter, and the signature becomes:

```
res = kstest(v, 'norm')
```

where

- `v`: is the input data sample
- `norm`: is the cumulative density function, the sample v is tested against

returning a data tuple containing the t-statistic and a p_{value}.

The Kolmogorov-Smirnov (KS) Test can either be used as a one-tailed or two-tailed test procedure. By default, it is a two-tailed test.

5.3.1 Sample v is drawn from the normal distribution

```
v = np.random.normal(size=1000)
```

We compare the sample v against the cumulative density function cdf() and try to establish whether this distribution is similar to the normal distribution, at a chosen level of significance. We formulate the

Hypothesis

- H_0: the data series is normally distributed
- H_1: the data series is not normally distributed

level of significance

- $\alpha = 0.05$

Recall, that by default, the KS-Test is a two-tailed test, so we allocate $\frac{\alpha}{2}$ in either tail of the distribution.

In the following Python code section, this test is implemented and the results are presented and interpreted.

```
import numpy as np
from scipy.stats import kstest

# parameters
alpha = 0.05
# Sample was drawn from the normal distribution
np.random.seed(124)
v = np.random.normal(size=1000)
# KS test
res = kstest(v, "norm")
# results
print("Kolmogorov-Smirnov Test:")
print(f"KS-statistic          : {res.statistic:.6f}")
print(f"p-value               : {res.pvalue:.6f}")
print(f"level of significance : {alpha:.2f}")
print("two-tailed test")
print("Hypothesis")
print("H0: the distribution of the data is Normal")
print("H1: the distribution of the data is Not Normal")
if res.pvalue < alpha/2: # two tailed test
    print("reject H0")
    print("Not Normal")
else:
    print("fail to reject H0")
    print("Normal")
```

```
Kolmogorov-Smirnov Test:
KS-statistic           : 0.024044
p-value                : 0.601085
level of significance : 0.05
two-tailed test
Hypothesis
H0: the distribution of the data is Normal
H1: the distribution of the data is Not Normal
fail to reject H0
Normal
```

Interpretation

The KS-statistic is reported as 0.024044 and the associated p_{value} is 0.6011.

Since the p_{value} is larger than the $\frac{\alpha}{2}$ of 0.025, we fail to reject the null hypothesis H_0. The data sample provides sufficient evidence to conclude, that the sample v is indeed drawn from the normal distribution. At the chosen level of significance (α), we can make this claim with (1-α) or 95% confidence.

This result is hardly surprising, given the way we created the sample data.

5.3.2 Sample v is drawn from the log-normal distribution

```
v = np.random.lognormal(size=1000)
```

We compare this sample v against the cumulative density function cdf() and try to establish whether this distribution is similar to the normal distribution, at a chosen level of significance. We formulate the

Hypothesis

- H_0: the data series is normally distributed
- H_1: the data series is not normally distributed

level of significance

- α = 0.05

Recall, that the Kolmogorov-Smirnov (KS) Test is a two-tailed test by default, so we allocate $\frac{\alpha}{2}$ in each tail of the distribution.

In the following Python code section, this approach is presented and the results are interpreted.

```
import numpy as np
from scipy.stats import kstest

# parameters
```

(continues on next page)

(continued from previous page)

```
N = 3000
alpha = 0.05
# sample v drawn from the log-normal distribution
np.random.seed(1)
v = np.random.lognormal(size=N)
# KS test
res = kstest(v, "norm")
# results
print("Kolmogorov-Smirnov Test:")
print(f"sample size             : {N:.0f}")
print(f"KS-statistic            : {res.statistic:.6f}")
print(f"p-value                 : {res.pvalue:.6E}")
print("level of significance : {:.2f}".format(alpha))
print("two-tailed test")
print("Hypothesis")
print("H0: the distribution of the data is Normal")
print("H1: the distribution of the data is Not Normal")
if res.pvalue < alpha/2: # two tailed test
    print("reject H0")
    print("Not Normal")
else:
    print("fail to reject H0")
    print("Normal")
```

```
Kolmogorov-Smirnov Test:
sample size           : 3000
KS-statistic          : 0.532335
p-value               : 0.000000E+00
level of significance : 0.05
two-tailed test
Hypothesis
H0: the distribution of the data is Normal
H1: the distribution of the data is Not Normal
reject H0
Not Normal
```

Interpretation

The KS-statistic is reported as 0.532335 and the associated p_{value} as 0.00e0, almost zero.

Since the p_{value} is smaller $\frac{\alpha}{2}$ of 0.025 we can reject the null hypothesis H_0 in favor of the alternative hypothesis H_1. The data provides sufficient evidence to conclude, with 95% certainty, that sample v is not drawn from the normal distribution, which is exactly what we expect, given the way we created the sample dataset.

5.4 Extract summary statistics from the result object

The `describe()` function is available from the `scipy.stats` library provides a summary statistics table. It has the following signature:

```
scipy.stats.res = describe(v)
```

where `v` is the data series and returns the following elements:

- number of observations (nobs)
- minimum and maximum values
- expected value or mean
- variance
- skewness
- kurtosis

Remember that the `describe()` function reports the kurtosis measure in Fisher notation, which is 0 for a normal distribution. Whereas the Pearson notation reports a kurtosis of 3 for the normal distribution, which is just an offset of 3.

In the following Python segment, we demonstrate the usage and present the computed values.

```
import numpy as np
from scipy.stats import describe

# Sample was drawn from normal distribution
np.random.seed(124)
N = 1000
v = np.random.normal(size=N)
# describe object
des = describe(v)
# results
print("describe:")
print(f"nobs                 : {des.nobs:.0f}")
print(f"min                  : {des.minmax[0]:.6f}")
print(f"max                  : {des.minmax[1]:.6f}")
print(f"mean                 : {des.mean:.6f}")
print(f"variance             : {des.variance:.6f}")
print(f"skewness             : {des.skewness:.6f}")
print(f"kurtosis Fisher      : {des.kurtosis:.6f}")
print(f"kurtosis Pearson     : {des.kurtosis+3:.6f}")
```

```
describe:
nobs                 : 1000
min                  : -3.047625
```

(continues on next page)

(continued from previous page)

```
max                  : 2.883788
mean                 : 0.002333
variance             : 1.009813
skewness             : -0.134815
kurtosis Fisher      : -0.148352
kurtosis Pearson     : 2.851648
```

5.5 Skewness and Kurtosis

The skewness is a measure of symmetry in the data.

- For the normal distribution, it is 0
- A negative skew indicates that the mean of the data is off-center and to the left.
- A positive skew indicates that the mean of the data is off-center and to the right.

The kurtosis is a measure of the peakedness of the distribution. A low peakedness, or positive kurtosis, is indicated by heavy or fat tails in the distribution. Conversely, high peakedness, or negative kurtosis, refers to a slim and narrow distribution with light tails. In summary, positive kurtosis means heavy tails and negative kurtosis means light tails.

In Python, we implement the computation and present the results.

```python
import numpy as np
from scipy.stats import skew, kurtosis

# parameters
N = 10000
# Sample was drawn from normal distribution
np.random.seed(1)
v = np.random.normal(size=N)
# inspect
print("statistical moments:")
print(f"sample size           : {N:.0f}")
print(f"mean                  : {np.mean(v):.6f}")
print(f"std                   : {np.var(v):.6f}")
print(f"skew                  : {skew(v):.6f}")
print(f"kurtosis Fisher       : {kurtosis(v):.6f}")
print(f"kurtosis Pearson      : {kurtosis(v)+3:.6f}")
```

```
statistical moments:
sample size          : 10000
mean                 : 0.009773
```

(continues on next page)

(continued from previous page)

```
std                : 0.997573
skew               : 0.024905
kurtosis Fisher    : 0.028670
kurtosis Pearson   : 3.028670
```

5.6 Testing for Normality

To investigate if the presented data is drawn from the normal distribution, the `normaltest()` function, which is provided by the SciPy library, is used. Its signature becomes:

```
s,p = normaltest(a, axis=0, nan_policy='propagate')
```

where

- `a`: is the sample data series v
- `axis`: 0 optional, default is 0
- `nan_policy`: the setting 'propagate' returns `NaN` values if present

it returns a test statistics measure and the corresponding p_{value}.

Before we use the `normaltest()` function, we might want to bring up the documentation.

```
from scipy.stats import normaltest
# help(normaltest)
```

5.6.1 Sample v drawn from the normal distribution

We draw a sample from the normal distribution. Then we conduct a test for normality using the `normaltest()` function from the `scipy.stats` library packages, to confirm that the data is indeed drawn from a normal distribution, with a chosen level of significance. The `normaltest()` function has this signature:

```
v = np.random.normal(size=9000)
```

To formulate the statistical procedure, we write:

Hypothesis

- H_0: the data series is normally distributed
- H_1: the data series is not normally distributed

level of significance:

- $\alpha = 0.05$

The test is set up to be a two-tailed test, so we allocate $\frac{\alpha}{2}$ in either tail of the distribution.

It is expected, that the test confirms, that the sample v is indeed drawn from the normal distribution since we created the sample data that way. In the following Python code segment, this test is implemented and the results are interpreted.

```
import numpy as np
from scipy.stats import normaltest

# parameters
alpha = 0.05
# sample was drawn from the normal distribution
np.random.seed(1)
v = np.random.normal(size=9000)
# compute normaltest
res = normaltest(v)
# results
print("Normaltest Test:")
print(f"statistic             : {res.statistic:.4f}")
print(f"pvalue                : {res.pvalue:.4f}")
print(f"level of significance : {alpha:.2f}")
print("two-tailed test")
print("Hypothesis")
print("H0: the distribution of the data is Normal")
print("H1: the distribution of the data is Not Normal")
if res.pvalue < alpha/2:
    print("reject H0")
    print("Not Normal")
else:
    print("fail to reject H0")
    print("Normal")
```

```
Normaltest Test:
statistic             : 0.9558
pvalue                : 0.6201
level of significance : 0.05
two-tailed test
Hypothesis
H0: the distribution of the data is Normal
H1: the distribution of the data is Not Normal
fail to reject H0
Normal
```

Interpretation

The statistic is reported as 0.9558 and the associated p_{value} is 0.6201.

The p_{value} is larger than $\frac{\alpha}{2}$ of 0.025, so we fail to reject the null hypothesis

H_0. The tested data provides sufficient evidence to conclude, with (1-α) or 95% certainty, that the sample v is indeed drawn from the normal distribution, exactly what we expected.

To visualize the data, we plot the sample and create two corresponding histograms, side by side.

```
import matplotlib.pyplot as plt
import pandas as pd

df = pd.DataFrame({"sample": v})
# plot
fig, ax = plt.subplots(nrows=1, ncols=2, figsize=(8.5,3))
fig.suptitle("Sample drawn from normal distribution",
             fontsize=10)
# left
plt.subplot(1, 2, 1)
ax[0].set_title("sample v", fontsize=10)
ax[0].set_xlabel('count')
ax[0].set_ylabel('$\sigma$')
df["sample"].plot(ax=ax[0])
ax[0].grid()
# right
plt.subplot(1, 2, 2)
ax[1].grid()
ax[1].set_title("histogram", fontsize=10)
ax[1].set_xlabel('$\mu$')
ax[1].set_ylabel('frequency')
df["sample"].hist(bins=50,
                  ax=ax[1])
plt.show()
```

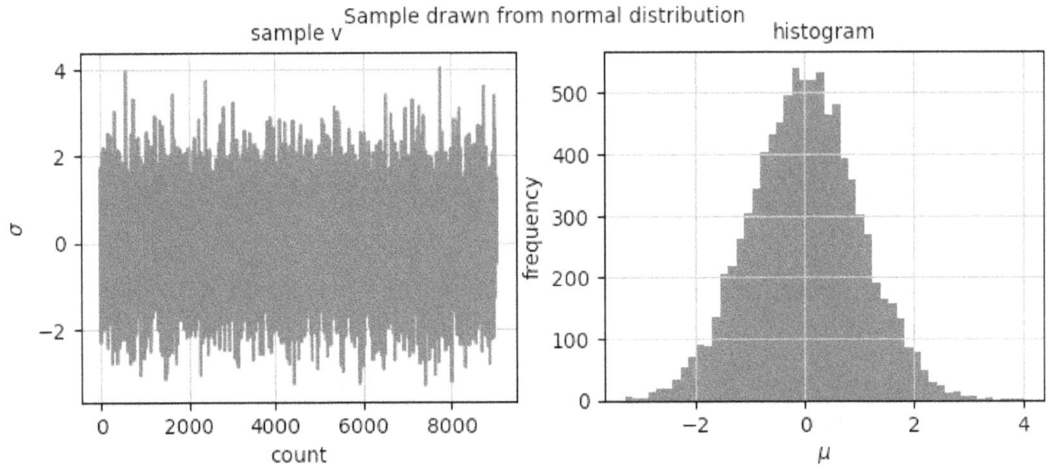

5.6.2 Sample v drawn from the log-normal distribution

The sample data is drawn from a log-normal distribution, by utilizing the `lognormal()` function of the NumPy random package, which has the following signature:

```
v = np.random.lognormal(size=3000)
```

We test for normality and expect, given the way we produced the test dataset, this test to fail. In Python, we implement this procedure and report and interpret the results.

```
import numpy as np
from scipy.stats import normaltest

# parameters
N = 3000
alpha = 0.05
# sample v drawn from log-normal distribution
np.random.seed(1)
v = np.random.lognormal(size=N)
# normaltest
res = normaltest(v)
# results
print("Normaltest-Test:")
print(f"sample size            : {N:.0f}")
print(f"statistics             : {res.statistic:.6f}")
print(f"p-value                : {res.pvalue:.6E}")
print(f"level of significance : {alpha:.2f}")
print("two-sided test")
print("Hypothesis")
print("H0: the distribution of the data is Normal")
print("H1: the distribution of the data is Not Normal")
if res.pvalue < alpha/2:
    print("reject H0")
    print("Not Normal")
else:
    print("fail to reject H0")
    print("Normal")
```

```
Normaltest-Test:
sample size           : 3000
statistics            : 4255.417554
p-value               : 0.000000E+00
level of significance : 0.05
two-sided test
Hypothesis
H0: the distribution of the data is Normal
H1: the distribution of the data is Not Normal
```

(continues on next page)

(continued from previous page)

```
reject H0
Not Normal
```

Interpretation

The statistic is reported as 4255.41 and the associated p_{value} as 0.0e0, almost zero.

The p_{value} is smaller than $\frac{\alpha}{2}$ of 0.025, we reject the null hypothesis H_0 in favor of the alternative hypothesis H_1. The data provides sufficient evidence to conclude, with (1-α) or 95% certainty, that the sample v is not drawn from the normal distribution. This is exactly as we expected, given the way the test data set was constructed.

To visualize this, we plot the data sample v along with the corresponding histogram, side by side.

```
import matplotlib.pyplot as plt
import pandas as pd

df = pd.DataFrame({"sample": v})
# plot
fig, ax = plt.subplots(nrows=1, ncols=2, figsize=(8.5,3))
fig.suptitle("Sample drawn from log-normal distribution",
             fontsize=10)
# left
df["sample"].plot(ax=ax[0])
ax[0].grid()
ax[0].set_title("sample v", fontsize=10)
ax[0].set_xlabel('count')
ax[0].set_ylabel('$\sigma$')
# right
ax[1].grid()
df["sample"].hist(bins=50,
                  ax=ax[1])
ax[1].set_title("histogram", fontsize=10)
ax[1].set_xlabel('$\mu$')
ax[1].set_ylabel('frequency')
# plt.tight_layout()
plt.show()
```

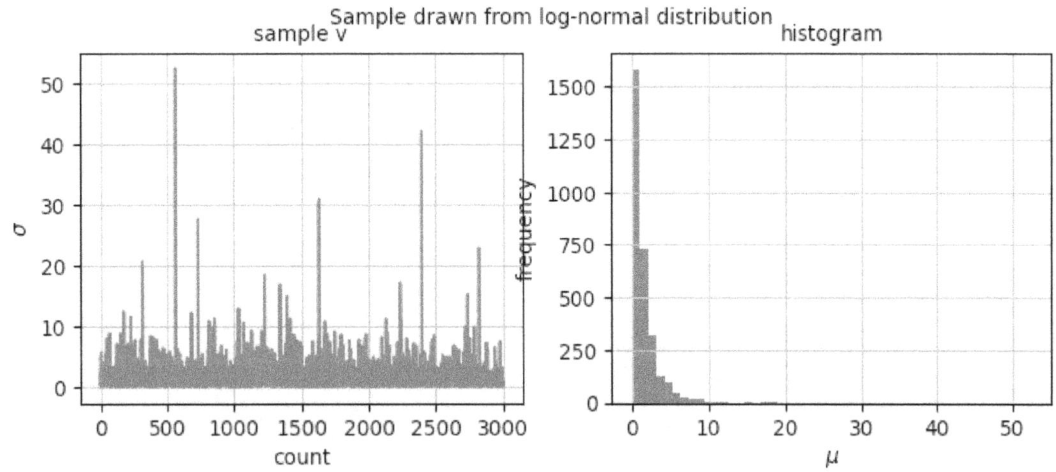
Sample drawn from log-normal distribution
sample v
histogram
σ
count
frequency
μ

CHAPTER 6

RUNS TEST TO CONFIRM RANDOMNESS

A run is defined as a series of increasing or decreasing values, and the number of consecutive up or down values determines the length of each run. A Runs Test for randomness is a statistical test that is applied to statistically assess the randomness of the sample data.

The Runs Test is non-parametric and uses runs of consecutive values to decide whether the presented sample is random or not, at the required level of significance.

Random numbers are a crucial part of many systems, like simulations, or cryptographic tools. Since a computer is not able to produce truly random numbers, they are known as pseudo-random numbers. The generated sequence depends on an initial value, called seed, which is to be passed into the algorithm.

One of the nice properties of these pseudo-random sequences is that they are reproducible, meaning that given a seed value, the algorithm produces an identical set of pseudo-random numbers, each time.

To ensure that the values generated by the pseudo-random number generator are as close to random as possible, several statistical tests for randomness can be applied, such as:

- Runs Test of randomness
- Chi-Square Test

In the following section, we discuss both test procedures.

6.1 Runs Test for Randomness with the runsTest() function

The number of increasing, or decreasing, values determines the length of the run. The first step in this Runs Test implementation is to count the number of runs in the data sample. In this case, the values above the median are treated as positive and values below the median as negative. A run is defined as a series of consecutive positive or negative values. We compute the test statistic like so.

Z-statistic:

$$Z = \frac{R - \bar{R}}{s_R}$$

where

- R: the number of observed runs
- $\bar{R}$: the number of expected runs

given as

$$\bar{R} = \frac{2n_1n_2}{n_1 + n_2} + 1$$

and

- s_R : standard deviation of the number of runs

$$s_R^2 = \frac{2n_1n_2(2n_1n_2 - n_1 - n_2)}{(n_1 + n_2)^2(n_1 + n_2 - 1)}$$

with

- n_1 and n_2: the number of positive and negative values in the series.

The computed $Z_{statistic}$ is compared with a critical value $Z_{critical}$, which corresponds to the chosen level of significance α, to determine the randomness of the provided pseudo-random sequence.

To compute the $Z_{critical}$ value, we make use of the percentage point function `ppf()`, provided by the stats module of the SciPy library. It can be used like so:

```
z_critical = abs(norm.ppf(q=alpha_half))
```

For interpretation, we compare the value of the calculated $Z_{statistic}$ with the $Z_{critical}$ value computed like $Z_{critical} = 1.96$, which corresponds to a level of significance of $\alpha = 0.025$. Since the applied Z-Test is a two-tailed test $\frac{\alpha}{2}$ is allocated in each tail of the distribution.

If $|Z_{statistic}| > Z_{critical}$ the sample provides us with sufficient evidence to conclude that the numbers are not random, otherwise we conclude that the numbers are random. Such a claim can be made, given the chosen level of significance α = 0.05 with (1-α) or 95% confidence.

Suppose we make use of a pseudo-random number generator to produce a set of 100 values drawn from the normal distribution. We assume that these values are randomly distributed and contain no "runs", which are defined as consecutive values up or consecutive values down.

```
for i in range(100):
    sample.append(random.normalvariate(10, 2))
```

To formally test the property of randomness, a Runs Test is conducted, to quantitatively assess the randomness of the sampled number sequence. We formulate:

Hypothesis

- H_0: The sequence was produced in a random manner
- H_1: The sequence was produced in a non-random manner

level of significance

- α = 0.05

Since the Runs Test is two-tailed, $\frac{\alpha}{2}$ is allocated in each tail of the distribution for the computation of the $Z_{critical}$ value.

6.1.1 Sample drawn from the normal distribution

We apply the custom build `runsTest()` function, which has the following signature:

```
median = statistics.median(sample)
Z = abs(runsTest(sample, median))
```

where:

- sample: the first parameter to the function
- median: the second parameter of the function

The test procedure is set up to be a two-tailed test, so we allocate $\frac{\alpha}{2}$ in either tail of the distribution, and the critical value $Z_{critical}$ is computed using the `ppf()` function, which is provided by the `stats.norm` package. It has the following signature:

```
z_critical = abs(norm.ppf(q=alpha/2))
```

where the q parameter is set to $\frac{\alpha}{2}$.

In the following Python code segment, this procedure is implemented and the results are interpreted.

```
import random
import math
import statistics
from scipy.stats import norm

def runsTest(l, median):
    """ runsTest: performs a runs test
    Hypothesis:
        H0: sequence is produced in a random manner
        H1: sequence is Not produced in a random manner
    Parameters:
        l = list or array of random numbers
        l_median = the statistical median of l
    Returns:
        z = Z-statistic for the runs """

    runs, n1, n2 = 0, 0, 0
    # checking the start of a run
    for i in range(len(l)):
        # no. of runs
        if (l[i] >= median and l[i - 1] < median) or (
            l[i] < median and l[i - 1] >= median):
            runs += 1
        # no. of positive values
        if (l[i]) >= median:
            n1 += 1
        # no. of negative values
        else:
            n2 += 1
    # expected and deviation
    runs_exp = ((2 * n1 * n2) / (n1 + n2)) + 1
    stan_dev = math.sqrt((2 * n1 * n2 * (2 * n1 * n2 - n1 - n2)) /
                         (((n1 + n2) ** 2) * (n1 + n2 - 1)))
    # Z-statistic
    z = (runs - runs_exp) / stan_dev
    return z

# parameters
N = 100
alpha = 0.05
# sample was drawn from the normal distribution
sample = []
random.seed(1) # reproducibility
for i in range(N):
    sample.append(random.normalvariate(10, 2))
# perform runsTest
median = statistics.median(sample)
```

(continues on next page)

(continued from previous page)

```
# custom function runsTest()
Z = abs(runsTest(sample, median))
# critical value
z_critical = abs(norm.ppf(q=alpha/2))
# results
print("runsTest:")
print(f"sample size              : {N:.0f}")
print(f"Z-statistic              : {Z:.4f}")
print(f"Z-critical               : {z_critical:.2f}")
print(f"level of significance    : {alpha:.2f}")
print('two-tailed test')
print('Hypothesis')
print("H0: sequence was produced in a Random manner")
print("H1: sequence was produced in a Non Random manner")
if Z < z_critical:
    print("failed to reject H0")
    print("Random")
else:
    print("reject H0")
    print("Non Random")
```

```
runsTest:
sample size              : 100
Z-statistic              : 0.6031
Z-critical               : 1.96
level of significance    : 0.05
two-tailed test
Hypothesis
H0: sequence was produced in a Random manner
H1: sequence was produced in a Non Random manner
failed to reject H0
Random
```

Interpretation

The $Z_{statistic}$ is reported at 0.6031. The $Z_{critical}$ value of 1.96 corresponds to the chosen level of significance α of 0.05, whereby $\frac{\alpha}{2}$ is used to compute this value.

Since the $Z_{statistic}$ value of 0.6031 is smaller than the $Z_{critical}$ value of 1.96, we fail to reject the null hypothesis H_0 at the chosen level of $\frac{\alpha}{2}$ of 0.025 allocated in each tail of the distribution.

The tested data sequence provides sufficient evidence to conclude that the sample is indeed random, at the desired level of significance α. We can make this claim with (1-α) or 95% confidence.

6.1.2 Sample drawn from the uniform distribution

The data sequence is generated by drawing 100 values from the uniform distribution and we test this sequence for randomness. For that, the custom build `runsTest()` function is applied, with this signature:

```
median = statistics.median(sample)
Z = abs(runsTest(sample, median))
```

In the next Python code segment, this approach is implemented and the results are interpreted.

```
from scipy.stats import norm

# parameters
N = 100
alpha = 0.05
# sample was drawn from a uniform distribution
sample = []
random.seed(1) # reproducibility
for i in range(N):
    sample.append(random.random()) # uniform
# perform runsTest
median = statistics.median(sample)
Z = abs(runsTest(sample, median))
# critical value
z_critical = abs(norm.ppf(q=alpha/2))
# results
print("runsTest:")
print(f"sample size                 : {N:.0f}")
print(f"Z-statistic                 : {Z:.4f}")
print(f"Z-critical                  : {z_critical:.2f}")
print(f"level of significance       : {alpha:.2f}")
print('two-tailed test')
print('Hypothesis')
print("H0: sequence was produced in a Random manner")
print("H1: sequence was produced in a Non Random manner")
if Z < z_critical:
    print("failed to reject H0")
    print("Random")
else:
    print("reject H0")
    print("Non Random")
```

```
runsTest:
sample size              : 100
Z-statistic              : 1.8092
Z-critical               : 1.96
level of significance    : 0.05
```

(continues on next page)

(continued from previous page)

```
two-tailed test
Hypothesis
H0: sequence was produced in a Random manner
H1: sequence was produced in a Non Random manner
failed to reject H0
Random
```

Interpretation

The $Z_{critical}$ value of 1.96 corresponds to the chosen level of significance α of 0.05, whereby $\frac{\alpha}{2}$ is used to compute this value.

Since the $Z_{statistic}$ value of 1.8092 is lower than the $Z_{critical}$ value of 1.96, we fail to reject the null hypothesis H_0 at the chosen level of significance α. The tested data sequence provides sufficient evidence to conclude that the sample is indeed random, at the desired level of significance α. We can make this claim with (1-α) or 95% confidence.

We might want to review the documentation of the custom-built `runsTest()` function.

```
# print(runsTest.__doc__)
# help(runsTest)
```

6.2 Runs Test for Randomness

The Runs test is a statistical test that is used to determine whether a dataset comes from a random process. To conduct a formal test, we formulate:

Hypothesis

- H_0: The data was produced in a random manner
- H_1: The data was not produced in a random manner

level of significance:

- $\alpha = 0.05$

We can perform a Runs Test on a given dataset by using the `runstest_1samp()` method from the statsmodels library, which has this signature:

```
runstest_1samp(x, cutoff='mean', correction=True)
```

where:

- `x`: Array of data values
- `cutoff`: threshold used to split the data into large and small values

- `correction`: for a sample size below 50, this function subtracts 0.5 as a correction

and it returns

- z_stat: test statistic, asymptotically normally distributed
- p_{value}: reject the null hypothesis if it is below the type 1 error level, α.

This function produces a $Z_{statistic}$ and a corresponding p_{value}.

In conjunction with the chosen level of significance α, we can draw statistical inferences regarding the randomness of the sample data.

To view the help documentation on the `runstest_1samp()` function.

```
from statsmodels.sandbox.stats.runs import runstest_1samp
# help(runstest_1samp)
```

6.2.1 Sample dataset containing "runs"

We produce a dataset of consecutive up values, by using the Python `range()` function. Since this dataset represents a single run of increasing numbers, we therefore know that the dataset cannot be considered random at any level of significance.

```
data = list(range(1,21))
```

We would like to confirm, that the set of numbers indeed is generated by a non-random process, at a chosen level of significance. For this purpose, we conduct the statistical test by applying the `runstest_1samp()` library method, with the following signature:

```
z, p = runstest_1samp(data_rnd, cutoff='mean', correction=False)
```

where

- `data_rnd`: dataset containing the test data
- `cutoff`: split the values into large and small values
- `correction`: set to False, meaning no correction

referring to the help function, to obtain a more detailed description.

In the following code segment in Python, we implement this test and interpret its results.

```
import numpy as np
from statsmodels.sandbox.stats.runs import runstest_1samp

# parameters
alpha = 0.05
# Experiment 1: with non-random data
data = list(range(1, 21))
z, p = runstest_1samp(data,
                      cutoff="mean",
                      correction=False)
# results
print("Runs-Test:")
print(f"sample size            : {len(data):.0f}")
print(f"Z-statistic            : {z:.4f}")
print(f"p-value                : {p:.2E}")
print(f"level of significance : {alpha:.2f}")
print("two-tailed test")
print("Hypothesis")
print("H0: data generated by random process")
print("H1: data generated by Non random process")
if p < alpha/2:
    print("reject H0")
    print("Not Random")
else:
    print("fail to reject H0")
    print("Random")
```

```
Runs-Test:
sample size            : 20
Z-statistic            : -4.1352
p-value                : 3.55E-05
level of significance : 0.05
two-tailed test
Hypothesis
H0: data generated by random process
H1: data generated by Non random process
reject H0
Not Random
```

Interpretation

The $Z_{statistic}$ is computed as -4.135 and the corresponding p_{value} is 3.55e-5, almost 0.

Since this $p_{value} \leq \frac{\alpha}{2}$, at the chosen level of significance α, we reject the null hypothesis H_0, in favor of the alternative hypothesis H_1. The tested sample provides sufficient evidence to say that the data sequence was produced in a non-random manner, and we can have (1-α) or 95% confidence in such a claim.

6.2.2 Sample dataset generated at "random"

We employ the NumPy random number generator to produce a set of randomly drawn integer numbers. For this, we make use of the `randint()` function of the NumPy package, which has the following signature.

```
data_rnd = np.random.randint(0,10, size=100000)
```

It is desirable to confirm, at a chosen level of significance, that a given set of numbers was indeed produced randomly. For this purpose, we make use of the `runtest_1samp()` method from the matplotlib library, which has this signature.

```
z, p = runstest_1samp(data_rnd, cutoff='mean', correction=False)
```

In the following Python code segment this idea is implemented and its results are interpreted.

```
import numpy as np
from statsmodels.sandbox.stats.runs import runstest_1samp

# parameters
alpha = 0.05
N = 100000
# Experiment 2: with random data
np.random.seed(1) # reproducibility
data_rnd = np.random.randint(0, 10, size=N) # random
z, p = runstest_1samp(data_rnd,
                      cutoff="mean",
                      correction=False)
# results
print("Runs-Test:")
print(f"sample size            : {N:.0f}")
print(f"Z-statistic            : {z:.6f}")
print(f"p-value                : {p:.2E}")
print(f"level of significance : {alpha:.2f}")
print("two-tailed test")
print("Hypothesis")
print("H0: data generated by Random process")
print("H1: data generated by Non Random process")
if p < alpha/2:
    print("reject H0")
    print("Not Random")
else:
    print("fail to reject H0")
    print("Random")
```

```
Runs-Test:
sample size            : 100000
Z-statistic            : -0.874315
```

(continues on next page)

(continued from previous page)

```
p-value                 : 3.82E-01
level of significance : 0.05
two-tailed test
Hypothesis
H0: data generated by Random process
H1: data generated by Non Random process
fail to reject H0
Random
```

Interpretation

The $z_{statistic}$ turns out to be -0.8743 and the corresponding p_{value} is reported as 3.82e-1.

As the test is set up to be a two-tailed test, $\frac{\alpha}{2}$ is allocated in either tail of the distribution. Since the $p_{value} > \frac{\alpha}{2}$ of 0.025, we fail to reject the null hypothesis H_0 and conclude that the analyzed sample provides sufficient evidence to say that the data was produced randomly. With the chosen level of significance α of 0.05, we can have (1-α) or 95% confidence in this assessment.

CHAPTER 7

KOLMOGOROV-SMIRNOV (KS) TEST

The Kolmogorov-Smirnov (KS) Test represents a very efficient way to determine if two samples are significantly different from each other. It can also be used to test the uniformity of numbers generated by a pseudo-random number generator.

The KS-statistic quantifies the distance between the empirical distribution function of a sample and the cumulative distribution function of a reference distribution. Alternatively, a test for equality of two distributions can be constructed by testing two samples against each other.

For example, to test and verify the uniformity of pseudo-random numbers, we use the cumulative distribution function `cdf()` of uniformly distributed data of type $U[0, 1]$, as the reference distribution, and we formulate:

cumulative density function

$$F(x) = x$$

is defined in the $0 \leq x \leq 1$ interval.

The data series of pseudo-random numbers, we want to test, must also be in the $[0, 1]$ range, and we compute the Sn values, like so:

$$Sn(x) = \frac{(R1, R2...Rn < x)}{N}$$

The Kolmogorov-Smirnov (KS) Test can be used in two different ways, and we explore several examples of both.

- One Sample KS Test - sample `v` versus reference distribution
- Two Sample KS Test - sample `v1` versus sample `v2`

Before using the random generator, we might want to bring up its documentation and understand its properties and limitations.

```
import random
# print(help(random.random))          # uniform
# print(help(random.normalvariate))   # normal
# print(help(random.gauss))           # Gaussian
# print(help(random.lognormvariate))  # log-normal
```

7.1 One Sample Kolmogorov-Smirnov (KS) Test

7.1.1 KS-Test for uniformity of pseudo-random numbers with plot

The pseudo-random number generator from the NumPy package is applied, to build the datasets of random numbers. To statistically confirm the randomness of those numbers, a Kolmogorov-Smirnov Test is performed, and for this, the `kstest()` function, provided by the SciPy package is used. It has following signature:

```
scipy.stats.kstest(dataset, 'uniform')
```

where:

- `dataset`: the first parameter denotes the dataset to be tested
- `uniform`: the second parameter denotes the reference distribution, to test against

For the statistical test, we formulate:

Hypothesis

- H_0: the numbers are uniformly distributed
- H_1: the numbers are not uniformly distributed

level of significance

- $\alpha = 0.05$

For a perfectly uniform distribution, the p_{value} is 1 and the KS-statistic is 0.

If the reported $p_{value} \leq \frac{\alpha}{2}$, we reject the null hypothesis H_0, in favor of the alternative hypothesis H_1, and conclude that the numbers are not uniformly distributed. Otherwise, if $p_{value} > \frac{\alpha}{2}$, we fail to reject the null hypothesis H_0 and conclude that the numbers are uniformly distributed.

The level of significance (α) is defined as the probability of rejecting the null hypothesis H_0, given the null hypothesis is true. For practical applications, α is often chosen to be 0.10, 0.05, or 0.01. The chosen level of significance (α) is allocated in either tail of the distribution as $\frac{\alpha}{2}$ of 0.025 for a two-sided test.

In the following Python code segment, we demonstrate this implementation and visualize the outcome with a histogram plot.

```
import random
import pandas as pd
from scipy.stats import kstest
import matplotlib.pyplot as plt
%matplotlib inline

# parameters
N = 5000
alpha = 0.05
# dataset
actual = []
random.seed(2)
for i in range(N):
    actual.append(random.random()) # random
# KS Test
x = kstest(actual, "uniform")
# results
print('Kolmogorov-Smirnov Test:')
print(f'sample size              : {N:.0f}')
print(f'KS-statistic             : {x.statistic:.6f}')
print(f'p-value                  : {x.pvalue:.6f}')
print(f'level of significance : {alpha:.2f}')
print('two-tailed test')
print('Hypothesis')
print('H0: the numbers are uniform distributed')
print('H1: the numbers are not uniform distributed')
if x.pvalue < alpha/2:
    print('reject H0')
    print('Not Uniform')
else:
    print('fail to reject H0')
    print('Uniform')
# plot
df = pd.DataFrame(actual)
bins = int(N/100)
fig, ax =  plt.subplots(1, 1, figsize=(6,2))
ax.set_xlabel('range')
ax.set_ylabel('frequency')
df[0].hist(bins=bins,
           ax=ax,
           color='lightblue') # uniform
plt.title('uniformly distributed pseudo-random numbers')
plt.show()
```

```
Kolmogorov-Smirnov Test:
sample size            : 5000
KS-statistic           : 0.009097
p-value                : 0.798819
level of significance : 0.05
two-tailed test
Hypothesis
H0: the numbers are uniform distributed
H1: the numbers are not uniform distributed
fail to reject H0
Uniform
```

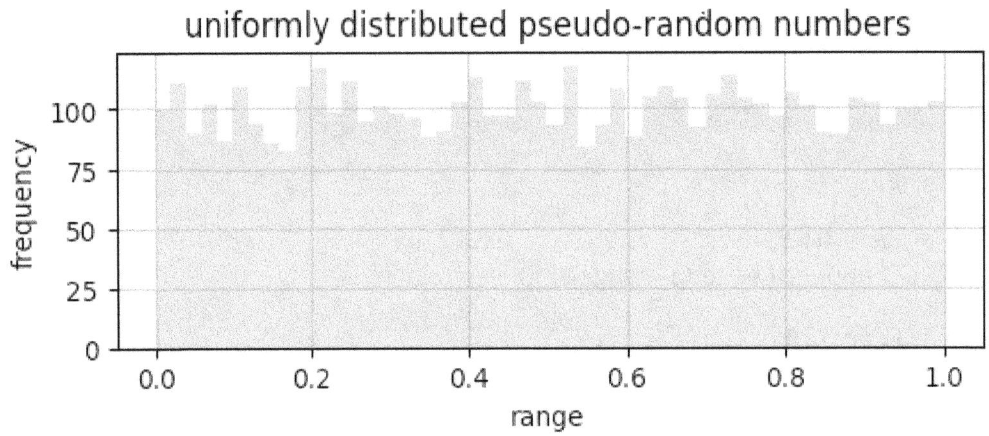

Interpretation

The KS-statistic is reported as 0.0091 and the associated p_{value} is 0.7988.

The chosen level of significance α = 0.05 is allocated in either tail of the distribution $\frac{\alpha}{2}$ = 0.025 for a two-sided test.

Since the p_{value} is larger than $\frac{\alpha}{2}$ of 0.025, we fail to reject the null hypothesis H_0. The tested sample provides sufficient evidence, to say that the data is uniformly distributed, which means, that the pseudo-random numbers are generated by a random process. We can make this claim with (1-α) or 95% confidence.

We might want to invoke the help function to bring up the documentation on the `kstest()` method.

```
from scipy.stats import kstest
# help(kstest)
```

7.1.2 KS-Test for uniform distribution with plot

In this example, we create a dataset of N numbers, drawn from the uniform distribution, and we are using the Kolmogorov-Smirnov (KS) Test to confirm the uniformity property of the data. To set up the statistical test, we formulate:

Hypothesis

- H_0 the numbers are uniformly distributed
- H_1 the numbers are not uniformly distributed

level of significance

- $\alpha = 0.05$

The level of significance α is defined as the probability of rejecting the null hypothesis H_0, given the null hypothesis is true. For most of the practical applications, α is chosen to be 0.05. Other popular choices are 0.1 or 0.01.

If we can reject the null hypothesis H_0, this means that the numbers are not uniformly distributed $U[0, 1]$. Failure to reject the null hypothesis implies that the numbers follow the uniform distribution, and such a claim can be made with (1-α) or 95% confidence.

In the next code segment, this test is implemented and the results are reported. Additionally, for visual inspection, a plot of the resulting distribution is presented as a histogram.

```
import random
import pandas as pd
from scipy.stats import kstest
import matplotlib.pyplot as plt
%matplotlib inline

# parameters
N = 5000
alpha = 0.05
random.seed(2)
# KS test on uniform sample
actual = []
for i in range(N):
    actual.append(random.random()) # uniform
x = kstest(actual, "uniform")
# results
print('Kolmogorov-Smirnov Test:')
print(f'sample size            : {N:.0f}')
print(f'KS-statistic           : {x.statistic:.6f}')
print(f'p-value                : {x.pvalue:.6f}')
print(f'level of significance : {alpha:.2f}')
print('two-tailed test')
print('Hypothesis')
```

(continues on next page)

(continued from previous page)

```
print('H0: the numbers are uniform distribution')
print('H1: the number are not uniform distributed')
if x.pvalue < alpha/2:
    print('reject H0')
    print('Not Uniform')
else:
    print('fail to reject H0')
    print('Uniform')
# plot
df = pd.DataFrame(actual)
bins = int(N/100)
fig, ax = plt.subplots(1,1,figsize=(6,2))
ax.set_xlabel('range')
ax.set_ylabel('frequency')
df[0].hist(bins=bins,
           ax=ax,
           color='lightgreen') # uniform
plt.title('KS test -- Uniform vs. Uniform')
plt.show()
```

```
Kolmogorov-Smirnov Test:
sample size             : 5000
KS-statistic            : 0.009097
p-value                 : 0.798819
level of significance : 0.05
two-tailed test
Hypothesis
H0: the numbers are uniform distribution
H1: the number are not uniform distributed
fail to reject H0
Uniform
```

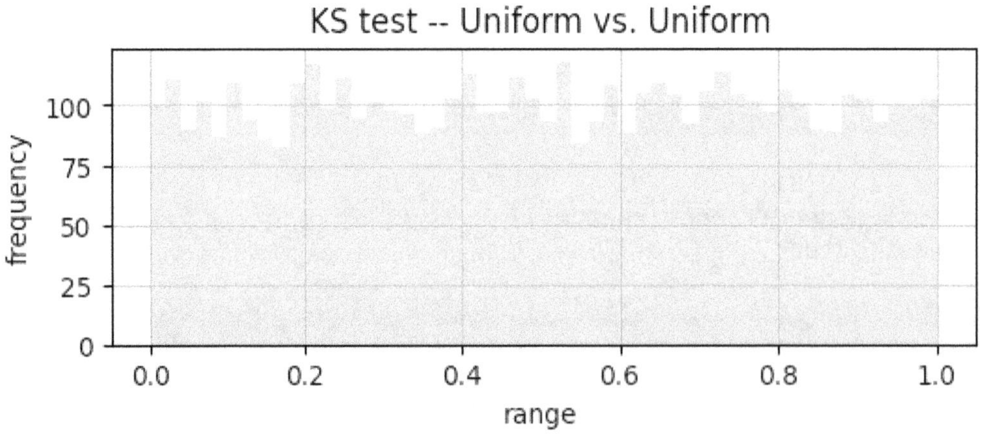

Interpretation

The KS-statistic is reported as 0.0091 and the associated p_{value} of 0.7988.

The chosen level of significance $\alpha = 0.05$ is allocated in either tail of the distribution $\frac{\alpha}{2} = 0.025$ for a two-sided test.

Since the $p_{value} \geq \frac{\alpha}{2}$ of 0.025, we fail to reject the null hypothesis H_0 and conclude that the sample is uniformly distributed. We can have (1-α) or 95% confidence in this assessment.

7.1.3 KS-Test for normal distribution with plot

A sample is drawn from the normal distribution and we test if this sample indeed comes from a normal distribution. To perform a Kolmogorov-Smirnov Test the `kstest()` function from the SciPy package is used, which has this signature:

```
s,p = scipy.stats.kstest(data, "norm")
```

where:

- `data`: the first parameter is the data sample to be tested
- `norm`: the second parameter, refers to the reference distribution, to test against

The function returns the KS-statistic and the corresponding p_{value}.

To set up the test procedures, we formulate:

Hypothesis

- H_0 the numbers follow the normal distribution
- H_1 the numbers are not from the normal distribution

level of significance

- $\alpha = 0.05$

Since this test is set up to be a two-tailed test, we allocate $\frac{\alpha}{2}$ in either tail of the distribution. To visually inspect the results, a histogram plot is produced and in the following Python code section this approach is implemented.

```
import random
import numpy as np
import pandas as pd
from scipy.stats import kstest
import matplotlib.pyplot as plt
%matplotlib inline

N = 10000
alpha = 0.05
random.seed(2)
```

(continues on next page)

(continued from previous page)

```
# KS test on normally distributed sample
actual = []
for i in range(N):
    actual.append(np.random.normal(0, 1)) # normal
x = kstest(actual, "norm")
# results
print("Kolmogorov-Smirnov Test:")
print(f'sample size            : {N:.0f}')
print(f'KS-statistic           : {x.statistic:.6f}')
print(f'p-value                : {x.pvalue:.6f}')
print(f'level of significance : {alpha:.2f}')
print('two-tailed test')
print('Hypothesis')
print("H0: numbers are normal distributed")
print("H1: numbers are not normal distributed")
if x[1] < alpha/2:
    print("reject H0")
    print("Not Normal")
else:
    print("fail to reject H0")
    print("Normal")
# plot
fig, ax = plt.subplots(1,1,figsize=(6,3))
ax.set_xlabel('$\mu$')
ax.set_ylabel('frequency')
bins = int(N / 100)
pd.DataFrame(actual).hist(bins=bins, ax=ax)
plt.title("KS test -- Normal vs. Normal")
plt.show()
```

```
Kolmogorov-Smirnov Test:
sample size            : 10000
KS-statistic           : 0.012333
p-value                : 0.094694
level of significance : 0.05
two-tailed test
Hypothesis
H0: numbers are normal distributed
H1: numbers are not normal distributed
fail to reject H0
Normal
```

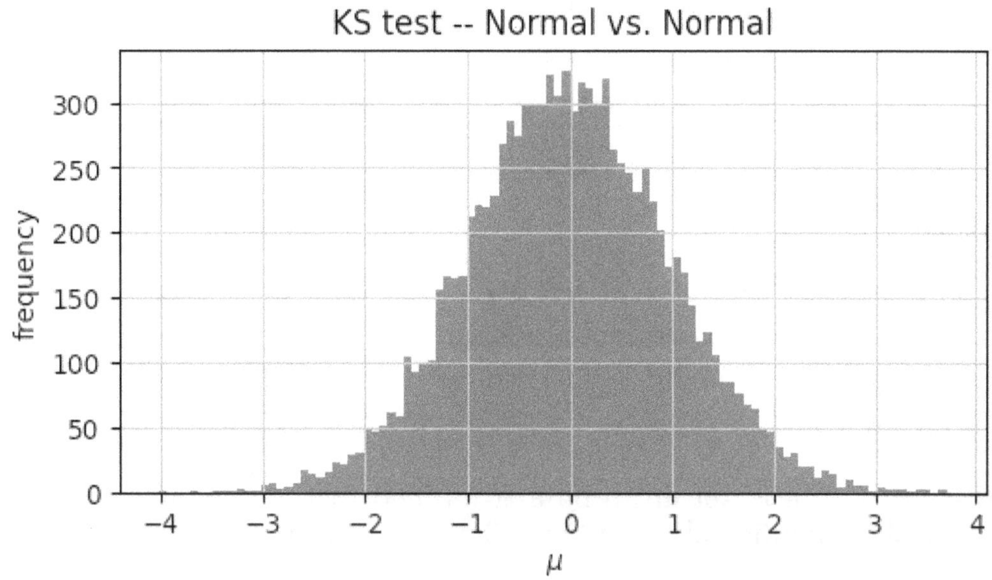

Interpretation

The KS-statistic is reported as 0.0134 and the associated p_{value} of 0.0551.

The chosen level of significance α = 0.05 is allocated in either tail of the distribution $\frac{\alpha}{2}$ = 0.025 for a two-sided test.

Since the $p_{value} \geq \frac{\alpha}{2}$ of 0.025, we fail to reject the null hypothesis H_0, and it can be concluded that the sample is indeed normally distributed. We can make this claim with (1-α) or 95% confidence.

7.2 Two Sample Kolmogorov-Smirnov (KS) Test

Suppose we have the following two sample data series, drawn from two different distributions. To explore this idea further, we generate data series, drawn from the:

- Uniform distribution, and a second from the log-normal distribution
- Normal distribution, and the second from the log-normal distribution
- Uniform distribution, and a second from the uniform distribution
- Normal distribution, and a second from the normal distribution

To perform a two-sample Kolmogorov-Smirnov (KS) Test we make use of the `ks_2samp()` function, provided by the SciPy package, which has this signature:

```
r = ks_2samp(uniform_sample, lognormal_sample)
```

where:

- `uniform_sample`: the first data sample
- `lognormal_sample`: the second data sample

the function returns a tuple with the KS-statistic and corresponding p_{value}.

To set up the statistical procedure, we formulate:

Hypothesis

- H_0 both distributions are identical
- H_1 both distributions are not identical

level of significance

- $\alpha = 0.05$

The test procedure is set up to be a two-tailed test, so we allocate $\frac{\alpha}{2}$ of the chosen level of significance in either tail of the distribution.

We might want to invoke the help function to bring up the documentation on the `ks_2samp()` method.

```
from scipy.stats import ks_2samp
# help(ks_2samp)
```

7.2.1 KS-Test on uniform vs. log-normal distributed samples

Now we perform the two-sample Kolmogorov-Smirnov (KS) Test on these two samples, to statistically assess if they came from the same distribution.

Since we know how the datasets were constructed, we expect the test to conclude the two datasets are not drawn from the same distribution.

```
from scipy.stats import ks_2samp
from numpy.random import seed
from numpy.random import randn
from numpy.random import lognormal
from numpy.random import randint

# parameters
N = 1000
alpha = 0.05
seed(0)  # reproducibility
# Two Sample Kolmogorov-Smirnov test
normal_sample = randn(N)
lognormal_sample = lognormal(3, 1, N)
uniform_sample = randint(0, 10, N)
r = ks_2samp(uniform_sample, lognormal_sample)
# results
print("Kolmogorov-Smirnov Test:")
```

(continues on next page)

(continued from previous page)

```
print(f"sample size             : {N:.0f}")
print(f"KS-statistic            : {r.statistic:.6f}")
print(f"p-value                 : {r.pvalue:.2E}")
print(f'level of significance : {alpha:.2f}')
print('two-tailed test')
print('Hypothesis')
print('H0: both distributions are identical')
print('H1: both distributions are not identical')
if r.pvalue < alpha/2:
    print("reject H0")
    print("Not Identical")
else:
    print("fail to reject H0")
    print("Identical")
```

```
Kolmogorov-Smirnov Test:
sample size             : 1000
KS-statistic            : 0.792000
p-value                 : 2.38E-312
level of significance : 0.05
two-tailed test
Hypothesis
H0: both distributions are identical
H1: both distributions are not identical
reject H0
Not Identical
```

Interpretation

From the output, we see that the KS-statistic is 0.7920 and the corresponding p_{value} is 2.38e-312, almost 0.

The chosen level of significance $\alpha = 0.05$ is allocated in either tail of the distribution $\frac{\alpha}{2} = 0.025$ for a two-sided test.

Since the $p_{value} \leq \frac{\alpha}{2}$ of 0.025, we reject the null hypothesis H_0, in favor of the alternative hypothesis H_1.

The samples provide sufficient evidence to conclude, that both data series are not drawn from the same distribution. This result is hardly surprising, as we tested the uniform distribution against the log-normal distribution.

7.2.2 KS-Test on log-normal vs. log-normal distributed samples

```
from scipy.stats import ks_2samp

# parameters
alpha = 0.05
# Two Sample Kolmogorov-Smirnov test
r = ks_2samp(lognormal_sample, lognormal_sample)
# results
print("Kolmogorov-Smirnov Test:")
print(f"sample size            : {N:.0f}")
print(f"KS-statistic           : {r.statistic:.6f}")
print(f"p-value                : {r.pvalue:.6f}")
print(f"level of significance : {alpha:.2f}")
print("two-tailed test")
print("Hypothesis")
print("H0: both distributions are identical")
print("H1: both distributions are not identical")
if r.pvalue < alpha/2:
    print("reject H0")
    print("Not Identical")
else:
    print("fail to reject H0")
    print("Identical")
```

```
Kolmogorov-Smirnov Test:
sample size            : 1000
KS-statistic           : 0.000000
p-value                : 1.000000
level of significance : 0.05
two-tailed test
Hypothesis
H0: both distributions are identical
H1: both distributions are not identical
fail to reject H0
Identical
```

Interpretation

From the output, it can be observed that the KS-statistic is 0.0 and the corresponding p_{value} is 1.0.

The chosen level of significance $\alpha = 0.05$ is allocated in either tail of the distribution $\frac{\alpha}{2} = 0.025$ for a two-sided test.

Since the $p_{value} \geq \frac{\alpha}{2}$ of 0.025, we fail to reject the null hypothesis H_0. The analyzed samples provide sufficient evidence to say that both samples are not drawn from the same distribution. We can have (1-α) or 95% confidence in making such a claim.

7.2.3 KS-Test on uniform vs. uniform distributed samples

```
from scipy.stats import ks_2samp

# parameters
alpha = 0.05
# Two Sample Kolmogorov-Smirnov test
r = ks_2samp(uniform_sample, uniform_sample)
# results
print("Kolmogorov-Smirnov Test:")
print(f"sample size              : {N:.0f}")
print(f"KS-statistic             : {r.statistic:.6f}")
print(f"p-value                  : {r.pvalue:.6f}")
print(f"level of significance : {alpha:.2f}")
print("two-tailed test")
print("Hypothesis")
print("H0: both distributions are identical")
print("H1: both distributions are not identical")
if r.pvalue < alpha/2:
    print("reject H0")
    print("Not Identical")
else:
    print("fail to reject H0")
    print("Identical")
```

```
Kolmogorov-Smirnov Test:
sample size           : 1000
KS-statistic          : 0.000000
p-value               : 1.000000
level of significance : 0.05
two-tailed test
Hypothesis
H0: both distributions are identical
H1: both distributions are not identical
fail to reject H0
Identical
```

Interpretation

From the output we have the KS-statistic of 0.0 and the corresponding p_{value} of 1.

The chosen level of significance $\alpha = 0.05$ is allocated in either tail of the distribution $\frac{\alpha}{2} = 0.025$ for a two-sided test.

Since $p_{value} > \frac{\alpha}{2}$ of 0.025, we fail to reject the null hypothesis H_0. The data provides sufficient evidence to say that the samples are drawn from the same distribution. At the chosen level of significance $\alpha = 0.05$, this claim can be made with 95% confidence.

7.2.4 KS-Test on normal vs. normal distributed samples

```
from scipy.stats import ks_2samp

# parameters
alpha = 0.05
# Two Sample Kolmogorov-Smirnov test
r = ks_2samp(normal_sample, normal_sample)
# results
print("Kolmogorov-Smirnov Test:")
print(f"sample size            : {N:.0f}")
print(f"KS-statistic           : {r.statistic:.6f}")
print(f"p-value                : {r.pvalue:.6f}")
print(f"level of significance : {alpha:.2f}")
print("two-tailed test")
print("Hypothesis")
print("H0: both distributions are identical")
print("H1: both distributions are not identical")
if r.pvalue < alpha/2:
    print("reject H0")
    print("Not Identical")
else:
    print("fail to reject H0")
    print("Identical")
```

```
Kolmogorov-Smirnov Test:
sample size            : 1000
KS-statistic           : 0.000000
p-value                : 1.000000
level of significance : 0.05
two-tailed test
Hypothesis
H0: both distributions are identical
H1: both distributions are not identical
fail to reject H0
Identical
```

Interpretation

In the output, the KS-statistic of 0.0 and the corresponding p_{value} of 1 are reported.

The chosen level of significance $\alpha = 0.05$ is allocated in either tail of the distribution $\frac{\alpha}{2}$ of 0.025 for a two-sided test.

Since the reported $p_{value} > \frac{\alpha}{2}$ of 0.025, we fail to reject the null hypothesis H_0. We have sufficient evidence to say that the samples are drawn from the same distribution. With the chosen level of significance $\alpha = 0.05$, we can make this claim with (1-α) or 95% confidence.

CHAPTER 8

Z-SCORE AND Z-CRITICAL VALUES

8.1 Z-score Values

In statistics, a Z_{score} value tells us how many standard deviations away a value is from the mean. We can use the following formula to calculate the

Z_{score} values:

$$Z_i = \frac{(X_i - \mu)}{\sigma}$$

where:

- X_i: is a single raw data value
- μ: is the population mean
- σ: is the population standard deviation

The Z_{scores} can be computed by using the `zscore()` function, provided by the scipy.stats library, which has the following signature:

```
scipy.stats.zscore(a, axis=0, ddof=0, nan_policy='propagate')
```

where:

- `a`: input data array
- `axis`: axis along which to calculate the Z_{score} values. The default is 0

- `ddof`: degrees of freedom correction in the calculation of the standard deviation. Default 0
- `nan_policy`: how to handle input containing NaN Values

The `nan_policy` parameter has three options:

- `propagate`: returns NaN values, which is the default behavior
- `raise`: throws an error, and
- `omit`: performs calculations, while ignoring NaN values.

In the following code section, we illustrate how to use these functions to calculate Z_{score} values for a one-dimensional NumPy array, a multidimensional NumPy array, and a Pandas DataFrame. In the following Python code segment, an example is given for each.

8.1.1 Compute Z-score values in a one-dimensional NumPy array

The Z_{score} measure tells us how many standard deviations away an individual value is from the mean or expected value.

```
import numpy as np
import scipy.stats as stats

# create dataset
data = np.array([6, 7, 7, 12, 13, 13, 15, 16, 19, 22])
# compute Z-scores
z = stats.zscore(data)
# statistics
mean = data.mean()
std = np.sqrt(data.var())
# inspect
print("data :", data)
print("mean : {:.6f}".format(mean))
print("std  : {:.6f}".format(std))
print()
print("Z-scores:")
print(z)
print()
# recover
print('data')
print(data)
print()
print("recover:")
print(["%.0f" % (mean + item * std) for item in z])
```

```
data : [ 6  7  7 12 13 13 15 16 19 22]
mean : 13.000000
```

(continues on next page)

(continued from previous page)

```
std  : 5.019960

Z-scores:
[-1.39443338 -1.19522861 -1.19522861 -0.19920477  0.          0.
  0.39840954  0.5976143   1.19522861  1.79284291]

data
[ 6  7  7 12 13 13 15 16 19 22]

recover:
['6', '7', '7', '12', '13', '13', '15', '16', '19', '22']
```

Interpretation

The first value of 6 is 1.394 standard deviations below the mean.

$$13 - 1.394 \cdot 5.0199 = 6$$

The second value of 7 is 1.1952 standard deviations below the mean.

$$13 - 1.1952 \cdot 5.0199 = 7$$

The last value of 22 is 1.793 standard deviations above the mean.

$$13 + 1.793 \cdot 5.0199 = 22$$

8.1.2 Compute Z-score values in a multidimensional NumPy array

If we have a multidimensional NumPy array, the `axis` parameter can be used to specify that we want to calculate each Z_{score} value relative to its array. We make use of the `zscore()` function from the scipy.stats library, which has this signature:

```
z = stats.zscore(data, axis=1)
```

where

- `data`: is the array of input data
- `axis`: along which to operate. The default is 0. If None, compute over the whole data array

Before using the `zscore()` function, we might want to bring up its documentation.

```
import scipy.stats as stats
# print(help(stats.zscore))
```

The following multidimensional NumPy array with sample data is created, then we apply the `zscore()` function to calculate the Z_{score} values for each of the matrix elements.

```
import numpy as np
import scipy.stats as stats

# dataset
data = np.array([[5, 6, 7, 7, 8],
                 [8, 8, 8, 9, 9],
                 [2, 2, 4, 4, 5]])
# compute Z-scores
z = stats.zscore(data, axis=1)
# results
print('shape    :', data.shape)
print("mean     : {:.5f}".format(data.mean()))
print("std      : {:.5f}".format(np.sqrt(data.var())))
print()
print("original data:")
print(data)
print()
print("Z-scores:")
print(z)
```

```
shape    : (3, 5)
mean     : 6.13333
std      : 2.27645

original data:
[[5 6 7 7 8]
 [8 8 8 9 9]
 [2 2 4 4 5]]

Z-scores:
[[-1.56892908 -0.58834841  0.39223227  0.39223227  1.37281295]
 [-0.81649658 -0.81649658 -0.81649658  1.22474487  1.22474487]
 [-1.16666667 -1.16666667  0.5         0.5         1.33333333]]
```

Interpretation

The Z_{score} value for each data item is shown relative to the array they are in.

The first value of 5 in the first array is -1.159 standard deviations below the mean of its array.

$$6.1333 - 1.159 \cdot 2.2764 = 5$$

The first value of 8 in the second array is -0.816 standard deviations below the mean of its array.

$$6.1333 - 0.816 \cdot 2.2764 = 8$$

The first value of 2 in the third array is -1.167 standard deviations below the mean of its array.

$$6.1333 - 1.167 \cdot 2.2764 = 2$$

8.1.3 Compute Z-score values in a Pandas DataFrame

Suppose we have a Pandas DataFrame containing the dataset. We make use of the `zscore()` function from the stats library, which has this signature:

```
z = stats.zscore(data, ddof=1, axis=0)
```

where:

- `data`: the input data
- `ddof`: degrees of freedom
- `axis`: determines along which dimension to operate

the function returns a DataFrame z with corresponding Z_{score} values for each data item.

In the following Python code section, this approach is implemented and the results are presented and interpreted.

```
import scipy.stats as stats
# help(stats.zscore)
# print(stats.zscore.__doc__[:1300])
```

```
import numpy as np
import scipy.stats as stats
import pandas as pd

# reproducibility
np.random.seed(2)
# random data set
data = pd.DataFrame(
    np.random.randint(0,10,size=(10,3)),
                 columns=["A", "B", "C"])
# DataFrame
print("data:")
print(data)
print()
# Z-scores
z = stats.zscore(data, ddof=1, axis=0)
```

(continues on next page)

(continued from previous page)

```
# inspect
print("describe:")
print(data.describe())
print()
print("Z-scores:")
print(z)
```

```
data:
   A  B  C
0  8  8  6
1  2  8  7
2  2  1  5
3  4  4  5
4  7  3  6
5  4  3  7
6  6  1  3
7  5  8  4
8  6  3  9
9  2  0  4

describe:
               A          B          C
count  10.000000  10.000000  10.000000
mean    4.600000   3.900000   5.600000
std     2.170509   3.071373   1.776388
min     2.000000   0.000000   3.000000
25%     2.500000   1.500000   4.250000
50%     4.500000   3.000000   5.500000
75%     6.000000   7.000000   6.750000
max     8.000000   8.000000   9.000000

Z-scores:
          A         B         C
0  1.566453  1.334908  0.225176
1 -1.197875  1.334908  0.788116
2 -1.197875 -0.944203 -0.337764
3 -0.276433  0.032559 -0.337764
4  1.105731 -0.293029  0.225176
5 -0.276433 -0.293029  0.788116
6  0.645010 -0.944203 -1.463644
7  0.184289  1.334908 -0.900704
8  0.645010 -0.293029  1.913996
9 -1.197875 -1.269790 -0.900704
```

Interpretation

The Z_{score} value for each feature is shown relative to their column. We can observe, that:

The first value of 8 in the first column is 1.2937 standard deviations above the mean value of its column.

$$4.6 + 1.5665 * 2.1705 = 8$$

The first value of 8 in the second column is 1.2469 standard deviations above the mean value of its column.

$$3.9 + 1.3349 * 3.0714 = 8$$

The first value of 6 in the third column is 0.2252 standard deviations above the mean value of its column.

$$5.6 + 0.2252 * 1.7763 = 6$$

We attempt to recover the original data items by performing the following matrix operations:

```
recover = data.mean() + z * data.std()
```

In Python, we implement this idea, like so:

```
# recover
recover = data.mean() + z * data.std()
print('input data:')
print(data)
print()
print("recover:")
print(recover)
```

```
input data:
   A  B  C
0  8  8  6
1  2  8  7
2  2  1  5
3  4  4  5
4  7  3  6
5  4  3  7
6  6  1  3
7  5  8  4
8  6  3  9
9  2  0  4

recover:
     A    B    C
0  8.0  8.0  6.0
1  2.0  8.0  7.0
2  2.0  1.0  5.0
3  4.0  4.0  5.0
4  7.0  3.0  6.0
```

(continues on next page)

(continued from previous page)

```
5  4.0  3.0  7.0
6  6.0  1.0  3.0
7  5.0  8.0  4.0
8  6.0  3.0  9.0
9  2.0  0.0  4.0
```

8.2 Z-critical Values

When conducting a hypothesis test, a $Z_{statistic}$ is returned. To determine if the results of this test are statistically significant, we need to compare the $Z_{statistic}$ to a $Z_{critical}$ value.

If the absolute value of the $|Z_{statistic}|$ is greater than the $Z_{critical}$ value, we conclude that the results of the test are statistically significant, at the chosen level of significance of α.

To compute the $Z_{critical}$ values, we make use of the percentage point function `norm.ppf()` function from the scipy.stats package, which has this signature:

```
z = scipy.stats.norm.ppf(q)
```

where q is the lower tail probability.

Note, that for a one-tailed test, we might want to set the level of significance to $\alpha = 0.05$, which is in the lower tail only. In contrast, for a two-sided test, $\frac{\alpha}{2}$ of 0.025 is allocated in either tail of the distribution.

Before using the `norm.ppf()` function, you might want to bring up the documentation on this function. In particular, you might want to review the parameters, and return values, as well as any hints or suggestions about its applicability or limitations.

```
from scipy.stats import norm
# help(norm.ppf)
```

The following examples illustrate how to find the $Z_{critical}$ values:

- for a one-tailed test
- for a right-tailed test
- for a two-tailed test

8.2.1 Left-tailed test

Suppose we want to find $Z_{critical}$ for a left-tailed test with a significance level of $\alpha = 0.05$:

```
import scipy.stats

# parameters
alpha = 0.05
# compute Z-critical value, one-tailed test
z = scipy.stats.norm.ppf(alpha)
# results
print("Left-tailed test:")
print(f"level of significance : {alpha:.2f}")
print(f"Z-critical            : {z:.3f}")
print("one-tailed-test")
print()
```

```
Left-tailed test:
level of significance : 0.05
Z-critical            : -1.645
one-tailed-test
```

Interpretation

If the test $Z_{statistic} \leq Z_{critical}$ at the chosen level of significance $\alpha = 0.05$, the test results are deemed statistically significant.

8.2.2 Right-tailed test

Suppose we want to find the $Z_{critical}$ value for a right-tailed test with a significance level $\alpha = 0.05$.

```
import scipy.stats

# parameters
alpha = 0.05
# compute Z critical value
z = scipy.stats.norm.ppf(1 - alpha) # one-tailed
# results
print("Right-tailed test:")
print(f"level of significance : {alpha:.2f}")
print(f"Z-critical            : {z:.3f}")
print("one-tailed-test")
```

```
Right-tailed test:
level of significance : 0.05
```

(continues on next page)

(continued from previous page)

```
Z-critical                : 1.645
one-tailed-test
```

Interpretation

The $Z_{critical}$ value is +1.64485. If the test statistic $Z_{statistic}$ is greater than this $Z_{critical}$ value, the results of this right-tailed test are statistically significant.

8.2.3 Two-tailed test

Suppose we want to find the $Z_{critical}$ value for a two-tailed test with a significance level $\alpha = 0.05$, $\frac{\alpha}{2} = 0.025$ is allocated in either tail of the distribution.

Whenever a two-tailed test is performed, there will be two critical values - $Z_{critical}$ and $+Z_{critical}$.

```
import scipy.stats

# parameters
alpha = 0.05
# Z-critical value
z = scipy.stats.norm.ppf(1 - alpha/2)
# results
print("Two-tailed test:")
print(f"level of significance : {alpha:.2f}")
print(f"alpha half            : {alpha/2:.3f}")
print(f"Z-critical            : {z:.3f}, {-z:.3f}")
print("two-tailed-test")
```

```
Two-tailed test:
level of significance : 0.05
alpha half            : 0.025
Z-critical            : 1.960, -1.960
two-tailed-test
```

Interpretation

Recall, that this analysis is set up to be two-tailed, so we allocate $\frac{\alpha}{2}$ in either tail of the distribution.

In this case, the $Z_{critical}$ values are +1.96 and -1.96.

Therefore, if the test statistic $Z_{statistic}$ is less than -1.96 or greater than +1.96, the results of the two-tailed test are statistically significant, and we can make such a claim with (1-α) or 95% confidence.

CHAPTER 9

PEARSON CORRELATION COEFFICIENT

To quantify the relationship between variables the Pearson correlation coefficient p is computed, which measures the strength and direction of any linear association between those two variables.

Pearson correlation:

$$p = \frac{n \cdot (\sum xy) - (\sum x) \cdot (\sum y)}{\sqrt{[n \sum x^2 - (\sum x)^2] \cdot [n \sum y^2 - (\sum y)^2]}}$$

where

- p: Pearson correlation coefficient
- n: number of the pairs of the scores
- $\sum xy$: sum of products of the paired scores
- $\sum x$: sum of the x scores
- $\sum y$: sum of the y scores
- $\sum x^2$: sum of the squared x scores
- $\sum y^2$: sum of the squared y scores.

It takes on values between -1 and +1 where:

- -1: indicates a perfectly negative linear association between two variables
- 0: indicates no linear association between two variables

- $+1$: indicates a perfectly positive linear association between two variables

Remember, we denote the correlation coefficient with the letter p when the entire population is involved, and the letter r is used when dealing with samples.

The following topics are discussed:

- Compute correlation test
- Five underlying assumptions for the Pearson correlation analysis
- Comparison of three methods to compute Pearson correlation coefficient

9.1 Student-t Test for the correlation coefficient

To statistically confirm that a linear relationship indeed exists between two variables, we can perform a Student-t Test. As a result it returns a t-statistic and, for a chosen level of significance α, the corresponding p_{value}. To set up the test, we formulate:

Hypothesis

- H_0: No correlation exists between the two variables
- H_1: Correlation exists among the two variables

The formula for calculating the t-statistic $t_{df,\alpha}$ for the number of freedom `df` and the level of significance α.

t-statistic:

$$t_{df,\alpha} = r \cdot \frac{\sqrt{n-2}}{\sqrt{1-r^2}}$$

with

- `n`: number of observations
- `k`: number of feature variables
- `df`: degrees of freedom given as (n-k-1)
- α: level of significance

The computation returns a t-statistic and the corresponding p_{value}, are computed for a two-sided test.

For demonstration purposes, we set up two datasets of random uniform numbers x and y, and attempt the test if any significant correlation r_{xy} exists among those values. To determine if the correlation coefficient between two variables is statistically significant, we perform a Student-t test by using the `pearsonr()` function from the `SciPy` library, which has the following signature:

```
r, p = pearsonr(x, y)
```

where

- `x y`: the input vectors
- `r`: the pearson regression coefficient r
- `p`: the p_{value} measure as the tail probability

The `pearsonr()` function returns the correlation coefficient r_{xy} and the corresponding p_{value} for a two-tailed test, meaning that $\frac{\alpha}{2}$ is allocated in each tail of the distribution.

In the following Python code segment, this approach is implemented and the results are interpreted.

Before using the `pearsonr()` function, we might want to consult the documentation.

```
from scipy.stats import pearsonr
# help(pearsonr)
```

```
from scipy.stats import pearsonr
import numpy as np

# parameters
alpha = 0.05
N = 10
np.random.seed(1212)
# Pearson correlation coefficient
x = np.random.randint(0, 10, N) # uniform
y = np.random.randint(0, 10, N) # uniform
t, p = pearsonr(x, y)
# results
print("Student-t Test:")
print(f"t-statistic            : {t:.6f}")
print(f'p-value                : {p:.6f}')
print(f"level of significance : {alpha:.2f}")
print("two-tailed test")
print("Hypothesis")
print("H0: No correlation exists among the variables")
print("H1: Correlation exists among the variables")
if p < (alpha/2):
    print("reject H0")
    print("Correlated")
else:
    print("failed to reject H0")
    print("Not Correlated")
```

```
Student-t Test:
t-statistic           : 0.629151
p-value               : 0.051314
level of significance : 0.05
two-tailed test
Hypothesis
H0: No correlation exists among the variables
H1: Correlation exists among the variables
failed to reject H0
Not Correlated
```

Interpretation

The Pearson correlation coefficient r_{xy} is reported as 0.6291, and the associated p_{value} is 0.0513.

Remember that the Student-t Test is two-sided, meaning that the level of significance $\frac{\alpha}{2}$ is allocated in each tail of the distribution.

Since the $p_{value} \geq \frac{\alpha}{2}$ or 0.025, we fail to reject the null hypothesis H_0 and conclude, with the desired confidence (1-α) of 95%, that the two variables are not correlated with each other.

This conclusion is hardly surprising since we created the dataset as two randomly generated samples and attempted to confirm any significant relationship, which is likely not there.

9.2 Five underlying assumptions for the Pearson correlation analysis

Before we calculate the Pearson correlation coefficient r_{xy} between two samples we have to make sure that the following five assumptions are met, to arrive at valid and unbiased results for the regression analysis:

1. Level of Measurement: The two variables should be measured at the interval or ratio level.
2. Linear Relationship: The relationship should be linear.
3. Normality: Both variables should be approximately normally distributed.
4. Related Pairs: Each observation in the dataset should have a pair of values.
5. No Outliers: There should be no outlier observations in the data sample

We discuss each assumption and determine if these assumptions are satisfied.

9.2.1 Assumption 1: Level of Measurement

To calculate the Pearson correlation coefficient between two variables, both should be measured at the interval or ratio level.

Some examples of variables that can be measured on an `interval` scale include:

- Temperature: Measured in Fahrenheit or Celsius e.g 1600 degrees
- Credit Scores: Measured from 300 to 850 points
- SAT Scores: Measured from 400 to 1600 points

Some examples of variables that can be measured on a `ratio` scale include:

- Height: Measured in centimeters, inches, feet, etc.
- Weight: Measured in kilogram, pounds, etc.
- Length: Measured in centimeters, inches, feet, etc.
- Related: Levels of Measurement can be `nominal`, `ordinal`, `interval` and `ratio`

If the variables are measured at the ordinal scale, the Spearman correlation coefficient should be used instead.

9.2.2 Assumption 2: Linear Relationship

One of the underlying assumptions concerning the Pearson correlation coefficient is that a linear relationship exists between the two sampled variables. The regression model is only suitable for linearly related data, like $y = ax + b$, and it is not a valid procedure for non-linearly related data, such as $y = ax^3 + bx^2 + c$.

A visual inspection of a scatter plot might help determine if the linearity assumption is met. For example, if the points in the scatter plot fall roughly along a straight line, a linear relationship is likely to exist. In the following Python code segment, this is demonstrated.

```
import numpy as np
import pandas as pd
import matplotlib.pyplot as plt

# parameters
N = 100
x = np.arange(0, N)
# dataset
y1 = []; y2 = []
np.random.seed(1) # reproducibility
for i in x:
```

(continues on next page)

(continued from previous page)

```
    y1.append(10+i*2 + np.random.randn()*7) # linear
    y2.append(int(.02*i*i*i + np.random.randn() * 450))
# DataFrame
df = pd.DataFrame({"x": x, "y1": y1, "y2":y2})
# plot
fig, ax = plt.subplots(nrows=1,ncols=2, figsize=(10,4))
ax[0].scatter(df.x, df.y1,
              c="g", s=3)
ax[0].set_title('Linear + noise')
ax[0].set_xlabel('x')
ax[0].set_ylabel('y1')
ax[0].grid(True)
ax[1].scatter(df.x, df.y2,
              c="b", s=3)
ax[1].set_title('Nonlinear + noise')
ax[1].set_xlabel('x')
ax[1].set_ylabel('y2')
ax[1].grid(True)
plt.show()
```

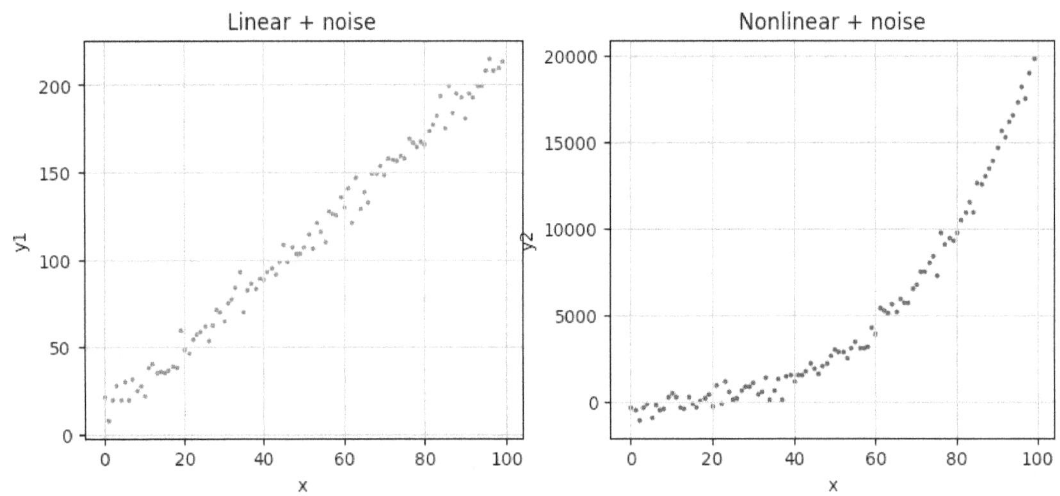

Interpretation

The left chart indicates the presence of a linear relationship between the values x and y_1. In this case, we can safely assume that the assumption of a linear relationship is met.

The right chart indicates that a non-linear relationship exists between the variables x and y_2, meaning that we cannot apply the Pearson correlation analysis to this data. The assumption of a linear relationship is not met.

In general terms, if the data points are randomly scattered about the plot or if they exhibit some other type of relationship (e.g. quadratic, logarithmic, etc.) the assumption of a linear relationship does not hold. In such cases, the Pearson correlation analysis cannot be used.

9.2.3 Assumption 3: Normal Distribution

The Pearson correlation analysis also assumes that both variables are approximately normally distributed. We can check this assumption visually by creating a histogram or a Q-Q plot for each variable. In the next code sections, we demonstrate both approaches.

Histogram

If a histogram for the data sample is approximately bell-shaped, likely, that the data is indeed normally distributed. In the following Python code segment, we produce the corresponding histograms to demonstrate this.

```
# parameters
N = 15000
# dataset normal and uniform
normal_a = np.random.normal(loc=30, scale=5, size=N)
uniform_b = np.random.uniform(low=3, high=30, size=N)
normalDf = pd.DataFrame({"normal": normal_a,
                        "uniform": uniform_b})
# plot
output = normalDf.plot.hist(bins=100, grid=True,
        title="Histogram for $N(30,5)$ and $U[3,30]$",
        figsize=(7,3), color=("grey", "lightgreen"),
        alpha=0.6)
```

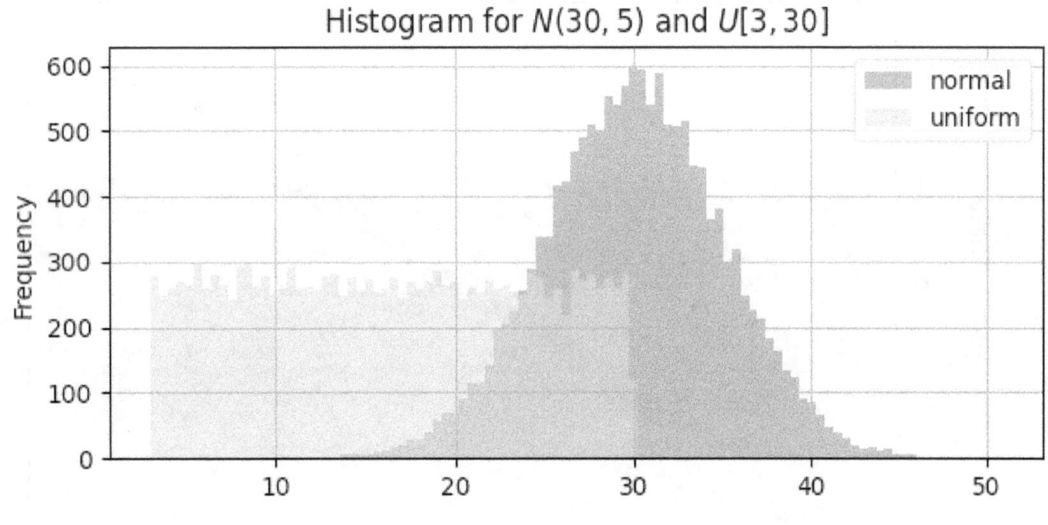

Interpretation

Observe that one histogram looks quite Gaussian in shape, with a mean μ_a = 300 and standard deviation σ = 5. The chart would satisfy the normality requirement of the correlation analysis.

In contrast, the second histogram $U[3, 30]$ is not even remotely bell-shaped and therefore does not meet the normality requirement.

Q-Q Plot

A Q-Q plot, short for quantile-quantile plot, is a type of plot that displays the theoretical quantile along the x-axis and the sample quantile along the y-axis. If the data points of the test sample fall along the straight diagonal line at a 45-degree angle, the data sample is considered to be normally distributed. In Python code, a Q-Q plot is produced.

```
import matplotlib as mpl
import matplotlib.pyplot as plt
import statsmodels.api as sm

# Normally distributed data points
np.random.seed(100)
data_points = np.random.normal(0, 1, 200)
# plot
fig, ax1 = plt.subplots(figsize=(6,4))
r = sm.qqplot(data_points, line="r", ax=ax1)
plt.grid(linestyle="--")
plt.title("Q-Q Plot", fontsize=12)
plt.show()
```

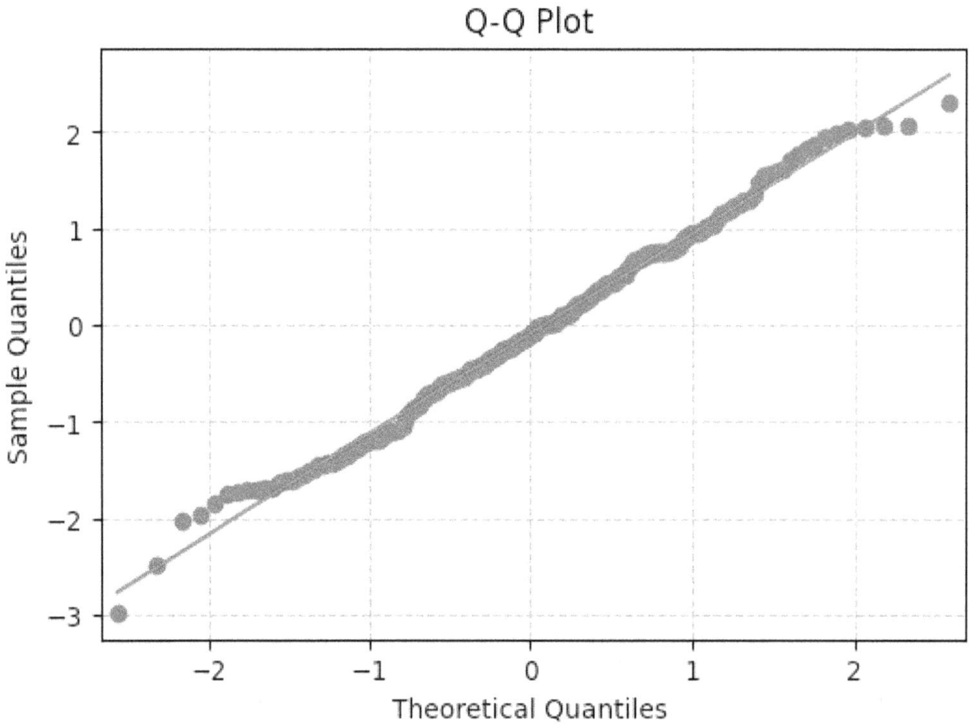

Perform a formal test for normality

We can also perform a more formal statistical test to determine if the data sample was drawn from the normal distribution. There are several tests available to assess normality of the data sample, such as:

- Jarque-Bera Test for Normality
- Shapiro-Wilk Test for Normality
- Kolmogorov-Smirnov Test for Normality

9.2.4 Assumption 4: Related Pairs

The Pearson correlation analysis assumes that each observation in the dataset consists of a pair of corresponding values. This assumption is easily confirmed.

For example, if we are calculating the correlation between weight and height of human beings, then verify that each observation in the dataset has one measurement for weight and one measurement for height in each data row.

```
# parameters
N = 2000
# Check related pairs
a = np.random.normal(loc=20, scale=5, size=N)
b = np.random.normal(loc=20, scale=5, size=N)
dataDf = pd.DataFrame({"x": a, "y": b})
print("length x :", dataDf.x.shape[0])
print("length y :", dataDf.y.shape[0])
# results
if len(dataDf.x) == len(dataDf.y):
    print('requirement: is satisfied')
else:
    print('requirement: not satisfied')
```

```
length x : 2000
length y : 2000
requirement: is satisfied
```

9.2.5 Assumption 5: No Outliers

The Pearson correlation analysis assumes that there are no significant outlier or extreme measurements, in the data sample. If outliers observations are present, they can adversely affect the calculation of the Pearson correlation analysis and produce invalid results. To illustrate this, consider the following dataset:

```
import scipy.stats as stats

# dataset, with no outliers
print('data without outlier:')
x = [12, 13, 13, 14, 15, 17, 19, 13, 14, 19]
y = [20, 25, 28, 30, 36, 34, 37, 30, 26, 36]
# Pearson correlation coefficient
r = stats.pearsonr(x, y)
# results
print('y:',y)
print("Pearson correlation:")
print("r_xy          : {:.5f}".format(r[0]))
print("p-value       : {:.5f}".format(r[1]))
```

```
data without outlier:
y: [20, 25, 28, 30, 36, 34, 37, 30, 26, 36]
Pearson correlation:
r_xy          : 0.84014
p-value       : 0.00234
```

The Pearson correlation coefficient r_{xy} of 0.84014 with the corresponding p_{value} of 0.00234 are reported. However, suppose we introduce one large outlier observation into the dataset (observe the value 100), and recompute.

```
# dataset, with outliers
print('data with outlier:')
y[4] = 100  # replace 36 with 100
# Pearson correlation coefficient
r = stats.pearsonr(x, y)
# inspect
print('y:',y)
print("Pearson correlation:")
print("r_xy          : {:.5f}".format(r[0]))
print("p-value       : {:.5f}".format(r[1]))
```

```
data with outlier:
y: [20, 25, 28, 30, 100, 34, 37, 30, 26, 36]
Pearson correlation:
r_xy          : 0.21757
p-value       : 0.54596
```

Interpretation

The Pearson correlation coefficient r_{xy} is now 0.21757 with the corresponding 0.54596 as p_{value}.

A few large outliers can significantly change the Pearson correlation coefficient and render the result invalid. In this case, it could make sense to remove the outlier from the dataset. However, great care must be taken when removing outliers observations. It is advised to study the data carefully before removing any outliers, they can easily belong to a second distribution from which the data was drawn.

9.3 Three methods to compute the correlation coefficient

We explore three library functions to calculate the correlation coefficient between two variables. We explore the usage of the:

- `corrcoef()`: method, provided by the NumPy library
- `pearsonr()`: method, provided by the Scipy library
- `corr()`: method, provided by the Pandas object

In the following code section, the usage of each method is demonstrated and the computed results are interpreted.

9.3.1 Pearson correlation coefficient using NumPy corrcoef()

To calculate the correlation between two variables, we can use the NumPy `corrcoef()` method, which has the following signature:

```
r = corrcoef(a,b)
```

where a and b are vectors of length n.

Before we use the `corrcoef()` method, we might want to bring up the documentation, to review the input parameters, output results, and any restrictions or limitations.

```
import numpy as np
# help(np.corrcoef)
# print(np.corrcoef.__doc__[:1530])
```

```
import numpy as np
import pandas as pd

# sample data
np.random.seed(129234)
data = pd.DataFrame(np.random.randint(0, 10,
          size=(5,3)), columns=["A", "B", "C"])
# inspect
print('dataset:')
print(data)
```

```
dataset:
   A  B  C
0  4  3  1
1  1  5  5
2  7  8  8
3  9  9  0
4  1  9  3
```

```
import numpy as np
import pandas as pd

np.random.seed(129234)
data = pd.DataFrame(np.random.randint(0, 10,
            size=(5,3)),columns=["A", "B", "C"])
# Pearson Correlation coefficient
r1 = np.corrcoef(data["A"], data["B"])
# inspect
print('results:')
print("r(AB) = {:.4f}".format(r1[0, 0])) # r(BC)
print("r(BC) = {:.4f}".format(r1[0, 1])) # r(BC)
print("matrix:\n",r1) # matrix
```

```
results:
r(AB) = 1.0000
r(BC) = 0.3490
matrix:
 [[1.         0.34895833]
 [0.34895833 1.        ]]
```

Interpretation

Observe that the correlation coefficient r_{AB} is $r = 1.0000$, and r_{BC} is 0.3490, which are both positive correlations.

By default, this function produces a matrix of correlation coefficients. If we require a test if the correlation is statistically significant, we can calculate the p_{value} associated with the Pearson correlation analysis by using the Scipy `pearsonr()` function.

9.3.2 Pearson correlation coefficient using Scipy pearsonr()

The same dataset as before is used and the `personr()` function, provided by the `Scipy` library is applied to the data. It has the following signature:

```
r2 = pearsonr(var1, var2)
```

where `var1` and `var2` are the two data vectors to be analyzed.

We perform a Student-t Test, to confirm the existence of a statistically significant linear relationship between the chosen variables A and B, at the desired level of significance. To formulate the test we write:

Hypotheses

- H_0: correlation Not significant
- H_1: correlation significant

level of significance

- $\alpha = 0.05$

Remember, that the Student-t Test is two-tailed, so we allocate $\frac{\alpha}{2}$ of the chosen level of significance in each tail of the distribution.

In the following Python code segment, this test procedure is implemented, and the results are discussed.

```
from scipy.stats import pearsonr
import numpy as np
import pandas as pd

# parameters
alpha = 0.05
np.random.seed(129234) # reproducibility
# sample dataset
data = pd.DataFrame(
    np.random.randint(0, 10,
        size=(5,3)),columns=["A", "B", "C"])
# Compute Pearson correlation coefficient
r2 = pearsonr(data["A"], data["B"])
# results
print('Student-t Test:')
print(f'r_AB                 : {r2[0]:.4f}')
print(f'p_AB                 : {r2[1]:.4f}')
print(f'level of significance : {alpha:.2f}')
print('two-tailed test:')
print('Hypothesis')
print('H0: correlation Not Significant')
print('H1: correlation Significant')
if r2[1] < alpha/2:
    print('reject H0')
    print('Significant')
else:
    print('fail to reject H0')
    print('Not Significant')
```

```
Student-t Test:
r_AB                  : 0.3490
p_AB                  : 0.5649
```

(continues on next page)

(continued from previous page)

```
level of significance : 0.05
two-tailed test:
Hypothesis
H0: correlation Not Significant
H1: correlation Significant
fail to reject H0
Not Significant
```

Interpretation

The correlation coefficient r_{AB} is reported as 0.3490 and the corresponding p_{value} is 0.5649.

Since $p_{value} \geq \frac{\alpha}{2}$ of 0.025, we fail to reject the null hypothesis H_0. The analyzed data provide sufficient evidence, to conclude that a statistically significant correlation between the two variables does not exist, and we can have (1-α) or 95% confidence in this assessment.

9.3.3 Pearson correlation coefficient using Pandas corr()

To calculate the correlation between multiple variables in a Pandas DataFrame, we can employ the `corr()` function, available on the DataFrame, which has this signature:

```
rDf = dataDf.corr()
```

where the `data` is a DataFrame containing the samples in each column. The `corr()` returns a DataFrame with the computed correlation coefficients.

```
import pandas as pd
import numpy as np

# sample dataset
np.random.seed(129234)
data = pd.DataFrame(
    np.random.randint(0, 10,
        size=(5,3)), columns=["A", "B", "C"])
# correlation for all pairwise combinations
rDf = data.corr()
# results
print('correlation matrix:')
print(rDf)
```

```
correlation matrix:
          A         B         C
A  1.000000  0.348958 -0.148056
```

(continues on next page)

(continued from previous page)

```
B  0.348958  1.000000  0.098704
C -0.148056  0.098704  1.000000
```

If we are interested in calculating the correlation between two specific variables in the DataFrame, we can specify the variables, like so:

```
r3 = rDf["B"].A
# results
print('results:')
print("r_BA : {:.5f}".format(r3))
```

```
results:
r_BA : 0.34896
```

9.3.4 Comparison of the three methods used

```
print('comparison:')
print(f'NumPy corrcoeff() method : {r1[0,1]:.5f}')
print(f'Scipy pearsonr() method  : {r2[0]:.5f}')
print(f'Pandas corr() method     : {r3:.5f}')
```

```
comparison:
NumPy corrcoeff() method : 0.34896
Scipy pearsonr() method  : 0.34896
Pandas corr() method     : 0.34896
```

We are pleased to see that all three methods compute Pearson correlation coefficient r with the same results.

CHAPTER 10

F-TEST FOR REGRESSION MODEL SIGNIFICANCE

The F-Test for regression model significance assesses whether current the regression model provides a better fit to a dataset than a model with no predictor variables or an intercept-only model.

To set up the F-Test procedure we formulate:

Hypothesis

- H_0: The intercept-only model with no predictor variables fits the data as well as our regression model.
- H_1: Our regression model fits the data better than the intercept-only model.

with a level of significance $\alpha = 0.05$.

Other common choices for α include 0.01, 0.05, and 0.1, corresponding to the confidence (1-α) of 99%, 95%, and 90%, respectively.

When we fit a regression model to a dataset, we receive a regression table with its output. This results table provides us with the F-statistic along with the corresponding p_{value} for it.

If the p_{value} is less than the significance level α, then we can reject the null hypothesis H_0 in favor of the alternative hypothesis H_1, and conclude that the studied data provides sufficient evidence to say that the regression model fits the data better than the intercept-only model.

That conclusion can be drawn with 95% confidence (1-α), given the level of significance is set to be $\alpha = 0.05$.

10.1 F-Test in regression analysis

> Suppose we have the dataset that shows the total number of hours studied `StudyHours`, number of prep exams taken `PrepExams`, and the final exam score `FinalScore` received for 12 students.

To analyze the relationship between `StudyHours` and `PrepExams` with the `FinalScore` that a student received, we run a multiple linear regression using the following specification:

$$Score = \beta_0 + \beta_1(Hours) + \beta_2(PrepExams) + \epsilon$$

with the input variables `StudyHours`, `PrepExams`, and the target variable `FinalScore`. In the following code segment, this regression model is implemented and its results are presented.

```
import pandas as pd

# dataset
data = {
    "StudentNo": [1,2,3,4,5,6,7,8,9,10,11,12],
    "StudyHours": [3,7,16,14,12,7,4,19,4,8,8,3],
    "PrepExams": [2,6,5,2,7,4,4,2,8,4,1,3],
    "FinalScore": [76,88,96,90,98,80,86,89,68,75,72,76]}
# DataFrame
df = pd.DataFrame(data)
df.set_index("StudentNo", inplace=True)
# inspect
print(df.head())
```

```
           StudyHours  PrepExams  FinalScore
StudentNo
1                   3          2          76
2                   7          6          88
3                  16          5          96
4                  14          2          90
5                  12          7          98
```

Before using the OLS methods, you might want to bring up the documentation for this function, along with the explanation of the parameters used and the results.

```
from statsmodels.formula.api import ols
# help(ols)
```

10.2 Ordinary least square OLS regression model

We perform the ordinary least square optimizing on this model specification. The `ols()` method, from the statsmodels package, has this signature:

```
model = ols('FinalScore ~ StudyHours + PrepExams',
            data=data).fit()
```

where the first parameter describes the model specification in the convenient formula notation and the data points to the input data.

In return, we receive a `summary()` report from the OLS optimizing process, and we can access this report table-by-table. Additionally, a second `summary2()` function is also available, which gives a more concise version of the computed results.

In the Python code, the regression model is implemented and the two reports are presented.

```
from statsmodels.formula.api import ols
import warnings
from quantlib import print_img
warnings.filterwarnings("ignore")

# fit model
model = None
model = ols("FinalScore ~ StudyHours + PrepExams",
            data=data).fit()
# inspect
print('<table 0>:')
print_img(model.summary().tables[0])
print('<summary2>:')
print_img(model.summary2())
```

```
<table 0>:

                            OLS Regression Results
==============================================================================
Dep. Variable:             FinalScore   R-squared:                       0.531
Model:                            OLS   Adj. R-squared:                  0.427
Method:                 Least Squares   F-statistic:                     5.091
Date:                Tue, 02 Jul 2024   Prob (F-statistic):             0.0332
Time:                        14:05:38   Log-Likelihood:                -39.200
No. Observations:                  12   AIC:                             84.40
Df Residuals:                       9   BIC:                             85.85
Df Model:                           2
Covariance Type:            nonrobust
==============================================================================
```

```
<summary2>:
```

```
                  Results: Ordinary least squares
=================================================================
Model:              OLS              Adj. R-squared:     0.427
Dependent Variable: FinalScore       AIC:                84.3992
Date:               2024-07-02 14:05 BIC:                85.8539
No. Observations:   12               Log-Likelihood:     -39.200
Df Model:           2                F-statistic:        5.091
Df Residuals:       9                Prob (F-statistic): 0.0332
R-squared:          0.531            Scale:              53.682
------------------------------------------------------------------
              Coef.   Std.Err.    t      P>|t|    [0.025   0.975]
------------------------------------------------------------------
Intercept    66.9901   6.2114  10.7849  0.0000  52.9388  81.0414
StudyHours    1.2999   0.4170   3.1172  0.0124   0.3566   2.2432
PrepExams     1.1173   1.0251   1.0899  0.3041  -1.2018   3.4363
-----------------------------------------------------------------
Omnibus:              0.859        Durbin-Watson:           1.201
Prob(Omnibus):        0.651        Jarque-Bera (JB):        0.690
Skew:                 -0.497       Prob(JB):                0.708
Kurtosis:             2.372        Condition No.:           32
=================================================================
```

10.3 Influence measures reported on the summary table

To identify influence and outlier measures, we make use of the get_influence() function provided by the statsmodels package, it has this signature:

```
r = model.get_influence().summary_table()
```

The function, when applied to the model object, returns a table of influence factors, and outlier measures like the Cook's distance.

In the following segment, we demonstrate this approach, and in Python code, we implement:

```
import pandas as pd

# influence measures
r = model.get_influence().summary_table()
# results
print('influence measures:')
r_csv = model.get_influence().summary_table().as_csv()
with open("data/temp/influence_stats.txt", "w") as o:
    o.write(str(r_csv))
```

(continues on next page)

(continued from previous page)

```
df = pd.read_csv("data/temp/influence_stats.txt")
# inspect
print_img(df.iloc[0:6:,0:5].to_string(index=False))
print_img(df.iloc[0:6:,5:].to_string(index=False))
```

influence measures:

obs	endog	fitted value	Cook's d	student. residual
0.0	76.0	73.1243562588255	0.030118738978833264	0.46681539927385823
1.0	88.0	82.79305797823739	0.039554810642859387	0.7773308404280564
2.0	96.0	93.3748857878561	0.024392668758859752	0.42477703425012503
3.0	90.0	87.42325982224438	0.01584826288687614	0.40044559542112934
4.0	98.0	90.40983470387903	0.2392675825895479	1.251128302407013

hat diag	dffits internal	ext.stud. residual	dffits
0.29310470138715844	0.3005931085978183	0.44554481037063826	0.2868964900842242
0.16414880804053492	0.3444770412212956	0.7587888980863492	0.33626011079196916
0.2885414070936124	0.2705143365453655	0.4045595450635566	0.257639062618251
0.22868905224686442	0.21804767520115506	0.3809527769673726	0.2074335898033873
0.3143948832959547	0.8472324048150212	1.2978238804469815	0.878853467819445

10.4 Analysis of Variation ANOVA

From the results table, we will focus on the F-statistic reported in the ANOVA table, along with the corresponding p_{value}, which is labeled as "Prob (F-statistic)".

To set up the statistical test, we formulate:

Hypothesis

- H_0: model is significantly better than the `intercept-only` model
- H_1: the model is not significantly better than the `intercept-only` model

We choose $\alpha = 0.05$ as the significance level.

In the following Python code segment, the ANOVA procedure is implemented and its results are discussed.

```
from statsmodels.formula.api import ols
import matplotlib.pyplot as plt
from quantlib import print_img

# parameters
alpha = 0.05
```

(continues on next page)

(continued from previous page)

```
# fit model
model = ols('FinalScore ~ StudyHours + PrepExams',
            data=data).fit()
# results
print_img(model.summary().tables[0])
# F-test
print('F-Test:')
print(f'F-statistic            : {model.fvalue:.4f}')
print(f'p-value                : {model.f_pvalue:.4f}')
print(f'level of significance : {alpha:.2f}')
print('one-tailed test')
print('Hypothesis')
print('H0: all params are simultaneously zero')
print('H1: at least one param differs from zero')
if (model.f_pvalue < alpha):
    print('reject H0')
    print('Significant')
else:
    print('fail to reject H0')
    print('Not Significant')
```

OLS Regression Results

Dep. Variable:	FinalScore	R-squared:	0.531
Model:	OLS	Adj. R-squared:	0.427
Method:	Least Squares	F-statistic:	5.091
Date:	Tue, 02 Jul 2024	Prob (F-statistic):	0.0332
Time:	14:05:40	Log-Likelihood:	-39.200
No. Observations:	12	AIC:	84.40
Df Residuals:	9	BIC:	85.85
Df Model:	2		
Covariance Type:	nonrobust		

```
F-Test:
F-statistic            : 5.0905
p-value                : 0.0332
level of significance : 0.05
one-tailed test
Hypothesis
H0: all params are simultaneously zero
H1: at least one param differs from zero
reject H0
Significant
```

Interpretation

Since the p_{value} is less than the significance level $\alpha = 0.05$, we reject H_0, and we can conclude that the regression model fits the data significantly better than the intercept-only model.

This further means that using our predictor variables `StudyHours` and `PrepEx-`

ams taken in the model allows us to fit the data better than if we have left them out and simply used the

Intercept-only model.

$$FinalScore = \beta_0 + \epsilon$$

where

- `FinalScore`: is the independent or target variable

```
import statsmodels.api as sm

print('reference:')
# suppress header and index
print_img(
    model.summary2().tables[0].to_string(header=False,
                                         index=False))
# compute ANOVA table
anova_table = sm.stats.anova_lm(model,
                        test="F", typ="I", robust=None)
print('anova table:')
print_img(anova_table)
# extract values for StudyHours and PrepExams
msr = anova_table.mean_sq[0] + anova_table.mean_sq[1]
msr = msr / model.df_model
# extract value for residual
mse = anova_table.mean_sq[2]
# results
print('results:')
print(f'df_model     : {model.df_model:.0f}')
print(f'msr          : {msr:.3f}')
print(f'mse          : {mse:.3f}')
print(f'F-statistic : {msr/mse:.3f}')
```

```
reference:

               Model:              OLS      Adj. R-squared:   0.427
  Dependent Variable:       FinalScore                 AIC: 84.3992
                Date: 2024-07-02 14:05                 BIC: 85.8539
    No. Observations:               12      Log-Likelihood: -39.200
            Df Model:                2         F-statistic:   5.091
        Df Residuals:                9 Prob (F-statistic):  0.0332
           R-squared:            0.531               Scale:  53.682
```

```
anova table:
```

```
             df     sum_sq    mean_sq         F    PR(>F)
StudyHours  1.0  482.769292  482.769292  8.993214  0.014984
PrepExams   1.0   63.763788   63.763788  1.187817  0.304090
Residual    9.0  483.133587   53.681510       NaN       NaN
```

```
results:
df_model     : 2
msr          : 273.267
mse          : 53.682
F-statistic  : 5.091
```

From the provided results table we extract the F-statistic as 5.091, and the corresponding p_{value} as 0.0332 is reported.

To perform the F-Test computation manually, we compute the

F-statistic:

$$F_{statistic} = \frac{MS_{regression}}{MS_{residual}}$$

where the $MS_{regression}$ is the mean squared regression, and the $MS_{residual}$ is the mean squared error or mean square residual.

In this case $\frac{MS_{regression}}{MS_{residual}} = \frac{(482.76+63.76)/2}{53.68} = 5.091.$

Bear in mind to compute the $MS_{regression}$ we add 482.76 for `StudyHours`, and 63.76 for `PrepExams` and divide the sum by the degrees of freedom of the model df_model = 2 which is one for each regressor variable.

Interpretation

If none of the predictor variables are statistically significant, the overall F-Test will also not be statistically significant.

It is possible, in some occasions, that this does not hold because the F-Test of overall significance, tests whether all of the predictor variables are jointly significant.

The Student-t Test of significance for each predictor variable, on the other hand, merely tests whether each predictor variable individually is significant. Therefore, the F-Test determines whether or not all of the predictor variables are jointly significant.

Each predictor variable might not be significant and yet the F-Test says that all of the predictor variables combined are jointly significant. In general, the more predictor variables we specify in the model, the higher the likelihood that the F-statistic and corresponding p_{value} will be statistically significant.

Another metric that we likely see in the output of regression is the coefficient of determination or R^2, which measures the strength of the linear relationship between the predictor variables and the response variable. Although R^2 can give us an idea of how strongly associated the predictor variables are with the response variable, it does not provide a formal statistical test for this relationship. This is why the F-Test is useful since it provides us with that formal statistical test.

In addition, if the overall F-Test is significant, we conclude that the coefficient of determination R^2 is not equal to 0, as the null hypothesis claims.

10.5 ANOVA table results

We make use of the `anova_lm()` method from the stats package to perform an analysis of variation (ANOVA). It has this signature:

```
table = sm.stats.anova_lm(model, test='F', typ='I', robust='hc3')
```

where:

- `model`: represents the result object of the fitted model
- `test`: set to "F" means that an F-Test is to be conducted
- `typ`: option are (I, II, III), default is I
- `robust`: options are (None, hc0, hc1, hc2, hc3)

In the following Python code segment we implement this approach.

Before using the `anova_lm()` function, we might want to bring up its documentation.

```
import statsmodels.api as sm
# help(sm.stats.anova_lm)
```

```
import statsmodels.api as sm
from statsmodels.formula.api import ols
from quantlib import print_img

# fit model
model = ols("FinalScore ~ StudyHours + PrepExams",
            data=data).fit()
# anova table
print("ANOVA table:")
anova_table = sm.stats.anova_lm(model, test="F",
                                typ="I",robust="hc3")
print_img(anova_table)
```

```
ANOVA table:
```

```
            df      sum_sq     mean_sq         F    PR(>F)
StudyHours  1.0  482.769292  482.769292  8.993214  0.014984
PrepExams   1.0   63.763788   63.763788  1.187817  0.304090
Residual    9.0  483.133587   53.681510       NaN       NaN
```

CHAPTER 11

F-REGRESSION (FR) AND MUTUAL INFORMATION (MI)

The F-regression only captures linear dependency among variables, and the Mutual Information method can recognize any kind of dependency between variables.

To demonstrate this, we compare and contrast the F-regression (FR) and Mutual Information (MI) methods, as we consider 3 feature variables *line*, *sine*, *rand* over the $[0, 1]$ interval, regressed onto the target variable y. We have this model specification:

$$\hat{y} = line + sin(6 \cdot \pi \cdot sine)$$
$$+ 0.1 \cdot N(0, 1) + \epsilon$$

The code below plots the dependent variable y against the features variables *line*, *sine*, and *rand*, individually in a combined plot. Then we compute the normalized values of the F-regression (FR) statistic and Mutual Information (MI) statistic, and we implement:

Before using the F-regression (FR) and Mutual Information (MI) functions, we might want to bring up the documentation and check for any restrictions or limitations

```
from sklearn.feature_selection import f_regression
from sklearn.feature_selection import mutual_info_regression
# print(f_regression.__doc__)
# print(mutual_info_regression.__doc__)
```

```
import numpy as np
import matplotlib.pyplot as plt

# features
np.random.seed(0) # reproducibility
X = np.random.rand(1000, 3)
line = X[:, 0]
sine = X[:, 1]
rand = np.random.randn(1000) # random noise
# target
y = line + np.sin(6 * np.pi * sine) + 0.1 * rand
# Check related pairs
print("x shape      :", X.shape)
print("y shape      :", y.shape)
print("observations :", len(X))
assert X.shape[0] == y.shape[0]
# results
print()
print("dataset:")
N = 15
print("  y    =  line  sine  rand")
for i in range(0,N):
    print(f"{y[i]:5.2f} = {line[i]:5.2f} \
{sine[i]:5.2f} {rand[i]:5.2f}")
print(N, 'of', len(X), 'observations shown')
```

```
x shape      : (1000, 3)
y shape      : (1000,)
observations : 1000

dataset:
  y    =  line  sine  rand
 1.52 =  0.55  0.72  1.80
 1.42 =  0.54  0.42 -1.20
-0.40 =  0.44  0.89  0.52
 1.13 =  0.38  0.79  0.41
-0.46 =  0.57  0.93 -0.42
 0.50 =  0.09  0.02  0.40
 0.19 =  0.78  0.87  0.50
 1.34 =  0.80  0.46 -1.22
-0.34 =  0.12  0.64  0.25
 0.45 =  0.94  0.52 -0.92
 1.10 =  0.26  0.77 -0.65
 0.74 =  0.57  0.02 -1.77
-0.24 =  0.61  0.62 -0.47
 1.14 =  0.68  0.36 -0.20
 1.66 =  0.70  0.06  0.55
15 of 1000 observations shown
```

11.1 F-regression (FR) analysis

```
# f_regression
f_regress, p_regression = f_regression(X, y)
f_regress /= np.max(f_regress)
# results
print("results:")
print("FR-statistic :", f_regress)
print("p-values     :", p_regression)
```

```
results:
FR-statistic : [1.          0.28024353 0.00252204]
p-values     : [3.19286906e-39 8.50243215e-13 4.91915197e-01]
```

Interpretation

The F-regression analysis reports the FR-statistic for `line`, `sine` and `rand` as 1.0, 0.28, and 0.0, respectively.

This means, that it identifies the `line` as the most important factor, and the `sine` as the second most important factor. As expected, the `rand` factor does not contribute to the result, since it is created as a random variable.

11.2 Mutual Information (MI) analysis

```
# compute mutual information
mi = mutual_info_regression(X, y)
mi /= np.max(mi)
# results
print("results:")
print("MI-statistic:", mi)
```

```
results:
MI-statistic: [0.36448455 1.          0.        ]
```

Interpretation

The Mutual Information analysis reports the MI-statistic for `line`, `sine`, and `rand` as 0.365, 1.00, and 0.0, respectively.

This means, that it identifies the `sine` as the most important factor, and the `line` as the second most important factor. Since the `rand` factor is created purely at random, it does not contribute to the regression result.

11.3 Visualizing data as scatter plots

Visualizing the data and the results in plots is the preferred way to inspect the data and the regression results. The plots provide a visual representation of the results previously computed.

```
# plot
plt.figure(figsize=(9,3))
features = ['line', 'sine', 'rand']
for i in range(3):
    plt.subplot(1, 3, i + 1)
    plt.grid()
    plt.scatter(X[:, i], y,
                edgecolor="green", s=20)
    plt.xlabel(features[i], fontsize=12)
    if i == 0: plt.ylabel("$y$", fontsize=12)
    plt.title("FR={:.2f}, \
             MI={:.2f}".format(f_regress[i], mi[i]),
             fontsize=12)
plt.show()
print('F-regression versus Mutual Information:')
```

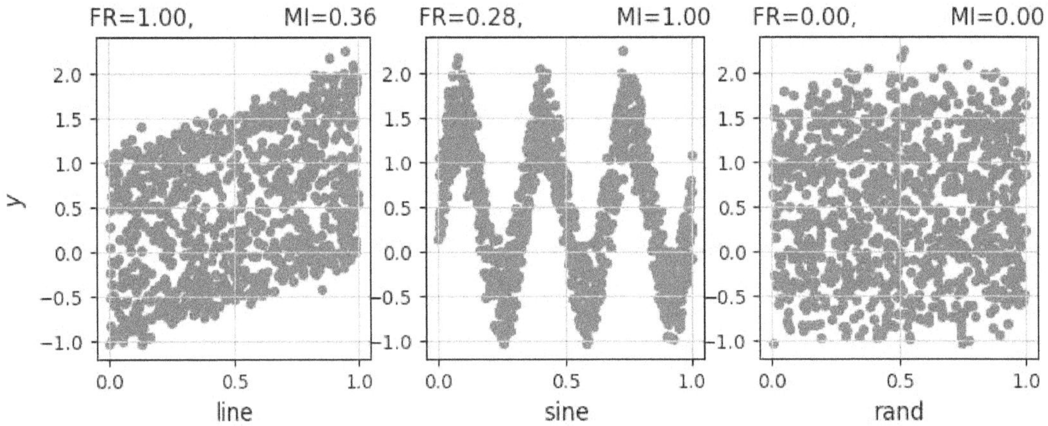


```
F-regression versus Mutual Information:
```

Interpretation

Remember that the F-regression analysis captures only linear dependency, and it identifies `line` as the most discriminative feature with a 1.0 FR-score

The Mutual Information method can capture any kind of dependencies, and it was able to identify `sine` as the most discriminative feature with a 1.0 MI-score

Both methods correctly identify the `rand` variable as irrelevant, with a low score of almost 0. This result is not surprising, since we generated the `rand` feature data at random.

CHAPTER 12

COEFFICIENT OF VARIATION CV

The coefficient of variation, often abbreviated as CV, is a way to measure how spread out values are in a dataset relative to its mean.

In financial analytics terms, it is a measure of risk σ per unit of return μ, and it provides a standardized measure in a risk-return framework.

Coefficient of variation:

$$CV_{ratio} = \sigma/\mu$$

where:

- σ: the standard deviation of the data series
- μ: the mean of the data series

The coefficient of variation or CV_{ratio}, as a ratio between the standard deviation and its mean, makes the CV_{ratio} comparable among different assets.

12.1 Usage of the coefficient of variation

It is often presented in financial analytics, to compare the standard deviation or risk σ, relative to its expected return μ of an investment. As such, this risk measure allows the investors to compare the risk-return trade-off between different investment alternatives.

For example, suppose an investor is considering investing in the following two mutual equities:

- Equity A : standard deviation = 12.4%, mean expected return = 9%

- Equity B : standard deviation = 8.20%, mean expected return = 5%

Upon calculating the coefficient of variation (CV-ratio) for each equity, the investor finds:

The CV_{ratio} for Equity A = $\frac{.124}{.09}$ = 1.38, and the corresponding CV_{ratio} for Equity B = $\frac{.820}{.05}$ = 1.64

Interpretation

Since Equity A has a lower coefficient of variation or CV_{ratio}, it offers a higher expected return per unit of risk and is considered the better investment.

12.2 Coefficient of variation custom function mycv()

We define a helper function `mycv()` to make the required computation. To calculate the coefficient of variation we make use of this function and apply it to the data.

In the following Python code segments, it is applied to a single NumPy array and a Pandas DataFrame.

12.3 Use mycv() on a single array

The following code shows how to calculate the CV_{ratio} for a single array.

```
import numpy as np

def mycv(x):
    """ coefficient of variation """
    return np.std(x, ddof=1) / np.mean(x)

# create a vector of data
data = [88, 85, 82, 97, 67, 77, 74, 86, 81, 95,
        77, 88, 85, 76, 81, 82]
# calculate CV
r = mycv(data)
# results
print("CV-ratio : {:.3f}".format(r))
```

```
CV-ratio : 0.092
```

The coefficient of variation turns out to be 0.092, or 9.2% in percentage terms.

12.4 Apply mycv() on a Pandas DataFrame

The following code segment demonstrates the calculation of the CV_{ratio} for multiple columns of a Pandas DataFrame.

```
import pandas as pd

# DataFrame
df = pd.DataFrame( {
        "Equity A": [88, 85, 82, 97, 67, 77, 74, 86, 81, 95],
        "Equity B": [77, 88, 85, 76, 81, 82, 88, 91, 92, 99],
        "Equity C": [67, 68, 68, 74, 74, 76, 76, 77, 78, 84] } )
# calculate CV-ratio for each column in the DataFrame
rDs = df.apply(mycv)
# results
print("coefficient of variation:")
print(rDs)
```

```
coefficient of variation:
Equity A    0.110129
Equity B    0.083308
Equity C    0.071540
dtype: float64
```

We can verify the result, by computing the CV_{ratio} manually.

```
# verify by manual computation
print("coefficient of variation:")
print(df.std() / df.mean())
```

```
coefficient of variation:
Equity A    0.110129
Equity B    0.083308
Equity C    0.071540
dtype: float64
```

We observe, that the results are identical.

12.5 Explore NaN or Missing Values in Pandas DataFrame

Note that missing `NaN` values will simply be ignored when calculating the coefficient of variation using a DataFrame as a data source.

Suppose we have the following dataset, containing missing values and the `cv-score` is computed. In the following Python code segment, the impact of

NaN values is explored.

```
import numpy as np
import pandas as pd

# DataFrame
df = pd.DataFrame({
        "Equity E": [88, 85, 82, 97, 67, 77, 74, 86, 81, 95],
        "Equity F": [77, 88, 85, 76, 81, 82, 88, 91, np.nan, 99],
        "Equity G": [67, 68, 68, 74, 74, 76, 76, 77, 78, np.nan] })
# inspect
print("check for missing values:")
print(df.isnull().any())
print("missing values count:", df.isnull().any().count())
print()
# calculate CV for each column in a DataFrame
rDs = df.apply(mycv)
# results
print("coefficient of variation:")
print(rDs)
```

```
check for missing values:
Equity E    False
Equity F     True
Equity G     True
dtype: bool
missing values count: 3

coefficient of variation:
Equity E    0.110129
Equity F    0.084976
Equity G    0.058609
dtype: float64
```

Interpretation

Although the coefficients of variation will be computed, however, the missing NaN values will simply be ignored in the computation. Great care must be taken, to determine if this behavior is permissible. Perhaps it is best to inspect the dataset before making any calculations and decide on how to treat missing data items.

CHAPTER 13

COVARIANCE AND CORRELATION MATRIX

The covariance cov(x,y) is a measure of how changes in one variable are associated with changes in a second variable, it quantifies the strength to which two variables are linearly associated.

The correlation `corr(x,y)` method is another way to quantify the linear relationship between two variables by computing the Pearson correlation coefficient, which is a normalized measure of linear association between two variables.

- A covariance matrix is a square matrix that shows the covariance coefficients between multiple variables.
- A correlation matrix is a square matrix that shows the Pearson correlation coefficients between multiple variables.

13.1 Covariance Matrix

This matrix can be useful in understanding the dataset and in particular how strong variables are related to each other. In the following Python code example, we demonstrate the creation of a covariance coefficient matrix.

13.1.1 Dataset

We create a dataset that records the final test results in `Math`, `Science` and `History` for 15 students on the three subjects taught, like so:

```
import numpy as np

# dataset
math = [84,82,81,89,73,94,92,70,88,95,92,91,82,87,68]
science = [85,82,72,77,75,89,95,84,77,94,92,94,78,83,88]
history = [97,94,93,95,88,82,78,84,69,78,79,83,78,92,88]
names = ["Math", "Science", "History"]
# NumPy array
data = np.array([math, science, history])
# inspect
print('dataset:')
print(names)
print(data)
```

```
dataset:
['Math', 'Science', 'History']
[[84 82 81 89 73 94 92 70 88 95 92 91 82 87 68]
 [85 82 72 77 75 89 95 84 77 94 92 94 78 83 88]
 [97 94 93 95 88 82 78 84 69 78 79 83 78 92 88]]
```

13.1.2 Create the covariance matrix using the cov() function

We compute the covariance matrix using the `cov()` function, provided by the `NumPy` library, which has the following signature:

```
r = np.cov(data, bias=True)
```

where

- `data`: is the dataset given as a Numpy array
- `bias`: set to `True` normalization is done by the number of observations `N`, and set to `False` normalization is done by $N-1$.
- `r`: the returns a NumPy array, containing the computed covariance coefficients

Before using the `cov()` function, we might want to bring up the documentation, to review the function signatures, its parameters, return values, and any information regarding restrictions.

```
import numpy as np
# help(np.cov)
```

```
# covariance matrix
r = np.cov(data, bias=True)
# inspect
print(type(r))
print("covariance matrix:")
print(names)
print(r)
```

```
<class 'numpy.ndarray'>
covariance matrix:
['Math', 'Science', 'History']
[[ 68.91555556  26.68888889 -20.97333333]
 [ 26.68888889  52.62222222 -18.06666667]
 [-20.97333333 -18.06666667  60.56      ]]
```

Interpretation

Recall, that the covariance of a variable with itself is its variance, that is the `cov(x,x)` is its `var(x)`. The values along the diagonal axis of the matrix are the variances of each variable.

- `Math`: covariance is 68.91
- `Science`: covariance is 52.62
- `History`: covariance is 60.56

The other values in the matrix represent the covariances between the three variables.

- For Math and Science the covariance is 26.69
- For Math and History the covariance is -20.97
- For Science and History the covariance is -18.07

A positive covariance indicates that two variables tend to increase or decrease in tandem, we say they walk lock-step with each other. For example, `Math` and `Science` have a positive covariance, which indicates that students who score high in `Math` also tend to score high in `Science`. Conversely, students who score low on `Math` also tend to score low in `Science`.

A negative covariance indicates that as one variable increases, a second variable tends to decrease. They walk in a counter-fashion with each other. For example, `Math` and `History` have a negative covariance, which indicates that students who score high in `Math` tend to score low in `History`. Conversely, students who score low in `Math` tend to score high in `History`.

13.1.3 Visualize the covariance matrix as a heatmap

We visualize the covariance matrix by using the `heatmap()` function from the seaborn package and for the plot we make use of the matplotlib package, which has the following signature:

```
sns.heatmap(cov, annot=True, fmt="g",
            xticklabels=names, yticklabels=names)
```

where:

- `cov`: is the computed covariance matrix
- `fmt`: formatting option to use when adding annotations
- `annot`: if set to `True`, write the data value in each cell
- `xticklabels`: the names of the variables along the x-axis
- `yticklabels`: the names of the variables along the y-axis

```
import seaborn as sns
import matplotlib.pyplot as plt

# covariance matrix
cov = np.cov(data, bias=True)
names = ["math", "science", "history"]
# plot
fig = plt.figure(figsize=(5,2))
sns.set(font_scale=1.1)
sns.heatmap(cov, annot=True,
            fmt="g", xticklabels=names,
            yticklabels=names)
plt.title("Covariance matrix as heatmap",
          fontsize=12)
plt.show()
# inspect
print("covariance matrix:")
print(cov)
print('shape:', cov.shape)
```

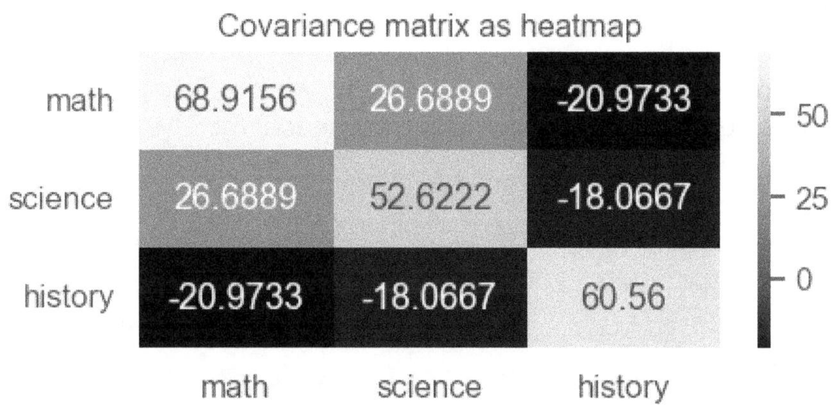


```
covariance matrix:
[[ 68.91555556  26.68888889 -20.97333333]
 [ 26.68888889  52.62222222 -18.06666667]
 [-20.97333333 -18.06666667  60.56      ]]
shape: (3, 3)
```

13.2 Correlation Matrix

The Pearson correlation coefficient is a measure of linear association between two variables. It takes on a value between -1 and +1 where:

- -1: indicates a perfectly negative linear correlation.
- 0 : indicates no linear correlation.
- $+1$: indicates a perfectly positive linear correlation.

The further away the correlation coefficient is from zero, the stronger the relationship between the two variables. However, in many cases, we want to understand the correlation between more than just one pair of variables simultaneously. This is where a correlation matrix comes in, which is a square table that shows the correlation coefficients between pairwise combinations of multiple variables.

We explore how to create a correlation matrix in the following Python code segment.

13.2.1 Dataset

We create a dataset containing 3 investment alternatives for Fund A, Fund B, and Fund C with 8 observations each for the expected returns.

```
import pandas as pd

data = {
    "Fund A": [4, 5, 5, 6, 7, 8, 8, 10],
    "Fund B": [12, 14, 13, 7, 8, 8, 9, 13],
    "Fund C": [22, 24, 26, 26, 29, 32, 20, 14]}
# DataFrame
df = pd.DataFrame(data, columns=["Fund A", "Fund B", "Fund C"])
# inspect
print('investment alternatives:')
print(df.head())
print('shape:', df.shape)
```

```
investment alternatives:
   Fund A  Fund B  Fund C
0       4      12      22
1       5      14      24
2       5      13      26
3       6       7      26
4       7       8      29
shape: (8, 3)
```

13.2.2 Create a correlation matrix using the corr() function

To calculate the correlation coefficients we make use of the `corr()` function, which is part of the Pandas DataFrame package. It has the following signature:

```
corr = df.corr()
```

where

- `df`: is the DataFrame containing the dataset

The `corr()` function returns a matrix of the correlation coefficient, corresponding to each input data element.

In Python code, this approach is implemented and the results are interpreted.

```
import pandas as pd

# correlation matrix
corr = df.corr()
```

(continues on next page)

(continued from previous page)

```
names = ["Fund A", "Fund B", "Fund C"]
# inspect
print("correlation matrix:")
print(corr)
print('shape:', corr.shape)
```

```
correlation matrix:
          Fund A    Fund B    Fund C
Fund A  1.000000 -0.244861 -0.329573
Fund B -0.244861  1.000000 -0.522092
Fund C -0.329573 -0.522092  1.000000
shape: (3, 3)
```

Interpretation

The correlation coefficients along the diagonal of the table are all equal to +1 because each variable is perfectly correlated with itself. All of the other correlation coefficients indicate the strength of the correlation between pairwise combinations of variables. For example, the correlation coefficient between:

- Fund A and Fund B is computed as -0.245
- Fund A and Fund C is computed as -0.330
- Fund B and Fund C is computed as -0.522

13.2.3 Visualize the correlation matrix as a heatmap

We can visualize the correlation matrix by using the styling options available in the Matplotlib package. By changing the argument of the `cmap` parameter, we control the appearance of the produced correlation matrix.

```
sns.heatmap(corr, annot=True, fmt="g", cmap="Oranges",
            xticklabels=names, yticklabels=names)
```

where:

- `corr`: is the computed correlation coefficients matrix
- `annot`: if set to `True`, write the data value in each cell
- `fmt`: formatting option to use when adding annotations
- `cmap`: denotes the color scheme to use
- `xticklabels`: the names of the variables along the x-axis
- `yticklabels`: the names of the variables along the y-axis

To further customize the appearance of the plot, we can change the color map by specifying the cmap argument, as demonstrated in the following section. Some available predefined styles for this cmap parameter include ('viridis', 'plasma', 'inferno', 'magma', 'cividis' 'Greys', 'Purples', 'Blues', 'Greens', 'Oranges', 'Reds', 'YlOrBr', 'YlOrRd' 'OrRd', 'PuRd', 'RdPu', 'BuPu', 'GnBu', 'PuBu', 'YlGnBu').

For a list of available cmap arguments, refer to the matplotlib documentation Matplotlib [2023].

```
import seaborn as sns
import matplotlib.pyplot as plt

# plot
fig = plt.figure(figsize=(5,2))
sns.set(font_scale=1.1)
sns.heatmap(corr, annot=True,
            fmt="g", cmap="YlOrBr",
            xticklabels=names,
            yticklabels=names)
plt.title("Correlation matrix as heatmap",
          fontsize=12)
plt.show()
```

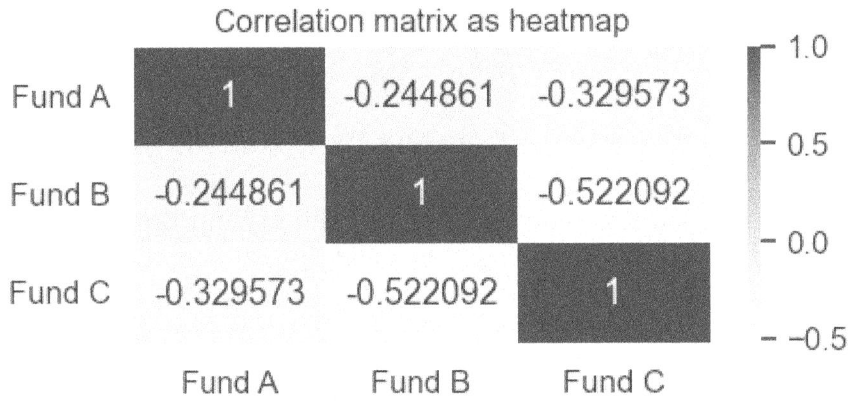

For demonstration purposes, we change the color scheme, by setting the cmap parameter to "Greens", like so.

```
# plot
fig = plt.figure(figsize=(5,2))
sns.set(font_scale=1.1)
sns.heatmap(corr, annot=True,
            fmt="g", cmap="Greens",
            xticklabels=names,
            yticklabels=names)
plt.title("Correlation matrix as heatmap",
          fontsize=12)
plt.show()
```

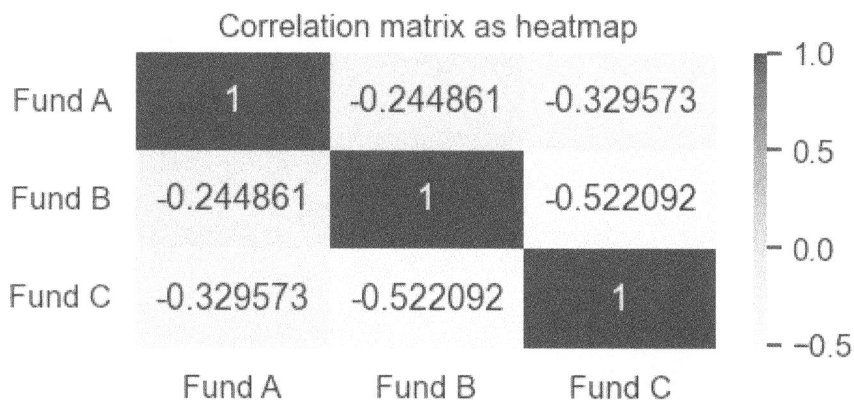
Correlation matrix as heatmap
Fund A
Fund B
Fund C
1
-0.244861
-0.329573
-0.244861
1
-0.522092
-0.329573
-0.522092
1
Fund A
Fund B
Fund C
1.0
0.5
0.0
−0.5

CHAPTER 14

BREUSCH-PAGAN TEST FOR HETEROSCEDASTICITY

In regression analysis, heteroscedasticity refers to the unequal scatter of residuals. Specifically, it refers to the case where there is a systematic change in the spread of the residuals over the range of measured values

Heteroscedasticity is a problem because ordinary least squares (OLS) regression assumes that the residuals come from a population that has homoscedasticity, which means constant error variance. When heteroscedasticity is present in a regression analysis, the results of the analysis become unreliable.

One way to determine if the regression analysis suffers from heteroscedasticity the Breusch-Pagan Test can be applied. In the following code segment, we explore the usage of the Breusch-Pagan Test on the small dataset.

```
import pandas as pd

# DataFrame
df = pd.DataFrame( {
   "rating": [90,85,82,88,94,85,80,75,87,86,82,88,84,90,85,82],
        "A": [25,20,14,16,27,19,21,15,14,19,17,13,14,25,20,14],
        "B": [5,7,7,8,5,7,6,9,9,5,6,8,6,5,7,7],
        "C": [11,8,10,6,7,9,8,10,10,7,9,6,9,11,8,10], })
# inspect
print('dataset:')
print(df.head())
print(df.shape)
```

```
dataset:
   rating   A  B   C
0      90  25  5  11
1      85  20  7   8
2      82  14  7  10
3      88  16  8   6
4      94  27  5   7
(16, 4)
```

We fit a multiple linear regression model using rating as the response or target variable and A, B and C as the explanatory or feature variables.

Regression model specification

$$\hat{y} = \beta_0 + \beta_1 A + \beta_2 B + \beta_3 C + \epsilon_t$$

where

- $\hat{y}$: response or target variable rating
- A: explanatory or feature variable A
- B: explanatory or feature variable B
- C: explanatory or feature variable C
- ϵ_t : residual or error term

We apply a regression analysis to estimate the model parameters β_0, β_1, β_2, and β_3. These estimates are achieved by minimizing the squared error term through the ordinary least squares regression framework.

Before we use the `ols()` method, we might want the bring up its documentation.

```
import statsmodels.formula.api as smf
# help(smf.ols)
```

14.1 Linear Multiple Regression model

We perform an ordinary least squares regression on the previously created DataFrame. We are using the `ols()` function from the statsmodels package, which has the following signature:

```
model = smf.ols('rating ~ A+B+C', data=df).fit()
```

where

- `("rating ~ A+B+C")`: refers to the model definition in formula notation

- data: specifies the source of the data to be df
- model: the resulting model object

The resulting OLS regression summary() function reports statistics and key metrics for further analysis and interpretation. In Python, this example is implemented and the results are presented.

```
import statsmodels.formula.api as smf
from quantlib import print_img
import warnings
warnings.filterwarnings("ignore")

# fit regression model
fit = smf.ols("rating ~ A+B+C", data=df).fit()
# results
print_img(fit.summary().tables[0])
print_img(fit.summary().tables[1])
print_img(fit.summary().tables[2])
```

```
                            OLS Regression Results
==============================================================================
Dep. Variable:                 rating   R-squared:                       0.391
Model:                            OLS   Adj. R-squared:                  0.239
Method:                 Least Squares   F-statistic:                     2.567
Date:                Tue, 02 Jul 2024   Prob (F-statistic):              0.103
Time:                        14:06:19   Log-Likelihood:                -42.356
No. Observations:                  16   AIC:                             92.71
Df Residuals:                      12   BIC:                             95.80
Df Model:                           3
Covariance Type:            nonrobust
==============================================================================

==============================================================================
                 coef    std err          t      P>|t|      [0.025      0.975]
------------------------------------------------------------------------------
Intercept     84.5414     13.562      6.234      0.000      54.992     114.091
A              0.5193      0.330      1.576      0.141      -0.199       1.237
B             -0.2956      1.089     -0.272      0.791      -2.667       2.076
C             -0.7928      0.630     -1.258      0.232      -2.166       0.580
==============================================================================

==============================================================================
Omnibus:                        2.108   Durbin-Watson:                   1.941
Prob(Omnibus):                  0.349   Jarque-Bera (JB):                1.104
Skew:                          -0.643   Prob(JB):                        0.576
Kurtosis:                       2.986   Cond. No.                         299.
==============================================================================
```

We can extract the residual term values from the regression model object, and visualize them in a scatter plot. This is demonstrated in the Python code below.

```
# results
print("residuals:")
```

(continues on next page)

(continued from previous page)

```
print(fit.resid)
```

```
residuals:
0     2.674033
1    -1.516575
2     0.185083
3     2.270718
4     2.464088
5    -0.204420
6    -7.331492
7    -6.743094
8     5.776243
9    -1.381215
10   -2.461326
11    3.828729
12    1.096685
13    2.674033
14   -1.516575
15    0.185083
dtype: float64
```

```
# DataFrame
df = pd.DataFrame({"x": range(0,
                    len(fit.resid)), "y": fit.resid})
# plot
ax1 = df.plot.scatter(x="x", y="y",
                      c="Maroon", figsize=(7,3))
ax1.set_title("Scatter plot of residual values",
              fontsize=12)
ax1.grid(True)
```

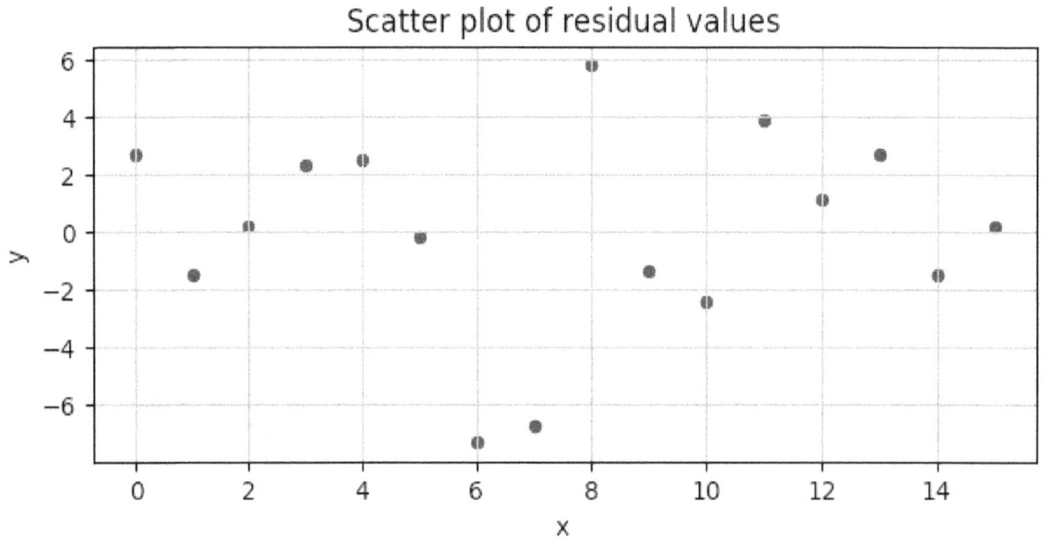

Although, the visual inspection of the scatter plot of the residual values, does not convince us that heteroscedasticity is a problem. Therefore, in the next step, we conduct a formal Breusch-Pagan Test, to arrive at a more objective assessment.

14.2 Breusch-Pagan Test for Heteroscedasticity

We perform a Breusch-Pagan Test to determine if heteroscedasticity is present in the dataset, we set up the statistical test procedure, and formulate:

Hypotheses

- H_0: data series exhibits no heteroscedasticity
- H_1: data series exhibits heteroscedasticity

level of significance

- α of 0.05

The test is set up to be a two-tailed test, so we allocate $\frac{\alpha}{2}$ in either tail of the distribution.

In the following Python code segment, we implement this approach:

Before we use the Breusch-Pagan Test function `het_breuschpagan()`, we might want the bring up the documentation.

```
import statsmodels.stats.api as sms
# help(sms.het_breuschpagan)
```

```
from statsmodels.compat import lzip
import statsmodels.stats.api as sms

# parameters
alpha = 0.05
# Breusch-Pagan test
test = sms.het_breuschpagan(fit.resid,
                             fit.model.exog)
names = ["Lagrange multiplier statistic",
         "p-value", "f-value", "f p-value"]
res = lzip(names, test)
# results
print("Breusch-Pagan Test:")
print(f"LM-statistic          : {res[0][1]:.4f}")
print(f"p-value               : {res[1][1]:.4f}")
print(f"level of significance : {alpha:.2f}")
print("two-tailed test")
print("Hypothesis")
print("H0: data exhibits no heteroscedasticity")
```

(continues on next page)

(continued from previous page)

```
print("H1: data exhibits heteroscedasticity")
if res[0][1] <= alpha/2:
    print("reject H0")
    print("Heteroscedastic")
else:
    print("fail to reject H0")
    print("Not Heteroscedastic")
```

```
Breusch-Pagan Test:
LM-statistic          : 3.6331
p-value               : 0.3039
level of significance : 0.05
two-tailed test
Hypothesis
H0: data exhibits no heteroscedasticity
H1: data exhibits heteroscedasticity
fail to reject H0
Not Heteroscedastic
```

Interpretation

The LM-statistic is reported as 3.6331 and the corresponding 0.3039 as p_{value}.

Because $p_{value} \geq \frac{\alpha}{2}$ of 0.025, we fail to reject the null hypothesis H_0, and we conclude that the data does not suffer from heteroscedasticity, meaning that the analyzed data does not provide sufficient evidence to say that heteroscedasticity is a problem. We can make such a claim with (1-α) or 95% confidence.

14.3 Correcting for Heteroscedasticity

Recall, that heteroscedasticity refers to the non-constant error variance, meaning that the scatter plot of the regression residuals or errors exhibits non-constant behavior like cyclically going up or down or exhibiting some form of trend.

In the previous example, we saw that heteroscedasticity was not present in the regression model. However, when the data series indeed suffers from heteroscedasticity, we have 3 ways to remedy the situation, as pointed out by Frost [2020].

One way to fix heteroscedasticity is to transform the dependent variable for example by taking the logarithm of the dependent variable. However this changes the model specification, and the resulting interpretation might change.

Another way to fix heteroscedasticity is to redefine the dependent variable. One common way to do so is to use a ratio value for the dependent variable, rather than the raw value. For example, we can use a per capita value in contrast to the absolute raw values.

A third way to correct for heteroscedasticity is to use a weighted regression model. This type of regression assigns a weight to each data point based on the variance of its fitted value. When the proper weights are used, this approach might eliminate the issue of heteroscedasticity.

CHAPTER 15

CHI-SQUARE TEST FOR INDEPENDENCE

A χ^2-Test for Independence is used to determine whether or not there is a significant association between two categorical variables. It is mostly concerned with categorical variables.

In the following examples, we are investigating, if

- gender is associated with political_party preference
- education_level and marital_status are somehow associated
- gender is associated with ice_cream_flavor preference
- favorite_color is associated with favorite_sport

In each of these cases, it is desirable to know if the two categorical variables are associated with each other in any significant way. To perform a formal test, we can use a χ^2-Test of Independence to assess, at a chosen level of significance, if there is an association between those two variables.

Suppose we conduct a survey and ask N people regarding their choices or preferences, and record the results in a dataset. To set up the statistical procedure, we formulate:

Hypothesis

- H_0: variables are independent (no association)
- H_1: variables are not independent (association)

level of significance:

- α = 0.05

Often used values for α are (0.01, 0.05, 0.10).

Remember, that the χ^2-Test for Independence is a one-tailed test, therefore we allocate α in one tail of the distribution.

We make use of the following formula to compute the

χ^2-statistic:

$$\tilde{\chi}^2 = \frac{1}{d}\sum_{k=1}^{n} \frac{(O_k - E_k)^2}{E_k}$$

where:

- 0: observed value
- E: expected value
- d: total number of observation

degrees of freedom:

- df = $(r-1)\cdot(c-1)$

and r denotes the number of rows, and c denotes the number of columns.

If the p_{value} that corresponds to the χ^2-statistic is less than your chosen level of significance, say α = 0.05 then we can reject the null hypothesis H_0 in favor of the alternative hypothesis H_1.

According to the test results, we can conclude that the two variables are not independent of each other, therefore we can say that there is an association between those two variables, and we can make such a claim with $(1-\alpha)$ or 95% confidence.

The data ca be further investigated, to gain a more in-depth understanding of this association.

Before we use the function, we might want to bring up the documentation for the `chi2_contingency()` function.

```
import scipy.stats as stats
# help(stats.chi2_contingency)
```

15.1 Gender versus ice-cream-flavor preference

Suppose we want to examine if gender is somehow associated with ice_cream_flavor preference.

> We take a sample of 250 customers ("male", "female") at a local ice cream shop and record the orders according to their flavor preference in the categories ("vanilla", "chocolate", "others").

The survey "gender versus ice_cream_flavor preference", has the following data.

```
        Vanilla Chocolate Others Total
Male      90      45        20     125
Female    55      38        23     125
Total    115      93        42     250
```

We attempt the test if `ice_cream_flavor` preference is somehow related to `gender`. To set up the statistical test procedure, we formulate:

Hypothesis

- H_0: The variables are independent
- H_1: The variables are not independent

level of significance:

- $\alpha = 0.05$

Use the following steps to perform a χ^2-Test for Independence in Python to determine if the two categorical variables are significantly related.

15.2 Compute the chi-square statistic

We perform the χ^2-Test for Independence by using the `chi2_contingency()` function from the SciPy library, which has the following signature:

```
r = chi2_contingency(observed)
```

where

- `observed`: the contingency table of the survey data points.

The function returns the computed χ^2-statistic, along with the degree of freedom `df` and the associated p_{value}.

In the following Python code segment, we implement this approach and the results are interpreted.

```python
import scipy.stats as stats

# parameters
alpha = 0.05
# contingency table
data = [[90, 45, 20], [55, 38, 23]]
# Chi-squared Test of Independence
r = stats.chi2_contingency(data)
# results
print("Chi-squared-Test:")
print(f"Chi-squared statistic    : {r[0]:.4f}")
print(f"p-value                  : {r[1]:.4f}")
print(f"degrees of freedom df    : {r[2]:.0f}")
print(f"level of significance    : {alpha:.2f}")
print("one-tailed test")
print("Hypothesis")
print("H0: two variables are independent (no association)")
print("H1: two variables are not independent (association)")
if r[1] < alpha:
    print("reject H0")
    print("Not Independent")
else:
    print("fail to reject H0")
    print("Independent")
```

```
Chi-squared-Test:
Chi-squared statistic    : 3.7123
p-value                  : 0.1563
degrees of freedom df    : 2
level of significance    : 0.05
one-tailed test
Hypothesis
H0: two variables are independent (no association)
H1: two variables are not independent (association)
fail to reject H0
Independent
```

Interpretation

The χ^2-statistic is reported as 3.7123 and the associated p_{value} is 0.1563.

Remember, the test is set up to be a one-tail test, so we allocate the full level of significance (α) in one tail of the distribution.

Since the $p_{value} \geq \alpha$ of 0.05, we fail to reject the null hypothesis H_0.

This means that the analyzed data does not provide sufficient evidence to conclude, that there is an association between the two variables gender and ice_cream_flavor preference. Therefore, the two variables are independent of each other, and we can make such a claim with $(1-\alpha)$ or 95% confidence.

15.3 A quarter of residency versus occupation type

A random sample of 650 residents of a city is taken from each quarter_of_residence within the city. The occupation_type of each subject is recorded as belonging to one of the three categories (WhiteCollar, BlueCollar, NoCollar). The quarter_of_residence variable has categories such as (NorthQuarter, EastQuarter, SouthQuarter, WestQuarter). The survey is adapted from the example given at Wikipedia [2023], and the data is presented in the following table:

The survey "quarter of residency" versus "occupation type", has the following data.

	NorthQuarter	EastQuarter	SouthQuarter	WestQuarter	Total
WhiteCollar	90	60	104	95	349
BlueCollar	30	50	51	20	151
NoCollar	30	40	45	35	150
Total	150	150	200	150	650

We attempt the test if the `quarter of residency` is somehow related to the `occupation type`. To set up the statistical test procedure, we formulate:

Hypothesis

- H_0: The variables are Independent
- H_1: The variables are Not Independent

level of significance:

- $\alpha = 0.05$

The test is set up to be a one-tailed test, therefore the entire α is allocated to one side of the distribution.

15.4 Compute the chi-square statistic

We make use of the `chi2_contigence()` function, provided by the Scipy library, which has the following signature:

```
r = stats.chi2_contingency(data)
```

This function returns the computed χ^2-statistic, along with the degree of freedom `df` and the associated p_{value}. In the following Python code segment, this approach is implemented and the results are interpreted.

```
import scipy.stats as stats

# parameters
alpha = 0.05
# contingency table
data = [[90, 60, 104, 95],
        [30, 50, 51, 20],
        [30, 40, 45, 35]]
# Chi-squared Test of Independence
r = stats.chi2_contingency(data)
# results
print("Chi-squared Test:")
print(f"Chi-squared statistic  : {r[0]:.4f}")
print(f"p-value                : {r[1]:.2E}")
print(f"degrees of freedom df  : {r[2]:.0f}")
print(f"level of significance  : {alpha:.2f}")
print("one-tailed test")
print("Hypothesis")
print("H0: two variables are Independent")
print("H1: two variables are Not Independent")
if r[1] < alpha:
    print("reject H0")
    print("Not Independent")
else:
    print("fail to reject H0")
    print("Independent")
```

```
Chi-squared Test:
Chi-squared statistic  : 24.5712
p-value                : 4.10E-04
degrees of freedom df  : 6
level of significance  : 0.05
one-tailed test
Hypothesis
H0: two variables are Independent
H1: two variables are Not Independent
reject H0
Not Independent
```

Interpretation

The χ^2-statistic is reported as 24.571 and the corresponding p_{value} is 4.1e-4, almost zero.

Since the p_{value} is less than the desired level of significance α = 0.05, we can reject the null hypothesis H_0, in favor of the alternative hypothesis H_1.

This means that the analyzed data does provide sufficient evidence to conclude, that there is a significant association between quarter_of_residency and occupation_type. The two variables are not independent of each other, and we can make such a claim with $(1 - \alpha)$ or 95% confidence.

CHAPTER 16

MANN-KENDALL TEST FOR TRENDS

The Mann-Kendall (MK) Test for Trends can be used to determine whether a trend exists in a data series in any significant way. It is a non-parametric test, meaning there are no underlying assumptions made regarding the normality of the data.

To set up the test procedure we formulate:

Hypothesis

- H_0: there is No Trend present in the data series
- H_1: there is a Trend present in the data series

level of significance

- $\alpha = 0.05$

Common choices for α are 0.1, 0.05, and 0.01, as a level of significance, corresponding to 90%, 95%, and 99% confidence.

This test is set up to be a two-tailed test, therefore we allocate $\frac{\alpha}{2}$ in either tail of the distribution.

If the p_{value} of the MK-Test is lower than the given level of significance, we reject the null hypothesis H_0 and conclude that there is a trend present in the data. If a trend is indicated, it could either be positive or negative.

Otherwise, if the p_{value} of the MK-Test is greater than the level of significance, we fail to reject the null hypothesis H_0 and conclude that there is no trend in the data series.

In the following Python code segment, a full example is implemented and its results are discussed.

We might want to bring up the inline documentation for the `original_test()` function. We can check the function call signature, as well as a detailed description of each parameter.

```
import pymannkendall as mk
print('version mk :', mk.__version__)
# help(mk.original_test)
```

```
version mk : 1.4.2
```

16.1 MK-Test on a sample containing no trend

The Mann-Kendall (MK) Test for Trends is applied to a given time series data set, to detect any trends within the data series.

We deliberately set up the data series containing no trend, and we performed a MK-Test to statistically confirm the absence of any trends, with a chosen level of significance.

We make use of the `original_test()` function, from the `pymannkendall` package, it has the following signature:

```
r = mk.original_test(data, alpha=alpha)
```

where

- `data`: is the input data
- `alpha`: the chosen level of significance

The function returns

- `trend_type`: The type of trend as (“no trend”, “increasing”, or “decreasing”)
- `h`: if a trend is indicated by `True`, and if no trend is indicated by `False`
- `p`: The p_{value} of the test
- `z`: The normalized test statistic

Please observe that the reported `trend_type` indicates the type of trend, either “no trend”, “increasing”, or “decreasing”, according to the chosen level of significance α.

Note: We have to install the package with "pip install pymannkendall", before we can use its functions.

In the following Python code segment, the usage of this function is demonstrated.

```
import pymannkendall as mk

# parameters
alpha = 0.05
# dataset, no trend
data = [19, 19, 18, 18, 17, 19, 18, 17, 18, 17, 18, 19,
        20, 19, 18, 19, 19]
# Mann-Kendall Test for Trends
r = mk.original_test(data, alpha=alpha)
# results
print("Mann-Kendall Test:")
print(f"MK-statistic            : {r.z:.4f}")
print(f"p-value                 : {r.p:.4f}")
print(f"level of significance : {alpha:.2f}")
print(f"trend type              : {r.trend:s}")
print("two-tailed test")
print("Hypothesis")
print("H0: there is No Trend present in the data series")
print("H1: there is a Trend present in the data series")
if r.p < alpha/2:
    print("reject H0")
    print("Trend")
else:
    print("fail to reject H0")
    print("No Trend")
```

```
Mann-Kendall Test:
MK-statistic          : 0.7947
p-value               : 0.4268
level of significance : 0.05
trend type            : no trend
two-tailed test
Hypothesis
H0: there is No Trend present in the data series
H1: there is a Trend present in the data series
fail to reject H0
No Trend
```

Interpretation

The MK-statistic is reported as 0.7947 and the corresponding p_{value} is 0.4268.

The p_{value} is greater than $\frac{\alpha}{2}$ of 0.025, the allocation of the level of significance in either tail, for a two-tailed test setup.

So we fail to reject the null hypothesis H_0, meaning that the data provides sufficient evidence to conclude that there is no trend in the data series. We can make such a claim with (1-α) or 95% confidence.

Exactly what we expected, given the way the dataset was created.

16.2 Plot the data series containing no trend

For visual inspection, we plot the data series using the matplotlib library, to intuitively confirm the absence of any trends.

```
import matplotlib.pyplot as plt
from matplotlib.lines import Line2D

# plot
fig = plt.figure(figsize=(8,3))
ax = fig.add_subplot(111)
ax.grid()
ax.set_title("Mann-Kendall Test for Trends @ data with no trend")
x = list(range(1, len(data) + 1))
line = Line2D(x, data)
ax.add_line(line)
ax.set_xlim(min(x), max(x))
ax.set_ylim(min(data) * 0.95, max(data) * 1.05)
plt.xlabel('number')
plt.ylabel('score')
plt.show()
```

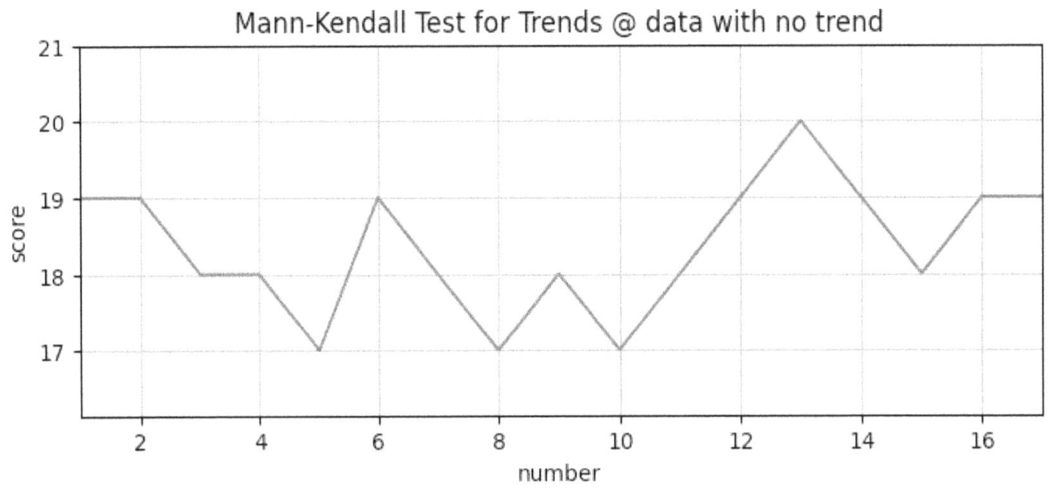

From the plot, it can be observed, that the data is a bit all over the place, which confirms that there is no clear trend in the data series.

16.3 MK-Test for Trends on the sample with a major trend

We deliberately set up a data series containing a major trend, and we perform a Mann-Kendall (MK) Test for Trends, to statistically confirm the presence of such a trend, at the chosen level of significance α.

In the following Python code segment, the MK-Test is implemented and its results are interpreted.

```
import pymannkendall as mk

# parameters
alpha = 0.05
# dataset, with trend
data = [19, 19, 22, 20, 23, 24, 22, 20, 23, 25, 23,
        26, 27, 30, 27, 28, 30]
# Mann-Kendall Test for Trends
r = mk.original_test(data, alpha=alpha)
# print(r)
# results
print("Mann-Kendall Test:")
print(f"MK-statistic          : {r.z:.4f}")
print(f"p-value               : {r.p:.2E}")
print(f"level of significance : {alpha:.2f}")
print(f"trend type            : {r.trend:s}")
print("two-tailed test")
print("Hypothesis")
print("H0: No Trend present in the data series")
print("H1: Trend present in the data series")
if r.p < alpha/2:
    print("reject H0")
    print("Trend")
else:
    print("fail to reject H0")
    print("No Trend")
```

```
Mann-Kendall Test:
MK-statistic          : 4.2744
p-value               : 1.92E-05
level of significance : 0.05
trend type            : increasing
two-tailed test
Hypothesis
H0: No Trend present in the data series
H1: Trend present in the data series
reject H0
Trend
```

Interpretation

The MK-statistic is reported as 4.2744 and the corresponding p_{value} is 1.92e-5, almost zero.

The p_{value} is almost 0, which is smaller than $\frac{\alpha}{2} = 0.025$, therefore we reject the null hypothesis H_0, in favor the the alternative hypothesis H_1.

The data does provide sufficient evidence to conclude, that there is a significant trend in the tested data series, and we can make this claim with (1-α) of 95% confidence.

Exactly what we expected, given the way we created the dataset.

16.4 Plot the data series containing a major trend

A visual inspection of the plot, confirms to us, that there is a trend present in the data series. This intuition is confirmed by the MK-Test for trend detection results.

```
import matplotlib.pyplot as plt

# plot
fig = plt.figure(figsize=(8,3))
ax = fig.add_subplot(111)
txt = "Mann-Kendall Test for Trends @ data containing a trend"
ax.set_title(txt)
x = list(range(1, len(data) + 1))
line = Line2D(x, data)
ax.add_line(line)
ax.set_xlim(min(x), max(x))
ax.set_ylim(min(data) * 0.95, max(data) * 1.05)
plt.xlabel('number')
plt.ylabel('score')
ax.grid()
plt.show()
```

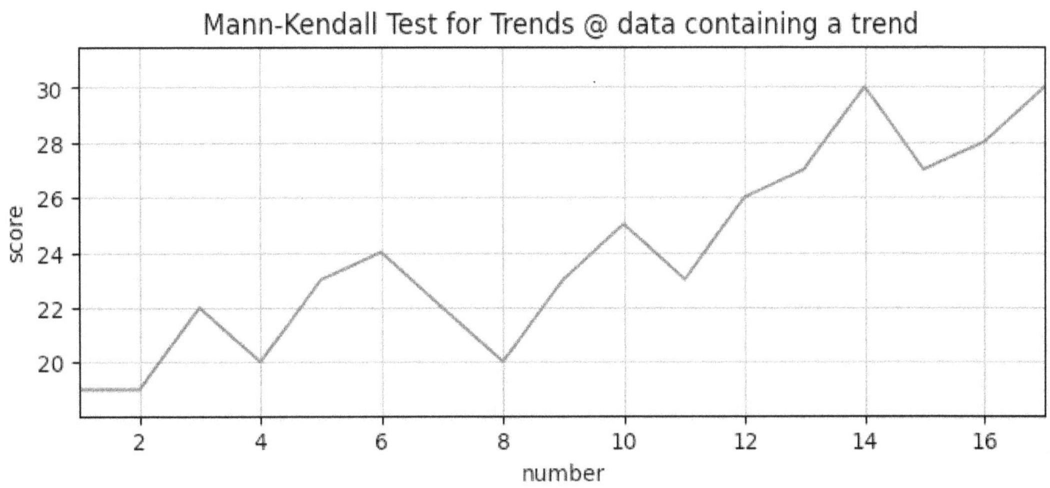
Mann-Kendall Test for Trends @ data containing a trend
score
30
28
26
24
22
20
2
4
6
8
10
12
14
16
number

CHAPTER 17

ANALYSIS OF VARIANCE ANOVA

Analysis of Variation (ANOVA) attempts to split the total variance into two portions. One part is explained by the regression model, and another part for the unexplained variation.

The analysis of the total variability of a data series, such as observations on the dependent variable in a regression model, into components representing different sources of variation. The ANOVA methodology provides the inputs for an `F-test`, which tests the significance of the regression as a whole.

17.1 Dataset: Moore Car Dataset

> The Moore data frame has 45 rows and 4 columns. The data are for subjects in a social-psychological experiment, who were faced with manipulated disagreement from a partner of either of low or high status. The subjects could either conform to the partner's judgment or stick with their own judgment.

This data frame contains the following columns:

- `partner_status`: Partner's status. A factor with levels: (high, low).
- `conformity`: Number of conforming responses in 40 critical trials.
- `fcategory`: F-Scale categorized with levels (high, low, medium).
- `fscore`: F-scale score for Authoritarianism

For more detailed information on this dataset, see Fox [2016], Fox and Weisberg [2019], Moore and Krupat [1971]. Additionally, the loaded dataset provides us with a built-in description of the data and its composition, which can be displayed in code, like so.

```
moore = sm.datasets.get_rdataset("Moore","carData",
                                  cache=True)
print(moore.__doc__)
```

We analyze the variance (ANOVA) of this dataset to gain a better understanding of it. Therefore, we apply the `get_rdataset()` function from the statsmodels library, which has the following signature:

```
moore = sm.datasets.get_rdataset("Moore","carData",
                                  cache=True)
```

where:

- `Moore`: specifies the data subset to be used
- `carData`: the class of data
- `cache`: use the cached version if available

The function returns an ANOVA table.

In the following Python code segment, an ANOVA analysis is performed on this `Moore` dataset and the results are presented in structured table-by-table format.

```
import statsmodels.api as sm

# Load dataset
moore = sm.datasets.get_rdataset("Moore", "carData",
                                  cache=True)
dataDf = moore.data
# inspect
print("dataset:")
print(dataDf.head())
print()
print('describe:')
print(dataDf.describe())
```

```
dataset:
  partner.status  conformity fcategory  fscore
0            low           8       low      37
1            low           4      high      57
2            low           8      high      65
3            low           7       low      20
4            low          10       low      36

describe:
       conformity     fscore
```

(continues on next page)

(continued from previous page)

```
count   45.000000  45.000000
mean    12.133333  43.111111
std      5.242310  14.249756
min      4.000000  15.000000
25%      8.000000  35.000000
50%     12.000000  43.000000
75%     15.000000  55.000000
max     24.000000  68.000000
```

```
import statsmodels.api as sm
from statsmodels.formula.api import ols

# load dataset
moore = sm.datasets.get_rdataset("Moore", "carData",
                                 cache=True)
# change invalid column names
data = moore.data.rename(
    columns={"partner.status":"partner_status"})
# inspect
print("dataset:")
print(data[-28:-20])
```

```
dataset:
   partner_status  conformity fcategory  fscore
17            low           7      high      61
18            low          23      high      57
19            low          13      high      55
20            low           8       low      17
21            low          12       low      35
22           high          19      high      68
23           high          12    medium      41
24           high          21       low      16
```

```
from io import StringIO
import sys
import pandas as pd
import lxml
from quantlib import print_img
import warnings
warnings.filterwarnings('ignore')

# model in formula notation
fstr = "conformity ~ C(fcategory, Sum)*C(partner_status, Sum)"
model = ols(fstr, data=data)
# fit
results = model.fit()
# inspect
print('table 0:')
```

(continues on next page)

(continued from previous page)

```
print_img(results.summary().tables[0])
print('table 1:')
print_img(results.summary().tables[1])
print('table 2:')
print_img(results.summary().tables[2])
```

table 0:

OLS Regression Results

Dep. Variable:	conformity	R-squared:	0.324
Model:	OLS	Adj. R-squared:	0.237
Method:	Least Squares	F-statistic:	3.734
Date:	Tue, 02 Jul 2024	Prob (F-statistic):	0.00740
Time:	14:06:40	Log-Likelihood:	-129.10
No. Observations:	45	AIC:	270.2
Df Residuals:	39	BIC:	281.0
Df Model:	5		
Covariance Type:	nonrobust		

table 1:

	coef	std err	t	P>|t|	[0.025	0.975]
Intercept	12.0508	0.728	16.564	0.000	10.579	13.522
C(fcategory, Sum)[S.high]	0.1903	0.999	0.191	0.850	-1.830	2.210
C(fcategory, Sum)[S.low]	1.0992	1.026	1.071	0.291	-0.977	3.175
C(partner_status, Sum)[S.high]	2.4591	0.728	3.380	0.002	0.988	3.931
C(fcategory, Sum)[S.high]:C(partner_status, Sum)[S.high]	-2.8431	0.999	-2.847	0.007	-4.863	-0.823
C(fcategory, Sum)[S.low]:C(partner_status, Sum)[S.high]	1.7909	1.026	1.745	0.089	-0.285	3.867

table 2:

Omnibus:	2.500	Durbin-Watson:	2.626
Prob(Omnibus):	0.287	Jarque-Bera (JB):	1.712
Skew:	0.465	Prob(JB):	0.425
Kurtosis:	3.216	Cond. No.	2.39

Before we compute the ANOVA table, we might want to bring up its documentation.

```
# help(sm.stats.anova_lm)
# print(sm.stats.anova_lm.__doc__[0:1900])
```

17.1.1 ANOVA table type 1

```
from quantlib import print_img

# formula notation
fstr = "conformity ~ C(fcategory, Sum)*C(partner_status, Sum)"
model = ols(fstr, data=data)
# fit
results = model.fit()
# anova analysis
table = sm.stats.anova_lm(results, test="F",
                          typ=1, robust="hc3")
# inspect
print('table <typ=1>:')
print_img(table)
```

```
table <typ=1>:
```

```
                                            df      sum_sq     mean_sq  \
C(fcategory, Sum)                          2.0    3.733333    1.866667
C(partner_status, Sum)                     1.0  212.213778  212.213778
C(fcategory, Sum):C(partner_status, Sum)   2.0  175.488928   87.744464
Residual                                  39.0  817.763961   20.968307

                                                  F    PR(>F)
C(fcategory, Sum)                          0.089023  0.915010
C(partner_status, Sum)                    10.120692  0.002874
C(fcategory, Sum):C(partner_status, Sum)   4.184623  0.022572
Residual                                        NaN       NaN
```

17.1.2 ANOVA table type 2

```
from quantlib import print_img

# formula notation
fstr = "conformity ~ C(fcategory, Sum)*C(partner_status, Sum)"
model = ols(fstr, data=data)
# fit
results = model.fit()
# anova analysis
table = sm.stats.anova_lm(results, test="F",
                          typ=2, robust="hc3")
# inspect
print('table <typ=2>:')
print_img(table)
```

```
table <typ=2>:
```

```
                                                 sum_sq    df          F  \
C(fcategory, Sum)                             15.793587   2.0   0.376606
C(partner_status, Sum)                       294.509091   1.0  14.045440
C(fcategory, Sum):C(partner_status, Sum)     118.653864   2.0   2.829362
Residual                                     817.763961  39.0        NaN

                                               PR(>F)
C(fcategory, Sum)                            0.688654
C(partner_status, Sum)                       0.000578
C(fcategory, Sum):C(partner_status, Sum)     0.071218
Residual                                          NaN
```

17.1.3 ANOVA table type 3

```
from quantlib import print_img

# formula notation
fstr = "conformity ~ C(fcategory, Sum)*C(partner_status, Sum)"
model = ols(fstr, data=data)
# fit
results = model.fit()
# anova analysis
table = sm.stats.anova_lm(results, test="F",
                          typ=3, robust="hc3")
# inspect
print('table <typ=3>:')
print_img(table)
```

```
table <typ=3>:
```

```
                                                 sum_sq    df           F  \
Intercept                                   4787.223834   1.0  228.307603
C(fcategory, Sum)                             38.205390   2.0    0.911027
C(partner_status, Sum)                       199.351458   1.0    9.507275
C(fcategory, Sum):C(partner_status, Sum)     118.653864   2.0    2.829362
Residual                                     817.763961  39.0         NaN

                                                  PR(>F)
Intercept                                   6.840958e-18
C(fcategory, Sum)                           4.104972e-01
C(partner_status, Sum)                      3.749020e-03
C(fcategory, Sum):C(partner_status, Sum)    7.121750e-02
Residual                                             NaN
```

As a reference we show the comprehensive report provided by the `summary()` function of the results object. Optionally, this report can be saved as an image, like so:

```
import matplotlib.pyplot as plt

# save as image
plt.rc('figure', figsize=(9,5))
plt.text(0.01, 0.05, str(results.summary()),
        {'fontsize':10}, fontproperties='monospace')
plt.axis('off')
plt.tight_layout()
# save to file
try:
    plt.savefig('data/temp/output.png')
    print('image saved')
except Exception as e:
    print(e)
```

```
image saved
```

```
                            OLS Regression Results
==============================================================================
Dep. Variable:             conformity   R-squared:                       0.324
Model:                            OLS   Adj. R-squared:                  0.237
Method:                 Least Squares   F-statistic:                     3.734
Date:                Tue, 02 Jul 2024   Prob (F-statistic):            0.00740
Time:                        14:06:43   Log-Likelihood:                -129.10
No. Observations:                  45   AIC:                             270.2
Df Residuals:                      39   BIC:                             281.0
Df Model:                           5
Covariance Type:            nonrobust
==================================================================================================================
                                                         coef    std err          t      P>|t|      [0.025      0.975]
------------------------------------------------------------------------------------------------------------------
Intercept                                             12.0508      0.728     16.564      0.000      10.579      13.522
C(fcategory, Sum)[S.high]                              0.1903      0.999      0.191      0.850      -1.830       2.210
C(fcategory, Sum)[S.low]                               1.0992      1.026      1.071      0.291      -0.977       3.175
C(partner_status, Sum)[S.high]                         2.4591      0.728      3.380      0.002       0.988       3.931
C(fcategory, Sum)[S.high]:C(partner_status, Sum)[S.high]   -2.8431      0.999     -2.847      0.007      -4.863      -0.823
C(fcategory, Sum)[S.low]:C(partner_status, Sum)[S.high]     1.7909      1.026      1.745      0.089      -0.285       3.867
==============================================================================
Omnibus:                        2.500   Durbin-Watson:                   2.626
Prob(Omnibus):                  0.287   Jarque-Bera (JB):                1.712
Skew:                           0.465   Prob(JB):                        0.425
Kurtosis:                       3.216   Cond. No.                         2.39
==============================================================================

Notes:
[1] Standard Errors assume that the covariance matrix of the errors is correctly specified.
```

CHAPTER 18

REGRESSION DIAGNOSTICS

We explore the usage of a few of the statsmodels regression diagnostic tests. Although, the majority of the tests described here merely return a result set of numbers, without any explicit explanation.

Recall, that a full description of parameters and options is always available in the docstring of each function used, as well as in the online statsmodels documentation. As given in Statsmodels [2023], we can find additional information on test specifications.

In the following code example, we discuss the `Guerry` dataset and investigate the regression diagnostics in detail.

18.1 Loading the dataset

> The dataset is available as part of the rdataset repository of the statsmodels library. The Guerry dataset, a collection of historical data used in support of Andre-Michel Guerry's 1833 Essay on the Moral Statistics of France.

Although, we make use of a previously downloaded local version of this data, like so:

```
import pandas as pd
%matplotlib inline

# load dataset
dat = pd.read_csv('data/Guerry.csv')
```

(continues on next page)

(continued from previous page)

```
# inspect
print('dataset:')
print(dat.iloc[:, 2:8].head()) # first 6 columns
print(dat.shape)
```

```
dataset:
   dept Region    Department  Crime_pers  Crime_prop  Literacy
0     1      E           Ain       28870       15890        37
1     2      N         Aisne       26226        5521        51
2     3      C        Allier       26747        7925        13
3     4      E  Basses-Alpes       12935        7289        46
4     5      E  Hautes-Alpes       17488        8174        69
(86, 25)
```

18.2 Ordinary Least Square (OLS) regression model

We make use of the `ols()` function, provided by the statsmodels library, to fit a linear regression model. It has the following signature:

```
fstr = "Lottery ~ Literacy + np.log(Pop1831)"
results = smf.ols(fstr, data=dat).fit()
```

where the first parameter represents the regression specification in the convenient `formula notation`, and the second parameter is the data used.

In the following Python code segment, this approach is implemented and the results are presented in table-by-table format.

```
import numpy as np
import statsmodels.formula.api as smf
from quantlib import print_img

# fit regression model
fstr = "Lottery ~ Literacy + np.log(Pop1831)"
results = smf.ols(fstr, data=dat).fit()
# inspect table-by-table
print('table 0:')
print(type(results.summary2().tables[0]))
print_img(results.summary2().tables[0].\
                 to_string(header=False, index=False))
print('table 1:')
print(type(results.summary2().tables[1]))
print_img(results.summary2().tables[1])
print('table 2:')
print(type(results.summary2().tables[2]))
```

(continues on next page)

(continued from previous page)

```
print_img(results.summary2().tables[2]\
                .to_string(header=False, index=False))
```

```
table 0:
<class 'pandas.core.frame.DataFrame'>

                 Model:                OLS     Adj. R-squared:    0.333
    Dependent Variable:            Lottery                AIC: 765.6463
                  Date: 2024-07-02 14:06                BIC: 773.0094
      No. Observations:                 86     Log-Likelihood:  -379.82
              Df Model:                  2        F-statistic:    22.20
          Df Residuals:                 83 Prob (F-statistic): 1.90e-08
             R-squared:              0.348              Scale:   416.02

table 1:
<class 'pandas.core.frame.DataFrame'>

                        Coef.   Std.Err.         t         P>|t|      [0.025  \
 Intercept         246.434135  35.232504  6.994511  6.260771e-10  176.358102
 Literacy           -0.488923   0.127588 -3.832038  2.462102e-04   -0.742692
 np.log(Pop1831)   -31.311392   5.976778 -5.238842  1.202925e-06  -43.198963

                       0.975]
 Intercept         316.510168
 Literacy           -0.235155
 np.log(Pop1831)   -19.423822

table 2:
<class 'pandas.core.frame.DataFrame'>


       Omnibus:  3.713    Durbin-Watson: 2.019
 Prob(Omnibus):  0.156 Jarque-Bera (JB): 3.394
          Skew: -0.487         Prob(JB): 0.183
      Kurtosis:  3.003    Condition No.:   702
```

18.3 Test for Residuals for Normality

The residuals are required to be normally distributed, for the regression model to produce valid results. This property needs to be confirmed before making any inferences or predictions based on the regression outputs.

We make use of two statistical procedures to confirm normality.

- Jarque-Bera (JB) Test for Normality

- χ^2 Omnibus Test for Normality

In the following Python code segment, both methods are used and their results are discussed.

18.3.1 Jarque-Bera (JB) Test for Normality

To set up the statistical test we formulate:

Hypothesis

- H_0: the data is Normal distributed
- H_1: the data is Not Normal distributed

level of significance:

- $\alpha = 0.05$

This is a two-tailed test, and we allocate $\frac{\alpha}{2}$ of the desired significance in each tail of the distribution.

In the following Python code segment, we make use of the `jarque_bera()` function with this signature:

```
test = sms.jarque_bera(results.resid)
```

it returns the JB-statistic and the p_{value}, corresponding to the chosen level of significance α.

```
import statsmodels.stats.api as sms

# Jarque-Bera Test
test = sms.jarque_bera(results.resid)
# parameters
alpha = 0.05
# results
print("Jarque-Bera (JB) Test:")
print(f"JB-statistic           : {test[0]:.4f}")
print(f"p-value                : {test[1]:.4f}")
print(f"level of significance : {alpha:.2f}")
print("two-tailed test")
print("Hypothesis")
print("H0: the sample is normally distributed")
print("H1: the sample is not normally distributed")
if test[1] < alpha/2:
    print("reject H0")
    print("Not Normal")
else:
    print("fail to reject H0")
    print("Normal")
```

```
Jarque-Bera (JB) Test:
JB-statistic           : 3.3936
p-value                : 0.1833
level of significance : 0.05
two-tailed test
Hypothesis
H0: the sample is normally distributed
H1: the sample is not normally distributed
fail to reject H0
Normal
```

Interpretation

The JB-statistic is reported as 3.3936 along with the associated p_{value} or 0.1833.

Since the $p_{value} \geq \frac{\alpha}{2}$ of 0.025, we fail to reject the null hypothesis H_0. The tested data sample, provides sufficient evidence to conclude, that the data is indeed normally distributed, at the chosen level of significance α, and we can make this claim with (1-α) or 95% confidence.

18.3.2 Chi-square Omnibus Test for Normality

To set up the χ^2 Omnibus Test for Normality, we formulate:

Hypothesis

- H_0: the data is Normal distributed
- H_1: the data is Not Normal distributed

level of significance:

- α = 0.05

Recall that this is a two-tailed test, and we allocate $\frac{\alpha}{2}$ of the desired significance in each tail of the distribution.

In Python, we make use of the `omni_normtest()` function, with this signature.

```
test = sms.omni_normtest(results.resid)
```

it returns the χ^2-statistic along with the p_{value}, corresponding to the chosen level of significance α.

```
# Omni-Norm Test
test = sms.omni_normtest(results.resid)
# parameters
alpha = 0.05
# results
print("Chi-squared Test:")
```

(continues on next page)

(continued from previous page)

```
print(f"X2-statistic           : {test[0]:.4f}")
print(f"p-value                : {test[1]:.4f}")
print(f"level of significance : {alpha:.2f}")
print("two-tailed test")
print("Hypothesis")
print("H0: the sample is normally distributed")
print("H1: the sample is not normally distributed")
if test[1] < alpha/2:
    print("reject H0")
    print("Not Normal")
else:
    print("fail to reject H0")
    print("Normal")
```

```
Chi-squared Test:
X2-statistic           : 3.7134
p-value                : 0.1562
level of significance : 0.05
two-tailed test
Hypothesis
H0: the sample is normally distributed
H1: the sample is not normally distributed
fail to reject H0
Normal
```

Interpretation

The X^2-statistic is reported as 3.7134 along with the associated p_{value} of 0.1562.

Since the $p_{value} \geq \frac{\alpha}{2}$ of 0.025, we fail to reject the null hypothesis H_0. The tested data sample, provides sufficient evidence to conclude, that the data is indeed normally distributed, at the chosen level of significance α, and we can make this claim with (1-α) or 95% confidence.

18.4 Influence Analysis

18.4.1 Influence analysis of the observations

Once the `OLSInfluence` object has been created, it provides additional functions, allowing us to assess the individual components of the result object. Available functions, include: `summary_table()`, `dbbetas()`, `cooks_distance()`, `resid_press()`, and `influence()`.

In the following code example, we demonstrate the usage of these functions, and in Python we have:

We might want to bring up the documentation on the OLSInflucence object and review its parameters, options and limitations.

```
from statsmodels.stats.outliers_influence import OLSInfluence
# print(help(OLSInfluence))
# print(dir(test_class))
```

A full description of the available report tables can be found at Statsmodels [2023].

```
def print_img(data, width=1, height=1, fontsize=10,
                        px=0, py=0):
    """ print data as image """

    fig = plt.figure(figsize=(width, height))
    plt.text(px, py,
             str(data),
             {'fontsize':fontsize},
             fontproperties='monospace')
    plt.axis('off')
    plt.show()

    return
```

```
from statsmodels.stats.outliers_influence import OLSInfluence
import matplotlib.pyplot as plt
import statsmodels

print('statsmodels version:', statsmodels.__version__)

# parameters
N = 5
K = 3000
# fit model
fstr = "Lottery ~ Literacy + np.log(Pop1831)"
results = smf.ols(fstr, data=dat).fit()
# OLSInflucence object
test_class = OLSInfluence(results)
print(type(test_class))
# results
print("dfbetas:")
print(test_class.dfbetas[0:N]) # N only
print()
print("cooks_distance:")
for i in range(len(test_class.cooks_distance[0][0:N])):
    print(test_class.cooks_distance[0][i])
print()
print("resid_press:")
print(test_class.resid_press[0:N])
print()
```

(continues on next page)

(continued from previous page)

```
print("influence:")
print(test_class.influence[0:N])
print()
print("endog:")
print(test_class.endog[0:N])
print()
print("fitted values:")
print(test_class.results.fittedvalues[0:N])
print()
print('summary frame:')
print(type(test_class.summary_frame()))
print_img(
    test_class.summary_frame()[['dfb_Intercept',
            'dfb_Literacy', 'cooks_d','standard_resid',
            'hat_diag']].head(10)) # 10 only
print()
print("summary table:")
print(type(test_class.summary_table()))
# first K chars only
print_img(
    test_class.summary_table("%.3f").as_text()[0:K])
```

```
statsmodels version: 0.13.2


<class 'statsmodels.stats.outliers_influence.OLSInfluence'>
dfbetas:


[[-0.00301154  0.00290872  0.00118179]
 [-0.06425662  0.04043093  0.06281609]
 [ 0.01554894 -0.03556038 -0.00905336]
 [ 0.17899858  0.04098207 -0.18062352]
 [ 0.29679073  0.21249207 -0.3213655 ]]

cooks_distance:
0.00017833876829961802
0.0033662554565919707
0.0006568278989434975
0.013437424249733149
0.051513808844836084

resid_press:
0    -4.332489
1    12.236036
2     4.514681
3    15.253730
4    21.485655
dtype: float64
```

(continues on next page)

(continued from previous page)

```
influence:
0   -0.051374
1    0.343351
2    0.181575
3    1.099443
4    2.992317
dtype: float64

endog:
[41. 38. 66. 80. 79.]

fitted values:
[45.28111552 26.10731517 61.66689491 65.84571262 60.50666251]

summary frame:
<class 'pandas.core.frame.DataFrame'>

   dfb_Intercept  dfb_Literacy  cooks_d  standard_resid  hat_diag
0      -0.003012      0.002909 0.000178       -0.211150  0.011858
1      -0.064257      0.040431 0.003366        0.591432  0.028061
2       0.015549     -0.035560 0.000657        0.216849  0.040219
3       0.178999      0.040982 0.013437        0.720404  0.072077
4       0.296791      0.212492 0.051514        0.977296  0.139270
5       0.023455     -0.073419 0.005448        0.956941  0.017535
6      -0.012998     -0.046826 0.001095       -0.260324  0.046250
7       0.062255     -0.068935 0.003673        0.531701  0.037518
8      -0.087755     -0.112952 0.010101       -0.858554  0.039489
9      -0.019590      0.006412 0.000315       -0.222777  0.018659

summary table:
<class 'statsmodels.iolib.table.SimpleTable'>
```

obs	endog	fitted value	Cook's d	student. residual	hat diag	dffits internal	ext.stud. residual	dffits
0	41.000	45.281	0.000	-0.211	0.012	-0.023	-0.210	-0.023
1	38.000	26.107	0.003	0.591	0.028	0.100	0.589	0.100
2	66.000	61.667	0.001	0.217	0.040	0.044	0.216	0.044
3	80.000	65.846	0.013	0.720	0.072	0.201	0.718	0.200
4	79.000	60.507	0.052	0.977	0.139	0.393	0.977	0.393
5	70.000	50.654	0.005	0.957	0.018	0.128	0.956	0.128
6	31.000	36.185	0.001	-0.260	0.046	-0.057	-0.259	-0.057
7	75.000	64.361	0.004	0.532	0.038	0.105	0.529	0.105
8	28.000	45.162	0.010	-0.859	0.039	-0.174	-0.857	-0.174
9	50.000	54.501	0.000	-0.223	0.019	-0.031	-0.221	-0.031
10	81.000	47.057	0.014	1.676	0.014	0.202	1.695	0.204
11	3.000	43.599	0.016	-2.002	0.012	-0.218	-2.040	-0.222
12	13.000	26.756	0.004	-0.684	0.027	-0.114	-0.681	-0.113
13	82.000	57.335	0.011	1.223	0.022	0.184	1.227	0.185
14	60.000	44.311	0.002	0.774	0.012	0.086	0.772	0.085
15	35.000	36.409	0.000	-0.070	0.016	-0.009	-0.069	-0.009
16	44.000	66.444	0.020	-1.127	0.046	-0.247	-1.128	-0.247
17	84.000	62.518	0.017	1.076	0.043	0.227	1.077	0.227
18	33.000	31.445	0.000	0.077	0.029	0.013	0.077	0.013
19	72.000	38.374	0.060	1.700	0.059	0.426	1.719	0.431
20	85.000	60.435	0.014	1.222	0.028	0.208	1.225	0.208
21	77.000	44.145	0.036	1.643	0.039	0.331	1.660	0.334
22	18.000	35.970	0.019	-0.911	0.065	-0.240	-0.910	-0.240
23	54.000	47.352	0.001	0.328	0.014	0.040	0.327	0.039
24	47.000	32.055	0.004	0.740	0.019	0.104	0.738	0.104
25	48.000	43.731	0.000	0.212	0.026	0.034	0.211	0.034
26	36.000	43.0						

18.4.2 Plot Influence analysis with bubble plots

Visualizing the influence factor as a bubble plot, and in Python code this regression is implemented and its results interpreted.

```
import statsmodels.api as sm
import matplotlib.pyplot as plt
import statsmodels.formula.api as smf

# model fit
fstr = "Lottery ~ Literacy + np.log(Pop1831)"
results = smf.ols(fstr, data=dat).fit()
# plot
fig, axs = plt.subplots(1, 1, figsize=(8,4))
sm.graphics.influence_plot(results, ax=axs)
plt.title("Influence plot", fontsize=14)
plt.xlabel("High leverage", fontsize=10)
plt.ylabel("Normalized Residuals", fontsize=10)
plt.grid()
plt.tight_layout()
plt.show()
```

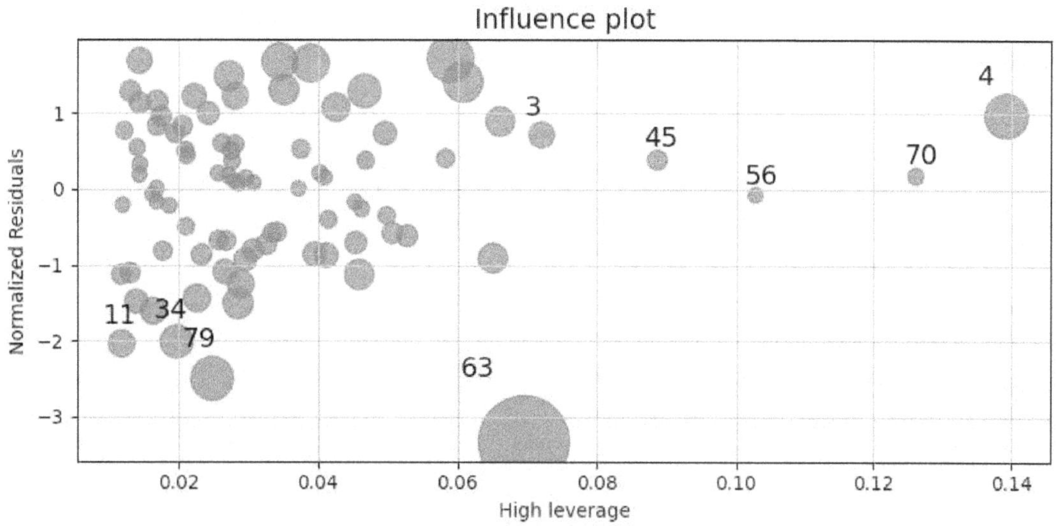

Interpretation

The larger the bubble is, the more influence the particular regressor variable has on the result.

18.4.3 Leverage versus Normalized residuals squared Analysis

We set up a fig and ax1 object for a given size, like so:

```
fig, ax1 = plt.subplots(figsize=(8,6))
```

Then we ask to plot_leverage_resid2() method to plot its output directly into the prepared ax1 object.

```
fig = plot_leverage_resid2(results, ax=ax1)
```

Before we use the plot_leverage_resid2() method, we might want to bring up its documentation and explore the parameters and options.

```
from statsmodels.graphics.regressionplots import plot_leverage_resid2
# print(help(plot_leverage_resid2))
```

```
# plot
fig, ax1 = plt.subplots(figsize=(8,4))
fig = plot_leverage_resid2(results, ax=ax1)
plt.grid(True)
plt.xlabel("normalized $\\mathsf{Residuals^2}$", fontsize=10)
plt.ylabel("$\\mathsf {Leverage}$", fontsize=10)
txt = "Leverage vs. normalized $\\mathsf {Residuals^2}$"
plt.title(txt, fontsize=14)
```

(continues on next page)

(continued from previous page)

```
plt.tight_layout()
plt.show()
```

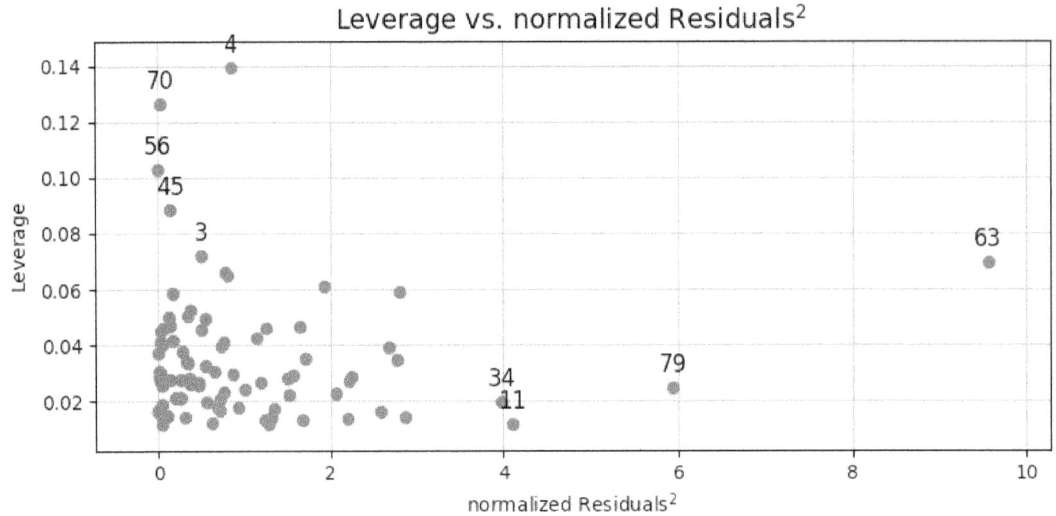

Further plotting and customization options can be found in Statsmodels [2023].

18.5 Detecting Multicollinearity

Recall, that multicollinearity refers to the condition where a high correlation exists among two or more of the regressor variables. This condition influences the standard error of estimate SEE, which distorts the coefficient standard error SE, resulting in incorrect t-statistic for the significance of parameters.

As a result of multicollinearity, there is an inflated probability that we will incorrectly conclude that a variable is not statistically significant, hence making a Type II error.

As a general rule, multicollinearity is usually present in most economic models. So great care must be taken to detect this condition and correct it.

18.5.1 Evaluate Condition Number to detect multicollinearity

A condition number greater than 30 is deemed to indicate the presence of multicollinearity, however, this is not a full hypothesis test.

In the following code segment, this approach is implemented and the results are interpreted.

```
from quantlib import print_img

# Conditional Number
cn = np.linalg.cond(results.model.exog)
# results
print_img(results.summary().tables[2])
print("conditional number : {:.2f}".format(cn))
print("results:")
if (cn) > 30:
    print("Multicollinearity is present")
else:
    print("No Multicollinearity is present")
```

```
==============================================================================
Omnibus:                        3.713   Durbin-Watson:                   2.019
Prob(Omnibus):                  0.156   Jarque-Bera (JB):                3.394
Skew:                          -0.487   Prob(JB):                        0.183
Kurtosis:                       3.003   Cond. No.                         702.
==============================================================================
```

```
conditional number : 702.18
results:
Multicollinearity is present
```

Interpretation

The condition number is reported to be 702, which indicates the presence of multicollinearity.

This means, that we cannot apply the regression model, to draw unbiased statistical inferences or make valid predictions. We have to address the multicollinearity issue, by altering the model specification. For example, we can successively drop any regressor variable from the regression specification and recompute the model to determine if the issue persists.

18.6 Detecting Heteroscedasticity

The term heteroscedasticity refers to the non-constant error variance. One of the underlying assumptions of linear regression is that the tested data is to be homoscedastic. Meaning if this requirement is not met, we cannot use the model to draw valid inferences.

In the following Python code segment we conduct a formal statistical test, to detect the presence of heteroscedasticity, and we demonstrate two statistical tests to detect heteroscedasticity:

- Breusch-Pagan Test for Heteroscedasticity
- Goldfeld-Quandt Test for Heteroscedasticity

18.6.1 Breusch-Pagan Test for Heteroscedasticity

To set up the statistical test, we formulate:

Hypothesis

- H_0: the data series is Not Heteroscedastic
- H_1: the data series is Heteroscedastic

level of significance:

- $\alpha = 0.05$

This is a two-tailed test, and we allocate $\frac{\alpha}{2}$ of the desired significance in each tail of the distribution.

In Python code, this approach is implemented and its results are discussed.

```
from statsmodels.compat import lzip
import statsmodels.stats.api as sms

# Breusch-Pagan Test
test = sms.het_breuschpagan(results.resid, results.model.exog)
names = ["Lagrange multiplier statistic",
         "p-value", "f-value", "f p-value"]
res = lzip(names, test)
# parameters
alpha = 0.05
# results
print("Breusch-Pagan Test:")
print(f"LM-statistic          : {res[0][1]:.4f}")
print(f"p-value               : {res[1][1]:.4f}")
print(f"level of significance : {alpha:.2f}")
print("two-tailed test")
print("Hypothesis")
print("H0: the sample is Not Heteroscedastic")
print("H1: the sample is Heteroscedastic")
if res[0][1] <= alpha/2:
    print("reject reject H0")
    print("Heteroscedastic")
else:
    print("fail to reject H0")
    print("Not Heteroscedastic")
```

```
Breusch-Pagan Test:
LM-statistic          : 4.8932
p-value               : 0.0866
level of significance : 0.05
two-tailed test
Hypothesis
H0: the sample is Not Heteroscedastic
```

(continues on next page)

(continued from previous page)

```
H1: the sample is Heteroscedastic
fail to reject H0
Not Heteroscedastic
```

Interpretation

The LM-statistic is reported as 4.8932 along with the associated p_{value} of 0.0866.

Since the $p_{value} \geq \frac{\alpha}{2}$ of 0.025, we fail to reject the null hypothesis H_0. The tested data sample, provides sufficient evidence to conclude, that the data has the desired property of being homoscedastic, at the chosen level of significance α, and we can make this claim with (1-α) or 95% confidence.

18.6.2 Goldfeld-Quandt Test for Heteroscedasticity

To set up the statistical test, we formulate:

Hypothesis

- H_0: the data series is Homoscedastic
- H_1: the data series is Not Homoscedastic (Heteroscedastic)

level of significance:

- $\alpha = 0.05$

This is a two-tailed test, and we allocate $\frac{\alpha}{2}$ of the desired significance in each tail of the distribution.

```
# Goldfeld-Quant Test
test = sms.het_goldfeldquandt(results.resid, results.model.exog)
# parameters
alpha = 0.05
# results
print("Goldfeld-Quandt Test:")
print(f"F-statistic            : {test[0]:.4f}")
print(f"p-value                : {test[1]:.4f}")
print(f"level of significance : {alpha:.2f}")
print("two-tailed test")
print("Hypothesis")
print("H0: the data series is Not Heteroscedastic")
print("H1: the data series is Heteroscedastic")
if test[1] > alpha/2:
    print("fail to reject H0")
    print("Not Heteroscedastic")
else:
    print("reject H0")
    print("Heteroscedastic")
```

```
Goldfeld-Quandt Test:
F-statistic          : 1.1002
p-value              : 0.3820
level of significance : 0.05
two-tailed test
Hypothesis
H0: the data series is Not Heteroscedastic
H1: the data series is Heteroscedastic
fail to reject H0
Not Heteroscedastic
```

Interpretation

The F-statistic is reported as 1.1002 along with the associated p_{value} or 0.3820.

Since the $p_{value} \geq \frac{\alpha}{2}$ of 0.025, we fail to reject the null hypothesis H_0. The tested data sample, provides sufficient evidence to conclude, that the data has the desired property of being homoscedastic, at the chosen level of significance α, and we can make this claim with (1-α) or 95% confidence.

18.7 Testing for Linear Model Specification

The term linearity refers to the requirement, that any relationship among any two variables is linear. The linear regression model, in general, is not suitable for non-linear relations between regressor variables and the target variable. This requirement can be statistically confirmed with a:

- Harvey-Collier Multiplier Test for Linear Specification

In the following Python code segment, this test is implemented and its results are discussed.

18.7.1 Harvey-Collier Multiplier Test for Linear Specification

To set up the statistical test, we formulate:

Hypothesis

- H_0: model linear specification is Correct
- H_1: model linear specification is Not Correct

level of significance:

- α = 0.05

This is a two-tailed test, and we allocate $\frac{\alpha}{2}$ of the desired significance in each tail of the distribution.

```
from statsmodels.compat import lzip

# parameters
alpha = 0.05
# Harvey-Collier Test
test = sms.linear_harvey_collier(results)
# results
print("Harvey-Collier Test:")
print(f"t-statistic           : {test[0]:.4f}")
print(f"p-value               : {test[1]:.4f}")
print(f"level of significance : {alpha:.2f}")
print("two-tailed test")
print("Hypothesis")
print("H0: model linear specification is Correct")
print("H1: model linear specification is Not Correct")
if test[1] > alpha/2:
    print("fail to reject H0")
    print("Correct")
else:
    print("reject H0")
    print("Not Correct")
```

```
Harvey-Collier Test:
t-statistic           : -1.0796
p-value               : 0.2835
level of significance : 0.05
two-tailed test
Hypothesis
H0: model linear specification is Correct
H1: model linear specification is Not Correct
fail to reject H0
Correct
```

Interpretation

The t-statistic is reported as -1.0796 along with the associated p_{value} of 0.2835.

Since the $p_{value} \geq \frac{\alpha}{2}$ of 0.025, we fail to reject the null hypothesis H_0. The sample, provides sufficient evidence to conclude, at the chosen level of significance α, that the model is correctly specified, and we can make this claim with (1-α) or 95% confidence.

CHAPTER 19

TEST FOR STATIONARITY AND DETRENDING

Stationary means that the statistical properties of a time series i.e. mean, variance and covariance do not change over time.

Many statistical models require a time series to be stationary to draw unbiased inferences and to make valid predictions. Two statistical tests can be used to check for stationarity of a time series. We discuss the

- Augmented Dickey-Fuller (ADF) Test, and
- Kwiatkowski-Phillips-Schmidt-Shin (KPSS) Test.

Additionally, a procedure called first-differencing, to convert a non-stationary time series into a stationary one, is also discussed.

19.1 Loading dataset

> The Sunspots dataset is used. It contains yearly (1700-2008) data on sunspots from the National Geophysical Data Center. The details of the dataset can be inspected at Center [2023].

Some pre-processing and clean-up are carried out on the data. For example, the `YEAR` column is removed, since the Pandas DataFrame uses the internal index within the data structure to represent the years. This allows us to change the analysis by resampling, say we want to study quarterly instead of annual sunspot cycles.

```
import matplotlib.pyplot as plt
import numpy as np
import pandas as pd
import statsmodels.api as sm
%matplotlib inline

# load data set
sunspots = sm.datasets.sunspots.load_pandas().data
# set index
sunspots.index = pd.Index(
    sm.tsa.datetools.dates_from_range("1700", "2008"))
del sunspots["YEAR"]
# inspect
print("dataset:")
print(sunspots.head(10))
```

```
dataset:
            SUNACTIVITY
1700-12-31          5.0
1701-12-31         11.0
1702-12-31         16.0
1703-12-31         23.0
1704-12-31         36.0
1705-12-31         58.0
1706-12-31         29.0
1707-12-31         20.0
1708-12-31         10.0
1709-12-31          8.0
```

19.2 Visualize and inspect the dataset with plots

```
# plot
ax = sunspots.plot(figsize=(9,2), grid=True,
                   style="grey", ylabel="spots",
                   title="SunSpot activity",
                   xlabel="Years")
```

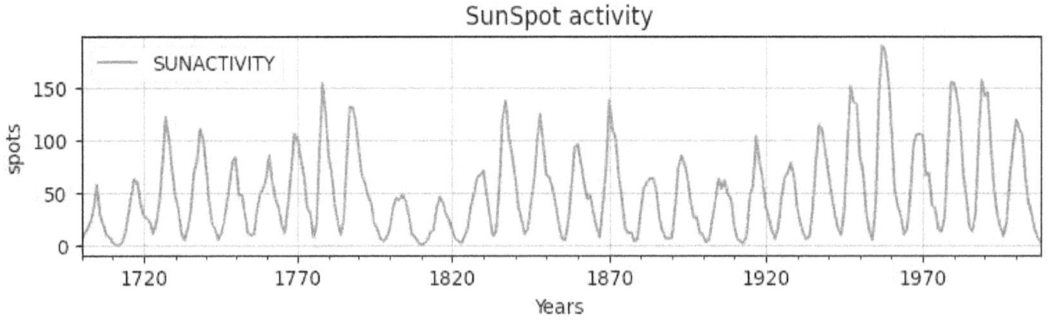

19.3 Assess Stationarity

19.3.1 Augmented Dickey-Fuller (ADF) Test

The ADF-Test is used to determine the presence of `unit root` in the series and hence helps in understanding if the series is stationary or non-stationary. A `unit root`, at a given significant level, indicates a non-stationary data series. Non-stationary, in this context, means that the data series has some sort of trend or seasonal structure.

We conduct a formal statistical ADF-Test, and formulate:

Hypothesis

- H_0: data series has Unit Root and is Non-Stationary
- H_1: data series has No Unit Root and is Stationary

level of significance:

- $\alpha = 0.05$

This is a two-tailed test, and we allocate $\frac{\alpha}{2}$ of the desired significance in each tail of the distribution.

If the p value from the ADF-Test is greater than the chosen level of significance $\frac{\alpha}{2} = 0.025$, the null hypothesis H_0 cannot be rejected, and we conclude that the data provides sufficient evidence to determine that the series is non-stationary.

```
from statsmodels.tsa.stattools import adfuller

def adf_test(timeseries):
    """ Augmented Dickey-Fuller Test """

    dftest = adfuller(timeseries, autolag="AIC")

    dfoutput = pd.Series(
        dftest[0:4],
        index=["Test Statistic", "p-value",
        "Number of Lags Used",
        "Number of Observations Used",],)

    for key, value in dftest[4].items():
        dfoutput["Critical Value (%s)" % key] = value

    return dfoutput
```

The custom `adf_test()` method is based on the stattools library and it has the following signature:

```
res = adf_test(sunspots["SUNACTIVITY"])
```

it returns ADF-statistic and the p_{value}, corresponding to the chosen level of significance α, the critical value at 1%, 5% , and 10% confidence levels are also returned.

We demonstrate the use of the Augmented Dickey-Fuller (ADF) Test on the Sunspots dataset.

```
# parameters
alpha = 0.05
# ADF-Test
res = adf_test(sunspots["SUNACTIVITY"])
print("Augmented Dickey-Fuller Test:")
print(f"ADF-statistic              : {res[0]:.4f}")
print(f"p-value                    : {res[1]:.4f}")
print(f"Number of Lags Used        : {res[2]:.0f}")
print(f"Number of Observations : {res[3]:.0f}")
print(f"level of significance      : {alpha:.2f}")
print("two-tailed test")
print("Hypothesis")
print("H0: sample has Unit Root and is Non Stationary")
print("H1: sample has No Unit Root and is Stationary")
if res[1] < alpha/2:
    print("reject H0")
    print("No Unit Root")
    print("Stationary")
else:
    print("fail to reject H0")
    print("Unit Root detected")
    print("Not Stationary")
```

```
Augmented Dickey-Fuller Test:
ADF-statistic          : -2.8378
p-value                : 0.0531
Number of Lags Used    : 8
Number of Observations : 300
level of significance  : 0.05
two-tailed test
Hypothesis
H0: sample has Unit Root and is Non Stationary
H1: sample has No Unit Root and is Stationary
fail to reject H0
Unit Root detected
Not Stationary
```

Interpretation

The ADF-statistic is reported as -2.8378 along with with p_{value} of 0.0531.

The p_{value} is greater then $\frac{\alpha}{2} = 0.025$, so we fail to reject the null hypothesis H_0.

Therefore, we conclude that the data series is non-stationary. We can make this claim with (1-α) or 95% confidence.

This means that we cannot use this data time series to make valid statistical inferences. We have to address the issue of `unit root` before we can use the data in any regression model.

19.3.2 Kwiatkowski-Phillips-Schmidt-Shin (KPSS) Test

The KPSS-Test is a way to determine if a given time series is stationary.

Note: The null hypothesis and alternative hypothesis for the KPSS-Test are opposite to that of the ADF-Test.

We formulate:

Hypothesis

- H_0: The series is trend stationary and is stationary
- H_1: The series has a unit root and is non-stationary

level of significance:

- $\alpha = 0.05$

This is a two-tailed test, and we allocate $\frac{\alpha}{2}$ of the desired significance in each tail of the distribution.

If the reported p value from the KPSS-Test is greater than the chosen level of significance $\frac{\alpha}{2} = 0.025$, we fail to reject the null hypothesis and conclude that the data provides sufficient evidence to say that the series is stationary.

In the following code segment, this test is implemented and its results are explored.

```
from statsmodels.tsa.stattools import kpss

def kpss_test(timeseries):
    """ Kwiatkowski-Phillips-Schmidt-Shin Test """

    kpsstest = kpss(timeseries,
                    regression="c",
                    nlags="auto")
    kpss_output = pd.Series(
        kpsstest[0:3], index=["KPSS-statistic",
                              "p-value",
                              "Lags Used"])
    for key, value in kpsstest[3].items():
        kpss_output["Critical Value (%s)" % key] = value
```

(continues on next page)

(continued from previous page)

```
    return kpss_output
```

The KPSS-Test procedure provides the following results

- KPSS-statistic,
- the p_{value} and the critical value at 1%, 5% , and 10% significance levels.

In the following code example, the KPSS-Test is applied to the dataset, and we implement:

```
# parameters
alpha = 0.05
# KPSS Test
res = kpss_test(sunspots["SUNACTIVITY"])
# results
print("Kwiatkowski-Phillips-Schmidt-Shin Test:")
print(f"KPSS-statistic         : {res[0]:.4f}")
print(f"p-value                : {res[1]:.4f}")
print(f"lags used              : {res[2]:.0f}")
print(f"level of significance : {alpha:.2f}")
print("two-tailed test")
print("Hypothesis")
print("H0: The process is stationary")
print("H1: The series has a unit root and is non-stationary")
if res[1] <= alpha/2:
    print("reject H0")
    print("unit root")
    print("Non Stationary")
else:
    print("fail to reject H0")
    print("Trend Stationary")
```

```
Kwiatkowski-Phillips-Schmidt-Shin Test:
KPSS-statistic         : 0.6699
p-value                : 0.0163
lags used              : 7
level of significance : 0.05
two-tailed test
Hypothesis
H0: The process is stationary
H1: The series has a unit root and is non-stationary
reject H0
unit root
Non Stationary
```

Interpretation

The KPSS-statistic is reported as 0.6699 and the associated p_{value} is 0.0163.

Since the $p_{value} \leq \frac{\alpha}{2}$ of 0.025, the data provides sufficient evidence for rejecting the null hypothesis H_0 in favor of the alternative hypothesis H_1, and we conclude that the series is non-stationary.

This further means that we cannot use this time series to make valid statistical inferences before we address the unit root issue, for example by first differencing the data series.

To arrive at a more solid assessment of stationarity, it is preferable to apply both tests, so we can be certain that the data series is indeed stationary. Therefore, possible outcomes of applying the ADF-Test and KPSS-Test for stationarity are as follows:

- `non-stationary`: both, the ADF-Test and KPSS-Test indicate non-stationarity
- `stationary`: both ADF-Test and KPSS-Test indicate stationary
- `trend-stationary`: the KPSS-Test indicates stationary and ADF-Test indicates non-stationary
- `strictly-stationary`: Like trend-stationary, although trend patterns are removable by first-differencing

Keep in mind that after first differencing, to remove the trend pattern, the test is to be recomputed to confirm stationarity.

In the following code section, this procedure is demonstrated and its results are interpreted.

19.3.3 Detrending by First Differencing

The first-differencing is a simple procedure for detrending a time series, by which a new series is created where the value at the current time step is calculated as the difference between the current and the previous value.

The method of first-differencing is applied to the dataset and the results are plotted, and subsequent visual inspection reveals the impact the first-differencing procedure has on the time series.

```
# detrending by 1st-differencing
sunspots["SUNACTIVITY_diff"] = sunspots["SUNACTIVITY"] - \
sunspots["SUNACTIVITY"].shift(1)
# inspect
print('detrending:')
print(sunspots.head())
```

```
detrending:
            SUNACTIVITY  SUNACTIVITY_diff
1700-12-31          5.0               NaN
```

(continues on next page)

(continued from previous page)

```
1701-12-31          11.0                6.0
1702-12-31          16.0                5.0
1703-12-31          23.0                7.0
1704-12-31          36.0               13.0
```

Visualize the detrended dataset with plots

To visualize detrending we plot the original data series and the detrended data series, and visually inspect the result.

```
# plots
fig, ax = plt.subplots(nrows=2, ncols=1, figsize=(8,5))
sunspots["SUNACTIVITY"].plot(ax=ax[0],
                            style="grey",
                            label="original")
ax[0].set_title("Sunspots activity")
ax[0].set_ylabel("number of spots")
ax[0].legend()
ax[0].grid()
sunspots["SUNACTIVITY_diff"].plot(ax=ax[1],
                                 style="blue",
                                 label="1st differenced")
ax[1].set_title("Sunspots activity")
ax[1].set_ylabel("change in spots")
ax[1].grid()
plt.tight_layout()
ax[1].legend()
plt.show()
```

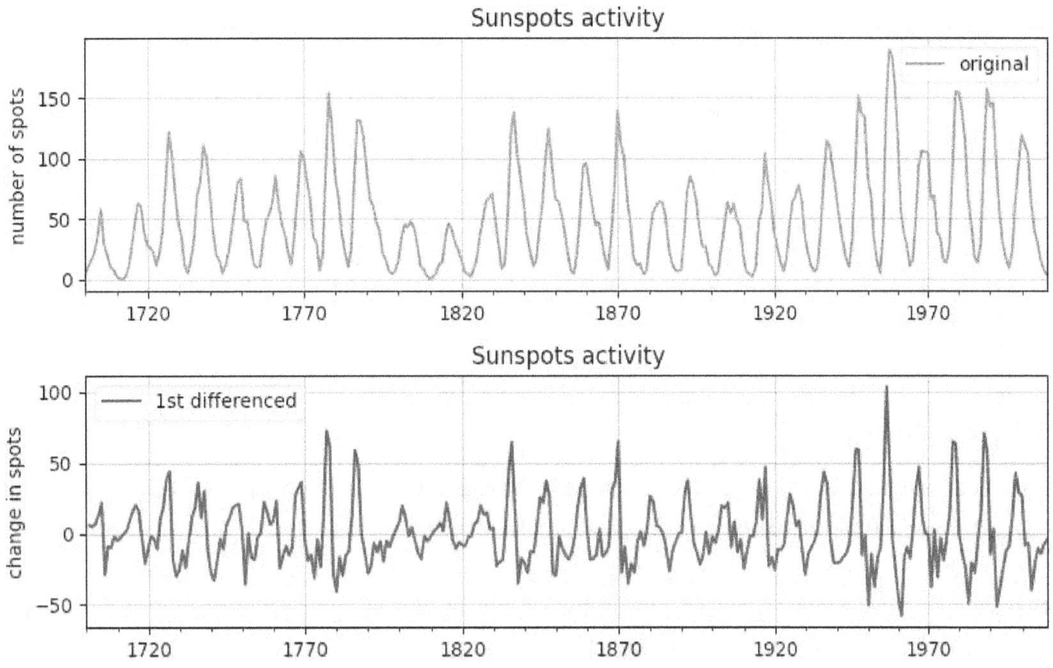

Recompute ADF-Test on the detrended data series

To confirm stationarity, the ADF-Test is applied to the detrended time series, and the resulting data series is re-checked for stationarity.

```
# parameters
alpha = 0.05
# ADF-Test
res = adf_test(sunspots["SUNACTIVITY_diff"].dropna())
# print(res)
print("Augmented Dickey-Fuller Test:")
print(f"ADF-statistic           : {res[0]:.4f}")
print(f"p-value                 : {res[1]:.2E}")
print(f"level of significance : {alpha:.2f}")
print("two-tailed test")
print("Hypothesis")
print("H0: Series has Unit Root and is Non Stationary")
print("H1: Series has No Unit Root and is Stationary")
# reverse to KPSS
if res[1] < alpha/2:
    print("reject H0")
    print("No Unit Root")
    print("Stationary")
else:
    print("fail to reject H0")
    print("Unit Root detected")
    print("Not Stationary")
```

```
Augmented Dickey-Fuller Test:
ADF-statistic            : -14.8617
p-value                  : 1.72E-27
level of significance : 0.05
two-tailed test
Hypothesis
H0: Series has Unit Root and is Non Stationary
H1: Series has No Unit Root and is Stationary
reject H0
No Unit Root
Stationary
```

Interpretation

The test procedure reports the ADF-statistic as -14.8617 and the associated p_{value} of 1.72e-27, almost zero, respectively.

Since the $p_{value} <= \frac{\alpha}{2}$ at the chosen level of significance $\alpha = 0.05$, there is evidence for rejecting the null hypothesis H_0, in favor of the alternative hypothesis H_1. Therefore, we conclude that the data series is stationary now. We can have (1-α) or 95% confidence in this assessment.

Recompute KPSS-Test on the detrended data series

A second KPSS-Test is applied on the now detrended time series to confirm stationarity. In the following Python code segment, this test procedure is implemented and its results are interpreted.

```python
import warnings
warnings.filterwarnings("ignore")

# parameters
alpha = 0.05
# KPSS Test
res = kpss_test(sunspots["SUNACTIVITY_diff"].dropna())
# print(res)
print("Kwiatkowski-Phillips-Schmidt-Shin Test:")
print(f"KPSS-statistic          : {res[0]:.4f}")
print(f"p-value                 : {res[1]:.4f}")
print(f"level of significance : {alpha:.2f}")
print("two-tailed test")
print("Hypothesis")
print("H0: Series is trend stationary and is stationary")
print("H1: Series has a unit root and is non-stationary")
# reverse to ADF
if res[1] < alpha/2:
    print("reject H0")
    print("Unit Root")
```

(continues on next page)

(continued from previous page)

```
    print("Non Stationary")
else:
    print("fail to reject H0")
    print("No Unit Root")
    print("Stationary")
```

```
Kwiatkowski-Phillips-Schmidt-Shin Test:
KPSS-statistic         : 0.0212
p-value                : 0.1000
level of significance : 0.05
two-tailed test
Hypothesis
H0: Series is trend stationary and is stationary
H1: Series has a unit root and is non-stationary
fail to reject H0
No Unit Root
Stationary
```

Interpretation

The KPSS-statistic is reported as 0.0212 along with the p_{value} of 0.10.

Since the $p_{value} \geq \frac{\alpha}{2}$, we fail to reject the null hypothesis H_0. The detrended data series provides sufficient evidence, to conclude that the time series is stationary now after we applied the first-differencing to remove the trend. We can make this claim with (1-α) or 95% confidence.

Recall, that the ADF-Test indicated stationarity and the KPSS-Test also indicates stationarity, therefore we can conclude that the detrended data series is stationary, and the data series can now be used in prediction models which have data stationarity as a prerequisite requirement.

Part II

Visualization

CHAPTER 20

PLOTS AND CHARTS FROM DATAFRAME

In Pandas, the DataFrame is the most important data structure. In this section, we explore the methods for plotting and visualization, which are built into the DataFrame object.

We might want to bring up the documentation for the `plot()` method of the DataFrame object and review its properties.

```
import pandas as pd
# help(pd.DataFrame.plot)
# print(pd.DataFrame.plot.__doc__[:4000])
```

20.1 Scatter Plots

Scatter plots or diagrams are used to visualize the relationship between two variables. For example, we have the following DataFrame containing two data rows, and we want to investigate any relationship among these variables.

```
unemployment_rate  index_price
6.1                1500
5.8                1520
5.7                1525
5.7                1523
5.8                1515
5.6                1540
```

(continues on next page)

(continued from previous page)

```
    5.5                 1545
    5.3                 1560
    5.2                 1555
    5.2                 1565
```

We make use of the `plot()` method from the Pandas DataFrame object, which has the following signature:

```
df.plot(x='unemployment_rate', y='index_price', kind='scatter')
```

where

- `df`: is the DataFrame containing the source data
- `x`: is the x-axis of the data pair
- `y`: is the y-axis of the data pair
- `kind`: set to "scatter", to indicate the type of plot to produce

We plot the `unemployment_rate` against the `index_price`, thereby creating a scatter diagram. In the following Python code segment, this is implemented and the results are interpreted.

```
import matplotlib.pyplot as plt
import pandas as pd

# dataset
data = {
    "unemployment_rate": [6.1, 5.8, 5.7, 5.7, 5.8,
                          5.6, 5.5, 5.3, 5.2, 5.2],
    "index_price": [1500, 1520, 1525, 1523, 1515,
                    1540, 1545, 1560, 1555, 1565],}
# DataFrame
df = pd.DataFrame(data)
# plot
df.plot(x="unemployment_rate", y="index_price",
        kind="scatter", figsize=(5,3))
plt.title("Scatter Plot", fontsize=14)
plt.xlabel("Unemployment rate")
plt.ylabel("Index price")
plt.grid(True)
plt.show()
```

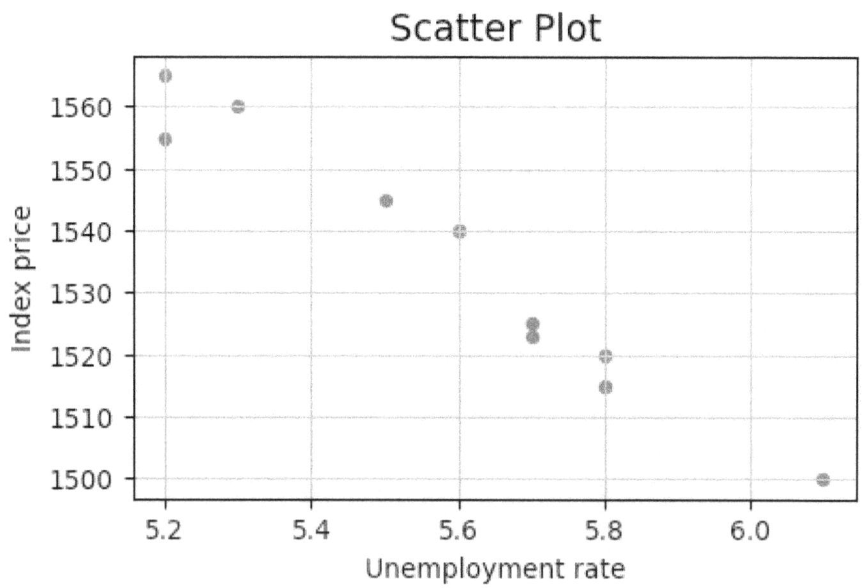

Interpretation

We can see that there is a negative linear relationship between the two variables, `unemployment_rate` and the `index_price`. A more formal regression analysis quantifies the direction and strength of this relationship, and by setting a level of significance, we can draw inferences from such analysis, with confidence.

20.2 Line Charts

Line charts are often used to display trends over time. To start, prepare your data for the line chart, and create a DataFrame of the `unemployment_rate` over 90 years. Here is an example of a dataset:

```
year        unemployment_rate
1920        9.8
1930        12
1940        8
1950        7.2
1960        6.9
1970        7
1980        6.5
1990        6.2
2000        5.5
2010        6.3
```

We plot the DataFrame by utilizing the `plot()` method from the DataFrame object, with the following parameters:

```
df.plot(x ='year', y='unemployment_rate', kind='line')
```

where

- `df`: is the DataFrame containing the data columns
- `x`: is the data column on the x-axis
- `y`: is the data column on the y-axis
- `kind`: set to "line", to indicate the type of chart to produce

```
import pandas as pd
import matplotlib.pyplot as plt

data = {
    "year": [1920, 1930, 1940, 1950, 1960,
             1970, 1980, 1990, 2000, 2010],
    "unemployment_rate": [9.8, 12, 8, 7.2, 6.9, 7,
                          6.5, 6.2, 5.5, 6.3]}
# DataFrame
df = pd.DataFrame(data)
# plot
df.plot(x="year", y="unemployment_rate",
        kind="line", figsize=(8,2.5))
plt.title("Line Chart", fontsize=16)
plt.xlabel("Years")
plt.ylabel("Unemployment rate")
plt.grid(True)
plt.show()
```

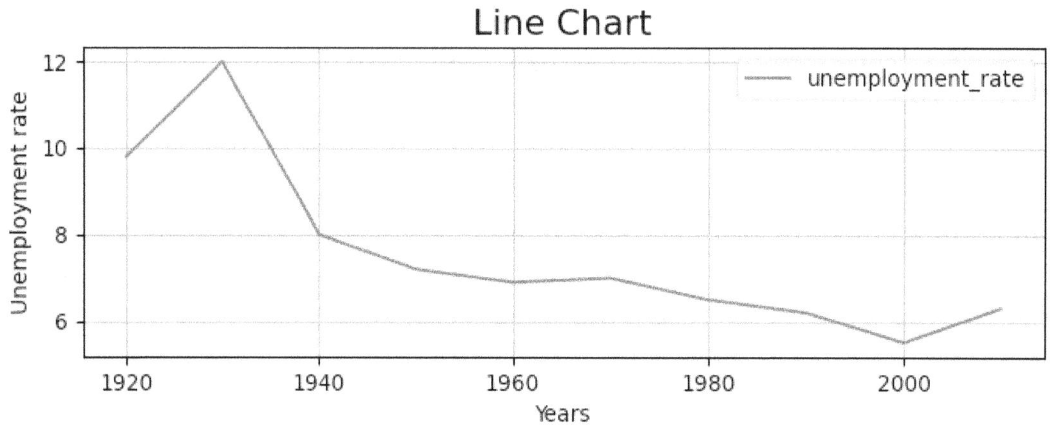

The line chart shows the `unemployment_rate` over the last 90 years, in 10-year steps.

20.3 Bar Charts

A Bar chart is mainly used to display categorical data. The following example dataset is used to create the bar chart, as it lists the gross domestic product per capita `gdp_per_capita` versus `eu_country` for several European countries.

```
eu_country gdp_per_capita
Austria    53637
Belgium    51247
 Canada    51987
Denmark    68007
Estonia    27943
 France    43659
Germany    51203
Hungary    18728
```

We make use of the `plot()` method from the DataFrame object, with the following signature:

```
df.plot(x='eu_country', y='gdp_per_capita', kind='bar')
```

where

- `df`: is the DataFrame containing the data columns
- x: is the country on the x-axis
- y: is the gdp_per_capita on the y-axis
- `kind`: indicates the type of the plot, we specify "bar" for a bar chart

Note, that we set the `kind='bar'` to plot the bar chart, and in Python we write:

```
import pandas as pd
import matplotlib.pyplot as plt

# dataset
data = {"eu_country": ["Austria", "Belgium", "Canada",
                        "Denmark", "Estonia", "France",
                        "Germany", "Hungary",],
    "gdp_per_capita": [53637, 51247, 51987, 68007,
                       27943, 43659,51203,18728]}
# DataFrame
df = pd.DataFrame(data)
# plot
df.plot(x="eu_country", y="gdp_per_capita",
        kind="bar", figsize=(7,3),
        legend=False, rot=0)
plt.title("Bar chart", fontsize=12)
plt.xlabel("EU country", fontsize=10)
plt.ylabel("GDP per capita", fontsize=10)
```

(continues on next page)

(continued from previous page)

```
plt.grid(True)
plt.show()
# inspect
print('data:')
print(df)
print(df.shape)
```

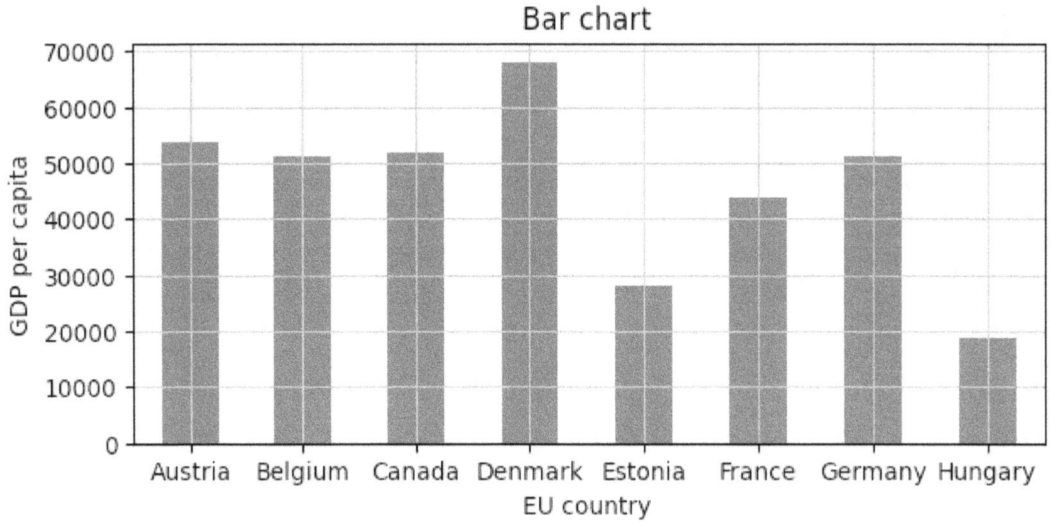


```
data:
  eu_country  gdp_per_capita
0    Austria           53637
1    Belgium           51247
2     Canada           51987
3    Denmark           68007
4    Estonia           27943
5     France           43659
6    Germany           51203
7    Hungary           18728
(8, 2)
```

The bar chart shows the `dgp_per_capita` versus `eu_country` for 8 European countries, and it provides a side-by-side comparison of the data provided.

20.4 Pie Charts

We attempt to visualize the jobs in our system's job queue. A sample of data is taken and the current status of the jobs in the queue is recorded in three categories, like so.

job queue data

```
             jobs
pending      110
running      217
completed    320
```

We plot the DataFrame by using the `plot.pie()` method of the DataFrame object, which has the following signature:

```
df.plot.pie(y='jobs', figsize=(3,3),
            autopct='%1.1f%%', startangle=90)
```

where

- `df`: is the DataFrame containing the data columns
- y: is the number of jobs in the queue per category
- `autopct`: indicates the formatting of the data items
- `startangle`: the angle of rotation

Observe, that we can set the `startangle` parameter to rotate the pie chart to make it look nice. In the following Python code segment, we implement this approach:

```
import pandas as pd
import matplotlib.pyplot as plt

# data
data = {"jobs": [110, 217, 320]}
# DataFrame
df = pd.DataFrame(data, index=["pending", "running", "completed"])
# plot
ax = df.plot.pie(y="jobs", figsize=(4,3.5), autopct="%1.1f%%",
                                    startangle=-20, fontsize=10)
plt.legend(loc="lower left", bbox_to_anchor=(0.85, 0))
plt.title("jobs queue status", fontsize=12, loc="center")
plt.ylabel("jobs", fontsize=10)
plt.xlabel("jobs status", fontsize=10)
plt.show()
# inspect
print(df)
print(df.shape)
```

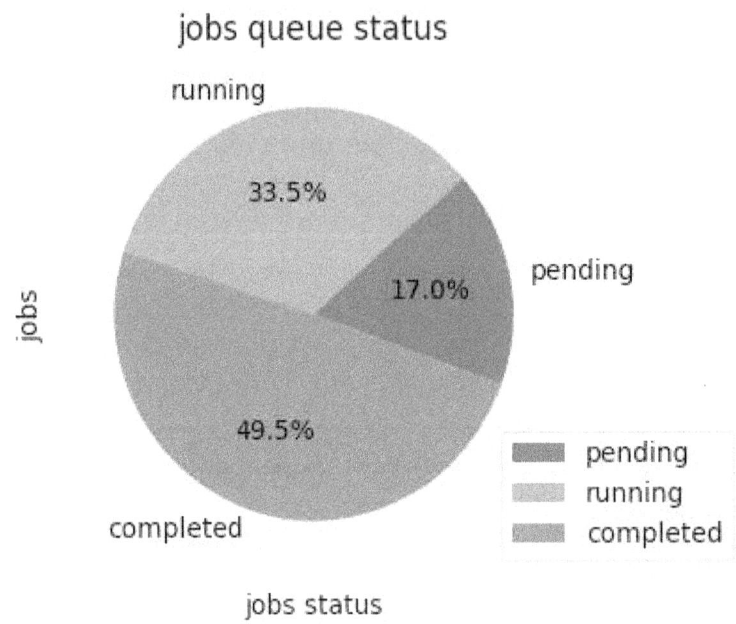


```
            jobs
pending      110
running      217
completed    320
(3, 1)
```

CHAPTER 21

HISTOGRAM PLOTS USING MATPLOTLIB

The matplotlib library is the workhorse when it comes to visualization in Python. It provides several plot and charting functions the data scientist can choose from.

- Plot the histogram using matplotlib `hist()` method of the DataFrame object
- Changing the style by using `plt.style.use('ggplot')`
- Computing statistical moments `skew()`, `kurtosis()` using Scipy.stats module

The `hist()` function computes the appropriate number of bins to use.

We secured a sample of peoples' ages and organized the observation in a Python `list()` for further analysis.

```
import numpy as np

# sample data set
sample = [1, 1, 2, 3, 3, 5, 7, 8, 9, 10, 10, 11, 11, 13,
          13, 15, 16, 17, 18, 18, 18, 19, 20, 21, 21, 23,
          24, 24, 25, 25, 25, 25, 26, 26, 26, 27, 27, 27,
          27, 27, 29, 30, 30, 31, 33, 34, 34, 34, 35, 36,
          36, 37, 37, 38, 38, 39, 40, 41, 41, 42, 43, 44,
          45, 45, 46, 47, 48, 48, 49, 50, 51, 52, 53, 54,
          55, 55, 56, 57, 58, 60, 61, 63, 64, 65, 66, 68,
          70, 71, 72, 74, 75, 77, 81, 83, 84, 87, 89, 90,
```

(continues on next page)

(continued from previous page)

```
        90, 91]
# inspect
print('results:')
print(f"observations       : {len(sample):.0f}")
print(f"range              : {max(sample)-min(sample):.0f}")
print(f"mean               : {np.mean(sample):.4f}")
print(f"standard deviation : {np.std(sample):.4f}")
```

```
results:
observations       : 100
range              : 90
mean               : 39.2600
standard deviation : 23.6003
```

Before we use the `hist()`` method from the matplotlib.pyplot library, we might want to check the documentation and review its properties.

```
import matplotlib.pyplot as plt
# help(plt.hist)
# print(plt.hist.__doc__)
```

histogram plots using the hist() method

We plot the histogram by using the matplotlib.pyplot package and the `hist()` method, which has the following signature:

```
plt.hist(sample, bins=8)
```

where

- `sample`: the data to be analyzed
- `bins`: the number of bins to use

We make use of the prepared `sample` list of data items. To visualize this example, we set the number of `bins` to 10, and in Python, we make use of the `hist()` method to produce the histogram chart, as shown below.

```
import matplotlib.pyplot as plt
import numpy as np
import pandas as pd
plt.style.use("ggplot")

# parameters
bins = 10
# plot
fig = plt.figure(figsize=(6,3))
plt.hist(sample,
         bins=bins,
```

(continues on next page)

(continued from previous page)

```
        edgecolor='r',
        color='grey',
        alpha=0.7)
plt.grid(True, color="lightgrey")
plt.title(f"Histogram, {bins:.0f} bins", fontsize=12)
plt.xlabel("observation")
plt.ylabel("frequency")
plt.show()
```

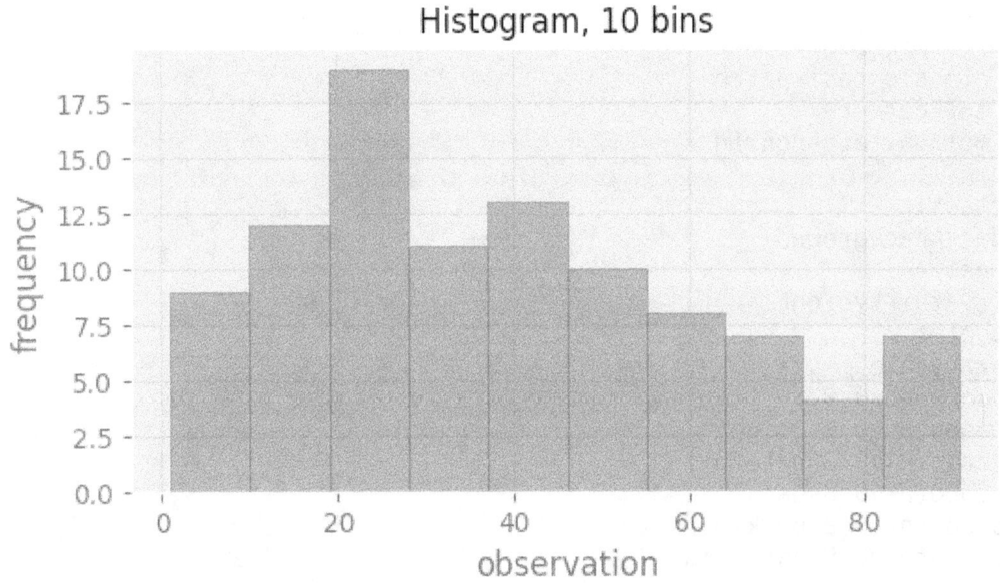

21.1 Change the styling with predefined styles

We can make use of a set of available predefined styles, to customize the appearance of the charts and plots. To set the style of the plot, we can make use of the following directive:

```
plt.style.use('ggplot')
```

where

- `style.use`: is set to `ggplot`, the name of the style to be used.

Remember to apply the `style.use` before any plotting, change to the title, or axis names takes place.

21.2 List all available styles

```
import matplotlib.pyplot as plt

# available styles
print('style options:')
for style in plt.style.available:
    print(style)
```

```
style options:
Solarize_Light2
_classic_test_patch
_mpl-gallery
_mpl-gallery-nogrid
bmh
classic
dark_background
fast
fivethirtyeight
ggplot
grayscale
seaborn-v0_8
seaborn-v0_8-bright
seaborn-v0_8-colorblind
seaborn-v0_8-dark
seaborn-v0_8-dark-palette
seaborn-v0_8-darkgrid
seaborn-v0_8-deep
seaborn-v0_8-muted
seaborn-v0_8-notebook
seaborn-v0_8-paper
seaborn-v0_8-pastel
seaborn-v0_8-poster
seaborn-v0_8-talk
seaborn-v0_8-ticks
seaborn-v0_8-white
seaborn-v0_8-whitegrid
tableau-colorblind10
```

We select the `style` from the list of available styling options, run the code, and observe the change in the histogram.

```
import matplotlib.pyplot as plt

plt.style.use("fivethirtyeight")

# parameters
bins = 8
# plot
```

(continues on next page)

(continued from previous page)

```
fig = plt.figure(figsize=(5,3.5))
plt.hist(sample,
         bins=bins,
         edgecolor='black')
plt.title(f"Histogram, {bins:.0f} bins", fontsize=14)
plt.xlabel("observation")
plt.ylabel("frequency")
plt.show()
```

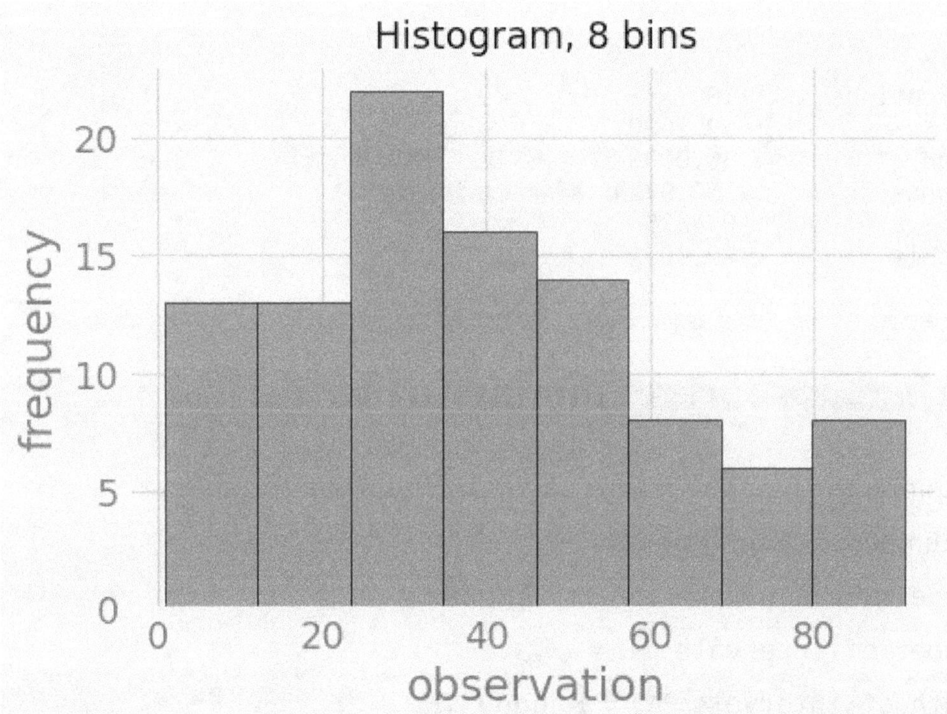

21.3 Statistical moments

To compute the statistical moments, we make use of the scipy.stats module, which provides functions for mean, standard deviation, skewness and kurtosis. We can use these functions like so:

```
scipy.stats.skew(sample)
```

In the following Python code segment, we demonstrate the usages of these methods, and implement them:

```
from scipy.stats import skew, kurtosis
import numpy as np
```

(continues on next page)

(continued from previous page)

```
# results
print("results:")
print(f"observations     : {len(sample):.0f}")
print(f"mean             : {np.mean(sample):.4f}")
print(f"median           : {np.median(sample):.4f}")
print(f"variance         : {np.std(sample) ** 2:.4f}")
print(f"skew             : {skew(sample):.4f}")
print(f"kurtosis         : {kurtosis(sample):.4f}")
```

```
results:
observations     : 100
mean             : 39.2600
median           : 36.0000
variance         : 556.9724
skew             : 0.4575
kurtosis         : -0.6091
```

21.4 The appropriate number of bins

We can derive the number of bins using the following formulas:

- N: number of observations
- Range: maximum value minus minimum value
- Number of intervals: NI = $\sqrt{n}$
- Width of intervals: WI = Range / NI

These formulas can then be used to create the frequency table followed by the histogram. Recall that our dataset contains 100 observations, and we compute using our formulas:

- N: number of observations = 100
- Range: maximum value and minimum value = 91 - 1 = 90
- Number of intervals: NI = $\sqrt{N} = \sqrt{100} = 10$
- Width of intervals: WI = Range / NI = 90 / 10 = 9

Based on this information, the frequency table would look like this:

```
Intervals (bins)  Frequency
0-9                9
10-19             13
20-29             19
30-39             15
```

(continues on next page)

(continued from previous page)

```
40-49             13
50-59             10
60-69              7
70-79              6
80-89              5
90-99              3
```

Note that the starting point for the first interval is 0, which is very close to the minimum observation of 1 in our dataset.

Note: If, for example, the minimum observation was 20 in another dataset, then the starting point for the first interval should be 20, rather than 0, and include the last value of 99.

We specify the values as a Python list of values, which we have computed before and pass this list into the `hist()` method as a parameter. Like so:

```
plt.hist(sample, bins=custom_bins)
```

where:

- bins: is set to a [] of custom_bins

21.5 Histogram plots using custom bins

```
import matplotlib.pyplot as plt
plt.style.use("tableau-colorblind10")

# plot
fig = plt.figure(figsize=(6,3))
custom_bins = [0, 10, 20, 30, 40, 50, 60, 70, 80, 90, 99]
plt.hist(sample, bins=custom_bins,
         color="green",
         alpha=0.5, edgecolor='black')
plt.title("Histogram, custom bins", fontsize=12)
plt.grid(color="grey", linestyle="--", linewidth=1, alpha=0.8)
plt.xlabel("observation")
plt.ylabel("frequency")
plt.show()
# inspect
print('results:')
print("custom bins            :", custom_bins)
print(f"number of bins          : {len(custom_bins):.0f}")
print(f"observations            : {len(sample):.0f}")
```

(continues on next page)

(continued from previous page)

```
print(f"mean                : {np.mean(sample):.4f}")
print(f"median              : {np.median(sample):.4f}")
print(f"std                 : {np.std(sample):.4f}")
print(f"variance            : {np.std(sample) ** 2:.4f}")
print(f"skew                : {skew(sample):.4f}")
print(f"kurtosis (Fisher)   : {kurtosis(sample, fisher=True):.4f}")
print(f"kurtosis (Pearson)  : {kurtosis(sample, fisher=False):.4f}")
print(f"check               : {kurtosis(sample, fisher=False)-3:.4f}")
```

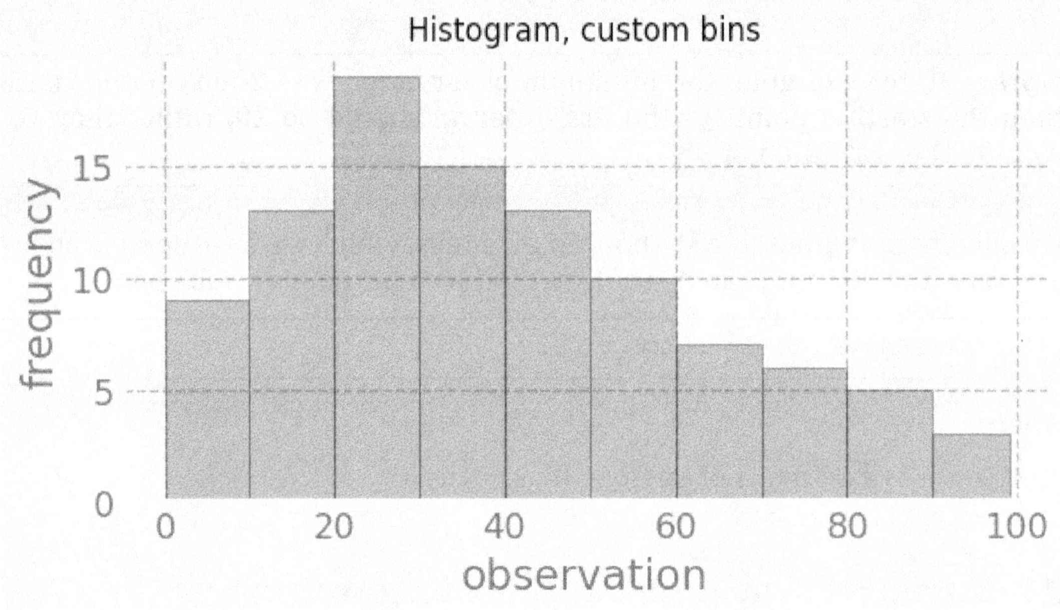


```
results:
custom bins        : [0, 10, 20, 30, 40, 50, 60, 70, 80, 90, 99]
number of bins     : 11
observations       : 100
mean               : 39.2600
median             : 36.0000
std                : 23.6003
variance           : 556.9724
skew               : 0.4575
kurtosis (Fisher)  : -0.6091
kurtosis (Pearson) : 2.3909
check              : -0.6091
```

Observe that the histogram is similar to the one we produced earlier. It exhibits a positive skew.

CHAPTER 22

CHARTS WITH MPLFINANCE LIBRARY

Creating Charts is a very effective way to visualize complex data series. We can use different chart types, for varying purposes.

According to Mplfinance [2023] there are many different ways to plot financial data. In this section, we explore several options to generate appealing charts and analysis:

- OHLC Charts on daily data
- Candle Charts on daily data
- Line Charts on daily data
- Renko Charts on daily data
- Point & Figure Charts on daily data
- OHLC Charts on daily data with moving average overlays
- Candle Charts on daily data with multiple moving averages overlays
- OHLC Charts on daily data with a volume in an extra diagram
- Candle Charts on daily data with multiple moving averages and extra volume diagram
- Candle Charts with 1 min resolution and multiple overlay studies
- Candle Charts with 1 min resolution
- Candle Charts with 1 min resolution

- OHLC Charts with 1 min resolution
- Line Charts with 1 min resolution, showing non-trading days
- Candle Charts on daily data with moving average overlay studies

```
import pandas as pd

# DataFrame
daily = pd.read_csv("data/SPY_20110701_20120630_Bollinger.csv",
                    index_col=0, parse_dates=True)
daily.index.name = "Date"
# inspect
print(type(daily))
print(daily[['Adj Close', 'Volume', 'UpperB',
             'LowerB', 'PercentB']].tail())
print(daily.shape)
```

```
<class 'pandas.core.frame.DataFrame'>
             Adj Close     Volume      UpperB      LowerB  PercentB
Date
2012-06-25  117.327911  146375700  136.498567  128.120436  0.381896
2012-06-26  117.917580  141634000  136.362697  128.084306  0.470585
2012-06-27  118.980804  108088000  136.447962  128.140042  0.605441
2012-06-28  118.641281  169242100  136.500761  128.219241  0.551922
2012-06-29  121.598610  212250900  136.721010  128.792993  0.921670
(252, 9)
```

Plotting OHLC (open, high, low, close) data into appealing charts is as simple as the calling `plot()` method, provided by the mplfinance library, on the DataFrame. In the following Python code segment, we demonstrate this approach on multiple examples.

22.1 Daily data

22.1.1 OHLC Charts on daily data

```
import mplfinance as mpf
import warnings
warnings.filterwarnings("ignore")

# parameters
start_date = "2011-11-01"
end_date = "2011-12-31"
# plot
mpf.plot( daily[start_date : end_date],
          type='ohlc',
```

(continues on next page)

(continued from previous page)

```
        xrotation=0,
        style="classic",
        figsize=(8,4.5),
        title="SPY, daily bars",
        tight_layout=True,)
```

The default plot type, as you can see above, is `ohlc`. Other plot types can be specified with the keyword argument type, for example, type='candle' or type='line' or type='renko' or type='pnf'.

22.1.2 Candle Charts on daily data

```
import mplfinance as mpf
import warnings
warnings.filterwarnings("ignore")

# parameters
start_date = "2011-07-01"
end_date = "2012-06-30"
# plot candle stick
mpf.plot(daily[start_date : end_date],
        type="candle",
        xrotation=0,
        figsize=(8,4.5),
        tight_layout=True,
        title="SPY, daily", )
```

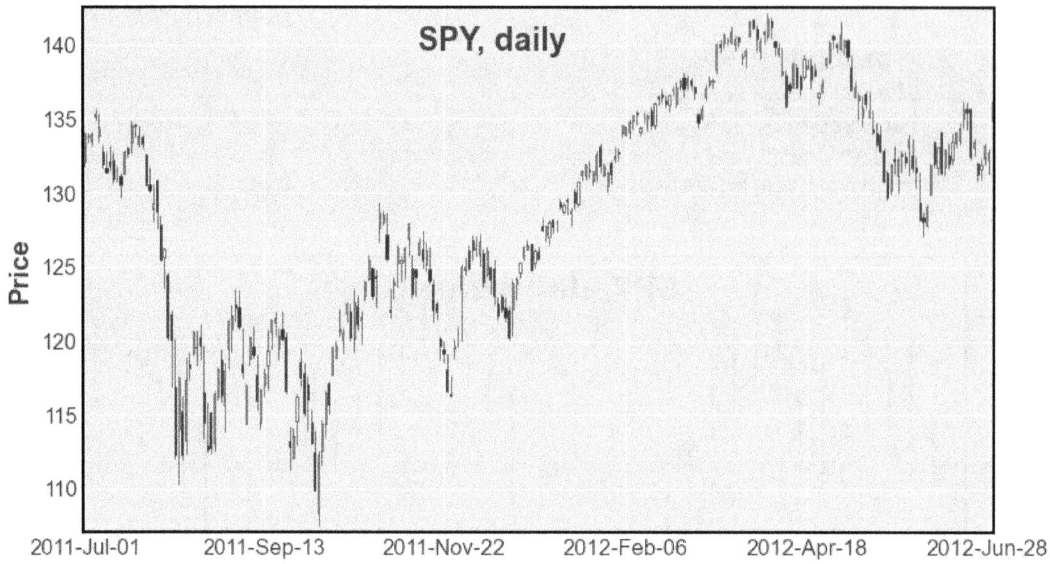

22.1.3 Line Charts on daily data

```
import mplfinance as mpf
import warnings
warnings.filterwarnings("ignore")

# parameters
start_date = "2011-07-01"
end_date = "2012-06-30"
# plot
mpf.plot(daily[start_date : end_date],
        type="line",
        xrotation=0,
        figsize=(8,4.5),
        title="SPY, daily",
        tight_layout=True, )
```

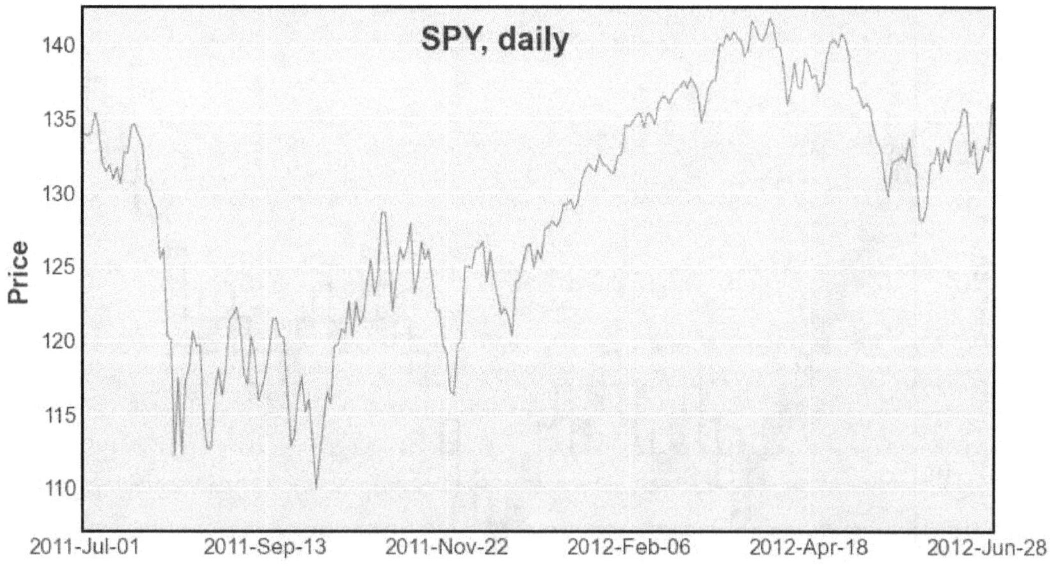

22.1.4 Renko Charts on daily data

```
import mplfinance as mpf
import warnings
warnings.filterwarnings("ignore")

# Load local file
year = pd.read_csv("data/SPY_20110701_20120630_Bollinger.csv",
                   index_col=0, parse_dates=True)
year.index.name = "Date"
# parameters
start_date = "2011-07-01"
end_date = "2012-06-30"
# plot
mpf.plot(year[start_date : end_date],
        type="renko",
        xrotation=0,
        figsize=(8,4.5),
        title=("SPY, renko"),
        tight_layout=True,)
```

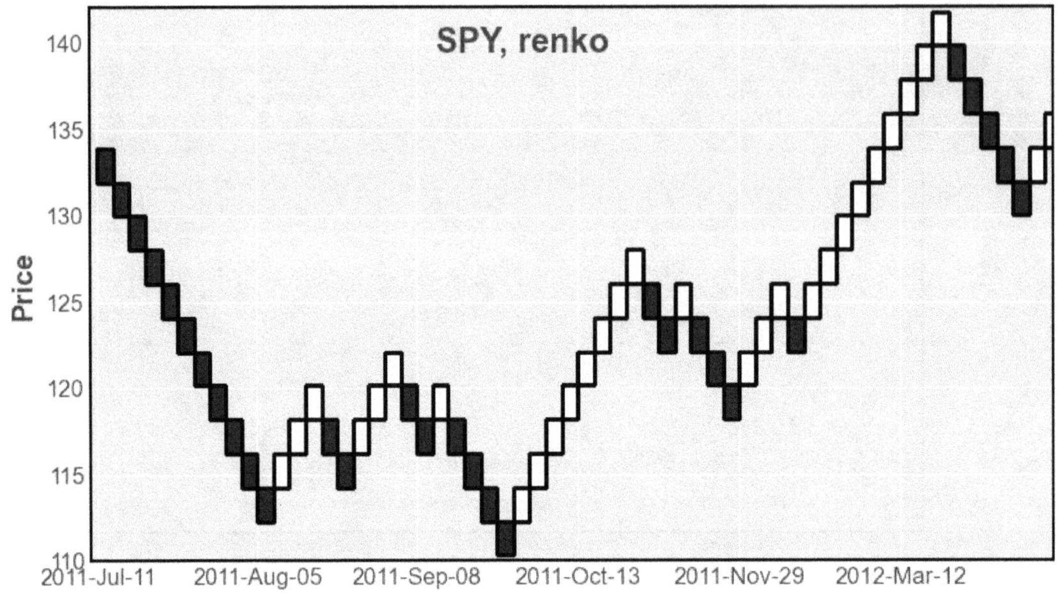

22.1.5 Point & Figure Charts on daily data

```
import mplfinance as mpf
import warnings
warnings.filterwarnings("ignore")

# parameters
start_date = "2011-07-01"
end_date = "2012-06-30"
# plot P&F
mpf.plot( year[start_date : end_date],
         type="pnf",
         xrotation=0,
         figsize=(9,4.5),
         title=("SPY, PF"),
         tight_layout=True)
```

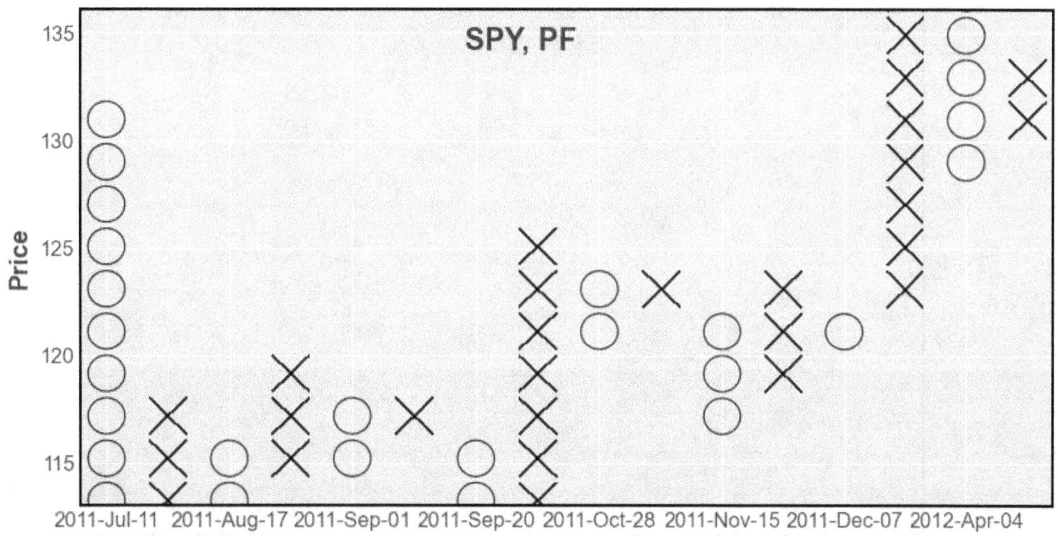

We can also superimpose moving averages with the mav positional argument onto the resulting plot, like so:

- mav=10: use a scalar for a single moving average
- mav=(10,20,90): use a tuple of scalar values for multiple moving averages
- mav=[10,20,90]: use a list of scalar values for multiple moving averages

22.1.6 OHLC Charts on daily data with moving average overlays

```
import mplfinance as mpf
import warnings
warnings.filterwarnings("ignore")

# parameters
start_date = "2011-07-01"
end_date = "2012-06-30"
# plot
mpf.plot(daily[start_date : end_date],
        type="ohlc",
        mav=4, # scalar
        xrotation=0,
        figsize=(8,4.5),
        title=("SPY, SMA(4)"),
        tight_layout=True,)
```

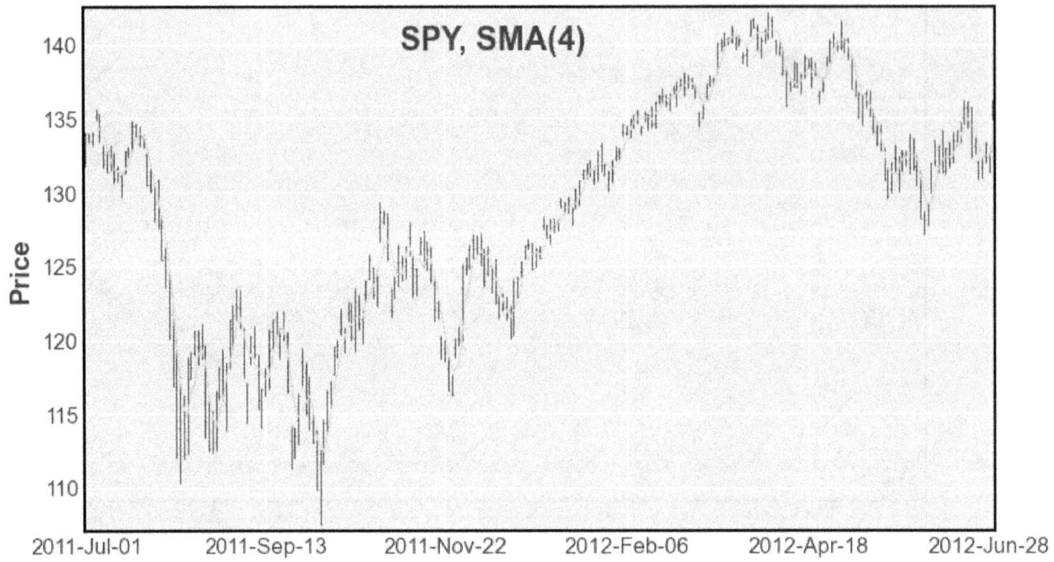

22.1.7 Candle Charts with multiple moving average overlays

```
import mplfinance as mpf
import warnings
warnings.filterwarnings("ignore")

# parameters
start_date = "2011-07-01"
end_date = "2012-06-30"
# plot
mpf.plot(daily[start_date : end_date],
        type="candle",
        mav=(3, 6, 9), # tuple of scalars
        xrotation=0,
        figsize=(8,4.5),
        title=("SPY, MA(3,6,9)"),
        tight_layout=True,)
```

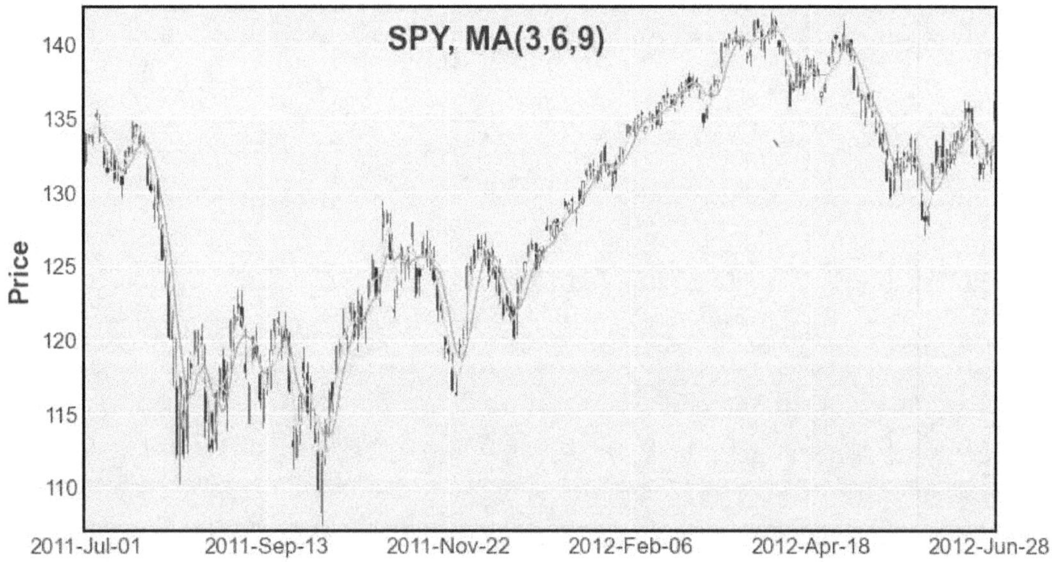

22.1.8 OHLC Charts on daily data with a volume in an extra diagram

```
import mplfinance as mpf
import warnings
warnings.filterwarnings("ignore")

# parameters
start_date = "2011-07-01"
end_date = "2012-06-30"
# plot
mpf.plot(daily[start_date : end_date],
        type="candle",
        mav=[3, 6, 9], # list of scalars
        volume=True,
        xrotation=0,
        figsize=(8,6.5),
        title=("SPY, MA(10,6)"),
        tight_layout=True)
```

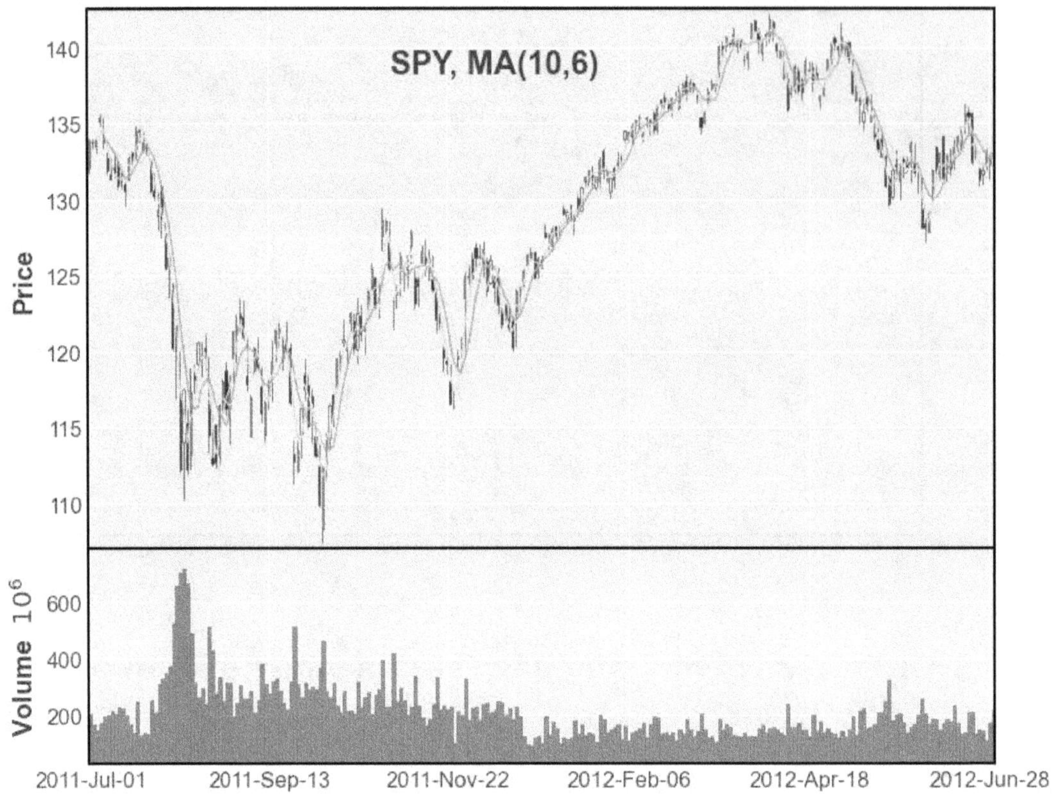

In the above chart, there are no gaps along the x-coordinate, even though there are days on which there was no trading. Non-trading days are simply not shown.

However, sometimes people like to see these gaps so that they can tell, with a glance, where the weekends and holidays fall.

Non-trading days can be displayed with the show_nontrading keyword.

Note that for these purposes non-trading intervals are those that are not represented in the data at all. There are simply no rows for those dates or datetime. This is because, when data is retrieved from an exchange or other market data source, that data typically will not include rows for non-trading days like weekends and holidays.

The parameter show_nontrading `True` will display all dates between the first time stamp and the last time stamp in the data, regardless of whether rows exist for those dates or datetime.

The parameter show_nontrading `False` (the default value) will show only dates that have actual rows in the data. This means that if there are rows in your DataFrame that exist but contain only `NaN` values, these rows will still appear on the plot.

For example, in the chart below, you can see weekends and the corresponding gap in the data.

22.1.9 Candle Charts with multiple moving averages and volume plot

```
import mplfinance as mpf
import warnings
warnings.filterwarnings("ignore")

# parameters
start_date = "2011-07-01"
end_date = "2012-06-30"
ymin = daily.Close.min() * 0.98
ymax = daily.Close.max() * 1.02
# plot
mpf.plot(daily[start_date : end_date],
         type="candle",
        mav=(90, 10, 20),
        volume=True,
        show_nontrading=True,
        xrotation=0,
        figsize=(8,6.5),
        title=("SP500, MA(90, 10, 20), daily bars"),
        tight_layout=True, ylim=(ymin, ymax))
```

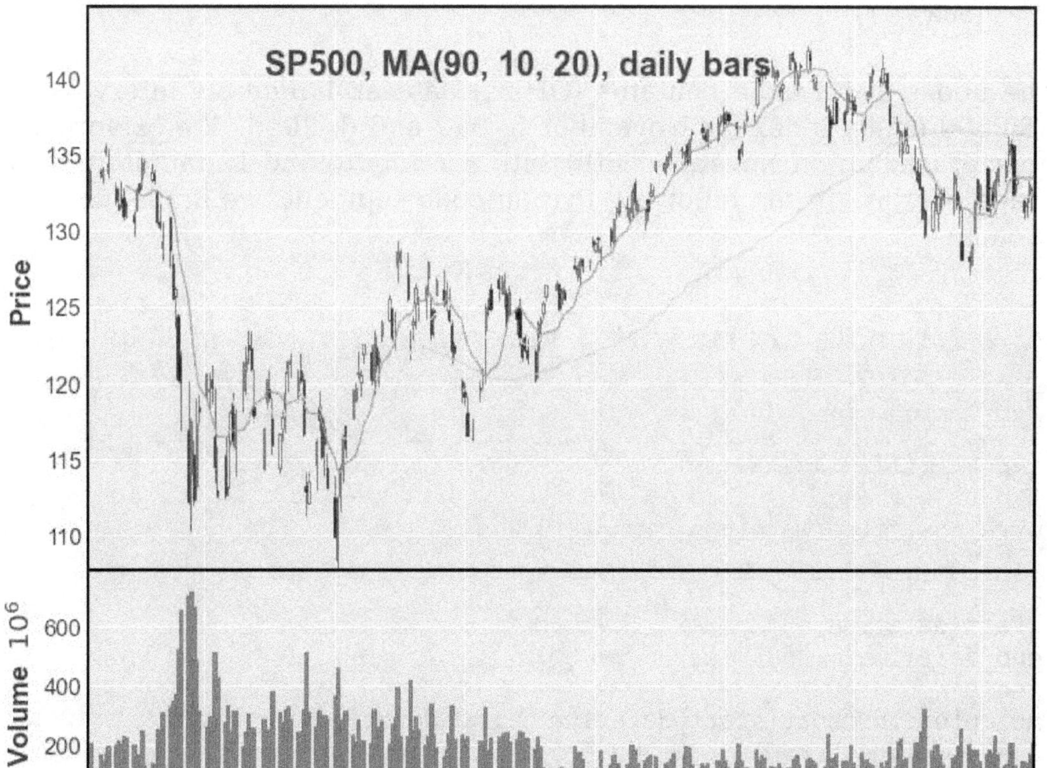

22.2 Intraday data

To facilitate plotting of intraday charts, we load a dataset for the S&P 500 Index in 1 minute resolution. This data allows us to produce intraday charts. In the following section, we explore several options.

```
import pandas as pd

# DataFrame
intraday = pd.read_csv("data/SP500_NOV2019_IDay.csv",
                       index_col=0, parse_dates=True)
intraday = intraday.drop("Volume", axis=1)
intraday.index.name = "Date"
# inspect
print(intraday.tail(3))
print(intraday.shape)
```

```
                        Open    Close     High      Low
Date
2019-11-08 15:57:00  3090.73  3090.70  3091.02  3090.52
2019-11-08 15:58:00  3090.73  3091.04  3091.13  3090.58
2019-11-08 15:59:00  3091.16  3092.91  3092.91  3090.96
(1563, 4)
```

The above DataFrame contains (OHLC) data at 1 minutes intervals for the S&P500 equity index for November 5, 6, 7 and 8, 2019. We explore the last hour of trading on November 6th, with a 7-minute and 12-minute moving average overlay. In the following Python code segment, we implement this approach:

22.2.1 Candle Charts with 1 min resolution and multiple overlay studies

```
import mplfinance as mpf
import warnings
warnings.filterwarnings("ignore")

# parameters
start_datetime = "2019-11-06 15:00"
end_datetime = "2019-11-06 16:00"
# plot
mpf.plot(intraday[start_datetime : end_datetime],
         type="candle",
         mav=(7, 12),
         title="SP500, 1min bars",
         xrotation=0,
```

(continues on next page)

(continued from previous page)

```
        figsize=(8,4.5),
        tight_layout=True,)
```

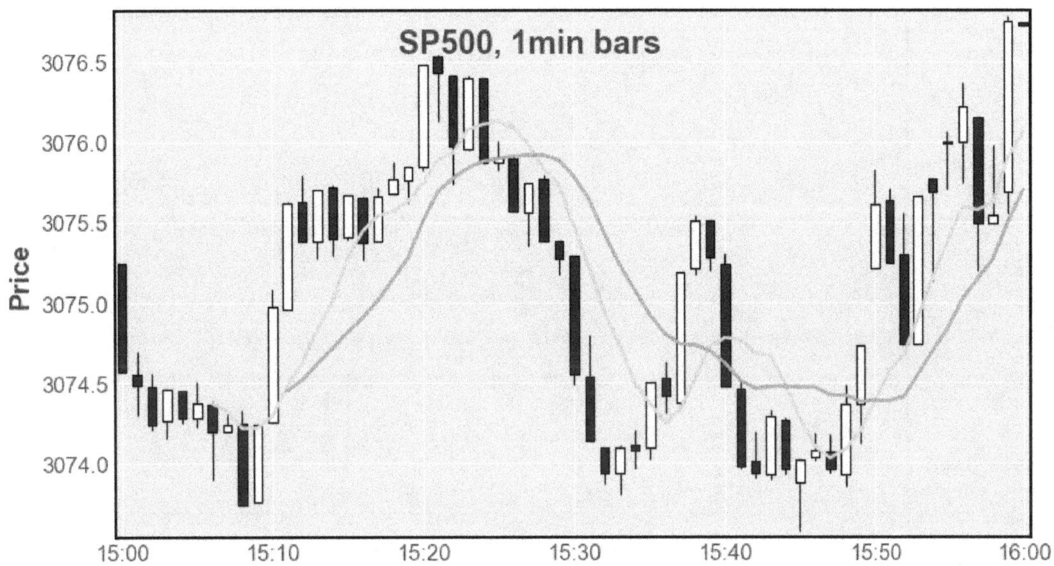

The time interpretation of the mav parameters depends on the frequency of the data because the mav integers are the number of data points used in the moving average and not the number of days or minutes.

Notice above that for intraday data the x-axis automatically displays time instead of date.

Below we see that if the intraday data spans two or more trading days, the x-axis automatically displays both time and data. In Python, this is demonstrated, in the following code section.

22.2.2 Candle Charts with 1 min resolution

```
import mplfinance as mpf
import warnings
warnings.filterwarnings("ignore")

# parameters
start_datetime = "2019-11-05 12:00"
end_datetime = "2019-11-06 16:00"
# plot
mpf.plot(intraday[start_datetime : end_datetime],
        type="candle",
        warn_too_much_data=10000,
        xrotation=0,
        figsize=(8,4.5),
```

(continues on next page)

(continued from previous page)

```
        title=("SP500, 1 mins bars"),
        tight_layout=True,)
```

In the plot below, we see what an intraday plot looks like. When we display non-trading periods by setting the show_nontrading parameter to True for intraday data spanning into two or more days.

22.2.3 Candle Charts with 1 min resolution

```
import mplfinance as mpf
import warnings
warnings.filterwarnings("ignore")

# parameters
start_datetime = "2019-11-06 12:00"
end_datetime = "2019-11-06 16:00"
# plot
mpf.plot(intraday[start_datetime : end_datetime],
        type="candle",
        show_nontrading=True,
        warn_too_much_data=10000,
        xrotation=0,
        figsize=(8,4.5),
        title=("SP500, 1 mins"),
        tight_layout=True,)
```

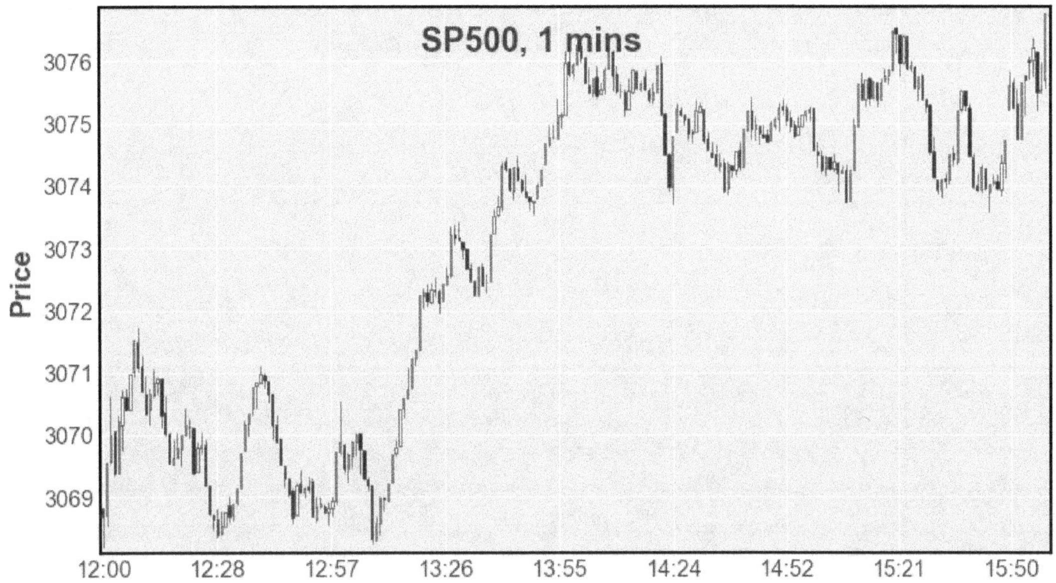

We plot 4 days of intraday data with the show_nontrading parameter set to True.

22.2.4 OHLC Charts with 1 min resolution

```
import mplfinance as mpf
import warnings
warnings.filterwarnings("ignore")

# parameters
start_datetime = "2019-11-06 12:00"
end_datetime = "2019-11-06 16:00"
# plot
mpf.plot(intraday[start_datetime : end_datetime],
        type="ohlc",
        show_nontrading=True,
        warn_too_much_data=10000,
        xrotation=0,
        figsize=(8,4.5),
        title=("SP500, 1 mins"),
        tight_layout=True,)
```

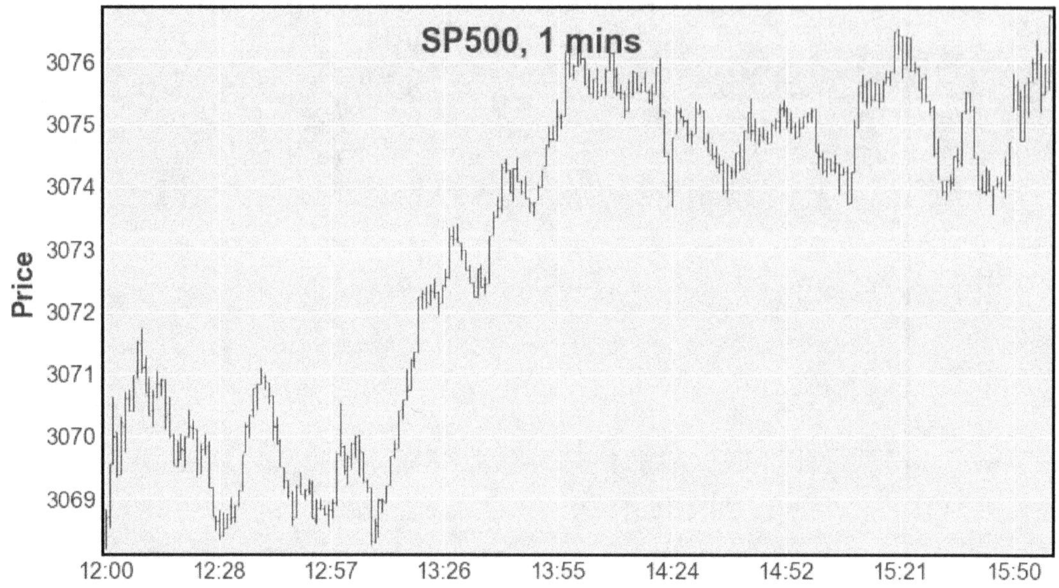

22.2.5 Line Charts with 1 min resolution, showing non-trading days

Below we present the same 4 days of intraday data with the show_nontrading parameter default is `False`.

```
import mplfinance as mpf
import warnings
warnings.filterwarnings("ignore")

# select data
iday = intraday.loc["2019-11-05 12:00":"2019-11-06 16:00", :]
# plot
mpf.plot(iday,
        type="line",
        xrotation=0,
        figsize=(8,4.5),
        title=("SP500, 1 mins"),
        tight_layout=True,)
```

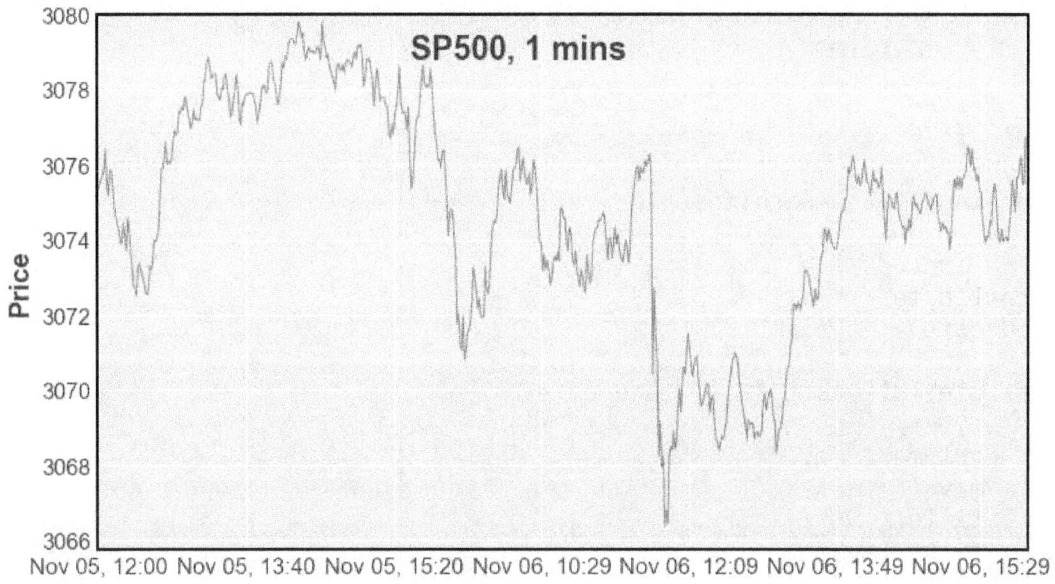

Daily data spanning across a year boundary automatically adds the year to the date format.

```
import pandas as pd

# daily data
df = pd.read_csv("data/yahoofinance-SPY-20080101-20180101.csv",
                 index_col=0, parse_dates=True)
# inspect
print(df.iloc[:, 3:6].tail()) # last 3 columns
print(df.shape)
```

```
                 Close   Adj Close    Volume
Date
2017-12-22  267.510010  267.510010  78720900
2017-12-26  267.190002  267.190002  45244400
2017-12-27  267.320007  267.320007  57751000
2017-12-28  267.869995  267.869995  45116100
2017-12-29  266.859985  266.859985  96007400
(2519, 6)
```

22.2.6 Candle Charts on daily data with moving average overlay studies

```
import mplfinance as mpf
import warnings
warnings.filterwarnings("ignore")

# parameters
start_date = "2011-02-01"
end_date = "2011-05-12"
# plot
mpf.plot(df[start_date : end_date],
    type="candle",
    volume=True,
    mav=(20,40),
    title=("SPY, daily, MA(20,40)"),
    tight_layout=True,
    xrotation=0,
    figsize=(8,6.5),)
```

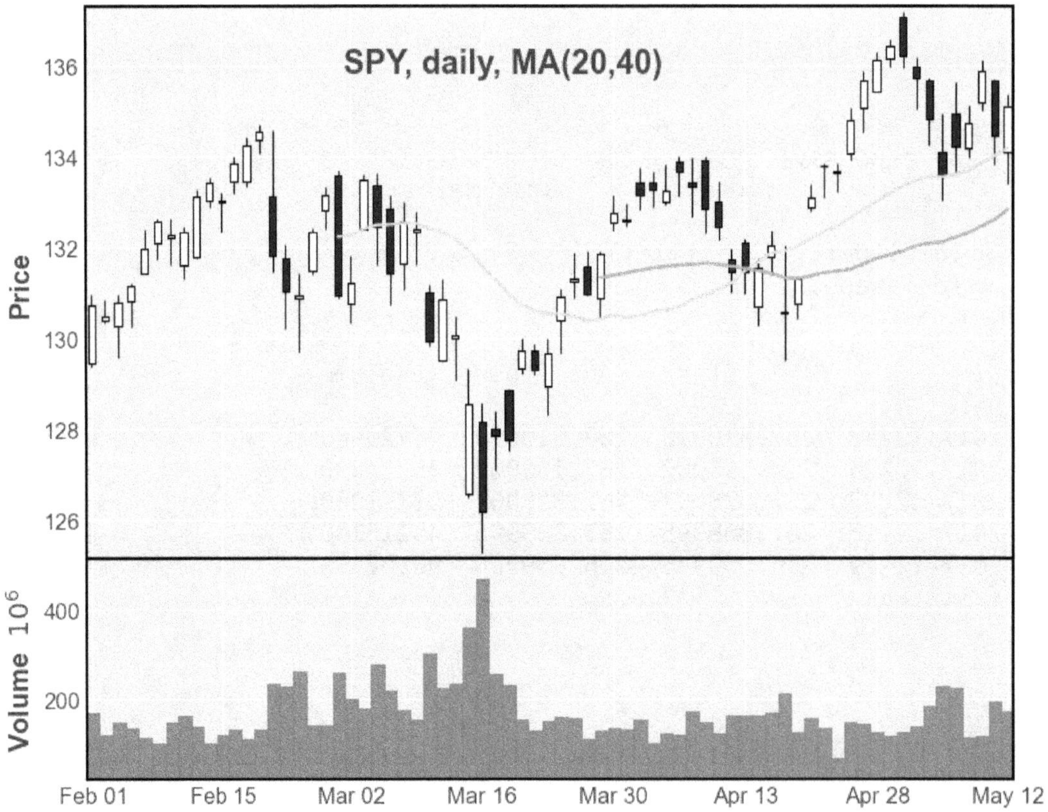

CHAPTER 23

LIVE CHART ANIMATION

The animation of charts is at times very helpful to visualize the development of a graph over time.

As introduced in John Hunter [2012], we explore the live chart animation functions of the matplotlib library with two examples.

23.1 Animated cosine function

We animate the `cos(x)` function for the specified interval. The animated function is defined as:

$$f(t) = \cos(t)$$

for the interval $t \in [0, 720]$ degree.

In the following Python code segment, a simulation approach is implemented.

```
import matplotlib.pyplot as plt
import numpy as np
from IPython.display import display, clear_output
from basic_units_lib import radians, degrees, cos
%matplotlib inline

# function
t = [val * radians for val in np.arange(0, 13, 0.15)]
x = cos(t)
# plot
```

(continues on next page)

(continued from previous page)

```
fig, ax = plt.subplots(figsize=(10, 3))
plt.grid(True)
(l,) = ax.plot(t, x, xunits=degrees)
ax.set_title("f(t) = cos(t)  t $\\in [0 - 720\\degree$]",
             fontsize=12)
ax.set_ylabel("amplitude")
# in-line function
animate = lambda i: l.set_data(t[:i], x[:i])
# animate
for i in range(len(x)):
    animate(i)
    clear_output(wait=True)
    display(fig)
    plt.show()
```

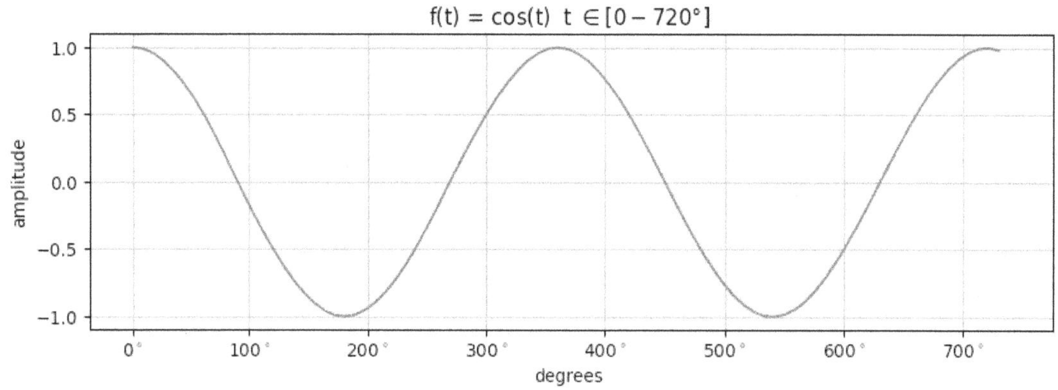

23.2 Animated arbitrary function

We animate the following function:

$$f(t) = \sin(t) + 0.2 \cdot \tan(t)$$

for the interval $t \in [0, 4\pi]$ rad.

In the following Python code segment, we implement this idea:

```
import matplotlib.pyplot as plt
import matplotlib.animation
import numpy as np
from IPython.display import display, clear_output
from basic_units_lib import radians, degrees
import math
%matplotlib inline
```

(continues on next page)

(continued from previous page)

```
def animate(i):
    """ animate this data """
    return l.set_data(t[:i], x[:i])

t = [val * radians for val in np.arange(0, 13, 0.15)]
tsteps = np.arange(0, 13, 0.15)
x = []
for i in tsteps:
    x.append(math.cos(i) + 0.2 * math.tan(i))
# plot
fig, ax = plt.subplots(figsize=(10, 3))
plt.grid(True)
(l,) = ax.plot(t, x, xunits=radians)
txt = "$f(t) = \\cos(t) + 0.2 * \\tan(t)$ $\\:\\: t \\in [0, 4\\pi]$"
ax.set_title(txt, fontsize=12)
ax.set_ylabel("amplitude")
# animate
for i in range(len(x)):
    animate(i)
    clear_output(wait=True)
    display(fig)
    plt.show()
```

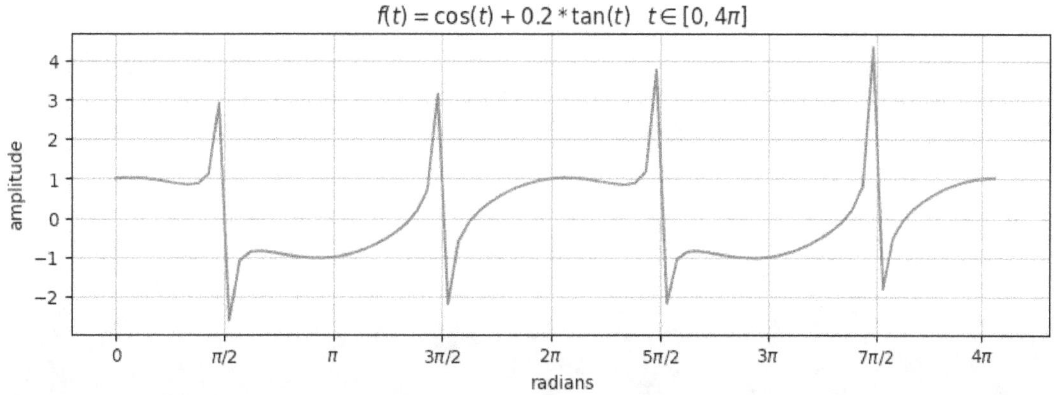

CHAPTER 24

CUSTOMIZE SIZE AND ORIENTATION OF CHARTS

The matplotlib figsize is a method from the pyplot class, which allows us to change the dimensions of the graph dynamically.

We understand how to make use of the figsize parameter of the matplotlib, to adjust the size of graphs and plots. By default, the drawing window is generated as 6.4 x 4.8 inches. Here we discuss ways to change the size of figures by setting the figsize parameter.

24.1 Syntax of Matplotlib Figsize

The `figsize` is a parameter in the figure class of the pyplot submodule of the matplotlib library. The `figure()` method is applied, with the following signatures:

```
matplotlib.pyplot.figure(figsize=(width, height))
```

where

- `width`: the width in inches. The default width is 6
- `height`: the height of the graph in inches. The default value is 4

Before using matplotlib, we might want to bring up the documentation.

```
import matplotlib.pyplot as mpp
# print(mpp.figure.__doc__)
```

24.2 Default Figsize

In Matplotlib all the diagrams are created at a default size of 6.4 by 4.8 inches, which can be changed using the figsize parameter. We can make use of the `rcParams` attribute of the figure. The default figure size values are stored as a tuple. For example:

```
plt.rcParams.update({'figure.figsize':(12,6)})
```

24.3 Customize figures using rcParams

The rcParams is a dictionary attribute in the matplotlib figure class, which allows us to customize the look and orientation of the produced output. This attribute holds data such as figure size, figure DPI, figure `facecolor`, and figure `edgecolor`, which can be set dynamically to alter the appearance of the output.

24.4 Set the figure size in centimeters instead of inches

For Figsize, the units of measure are inches by default. We can change this to centimeters, by using a helper function `centimeter_to_inches()`, like so:

```
def centimeter_to_inches(value):
    return value/2.54
```

We apply the helper function, like so:

```
plt.figure(figsize=(centimeter_to_inches(28),
                    centimeter_to_inches(16)))
```

In the next Python code segment, this approach is demonstrated.

```
import matplotlib.pyplot as plt
import numpy as np
```

(continues on next page)

(continued from previous page)

```
# helper function
def centimeter_to_inches(value):
    """ convert centimeters to inches """
    return value / 2.54

# data
x = np.arange(0, 15, 0.01)
y = 1.2 * np.sin(x) + 1.5 * np.exp(0.1*x)
# plot
plt.figure(figsize=(centimeter_to_inches(22),
                    centimeter_to_inches(8)))
plt.title("Plot size measured in cm vs. inches", fontsize=14)
plt.xlabel("time steps")
plt.ylabel("amplitude")
plt.plot(x, y, linewidth=3, color="blue", alpha=0.8)
plt.grid()
plt.show()
```

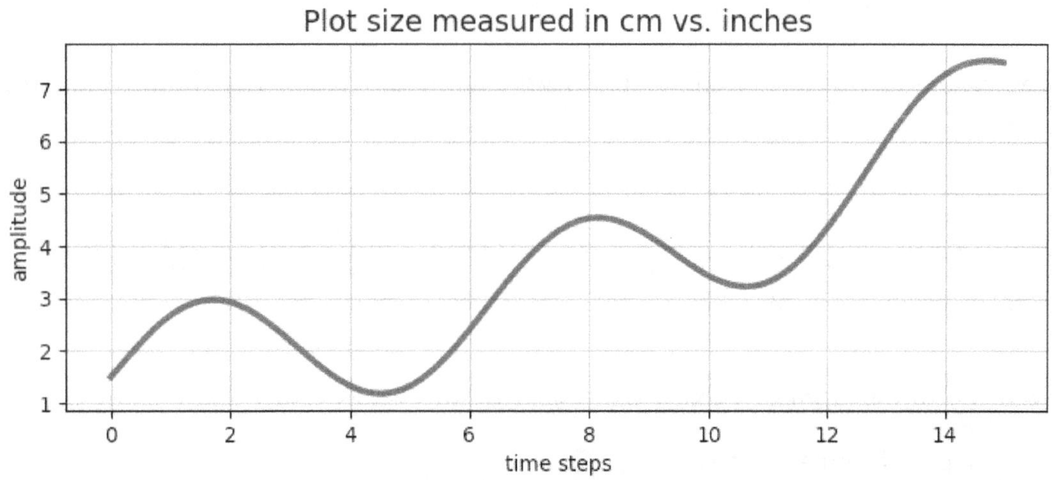

We obtain the function values by generating equidistant value for the x-axis and compute the corresponding y-values, according to the given formula, like so:

```
x = np.arange(0, 10, 0.1)
y = np.sin(x) + .2*np.tan(x)
```

We create an array of x axis whose value ranges from 0 to 10 in 0.1 increments. Then we compute the function values at each step and store the results in the y array.

The helper function `centimeter_to_inches()` converts all values from centimeters into inches.

```
plt.figure(figsize=(centimeter_to_inches(12),
                    centimeter_to_inches(6)))
```

We make use of this helper function to convert the inputs into inches and apply those values to the figsize method.

Additionally, we put the helper function in a dedicated `quantlib.py` file for future reuse.

In the following Python code segment is a brief demonstration of its usage.

```
from quantlib import centimeter_to_inches

# parameters
c = 10
i = centimeter_to_inches(c)
print(f'{c} centimeter are {i:.6f} inches')
```

```
10 centimeter are 3.937008 inches
```

Before using the `plt` module, we might want to review the documentation.

```
import matplotlib.pyplot as plt
# help(plt)
```

```
import matplotlib.pyplot as plt
import numpy as np

x = [1, 2, 3, 4, 5, 6, 7, 8, 9]
y = [15 * np.sin(t) + t**2 - 9 for t in x]
# plot
fig = plt.figure(figsize=(8,4))
plt.plot(x, y)
plt.grid()
plt.title(f"$f(t) = 15 \cdot sin(t) + t^2 - 9$",
          fontsize=12)
plt.xlabel("$t$")
plt.ylabel("$f(t)$")
plt.show()
```

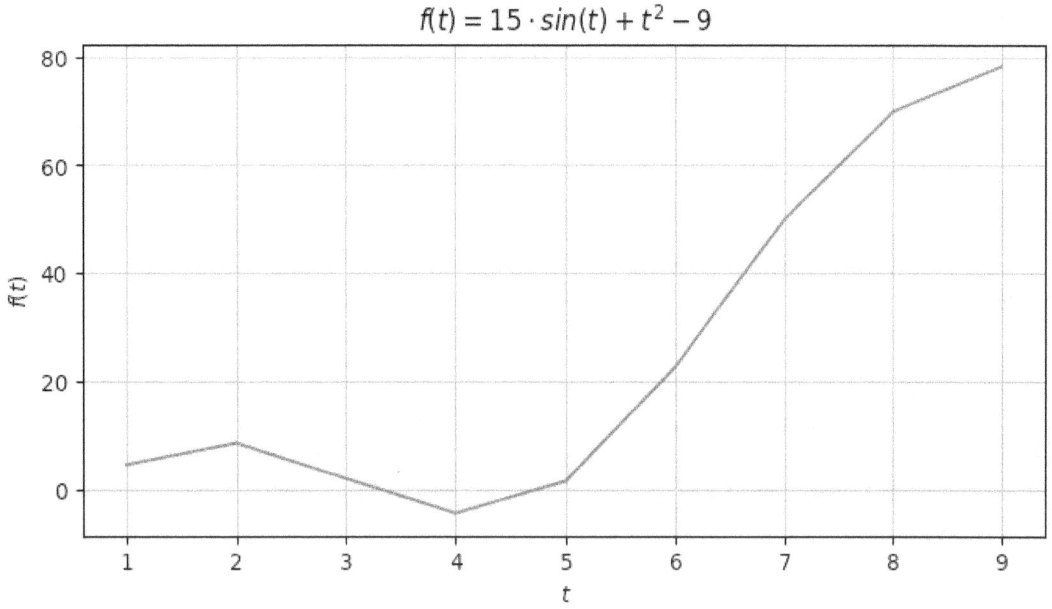

24.5 Change the height and width of the Charts

Suppose, we have 80 participants in the trading contest, and we want to make a bar chart of it.

However, when we have a lot of participants the vertical chart orientation will not be able to display all the participants. In such cases, it is preferable to rotate the chart by 90 degrees and have the names in the y axis and the scores as horizontal bars. This way, a great many participants can be displayed in a single chart.

24.6 Generate sample data using the Faker library

We can make use of the Faker Library to generate sample data. As explained in Faraglia [2014], we instantiate Faker to receive a faker object from which we can generate sample data.

```
faker = Faker()
```

In the following example, we produce 80 names and 80 corresponding score values for a fictitious trading tournament.

```
for _ in range(80):
    names.append(faker.name())
    counts.append(np.random.randint(40,400))
```

In the following Python code segment, the usage of the faker library is demonstrated.

```
import numpy as np
import pandas as pd
from faker import Faker

faker = Faker()
df = pd.DataFrame()
names = list()
scores = list()
for _ in range(80):
    names.append(faker.name())
    scores.append(np.random.randint(40,400))
df = pd.DataFrame({"names": names, "scores": scores})
df = df.sort_values(by=["scores"], ascending=True)
print(df)
```

```
                   names  scores
13          Janice Greer      46
25         Tracey Miller      56
11          Frank Bailey      59
53          Jenny Rivera      60
21         April Wallace      70
..                   ...     ...
23      Brandon Harrison     388
42           Blake Kelly     389
17   Dr. Walter Marshall     390
9            Tara Wright     395
73         Kaitlyn Brown     397

[80 rows x 2 columns]
```

To make 80 names fit into the chart, we might resort to making the font size for the names very small, like so:

```
plt.xticks(rotation=90, fontsize=8)
```

of course, this approach has its limitations. A better option is to rotate the chart by using the orientation parameter.

In the following Python code example, we implement this idea:

```
import matplotlib.pyplot as plt

# plot
plt.style.use('default')
plt.figure(figsize=(11, 6))
plt.bar(df.names, df.scores)
plt.xticks(rotation=90, fontsize=10) # very small
```

(continues on next page)

(continued from previous page)

```
plt.xlim(-1, len(names)) # 80
plt.grid(color='grey', linestyle='--',
        linewidth=1, alpha=0.5)
plt.title('Trading Competition 2021 Score board',
         fontsize=16)
plt.ylabel('score')
plt.show()
```

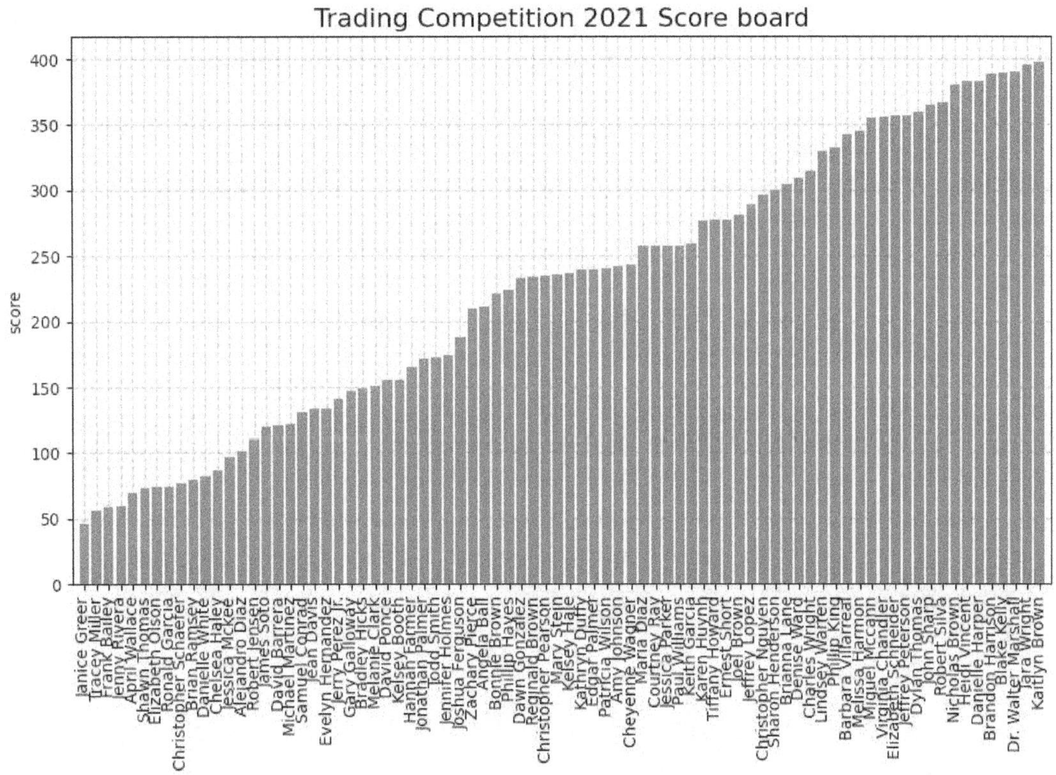

Changing the size of the graph has improved its readability, however by switching the orientation the readability and extendability might be improved even further.

24.7 Change the orientation of the Chart

In some cases, when we have many categories, it is better to change the orientation of the chart.

We can increase the height of the graph, by making use of the `figure()` method and passing in a second parameter for the chart size. The method has the following signature:

```
plt.figure(figsize=(15,10))
```

Additionally, the orientation can be changed with the `rotation` parameter, like so:

```
plt.xticks(rotation=90)
```

The changed orientation displays the names on the vertical axis and the scores on the horizontal axis, which allows us to accommodate a large number of names on the vertical axis. In the following Python code segment, we implement this idea:

```
import matplotlib.pyplot as plt

# plot
plt.style.use("default")
plt.figure(figsize=(10,17)) # inches
plt.barh(df.names, df.scores)
plt.xticks(rotation=0)
plt.ylim(-1, len(names) + 0.5)
plt.grid(linewidth=1, color="black",
         linestyle="--", alpha=0.3)
plt.title("Trading Competition 2021, score board",
          fontsize=16)
plt.grid(True)
plt.tight_layout = True
plt.xlabel("score")
plt.show()
```

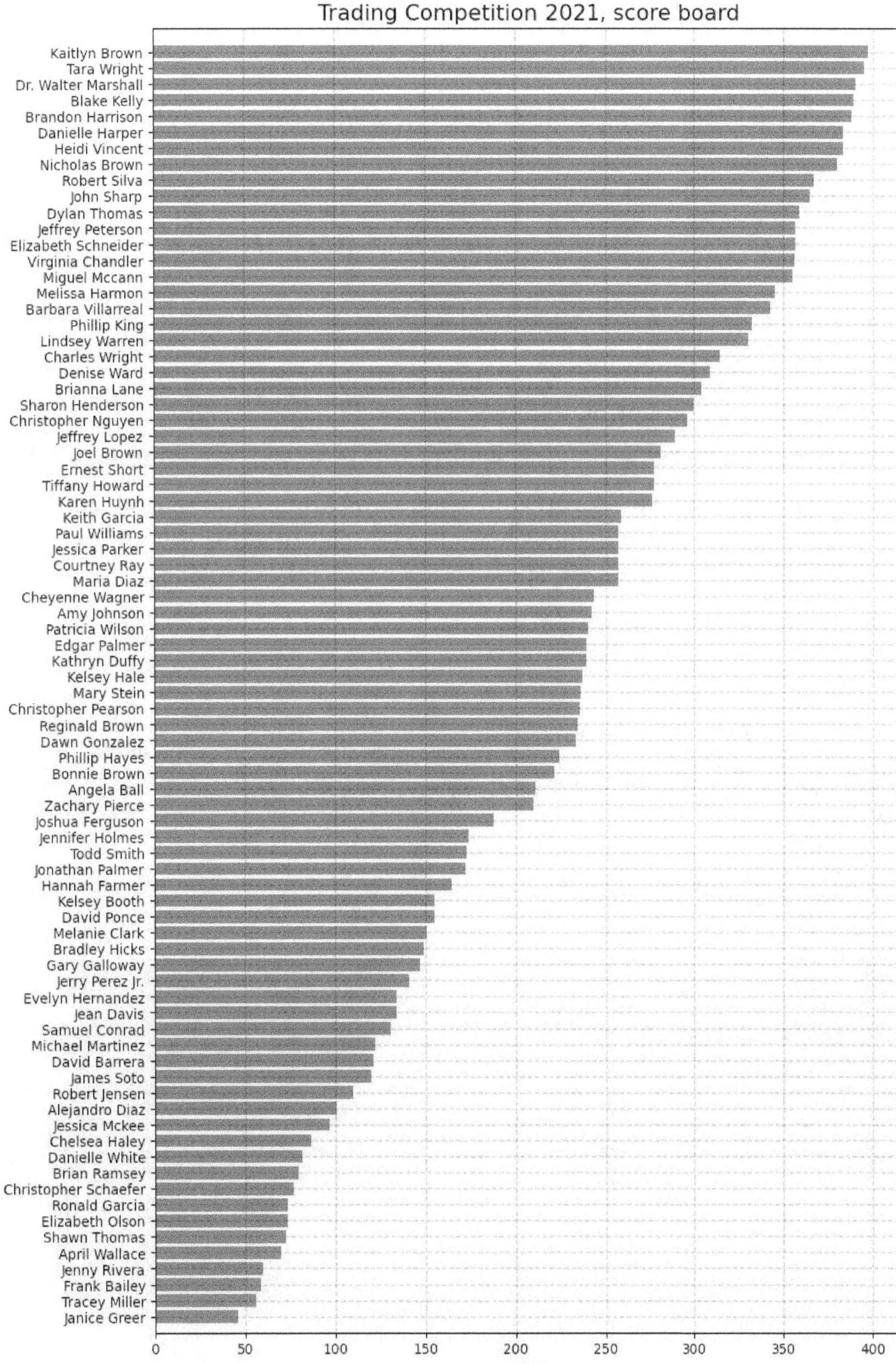

This changed orientation enables us to fit many more names to be properly displayed in a single plot.

24.8 Change the Figsize in Subplots

We can create multiple subplots in a single figure.

```
fig, (ax1,ax2) = plt.subplots(nrows=1, ncols=2, figsize=(10,3))
```

where

- `nrows`: the number of rows
- `ncols`: the number of columns
- `figsize`: is a tuple (height, width), this is shared among the subplots.

We set up subplots with 1 row and 2 columns and an overall figure size of 10 inches in width and 3 inches in height. The overall chart dimension is shared among the two individual charts.

```
import matplotlib.pyplot as plt

# data
x = range(10)
y = [i * i for i in range(10)]
# plot, subplots with 1 row and 2 cols.
fig, (ax1, ax2) = plt.subplots(nrows=1, ncols=2, figsize=(10,3.5))
ax1.plot(x, y)
ax1.grid()
ax1.set_title(f"$y(x)=x^2 \\:\\: x \\in [0,10]$")
ax1.set_xlabel("steps")
ax1.set_ylabel("continuous values")
ax2.bar(x, y)
ax2.grid()
ax2.set_title("Bar Chart")
ax2.set_xlabel("steps")
ax2.set_ylabel("discrete values")
plt.show()
```

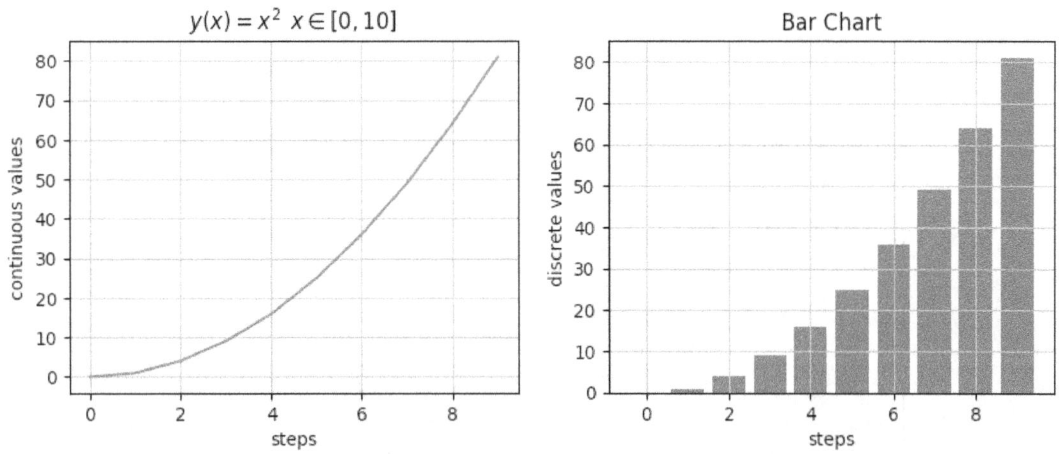

24.9 Set the figure size in pixels instead of inches

We want to set the size of a figure or chart in pixels. For that, we define the dots per inch (dpi=120) and set the number of pixels (640px) to arrive at the proper input (640/dpi) for the figsize attributes. Like so:

```
fig = plt.figure(figsize=(640/dpi,480/dpi), dpi=dpi)
```

```
import matplotlib.pyplot as plt

# data
x = [1, 2, 3, 4, 5, 6, 7, 8, 9, 10]
y = [10, 9, 8, 7, 6, 5, 4, 3, 2, 1]
# plot
dpi = 120
fig = plt.figure(figsize=(640 / dpi, 480 / dpi), dpi=dpi)
plt.bar(x, y, align="center")
plt.title("Bar chart, 640x480px, 120dpi", fontsize=12)
plt.xlabel("steps")
plt.ylabel("counts")
plt.grid()
plt.show()
```

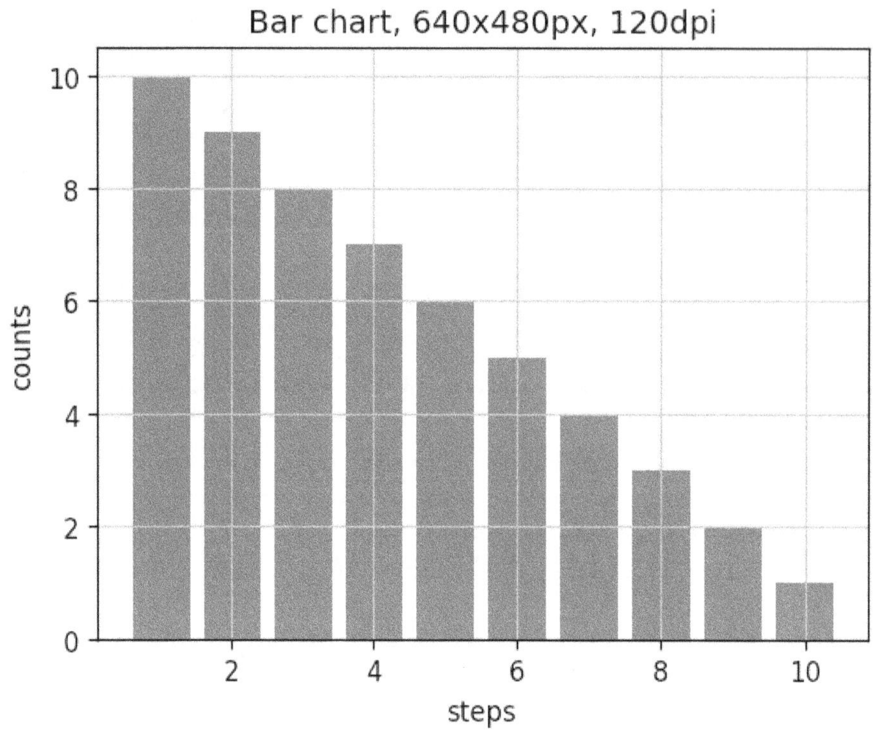

24.10 Choose a pre-defined style for the Charts

According to John Hunter [2012] there and many options to style and customize any given chart. To obtain a list of pre-defined style definitions, we can list them like so:

```
print(plt.style.available)
```

To demonstrate this we assign the style randomly to the subsequent plot and inspect the result. The function to randomly choose a style has the following signature:

```
choice = np.random.choice(plt.style.available)
print('choice:', choice)
plt.style.use(choice)
```

In Python code, we implement this approach, of selecting a pre-defined style at random, and visualize the results.

```
import numpy as np
import matplotlib.pyplot as plt

# style at random
```

(continues on next page)

(continued from previous page)

```
choice = np.random.choice(plt.style.available)
plt.style.use(choice)
# data
x = range(10)
y = [i * i for i in range(10)]
# plot
fig, (ax1, ax2) = plt.subplots(nrows=1,
                              ncols=2, figsize=(12,3.5))
ax1.plot(x, y)
ax1.grid()
ax1.set_title("Line Chart")
ax1.set_xlabel("steps")
ax1.set_ylabel("counts")
ax2.bar(x, y)
ax2.grid()
ax2.set_title("Bar Chart")
ax2.set_xlabel("steps")
ax2.set_ylabel("counts")
plt.show()
# set back to default
plt.style.use("default")
print("random style:", choice)
```

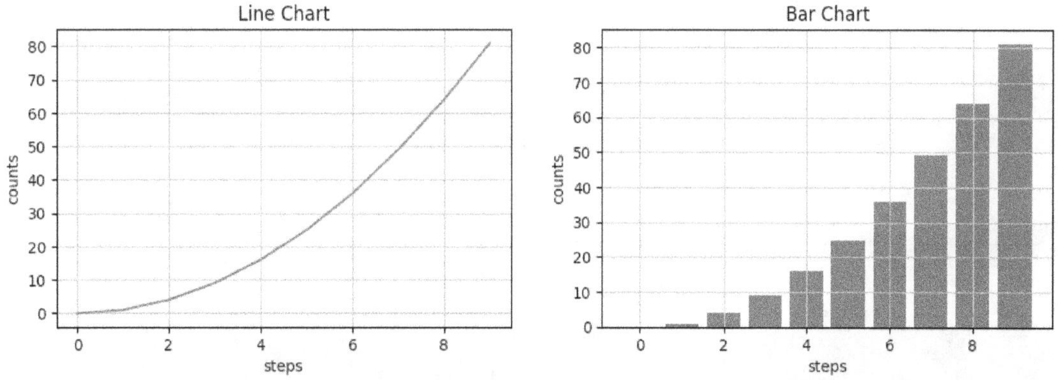


```
random style: seaborn-v0_8-colorblind
```

CHAPTER 25

RECEIVER OPERATING CHARACTERISTICS

Logistic Regression is a statistical method that we use to fit a regression model when the response variable is binary. To assess how well a logistic regression model fits a dataset, we can look at the sensitivity and specificity and plot them. This plot is called the Receiver Operating Characteristic curve or ROC curve for short.

The term `Sensitivity` refers to the probability that the model predicts a positive outcome for an observation when the outcome is indeed positive, and the term `Specificity` refers to the probability that the model predicts a negative outcome for an observation when the outcome is indeed negative.

A way to visualize these two metrics we can create an `ROC curve`, which is a plot that displays the sensitivity and specificity of the logistic regression model under consideration. Fawcett [2003].

25.1 Create a ROC Curve

Once we have computed the model fit for a logistic regression model, we can use the resulting regression equation to classify the observations from the testing data set into categories, to access the classification performance of the model.

The regression equation is defined as:

$$y = b_0 + b_1 \cdot A + b_2 \cdot B + b_3 \cdot C + \epsilon$$

where

- A is the first independent variable
- B is the second independent variable
- C is the third independent variable
- y is the binary response variable
- ϵ is the random error term

The true positive rate represents the proportion of observations that are predicted to be positive when indeed they are positive.

Conversely, the false positive rate represents the proportion of observations that are predicted to be positive when they are negative.

In the ROC curve, we plot pairs of the sensitivity (true positive rate) versus the specificity (false positive rate) for every possible decision threshold of a logistic regression model under consideration.

The outcome of this procedure is the Receiver Operating Characteristics or for short the ROC curve. In the following Python code segment this idea is implemented and the resulting plot is interpreted.

```
import pandas as pd
import matplotlib.pyplot as plt
import math
import numpy as np

# data
x, y = [], []
N = 80
for i in np.linspace(0, 1, N):
    x.append(float(i))
    y.append(1.0 - math.exp(-i * N / 8))
# DataFrame
df = pd.DataFrame({"specificity": x,
                   "sensitivity": y,
                   "diagonal_line": np.linspace(0, 1, N)})
# plot
fig = plt.figure(figsize=(8, 5))
plt.ylabel("True positive rate (sensitivity)")
plt.xlabel("False positive rate (1 - specificity)")
plt.xlim(0) # start at zero
txt = f"Receiver Operating Characteristics (ROC)"
plt.title(txt, fontsize=12)
plt.annotate("Area under the curve AUC",
             xy=(1,1), xytext=(0.15,0.65), fontsize=12)
plt.grid(linestyle="--")
plt.plot(df.specificity, df.sensitivity, linewidth=4)
plt.plot(df.specificity,df.diagonal_line,
```

(continues on next page)

(continued from previous page)

```
        linestyle=":",color="grey",linewidth=3)
plt.fill_between(df.specificity, df.sensitivity, alpha=0.1)
plt.show()
```

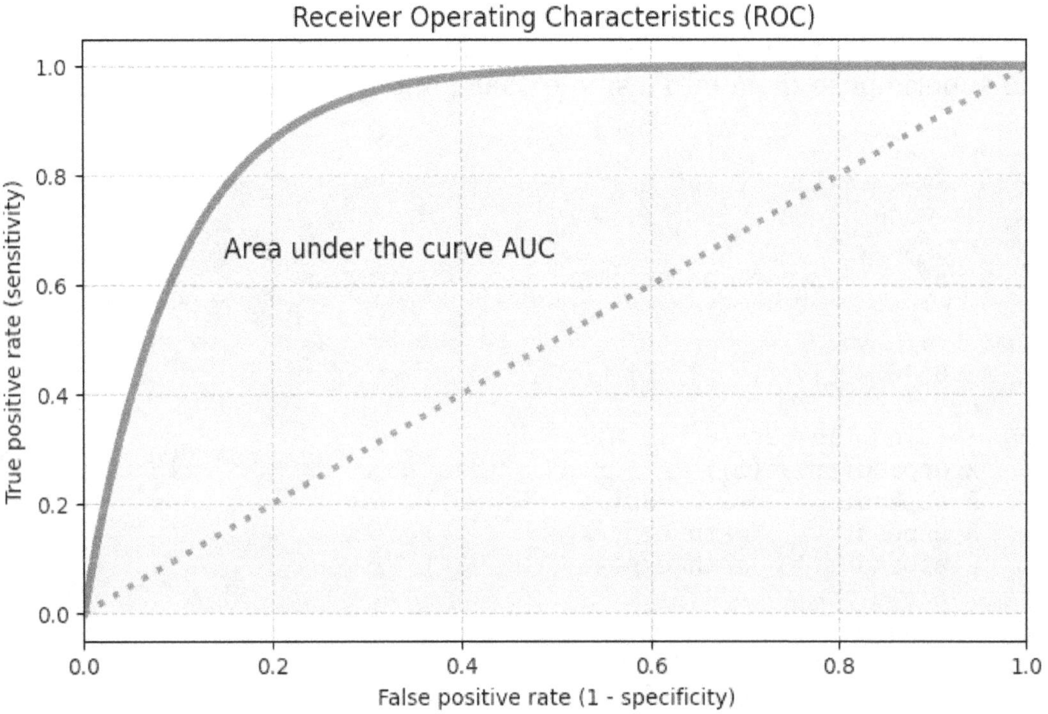

25.2 Interpreting the ROC Curve

The stronger the ROC curve reaches into the top left corner of the plot, the better the model does at classifying the data into the desired categories. To quantify this quality measure of the classification model, we can compute the area under the curve AUC.

The closer the AUC is to 1, the better the model is at classifying the data. A model with an AUC equal to 0.5 would be a perfectly diagonal line and it would represent a model that is no better than a model that makes random classifications.

As pointed out by Chire [2023], it is especially useful to calculate the AUC for multiple logistic regression models, and to compare the results. We can access the quality of different models, by visually inspecting the ROC curve and choosing the best model, with the highest area under the curve AUC value, for making actual predictions.

25.3 Comparing three logistic regression models

We fit 3 different logistic regression models and evaluate the classification competence of each model. A measure of competence is the area under the curve AUC.

To visualize their performance, we plot the ROC curve for each of the models and superimpose them into a single chart, and in Python, we implement:

```
import pandas as pd
import matplotlib.pyplot as plt
import math
import numpy as np
from quantlib import print_img

# generate data
x, A, B, C = [], [], [], []
N = 80
for i in np.linspace(0, 1, N):
    x.append(float(i))
    A.append(1.0 - math.exp(-i * N / 2))
    B.append(1.0 - math.exp(-i * N / 9))
    C.append(1.0 - math.exp(-i * N / 20))
# DataFrame
df = pd.DataFrame({
        "specificity": x,
        "sensitivity_A": A,
        "sensitivity_B": B,
        "sensitivity_C": C,
        "diagonal_line": np.linspace(0, 1, N),})
# plot
fig = plt.figure(figsize=(8,6))
plt.ylabel("True positive rate (sensitivity)")
plt.xlabel("False positive rate (1 - specificity)")
plt.xlim(0)  # start at zero
txt = "Receiver Operating Characteristic (ROC)"
plt.title(txt, fontsize=12)
plt.grid(linestyle="--")
plt.plot(df.specificity,
         df.sensitivity_A, linewidth=4)
plt.plot(df.specificity,
         df.sensitivity_B, linewidth=4)
plt.plot(df.specificity,
         df.sensitivity_C, linewidth=4)
plt.legend(["ROC A", "ROC B", "ROC C"])
plt.plot(df.specificity,
         df.diagonal_line,
         linestyle=":", color="grey",
         alpha=0.5, linewidth=3)
plt.show()
```

(continues on next page)

(continued from previous page)

```
# inspect
df2 = df.head().to_string(index=False)
print_img(df2)
print()
```

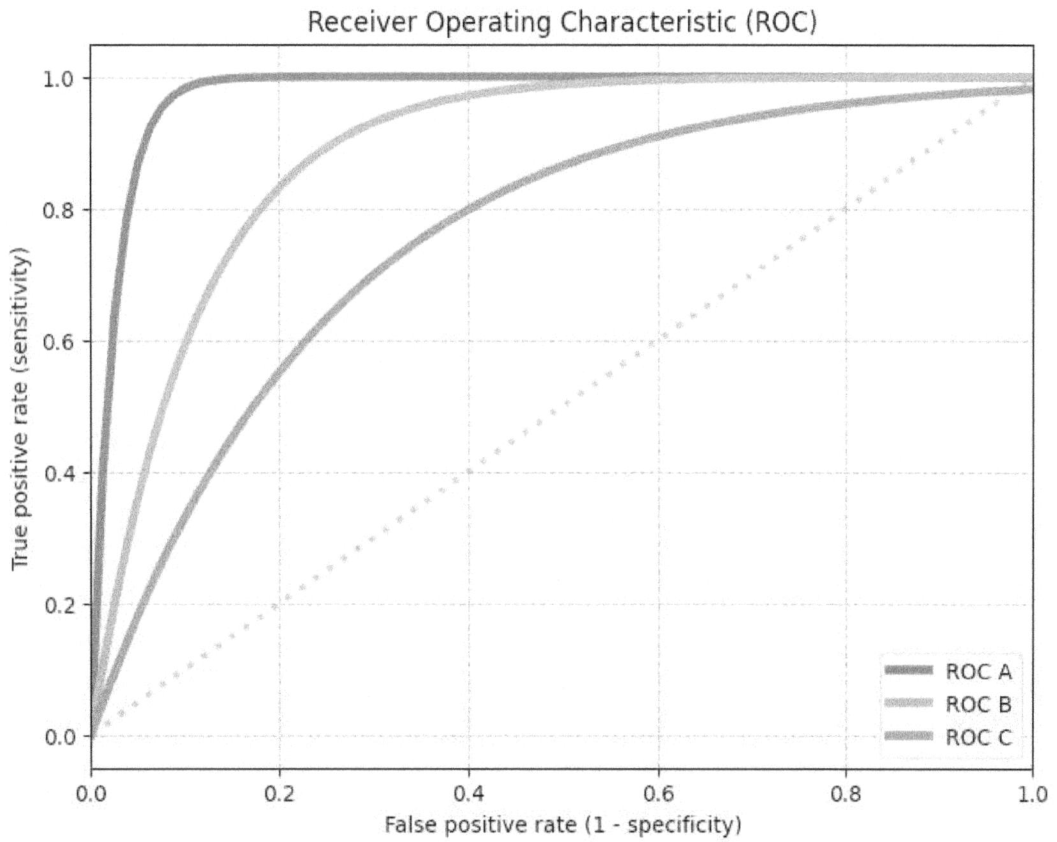

specificity	sensitivity_A	sensitivity_B	sensitivity_C	diagonal_line
0.000000	0.000000	0.000000	0.000000	0.000000
0.012658	0.397296	0.106418	0.049372	0.012658
0.025316	0.636748	0.201512	0.096307	0.025316
0.037975	0.781067	0.286486	0.140925	0.037975
0.050633	0.868048	0.362417	0.183339	0.050633

The ROC curves reveal the most promising model. As a quantitative measure, we compute the area under the curve AUC for each model, and the results are presented below.

- Model A : AUC = 0.923
- Model B : AUC = 0.794
- Model C : AUC = 0.588

Interpretation

Model A has the highest AUC of 0.923, therefore we conclude that this model has the highest competence in correctly classifying the presented observations into the desired categories.

Of course, the astute scientist needs to evaluate additional quality measures to arrive at a solid assessment of the model's competence.

CHAPTER 26

CREATE PLOTS FROM PANDAS DATAFRAMES

The Pandas DataFrame has substantial built-in plotting and charting capabilities, and here we demonstrate a few of them.

In the following sections, we demonstrate:

- Plot a histogram of a single column of the DataFrame
- Plot multiple columns of a DataFrame
- Horizontal Chart of a single column of the DataFrame
- Line Chart of the column of the DataFrame
- Box Plots from three columns of a DataFrame

26.1 Prepare sample dataset

We can use the `hist()` function from the Pandas DataFrame object, which has the following signatures:

```
df.hist(column='col_name')
```

where the `column` parameter is set to the desired column name, from which we want to draw the histogram.

To demonstrate the use of the Faker library for generating a sample data set, we first employ the Numpy random number generator to produce lists of random integers within a given range. Secondly, we instantiate a faker object, to produce a list of N random names.

In the following Python code segment, we demonstrate the usage of the Faker library to generate fake data items, like so:

Before you use the `hist()` function, we might want to bring up the documentation and review the usage.

```
import pandas as pd
# help(pd.DataFrame().hist)
# print(pd.DataFrame().hist.__doc__[:700]) # beginning only
```

```
import numpy as np
import pandas as pd
from faker import Faker

# parameters
N = 20
# Faker object
fake = Faker()
names = []
for _ in range(N):
    names.append(fake.name()) # N random names
np.random.seed(1) # reproducibility
df = pd.DataFrame({'months': range(N),
                   'names': names,
                   'points': np.random.randint(10, 23, N),
                   'revenues': sorted(np.random.randint(4, 19, N)),
                   'units': np.random.randint(5, 11, N)})
# results
print('dataset:')
print(df)
print(df.shape)
```

```
dataset:
    months              names  points  revenues  units
0        0       Teresa Davis      15         4     10
1        1   Michael Anderson      21         5      6
2        2      Robin Bennett      22         6      6
3        3     Cristina Stark      18         8      5
4        4         Mary Snow      19        10      9
5        5     Michael Gross      21        11      6
6        6   Joshua Martinez      15        11      5
7        7     Blake Schmidt      10        11      5
8        8        Paul Taylor      10        11     10
9        9       Bradley Cole      11        13      8
10      10        Cody Clark      22        13      7
11      11     Connie Bryant      17        13      6
12      12      Gary Mcdonald      22        14      5
```

(continues on next page)

(continued from previous page)

```
13      13          Andrew Weaver      16        15     8
14      14        Courtney Gamble      19        16    10
15      15   Christopher Campbell      12        16     6
16      16        Raymond Sanders      14        17     6
17      17            Anita Avila      15        17     8
18      18             Nancy Ryan      12        18     9
19      19         Matthew Duncan      14        18     5
(20, 5)
```

26.2 Plot histogram from a single column

In the following example, we demonstrate the creation of a histogram chart, directly from a specific column in a Pandas DataFrame. The `hist()` method is part of the DataFrame object and has this signature:

```
df.hist(column='points', rwidth=.9, ax=ax1)
```

where:

- `column`: is set to the points column as input data
- `rwidth`: parameter to set the width of the bars
- `ax`: is set to ax1, representing an axis object where to render the output in

```
import matplotlib.pyplot as plt

# plot
fig = plt.figure(figsize=(6,3))
ax1 = fig.add_subplot()
ax1.set_xlabel('points')
ax1.set_ylabel('frequency of points')
df.hist(column='points',
        rwidth=.9,
        ax=ax1)
plt.show()
```

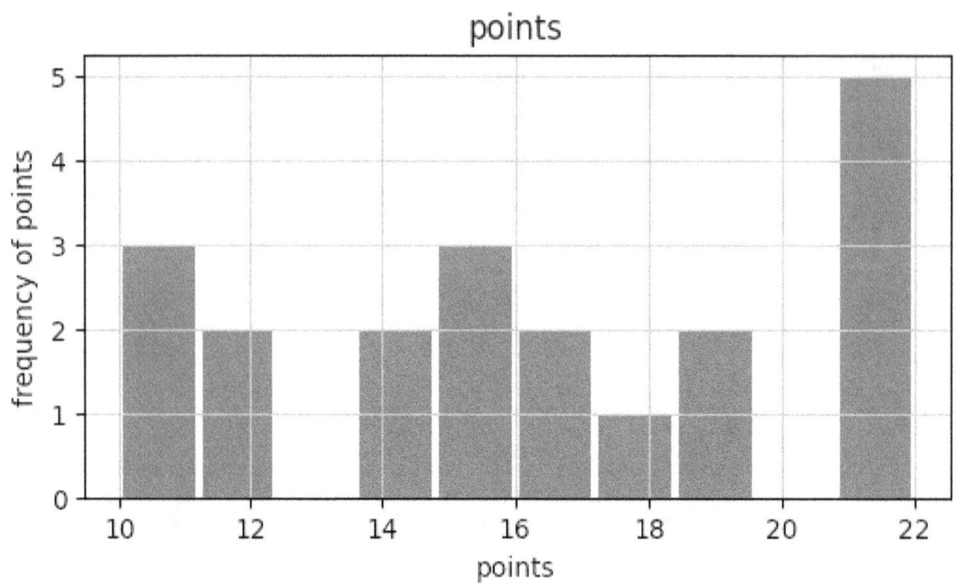

26.3 Plot histogram from multiple columns

By passing into the `hist()` method a list of column names, we can produce multiple charts at the same time. This can be achieved like so:

```
df.hist(column=['points','units'], rwidth=.9, ax=ax1)
```

Observe that we passed in as a parameter a list containing for example ['points','units']. Additionally, we make use of the `subplots()` method to create two plots side-by-side, like so:

```
fig, ax = plt.subplots(nrows=1, ncols=2, figsize=(8,3))
```

where

- `nrows`: the number of rows in the chart canvas
- `ncols`: the number of columns per row

Note that the figure size is shared among all of the sub-charts.

```
import matplotlib.pyplot as plt
import warnings
warnings.filterwarnings('ignore')
%matplotlib inline

# plot
fig, ax = plt.subplots(nrows=1, ncols=2, figsize=(8,3))
```

(continues on next page)

(continued from previous page)

```
df.hist(column=['points', 'units'],
        rwidth=.9,
        ax=ax)
ax[0].set_xlabel('points bin')
ax[0].set_ylabel('count')
ax[1].set_xlabel('units bin')
ax[1].set_ylabel('count')
plt.show()
```

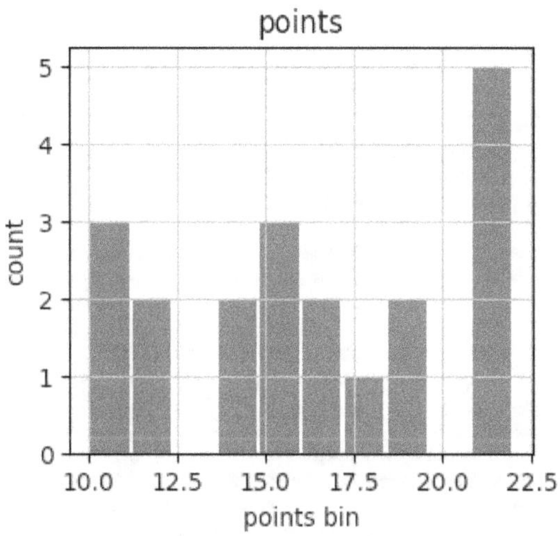

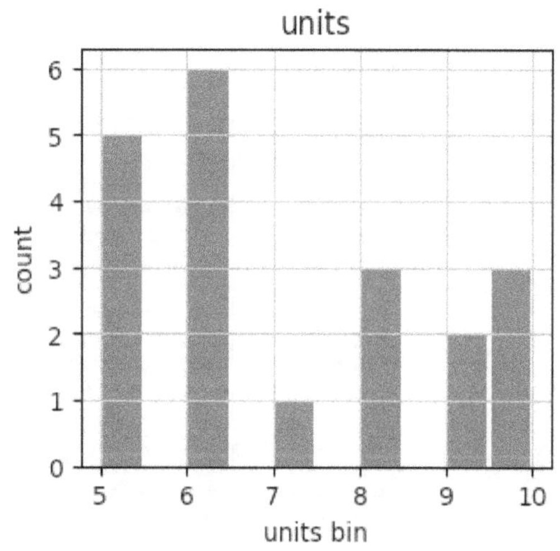

26.4 Horizontal histogram of two columns

According to PandasDocs [2023], the Pandas DataFrame has built-in facilities to plot bar charts and histograms. We make use of the `plot.barh()` method, which means that we want a horizontally oriented chart, with the `names` on the y-axis and the `points` on the x-axis.

```
df.plot.barh(x='names', y='points', color='grey', ax=ax1)
```

where

- `x`: the data source for the x-axis, we set this parameter to names
- `y`: the data source for the y-axis, we set this parameter to points
- `color`: denotes the color of the bars, which we set to grey
- `ax`: is the axis object, in which the output is rendered

Notice the `ax1` parameter argument tells the plot method to output the chart into the prepared axis object.

```
import matplotlib.pyplot as plt

# plot
fig = plt.figure(figsize=(8,4.5))
ax1 = fig.add_subplot()
df.plot.barh(x='names', y='points', color='grey', ax=ax1)
ax1.set_xlabel('points')
ax1.set_ylabel('names')
plt.title('Points per Employee', fontsize=12)
plt.grid(True)
plt.show()
```

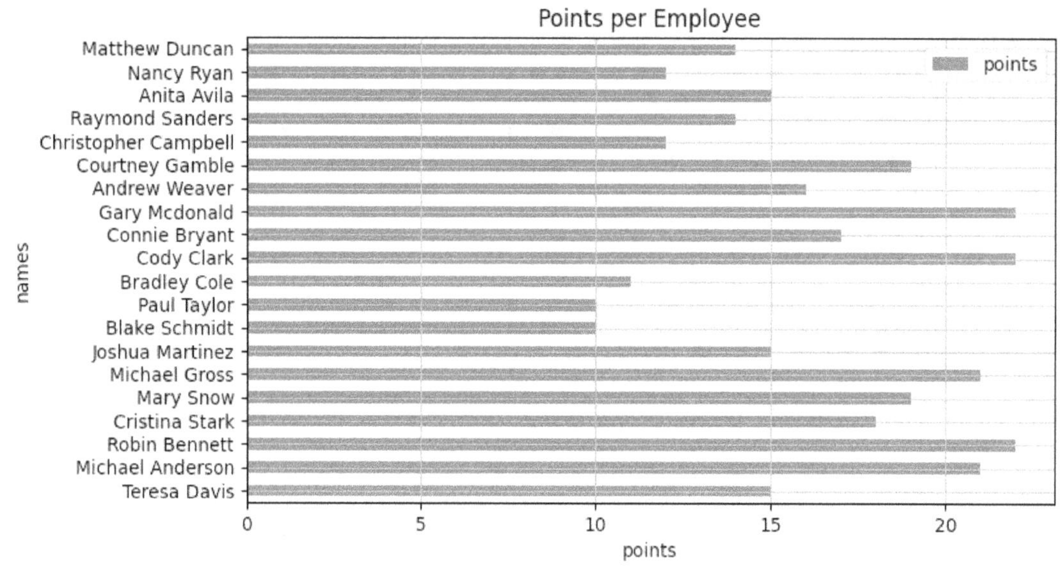

26.5 Line Chart of two columns

```
df.plot.line(x='months', y='revenues', color='maroon', ax=ax1)
```

where

- x: source data for the x-axis
- y: source data for the y-axis
- color: denotes the color of the bars, which we set to maroon
- ax: is the axis object, in which the output is rendered

```
import matplotlib.pyplot as plt

# plot
```

(continues on next page)

(continued from previous page)

```
fig = plt.figure(figsize=(6, 2.5))
ax1 = fig.add_subplot()
df.plot.line(x='months', y='revenues', color='maroon', ax=ax1)
ax1.set_xlabel('month')
ax1.set_ylabel('revenue')
plt.title('Cumulative revenue', fontsize=14)
plt.grid(True)
plt.show()
```

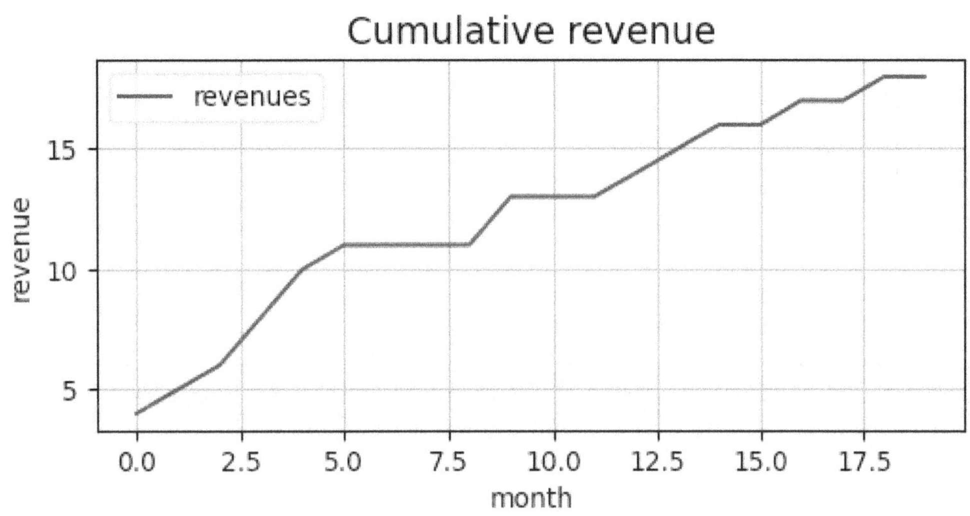

26.6 Box Plots from three columns

As highlighted in PandasDocs [2023], we demonstrate the creation of a Box plot from multiple DataFrame columns. For that, we make use of the slice [] operator to select the column names for which a box plot is to be shown. The signature of this method becomes:

```
df[['points','units','revenues']].plot.box(ax=ax1)
```

where

- df: the Pandas DataFrame containing the data with the slice [] operator applied
- ax: is set to ax1, an already existing axis object

```
import matplotlib.pyplot as plt

# plot
fig = plt.figure(figsize=(6,2.5))
```

(continues on next page)

(continued from previous page)

```
ax1 = fig.add_subplot()
df[['points', 'units', 'revenues']].plot.box(ax=ax1)
ax1.set_ylabel('values')
plt.title('Box plots', fontsize=14)
plt.grid(True, linestyle='--')
plt.show()
```

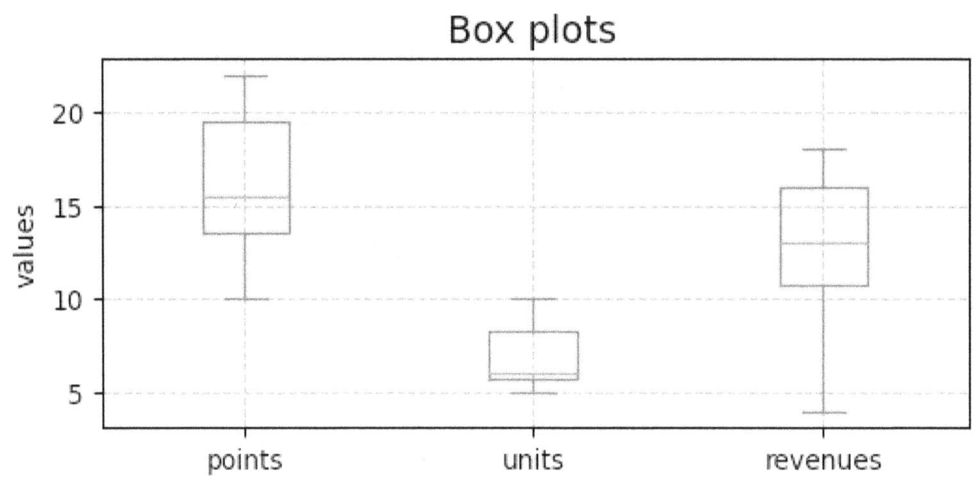

26.7 Three charts side-by-side using subplots

As described in John Hunter [2012], we make use of subplots to display three charts side-by-side in a single plot. The method has the following signature:

```
plt.subplot(nrows, ncols, index)
```

where

- rows: the number of rows in the resulting plot
- ncols: the number of columns in the resulting plot
- index: denotes the current plot area which receives the output

```
import numpy as np
import matplotlib.pyplot as plt
import pandas as pd

# data
x1 = np.linspace(0.0, 5.0)
y1 = np.cos(2 * np.pi * x1) * np.exp(-x1)
x2 = np.linspace(0.0, 2.0)
y2 = np.cos(2 * np.pi * x2)
```

(continues on next page)

(continued from previous page)

```
x3 = np.linspace(0.0, 2.0)
y3 = np.tanh(2 * np.pi * x2)
df = pd.DataFrame({'x1':x1, 'y1':y1, 'x2':x2,
                   'y2':y2, 'x3':x3, 'y3':y3})
# plot
fig = plt.figure(figsize=(10,4))
# subplots( rows, cols, current 1)
plt.subplot(1, 3, 1)
plt.plot(df.x1,
         df.y1,
         'ko-')
plt.ylabel('Damped oscillation')
plt.title('Subplot 1 of 3', fontsize=12)
plt.grid(True)
# subplots( rows, cols, current 2)
plt.subplot(1, 3, 2)
plt.plot(df.x2,
         df.y2,
         'r.-')
plt.xlabel('time (s)')
plt.ylabel('Undamped oscillation')
plt.title('Subplot 2 of 3', fontsize=12)
plt.grid(True)
# subplots( rows, cols, current 3)
plt.subplot(1, 3, 3)
plt.plot(df.x3,
         df.y3,
         'g.-')
plt.xlabel('time (s)')
plt.ylabel('Undamped oscillation')
plt.grid(True)
plt.title('Subplot 3 of 3', fontsize=12)
plt.show()
# inspect
print('dataset:')
print(df.head())
```

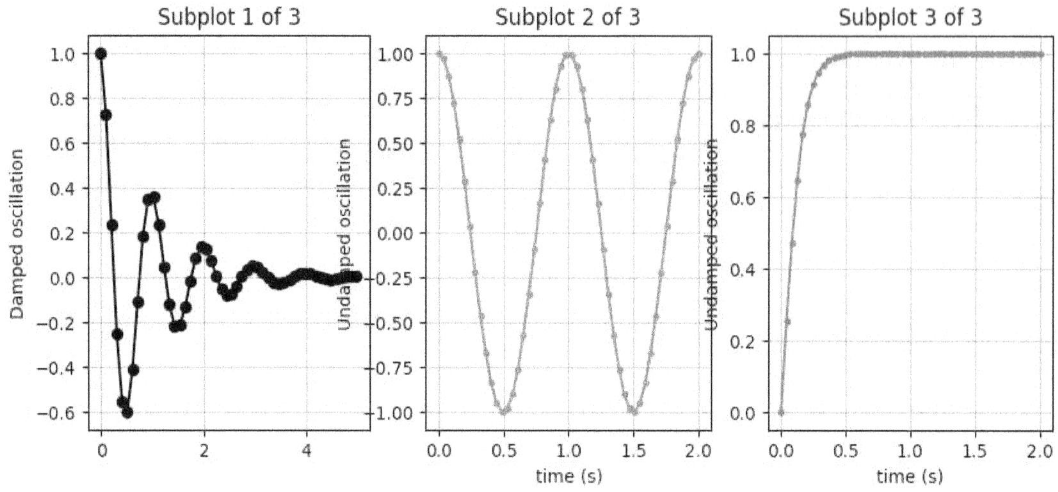


```
dataset:
         x1        y1        x2        y2        x3        y3
0  0.000000  1.000000  0.000000  1.000000  0.000000  0.000000
1  0.102041  0.723671  0.040816  0.967295  0.040816  0.250978
2  0.204082  0.232003  0.081633  0.871319  0.081633  0.472212
3  0.306122 -0.254291  0.122449  0.718349  0.122449  0.646563
4  0.408163 -0.557220  0.163265  0.518393  0.163265  0.772229
```

CHAPTER 27

VISUALIZE DIABETES DATASET

Visualizing the data is almost always the first step. Visual inspection of the data allows the quant analyst to gain some intuition about the data.

- creating a Pandas DataFrame with column names
- creating multiple Histograms plots
- creating grouped Histograms plots
- creating a Scatter matrix plots

```
import requests
import pandas as pd
import numpy as np
import matplotlib.pyplot as plt
%matplotlib inline

print('panda version:', pd.__version__)
print('numpy version:', np.__version__)
```

```
panda version: 1.5.2
numpy version: 1.22.4
```

> According to Smith J.W. [1988], the Pima Indians Diabetes dataset consists of several medical predictor variables and a class for the response variable. The data set contains 768 rows in 9 columns.

We demonstrate how to obtain the Pima Indians Diabetes dataset from an online resource, however, we make use of a local version of the dataset to study several aspects of data visualization.

```
from os import path

# parameters
url = '''https://raw.githubusercontent.com/
       jbrownlee/Datasets/master/pima-indians-diabetes.data.csv'''
target_file = "data/pima-indians-diabetes.data"
# checking
if not path.exists(target_file):
    try:
        print('attempting to download...')
        response = requests.get(url)
        response.raise_for_status()
        print(response.status_code)
        # save to local file
        with open(target_file, "wb") as f:
            f.write(response.content)
        print("download ok")
    except Exception as e:
        print(e)
else:
    print('file already downloaded')

print('using local file:', target_file)
```

```
file already downloaded
using local file: data/pima-indians-diabetes.data
```

27.1 Inspect the dataset

The first step in data analysis is to familiarize ourselves with the data set. For example, the `head()` function lists the first N records of the dataset, and the `tail()` function does the same with the last N records.

```
dataDf.head(N)
```

With the `describe()` method, a data summary is computed for all data columns. This summary report has this signature:

```
print(dataDf.describe().applymap(lambda x: f"{x:0.2f}"))
```

This function returns a summary table consisting of:

- `count`: the number of observations in the dataset
- `mean`: the expected value or average for each column
- `std`: the standard deviation for each column

- `min`: the smallest value in each column
- `25%`: the 25 percentile for each column
- `50%`: the 25 percentile for each column
- `75%`: the 25 percentile for each column
- `max`: the largest value in each column

Note that the output of reported floating point values can be formatted using the `applymap()` function, like so:

```
.applymap(lambda x: f"{x:0.2f}")
```

We load the local data file into a Pandas DataFrame using the `read_csv()` function available on the DataFrame object, which has this signature:

```
dataDf = pd.read_csv('data/pima-indians-diabetes.data', names=names)
```

Observe that we use the `names` parameter, to specify the names of the columns while reading the the dataset. This is often very helpful if the data set contains illegal column names, which can be corrected by supplying a `list()` of valid new names while creating the DataFrame.

```
import pandas as pd

# column names
names = ['preg', 'plas', 'pres', 'skin',
         'test', 'mass', 'pedi', 'age', 'class']
# DataFrame
dataDf = pd.read_csv('data/pima-indians-diabetes.data',
                     names=names)
# inspect
print('dataset:')
print(dataDf.head())
print()
print('describe:')
print(dataDf.describe().applymap(lambda x: f"{x:0.0f}"))
```

```
dataset:
   preg  plas  pres  skin  test  mass   pedi  age  class
0     6   148    72    35     0  33.6  0.627   50      1
1     1    85    66    29     0  26.6  0.351   31      0
2     8   183    64     0     0  23.3  0.672   32      1
3     1    89    66    23    94  28.1  0.167   21      0
4     0   137    40    35   168  43.1  2.288   33      1

describe:
      preg plas pres skin test mass pedi  age class
count  768  768  768  768  768  768  768  768   768
```

(continues on next page)

(continued from previous page)

```
mean     4  121   69   21   80   32   0  33   0
std      3   32   19   16  115    8   0  12   0
min      0    0    0    0    0    0   0  21   0
25%      1   99   62    0    0   27   0  24   0
50%      3  117   72   23   30   32   0  29   0
75%      6  140   80   32  127   37   1  41   1
max     17  199  122   99  846   67   2  81   1
```

Before we use the plot() function from the matplotlib library, we might want to bring up its documentation and review parameters and further options.

```
import matplotlib.pyplot as plt
# print(plt.__doc__)
```

27.2 Visualize the dataset with Box Plots

We make use of the boxplot() function from the Pylab library, which has this signature:

```
pylab.boxplot(dataDf, sym='')
```

where

- dataDF: is the DataFrame containing the dataset
- sym: indicates that we do not want to show outlier observation

In the following Python code segment this idea is implemented and resulting plots are produced.

```
import matplotlib.pyplot as plt
import pylab as pylab

# plot, without outliers
fig = plt.figure(figsize=(8,3))
pylab.boxplot(dataDf, sym='')
plt.title('Box plot without outliers', fontsize=14)
plt.grid(True)
plt.xlabel('class')
plt.ylabel('value')
plt.show()
# plot, with outliers
fig = plt.figure(figsize=(8,3))
pylab.boxplot(dataDf)
plt.title('Box plot with outliers', fontsize=14)
plt.grid(True)
```

(continues on next page)

(continued from previous page)

```
plt.xlabel('class')
plt.ylabel('value')
plt.show()
```

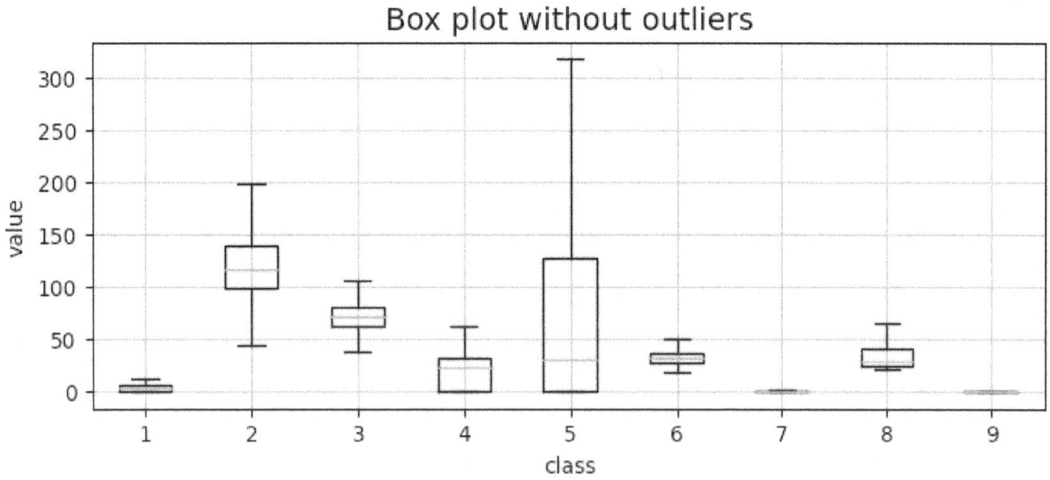

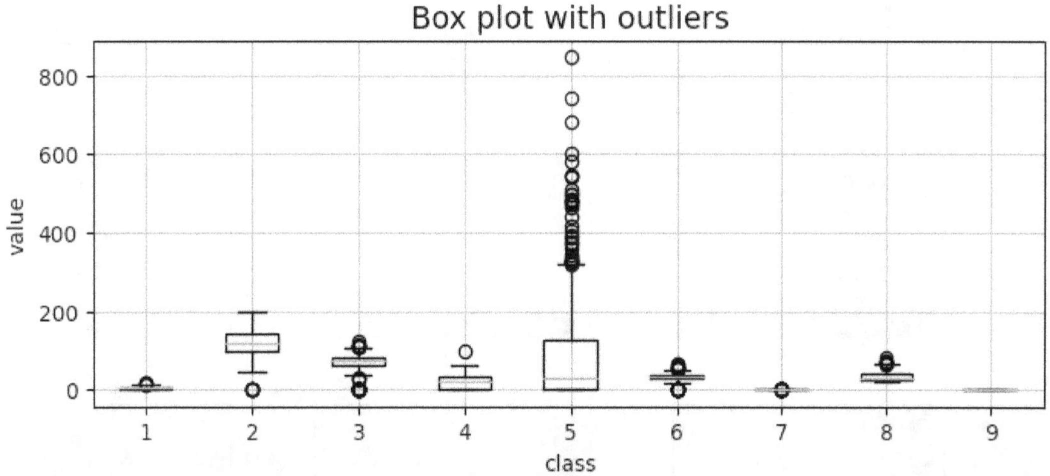

Interpretation

As demonstrated in the diagrams, by omitting the `sym` parameter, the outlier will be incorporated into the box plot, indicated by the black circles above and below the boxes.

27.3 Visualize with multiple histogram plots

Visualization of the dataset is often the first step in data analytics. Charts and plots help to better understand the data at hand. In the following example, we create a histogram chart, by making use of the built-in functionality of the Pandas DataFrame itself, and the signature of the `hist()` function is:

```
res = dataDf.hist(figsize=(10,8))
```

```
# histograms
res = dataDf.hist(figsize=(10,8))
plt.show()
```

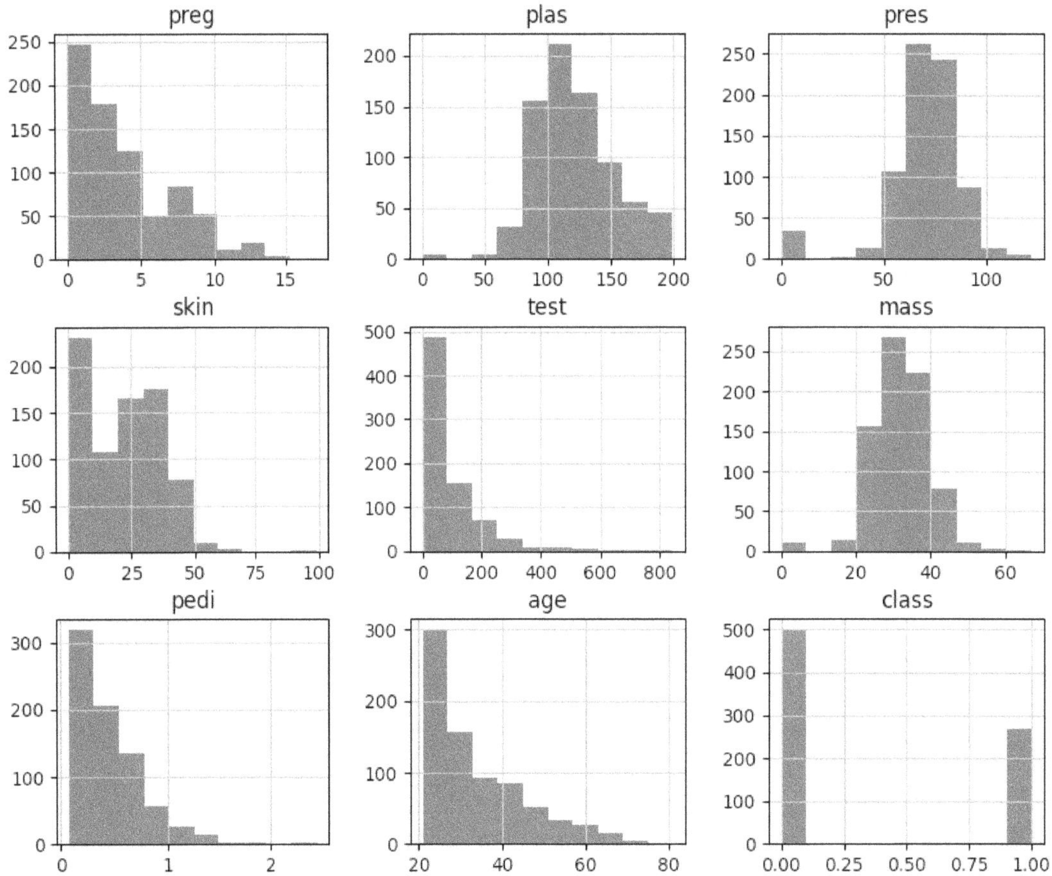

27.4 Extract a single plot from the scatter_matrix object

We can extract specific charts from the given chart matrix, by providing a columns parameter, like so:

```
res = dataDf.hist(column='pedi')
```

where

- `column`: is set to a specific chart name

It yields the specified chart. In the following code segment, we extract a single plot called the `pedi` chart.

```
# single histograms
res = dataDf.hist(column='pedi',
                  figsize=(4,3))
plt.show()
# inspect
print(res.shape)
```

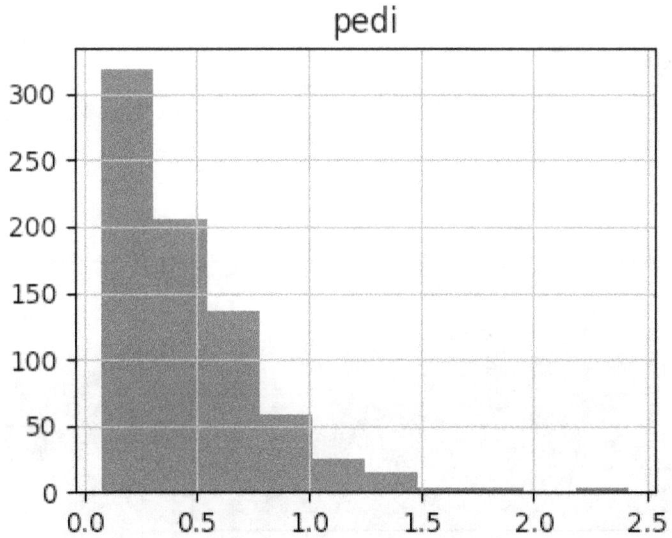


```
(1, 1)
```

27.5 Visualize with grouped histograms

An alternative visualization can be to compare two or more histograms in a single chart. In this way any similarities or differences become obvious. Creating grouped histograms can be obtained like so:

```
res = dataDf.groupby('class').plas.hist(alpha=0.8)
```

where dataDf is the DataFrame containing the sample data and the groupby() method is applied to specify the groupings of the data. The final hist() method produces the histogram plot.

In the following code example, this is demonstrated.

```
# plot
fig = plt.figure(figsize=(5,3))
res = dataDf.groupby('class').plas.hist(alpha=0.8)
plt.title('grouped histogram')
plt.show()
# inspect
print('describe:')
print(dataDf.groupby('class').plas.describe())
```

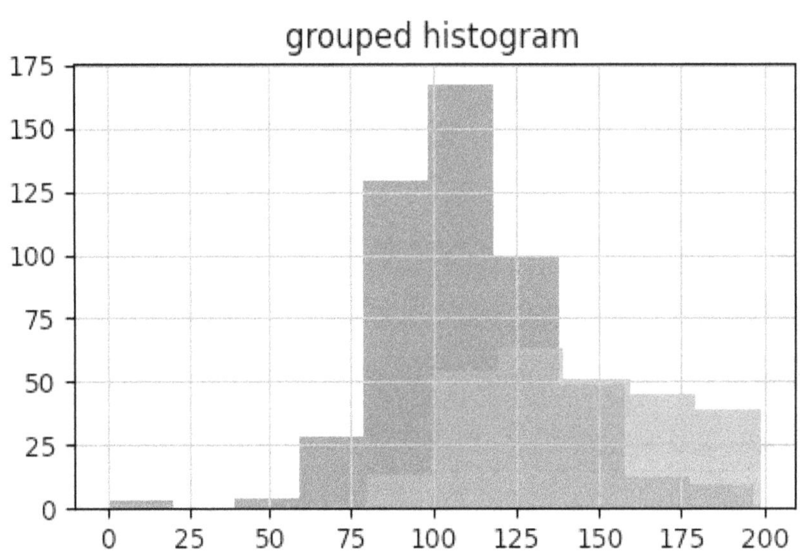


```
describe:
       count        mean        std  min    25%    50%    75%    max
class
0      500.0  109.980000  26.141200  0.0   93.0  107.0  125.0  197.0
1      268.0  141.257463  31.939622  0.0  119.0  140.0  167.0  199.0
```

Before using the scatter_matrix() method, we might want to bring up the relevant documentation and check the parameters and return values, as well as any extra requirements or limitations.

```
from pandas.plotting import scatter_matrix
# print(scatter_matrix.__doc__[:1080])
```

27.6 Visualize the dataset with a scatter matrix plot

The `scatter_matrix()` function is a convenience visualization tool, as part of the Pandas plotting module. To demonstrate we compute and visualize a partial scatter matrix, like so:

```
axs = scatter_matrix(dataDf[['preg','plas','pres','class']],
                     alpha=0.2, figsize=(8,7), diagonal='kde')
```

where

- `dataDf`: is the DataFrame containing the data sample
- `alpha`: the level of transparency of the diagrams
- `diagonal`: the parameter is set to estimate the kernel density function estimate (KDE)

Optional we can specify the diagonal parameter to `hist`, to show the small histograms in the diagonal elements. Further, notice that we select a subset by passing a list of names to the DataFrame. In the following Python code segment, we implement:

```
from pandas.plotting import scatter_matrix

# scatter plot
axs = scatter_matrix(dataDf[['preg', 'plas', 'pres',
                             'skin', 'class']],
                             alpha=0.2,
                             figsize=(8,6),
                             diagonal='kde')
plt.show()
# inspect
print('scatter matrix with KDE:')
print(axs.shape)
print(axs.diagonal())
```

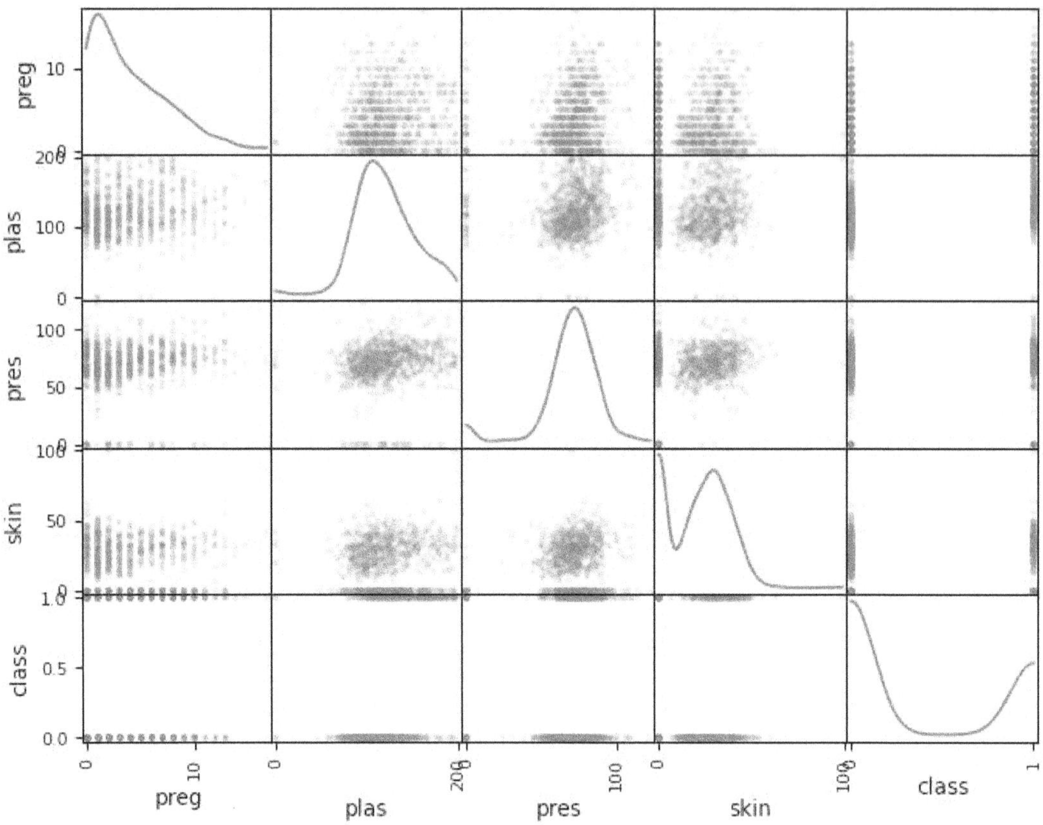


```
scatter matrix with KDE:
(5, 5)
[<AxesSubplot: xlabel='preg', ylabel='preg'>
 <AxesSubplot: xlabel='plas', ylabel='plas'>
 <AxesSubplot: xlabel='pres', ylabel='pres'>
 <AxesSubplot: xlabel='skin', ylabel='skin'>
 <AxesSubplot: xlabel='class', ylabel='class'>]
```

27.7 Extract a single plot from the scatter_matrix object

As noted by Deak [2017], we can extract a single kernel density estimate (KDE) out of the scatter matrix.

In the following example, we demonstrate this approach by extracting the first kernel density estimate chart. Then we access the underlying data (xd, yd) and place a marker for the nth data point onto the chart, like so:

```
import matplotlib.pyplot as plt
```

(continues on next page)

(continued from previous page)

```
N = 200 # data point
idx = 0 # first diagonal [0,0]
xd, yd = axs[idx,idx].get_lines()[0].get_data()
# plot
plt.figure(figsize=(4,3))
plt.grid()
plt.plot(xd,
         yd,
         '-')
plt.xlabel(dataDf.columns[idx])
plt.title("kernel density estimate KDE")
plt.text(xd[N]*0.921,
         yd[N]*0.921, "+",
         color='r',
         size=16)
plt.ylabel('estimated density')
plt.show()
# inspect
print('single KDE element:')
print('N  : {:.0f}'.format(N))
print('xd : {:.4f}'.format(xd[N]))
print('yd : {:.4f}'.format(yd[N]))
```

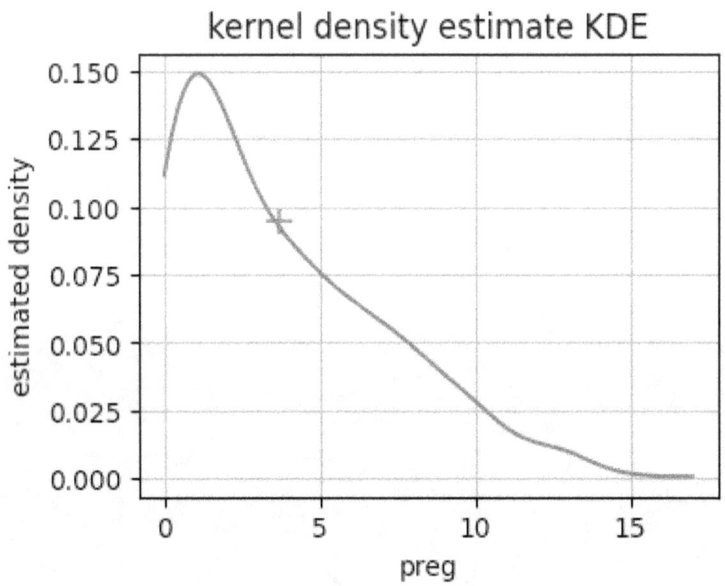


```
single KDE element:
N  : 200
xd : 3.4034
yd : 0.0977
```

Part III

Simple- & Multiple Linear Regression

CHAPTER 28

LINEAR REGRESSION MODELLING

Linear Regression Analysis is the workhorse of the quantitative discipline. We can quantitatively assess the strength of a linear relationship between one or multiple independent variables onto the dependent or target variable.

- Part I: Simple Linear Regression
- Part II: Multiple Linear Regression
- Part III: Multiple Linear Regression with scikit-learn
- Part IV: Categorical predictors

28.1 Part I: Simple Linear Regression

Simple linear regression is an approach for predicting a response variable by using a single feature or predictor variable as input.

Linear Regression model:

$$y_i = \beta_0 + \beta_1 \cdot x_i + \epsilon$$

where

- y_i: is the response variable
- x_i: is the feature variable

- β_0: is the intercept coefficient
- β_1: is the coefficient for the x feature variable
- ϵ: is the error or residual term

The β_0 and β_1 are called the model coefficients, which are to be estimated using the linear regression. Once we have estimated the coefficients, we can build the model equation, to forecast the future sales volume for a given set of new feature variable inputs.

28.1.1 Estimating model coefficients

The model coefficients (β_0, β_1) are estimated using the ordinary least squares method, which attempts to find the coefficients, in such a way, that it minimizes the sum of squared residuals, among the regression equation and the observed values. This results in the line of best fit.

The sum of squared residuals:

$$SS_{residuals} = \sum_{i=1}^{N}(\hat{y}_i - y_i)^2$$

where

- N: is the number of observation
- $\hat{y}_i$: is the value computed using the model
- y_i: is the current observation result

and

- $SS_{residuals}$: is the sum of squared residuals

28.1.2 Loading dataset

> The advertising dataset, lists 200 historical advertising budget figures for Ad spending in 3 different media channels, along with the corresponding Sales volume as target variable. The dataset was adapted from the version available at Ashish [2019], by reducing it to 200 records, deemed sufficient for this analysis.

We use linear regression analysis to study this reduced dataset, and in the first step, we load the data into a Pandas DataFrame for further processing and inspection.

```
import pandas as pd
import matplotlib.pyplot as plt
%matplotlib inline

# load dataset
data = pd.read_csv('data/advertising_200rows.csv')
# inspect
print('dataset:')
print(data.head())
print(data.shape)
```

```
dataset:
      TV  Radio  Newspaper  Sales
0  230.1   37.8       69.2   22.1
1   44.5   39.3       45.1   10.4
2   17.2   45.9       69.3    9.3
3  151.5   41.3       58.5   18.5
4  180.8   10.8       58.4   12.9
(200, 4)
```

28.1.3 Feature variables and response variable

The feature variables:

- `TV`: advertising dollars spent on TV ads
- `Radio`: advertising dollars spent on Radio Ads
- `Newspaper`: advertising dollars spent on Newspaper Ads

The response variable:

- `Sales`: Sales volume

28.1.4 Visual inspection of the data using a scatter diagram

We make use of a scatter diagram to visualize the feature variables individually against the response or target variable. The scatter plot function has the following signature:

```
data.plot(kind='scatter', x='TV', y='Sales', ax=axs[0])
```

where

- `kind`: set to 'scatter' for a scatter diagram
- `x`: data x-axis
- `y`: data y-axis

- ax: the prepared axis object, to render the results in

In the following Python code segment, a combined scatter diagram for all three categories is produced for visual inspection of the regression results.

```
import seaborn as sns
import matplotlib.pyplot as plt
# plot
fig, axs = plt.subplots(1, 3, sharey=True,
                     figsize=(10,4), sharex=False)
sns.regplot(x='TV', y='Sales',
            data=data, fit_reg=True,
            ax=axs[0], color='maroon')
sns.regplot(x='Radio', y='Sales',
            data=data, fit_reg=True,
            ax=axs[1], color='green')
sns.regplot(x='Newspaper', y='Sales',
            data=data, fit_reg=True,
            ax=axs[2], color='blue')
axs[0].grid(True)
axs[1].grid(True)
axs[2].grid(True)
axs[0].set_title('TV Ads', fontsize=12)
axs[1].set_title('Radio Ads', fontsize=12)
axs[2].set_title('Newspaper Ads', fontsize=12)
plt.show()
```

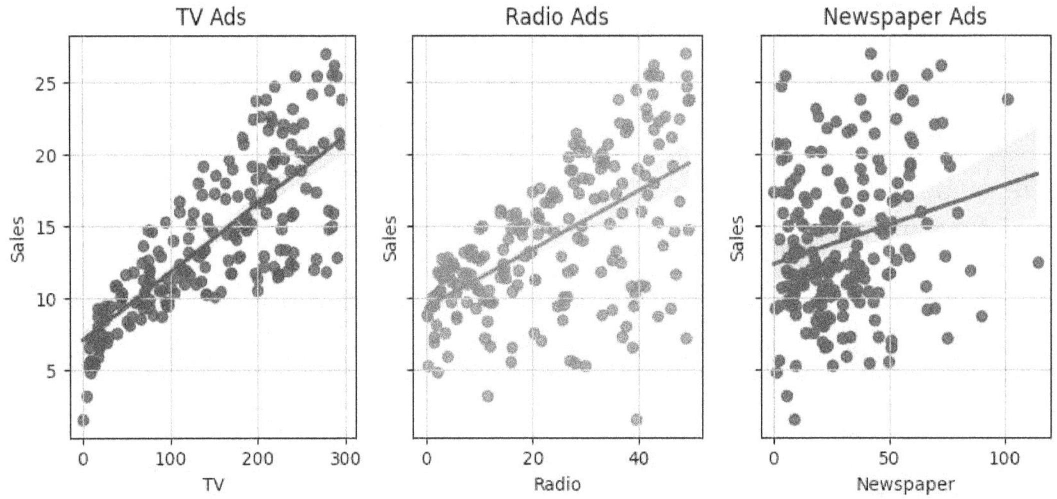

28.1.5 Visually inspecting the kernel density estimate

As demonstrated in PandasDocs [2023], we make use of the kde() function from the DataFrame plot module, to estimate the kernel density estimate (KDE) function. It has this signature:

```
data['TV'].plot.kde(ax=axs[0])
```

it produces the kernel density estimate plot from the provided data column.

In the following Python code section, we demonstrate this, and implement multiple kernel density estimates and present the results.

```
# plot
fig, axs = plt.subplots(1, 3, sharey=True, figsize=(10,4))
plt.suptitle('Kernel Density Estimate', fontsize=12)
data['TV'].plot.kde(ax=axs[0])
data['Radio'].plot.kde(ax=axs[1])
data['Newspaper'].plot.kde(ax=axs[2])
axs[0].grid(True)
axs[0].set_xlabel('$\mu_{TV}$')
axs[1].grid(True)
axs[1].set_xlabel('$\mu_{Radio}$')
axs[2].grid(True)
axs[2].set_xlabel('$\mu_{Newspaper}$')
axs[0].set_title('TV', fontsize=11)
axs[1].set_title('Radio', fontsize=11)
axs[2].set_title('Newspaper', fontsize=11)
plt.tight_layout()
plt.show()
```

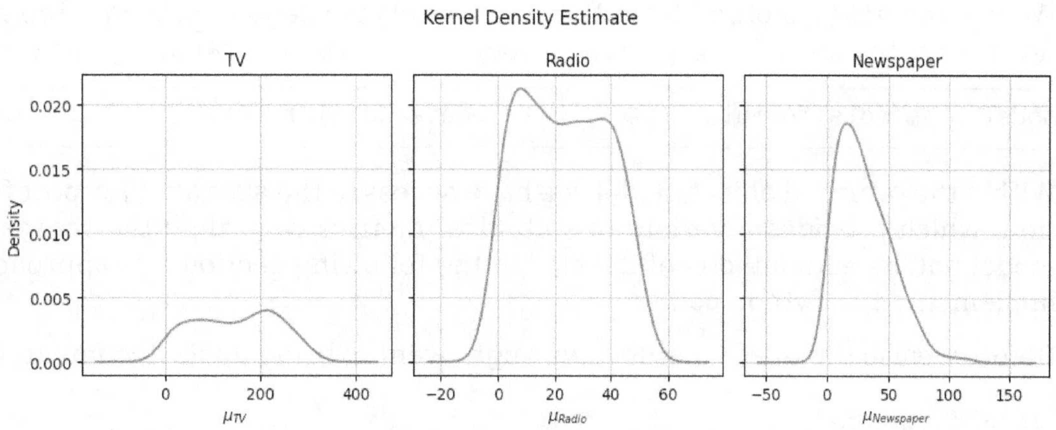

28.1.6 Study the impact of TV Ads on Sales

To better understand the data we perform a simple linear regression by considering only one of the 3 feature variables. In this first step, we study the relationship between TV Ad spending and Sales volume.

Simple Linear Regression model:

$$\hat{y} = \beta_0 + \beta_1 \cdot TV + \epsilon$$

where

- β_0: is the intercept (the value of y when TV=0)
- β_1: is the slope (the change in y divided by change in TV)

Regression coefficients:

$$\beta_0 = y(0)\ and\ \beta_1 = \frac{\Delta y}{\Delta TV}$$

Next, we investigate the relationship between ad spending and Sales volume and quantify the strength and direction of any relationship, and we ask which type of Ads have the biggest impact on Sales, and so on.

Once a satisfactory model is produced, we are providing next month's advertising budget in the Ads categories, to make a prediction or estimate of the corresponding Sales volume.

Estimating regression coefficients

We use the `ols()` method from the statsmodels package to estimate the coefficients for the specified regression model. It has the following signature:

```
model = smf.ols(formula='Sales ~ TV', data=data).fit()
```

Within the returned object model, we have access to the `summary()` report function, which provides a variety of statistical metrics regarding the regression model and its estimated coefficients. In the following section this approach is implemented in Python code:

Before we use the `ols()` method, we might want to bring up its documentation.

```
import statsmodels.formula.api as smf
# print(help(smf.ols)) # full documentation
```

```
import statsmodels.formula.api as smf
from quantlib import print_img

```

(continues on next page)

(continued from previous page)

```
# fit model
model = smf.ols(formula='Sales ~ TV', data=data).fit()
# inspect
print_img(model.summary().tables[0])
print_img(model.summary().tables[1])
print_img(model.summary().tables[2])
```

```
                            OLS Regression Results
==============================================================================
Dep. Variable:                  Sales   R-squared:                       0.612
Model:                            OLS   Adj. R-squared:                  0.610
Method:                 Least Squares   F-statistic:                     312.1
Date:                Tue, 02 Jul 2024   Prob (F-statistic):           1.47e-42
Time:                        14:00:16   Log-Likelihood:                -519.05
No. Observations:                 200   AIC:                             1042.
Df Residuals:                     198   BIC:                             1049.
Df Model:                           1
Covariance Type:            nonrobust
==============================================================================

==============================================================================
                 coef    std err          t      P>|t|      [0.025      0.975]
------------------------------------------------------------------------------
Intercept      7.0326      0.458     15.360      0.000       6.130       7.935
TV             0.0475      0.003     17.668      0.000       0.042       0.053
==============================================================================

==============================================================================
Omnibus:                        0.531   Durbin-Watson:                   1.935
Prob(Omnibus):                  0.767   Jarque-Bera (JB):                0.669
Skew:                          -0.089   Prob(JB):                        0.716
Kurtosis:                       2.779   Cond. No.                         338.
==============================================================================
```

Note: In later sections we will discuss each of the line items from the summary report in detail. We show how to compute those values manually, and how to extract values from the result object.

Interpretation

The TV coefficient β_1 can be interpreted as a 1-unit increase in TV Ad spending positively associated with a 0.0475-unit increase in Sales.

If the increase in TV Ad spending were associated with a decrease in Sales volume, indicated by a negative β_1 coefficient, the indicated Sales would drop.

```
from quantlib import print_img

print_img(model.summary().tables[1])
```

```
==============================================================================
                 coef    std err          t      P>|t|      [0.025      0.975]
------------------------------------------------------------------------------
Intercept      7.0326      0.458     15.360      0.000       6.130       7.935
TV             0.0475      0.003     17.668      0.000       0.042       0.053
==============================================================================
```

Using the fitted model to make a prediction

We assume that we have created a valid regression model, in which all the underlying assumptions of regression modeling are satisfied. Next, we utilize this model to make actual predictions. For example, we allocate a 50 thousand dollar TV Ads budget for the upcoming month and predict the expected Sales volume.

Linear regression equation:

$$y(x) = \beta_0 + \beta_1 \cdot TV + \epsilon$$

prediction for $x = 50$

$$y(50) = 7.033 + 0.048 \cdot 50 = 9.409$$

The manual calculation informs us that we would predict Sales of 9.409 thousand units.

Now, we can compute the equation and make this prediction using the statsmodels package. The TV Ads budget is stored in a DataFrame, since the `predict()` method expects it, like so:

```
X_new = pd.DataFrame({'TV':[50]})
```

Then, we apply `predict()` method to the fitted model, and pass in the X_{new} data item, like so:

```
r = model.predict(X_new)
```

In Python make a prediction, by using the regression model. We provide a new value into the estimated regression equation, like so:

```
# prediction
X_new = pd.DataFrame({'TV':[50]})
r = model.predict(X_new)
# inspect
print('TV Ads budget              :', X_new['TV'].values[0])
print("predicted Sales(TV=50)  : {:.4f}".format(r[0],3))
```

```
TV Ads budget         : 50
predicted Sales(TV=50) : 9.4094
```

Plot the scatter diagram with the least square line

To draw a line superimposed on the chart, we make predictions for the smallest and largest observed values for the TV coefficient and use such value pairs to plot a straight line onto the scatter plot. This line is known to be the least squared line.

In Python, this is implemented and the predicted Sales volume is shown.

```
# DataFrame
X_new = pd.DataFrame({'TV': [data.TV.min(), data.TV.max()]})
# prediction
preds = model.predict(X_new)
# inspect
print(f'predicted Sales(TV={X_new.TV[0]})   : {preds[0]:.4f}')
print(f'predicted Sales(TV={X_new.TV[1]}) : {preds[1]:.4f}')
```

```
predicted Sales(TV=0.7)   : 7.0659
predicted Sales(TV=296.4) : 21.1225
```

```
# plot
fig, ax1 = plt.subplots(1, figsize=(6,4))
data.plot(kind='scatter', x='TV',
          y='Sales',ax=ax1, color='maroon')
ax1.plot(X_new, preds, c='maroon',
        linewidth=4, alpha=0.8)
plt.grid(True)
plt.title('Simple Linear Regression (Sales ~ TV Ads)')
plt.show()
```

Confidence Interval

The statsmodels methods calculate the 95% confidence intervals for our model coefficients. If the population from which a sample was drawn was sampled 100 times, approximately 95 of those confidence intervals would contain the "true" coefficient value.

```
print_img(model._results.summary().tables[1])
```

	coef	std err	t	P>|t|	[0.025	0.975]
Intercept	7.0326	0.458	15.360	0.000	6.130	7.935
TV	0.0475	0.003	17.668	0.000	0.042	0.053

```
# confidence intervals
ci = model.conf_int()
# results
ci.columns = ['[0.025','0.975]']
print('confidence interval:')
print(ci)
```

```
confidence interval:
                [0.025     0.975]
Intercept  6.129719  7.935468
TV         0.042231  0.052843
```

Interpretation

Keep in mind that we only have a single sample of data, and not the entire population of data. The “true” coefficient is either within this confidence interval or it is not, but there is no way of actually knowing.

We estimate the coefficient with the sample data we have and reflect the uncertainty concerning that estimate, by providing a confidence interval or range for that coefficient, given the desired level of significance α.

A chosen level of significance α = 0.05 refers to a 95% confidence level, meaning that the given results are in an interval or range in which the “true” coefficient lies, with 95 percent certainty.

Student-t Test for coefficient significance

In general terms, we start with a null hypothesis H_0 and an alternative hypothesis H_1, these are assumptions, the researcher makes about the dataset. Then, we check whether the data sample supports either scenario: “rejecting the null hypothesis” or “failing to reject the null hypothesis”.

Note that “failing to reject” the null hypothesis H_0 is not the same as “accepting” the null hypothesis H_0. The alternative hypothesis H_1 may be true, except that we just don’t have enough evidence to support that.

t-statistic

$$t_i = \beta / SE_{i,i}$$

Hypothesis

- H_0 there is no relationship between TV ads and Sales (and thus β_1 equals zero)
- H_1 there is a relationship between TV ads and Sales (and thus β_1 is not equal to zero)

level of significance

- α = 0.05
- two-sided test

The Student-t Test is two-sided, so we allocate $\frac{\alpha}{2}$ or 0.025 in either tail of the distribution.

Intuitively, we reject the null hypothesis H_0 if the confidence interval does not include zero. The p_{value} represents the probability that the coefficient is zero, and if the 95% confidence interval includes zero, the p_{value} for that coefficient will be greater than $\frac{\alpha}{2} = 0.025$.

If the 95% confidence interval does not include zero, the p_{value} will be less than $\frac{\alpha}{2} = 0.025$, and we conclude that there is likely a relationship between the feature and the response variable.

In the following Python code example, we implement the Student-t Test with hypothesis and interpretation for the TV coefficient.

```
# parameters
alpha = 0.05
t = model._results.tvalues[1] # TV
p = model._results.pvalues[1] # TV
c = model._results.params[1] # TV
# confirmation
print_img(model._results.summary().tables[1])
# test procedure
print('Student-t Test:')
print(f't-statistic            : {t:.4f}')
print(f'p-value                : {p:.2E}')
print(f'level of significance : {alpha:.2f}')
print('two-tailed test')
print('Hypothesis')
print('H0: the TV variable contributes to the response')
print('H1: the TV variable does not contribute to the response')
if p < alpha/2:
    print('reject H0')
    print('TV is significant')
else:
    print('fail to reject H0')
    print('TV is not significant')
```

```
==============================================================================
                 coef    std err          t      P>|t|      [0.025      0.975]
------------------------------------------------------------------------------
Intercept      7.0326      0.458     15.360      0.000       6.130       7.935
TV             0.0475      0.003     17.668      0.000       0.042       0.053
==============================================================================
```

```
Student-t Test:
t-statistic            : 17.6676
p-value                : 1.47E-42
level of significance : 0.05
two-tailed test
Hypothesis
H0: the TV variable contributes to the response
H1: the TV variable does not contribute to the response
reject H0
```

(continues on next page)

(continued from previous page)

```
TV is significant
```

Interpretation

The t-statistic is reported as 17.6676, and the corresponding p_{value} is 1.47e-42, almost zero.

Remember, the test is designed to be a two-tailed test, so we allocate $\frac{\alpha}{2}$ in either tail of the distribution.

Since the p_{value} for the TV coefficient is far less than $\frac{\alpha}{2}$ of 0.025, we reject the null hypothesis H_0 in favor of the alternative hypothesis H_1. The analyzed sample provides sufficient evidence, to conclude that there is indeed a relationship among TV Ads spending and Sales volume, at the chosen level of significance α = 0.05, which corresponds to (1-α) or 95% confidence.

Assessing the goodness of fit of the model

The common way to evaluate the overall competence of a linear model is by computing the coefficient of determination or R^2 measure. It quantifies the proportion of variance in the data explained by the model or the improvement by the model compared to the intercept-only model, which has all β_i coefficients set to zero, except the Intercept term β_0.

We make use of the statsmodels package to compute the coefficient of determination, which is reported as the R^2 measure. The R^2 value lies between 0 and 1, and higher values are preferred, meaning that a greater portion of the variance is explained by the model.

In the following Python code segment, this approach is implemented, and the results are presented.

```
# report
print_img(model._results.summary().tables[0])
print()
print("R-squared        : {:.4f}".format(model.rsquared))
print("Adj. R-squared : {:.4f}".format(model.rsquared_adj))
```

```
                            OLS Regression Results
==============================================================================
Dep. Variable:                  Sales   R-squared:                       0.612
Model:                            OLS   Adj. R-squared:                  0.610
Method:                 Least Squares   F-statistic:                     312.1
Date:                Tue, 02 Jul 2024   Prob (F-statistic):           1.47e-42
Time:                        14:00:20   Log-Likelihood:                -519.05
No. Observations:                 200   AIC:                             1042.
Df Residuals:                     198   BIC:                             1049.
Df Model:                           1
Covariance Type:            nonrobust
==============================================================================
```

```
R-squared      : 0.6119
Adj. R-squared : 0.6099
```

Interpretation

The coefficient of determination or R^2 measure is reported as 0.612.

The threshold for a good R^2 value depends on the domain, however, a fairly large R^2 indicates that the model is significant, at the chosen level of significance (α). Therefore, this measure is most useful for comparing different regression models with each other and selecting the most appropriate model.

As demonstrated in later sections, a formal `F-Test` can be conducted to arrive at a more quantitative assessment of the goodness of fit for the regression model as a whole.

28.1.7 Study the impact of Radio Ads on Sales

To better understand the data we perform a simple linear regression by considering only one of the 3 feature variables. In this case, we study the relationship between Radio Ads expenditure on Sales volume.

Simple Linear Regression model:

$$\hat{y} = \beta_0 + \beta_1 \cdot Radio + \epsilon$$

where

- β_0 is the intercept (the value of y when $Radio$=0)
- β_1 is the slope (the change in y divided by change in $Radio$)

The regression coefficients are defined as:

$$\beta_0 = y(0)\ and\ \beta_1 = \frac{\Delta y}{\Delta Radio}$$

Estimate regression coefficients

We perform the regression analysis with the `ols()` method from the statsmodels package, to estimate the model coefficients for the linear regression model. It model has the following signature:

```
model = smf.ols(formula='Sales ~ Radio', data=data).fit()
```

In return we receive a model object, providing a summary report object, which lists statistical metrics regarding the regression model.

Before we use the `ols()` method, we might want to bring up its documentation.

```
import statsmodels.formula.api as smf
# print(help(smf.ols)) # full documentation
# print(smf.ols.__doc__[:1220]) # brief documentation
```

```
import statsmodels.formula.api as smf

# fit model
model = smf.ols(formula='Sales ~ Radio', data=data).fit()
# inspect
print_img(model.summary().tables[0])
print_img(model.summary().tables[1])
print_img(model.summary().tables[2])
```

```
                            OLS Regression Results
==============================================================================
Dep. Variable:                  Sales   R-squared:                       0.332
Model:                            OLS   Adj. R-squared:                  0.329
Method:                 Least Squares   F-statistic:                     98.42
Date:                Tue, 02 Jul 2024   Prob (F-statistic):           4.35e-19
Time:                        14:00:21   Log-Likelihood:                -573.34
No. Observations:                 200   AIC:                             1151.
Df Residuals:                     198   BIC:                             1157.
Df Model:                           1
Covariance Type:            nonrobust
==============================================================================

==============================================================================
                 coef    std err          t      P>|t|      [0.025      0.975]
------------------------------------------------------------------------------
Intercept      9.3116      0.563     16.542      0.000       8.202      10.422
Radio          0.2025      0.020      9.921      0.000       0.162       0.243
==============================================================================

==============================================================================
Omnibus:                       19.358   Durbin-Watson:                   1.946
Prob(Omnibus):                  0.000   Jarque-Bera (JB):               21.910
Skew:                          -0.764   Prob(JB):                     1.75e-05
Kurtosis:                       3.544   Cond. No.                         51.4
==============================================================================
```

Interpretation

The coefficient for Radio Ads β_1 is 0.2025, the t-statistic is reported as 9.921, and the corresponding p_{value} is almost 0.

The Radio Ads coefficient β_1 can be interpreted like, a 1 thousand-dollar increase in Radio Ads spending is associated with a 0.2025-unit increase in Sales volume. Of course, if the β_1 coefficient were to be negative, the increase in Radio ad spending would be associated with a decline in Sales volume of the same magnitude.

We can also conduct a formal Student-t Test, to quantitatively evaluate the significance of the Radio parameter, like demonstrated in the previous section.

Using the fitted model to make a prediction

We assume that we have created a valid regression model, in which all the underlying assumptions of regression modeling are satisfied.

Assuming there is a new market where we allocate a 25 thousand dollars Radio Ad advertising budget for the upcoming month. What would we predict for the Sales in that market?

Regression equation:

$$y(x) = \beta_0 + \beta_1 \cdot Radio + \epsilon$$

To conduct the manual computation, we report the estimated parameters for the model.

```
print_img(model.summary().tables[1])
```

	coef	std err	t	P>|t|	[0.025	0.975]
Intercept	9.3116	0.563	16.542	0.000	8.202	10.422
Radio	0.2025	0.020	9.921	0.000	0.162	0.243

We calculate the expected Sales volume, like so:

$$Sales(25) = 9.3116 + 0.2025 \cdot 25 = 14.374$$

Thus, we would predict Sales of 14.374 units in that specified market.

Instead of manually computing the predicted Sales volume, we can evaluate the equation and make this prediction using the statsmodels package. We make use of the `predict()` method, which has this signature:

```
r = model.predict(X_new)
```

where

- X_{new}: contains the input variable used in the prediction formula

The returned variable `r` contains the predicted Sales volume, given the X_{new} input.

```
# DataFrame
X_new = pd.DataFrame({'Radio':[25]})
# prediction
r = model.predict(X_new)
# inspect
print('prediction:')
print("new Radio budget:", X_new['Radio'].values)
print("estimated Sales(Radio=25) = {:.3f}".format(r[0]))
```

```
prediction:
new Radio budget: [25]
estimated Sales(Radio=25) = 14.374
```

Scatter diagram with the least square line

We make predictions for the smallest and largest observed values for the Radio coefficient and use those predicted values to plot the least squared line.

```
X_new = pd.DataFrame({'Radio': [data.Radio.min(),
                                 data.Radio.max()]})
# prediction
preds = model.predict(X_new)
# results
print(f'predicted Sales(Radio={X_new.Radio[0]:.4f})',end='')
print(f'  : {preds[0]:.4f}')
print(f'predicted Sales(Radio={X_new.Radio[1]:.4f})',end='')
print(f' : {preds[1]:.4f}')
```

```
predicted Sales(Radio=0.0000)  : 9.3116
predicted Sales(Radio=49.6000) : 19.3554
```

```
# plot
fig, ax1 = plt.subplots(1, figsize=(6,4))
data.plot(kind='scatter', x='Radio',
          y='Sales', ax=ax1, color ='green')
ax1.plot(X_new, preds, c='green', linewidth=4, alpha=0.8)
plt.grid(True)
plt.title('Simple Linear Regression (Sales ~ Radio Ads)')
plt.show()
```

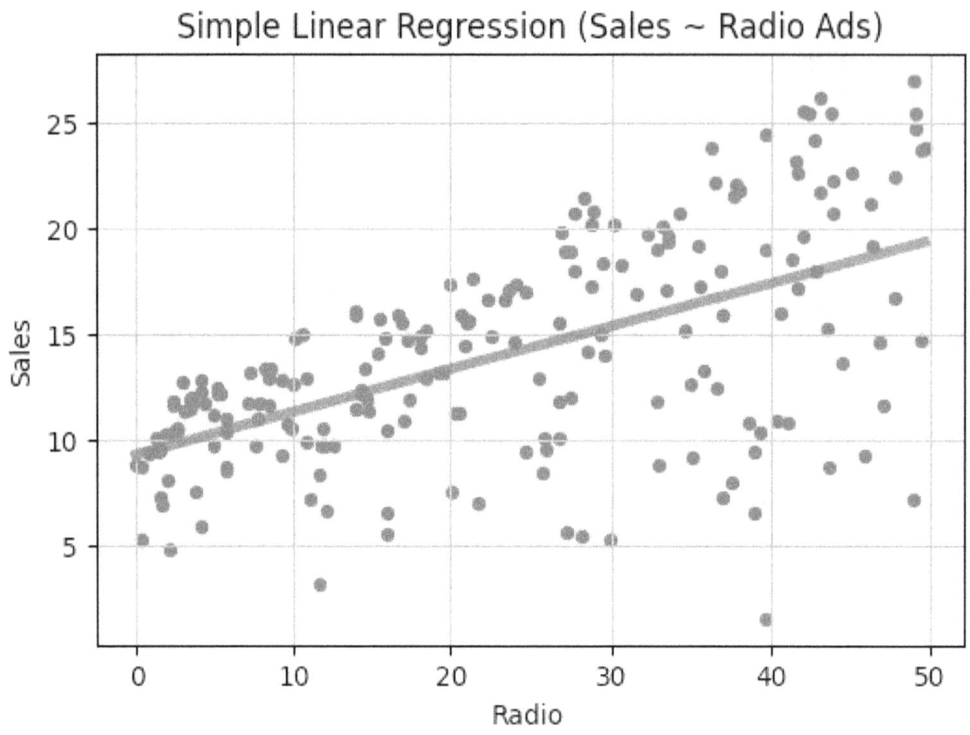

Confidence interval

The statsmodels package calculates the 95% confidence intervals for our model coefficients. We study the confidence interval in-depth in later sections. For example, if a population was sampled 100 times, given a chosen level of significance of $\alpha = 0.05$, approximately 95 of those reported confidence intervals would contain the "true" coefficient value, this is the basic intuition behind confidence intervals.

Variance versus bias

With repeated sampling, the line will remain almost the same, indicating a low variance of the model, which is desirable. On the other hand, a high bias is indicated, when the average of those models is not performing well in capturing the "true" relationship between the variables under consideration.

```
# confidence intervals
ci = model.conf_int()
# report
print_img(model._results.summary().tables[1])
print()
print('confidence interval:')
```

(continues on next page)

(continued from previous page)

```
ci.columns = ['[0.025','0.975]']
print(ci)
```

```
==============================================================================
                 coef    std err          t      P>|t|      [0.025      0.975]
------------------------------------------------------------------------------
Intercept      9.3116      0.563     16.542      0.000       8.202      10.422
Radio          0.2025      0.020      9.921      0.000       0.162       0.243
==============================================================================
```

```
confidence interval:
              [0.025     0.975]
Intercept  8.201588  10.421688
Radio      0.162244   0.242747
```

Since we only studied a single data sample, and not the entire population, which means that the "true" coefficient is either within this interval or it is not, but there is no way of actually knowing.

We estimate the coefficient with the sample we have and reflect the uncertainty about that estimate by giving a confidence interval in which the coefficient is probably within. Most often we give a 95% confidence interval.

Student-t Test for coefficient significance

We start with a null hypothesis H_0 and an alternative hypothesis H_1, these are assumptions with respect the the sample. Then, we check whether the data supports either rejecting the null hypothesis or failing to reject the null hypothesis.

Bear in mind that "failing to reject" the null hypothesis is not the same as "accepting" the null hypothesis, as the alternative hypothesis may still be true, but the given data sample does not provide enough evidence to support that conclusion.

Hypothesis

- H_0 there is no relationship between Radio Ads and Sales (and thus β_1 equals zero)
- H_1 there is a relationship between Radio Ads and Sales (and thus β_1 is not equal to zero)

level of significance

- $\alpha = 0.05$

The Student-t Test is two-sided, so we allocate $\frac{\alpha}{2}$ in either tail of the distribution.

Intuitively, we reject the null hypothesis if the 95% confidence interval does not include zero. Conversely, the p_{value} represents the probability that the coefficient is zero. If the 95% confidence interval includes zero, the p_{value} for that coefficient will be greater $\frac{\alpha}{2} = 0.025$.

If the 95% confidence interval does not include zero, the p_{value} will be less than $\frac{\alpha}{2} = 0.025$. Thus, a p_{value} less than $\frac{\alpha}{2}$ is one way to decide whether there is likely a relationship between the feature and the response variable.

In Python, a full Student-t Test is implemented and the results are interpreted.

```
# parameters
alpha = 0.05
t = model.tvalues[1]
p = model.pvalues[1]
# confirmation
print_img(model._results.summary().tables[1])
# results
print('Student-t Test:')
print(f't-statistic            : {t:.4f}')
print(f'p-value                : {p:.2E}')
print(f'level of significance : {alpha:.2f}')
print('two tailed test')
print('Hypothesis')
print('H0: Radio Ads do not contribute to Sales')
print('H1: Radio Ads do contribute to Sales')
if p < alpha/2:
    print('reject H0')
    print('Radio is significant')
else:
    print('fail to reject H0')
    print('Radio is not significant')
```

	coef	std err	t	P>|t|	[0.025	0.975]
Intercept	9.3116	0.563	16.542	0.000	8.202	10.422
Radio	0.2025	0.020	9.921	0.000	0.162	0.243

```
Student-t Test:
t-statistic            : 9.9208
p-value                : 4.35E-19
level of significance : 0.05
two tailed test
Hypothesis
H0: Radio Ads do not contribute to Sales
H1: Radio Ads do contribute to Sales
reject H0
Radio is significant
```

Interpretation

The t-statistic is reported as 9.9208 and the corresponding p_{value} as 4.35e-19, almost zero

Since the $p_{value} \leq \frac{\alpha}{2}$, we reject the null hypothesis H_0, in favor of the alternative hypothesis H_1. The data provides sufficient evidence, to conclude that there is a significant relationship between Radio Ads and Sales. We can make this claim with (1-α) or 95% confidence.

Assessing the goodness of fit of the model

The most common way to evaluate the overall fitness of a linear model is by computing the coefficient of determination or R^2 measure, which measures the proportion of variance explained by the regression model.

The portion of variance explained by the model is equivalent to saying a reduction in error compared to the intercept-only model, which just predicts the mean of the observed response, and has an intercept and no slope coefficient.

The coefficient of determination R^2 is between 0 and 1, and a higher value is better because it means that more variance is explained by the model. We make use of the statsmodels package to compute the coefficient of determination reported as R^2 measure.

In the following Python code segment, an example of this is implemented and its results are interpreted.

```
print_img(model._results.summary().tables[0])
# results
print('R-squared       : {:.4f}'.format(model.rsquared))
print('Adj. R-squared : {:.4f}'.format(model.rsquared_adj))
```

```
                            OLS Regression Results
==============================================================================
Dep. Variable:                  Sales   R-squared:                       0.332
Model:                            OLS   Adj. R-squared:                  0.329
Method:                 Least Squares   F-statistic:                     98.42
Date:                Tue, 02 Jul 2024   Prob (F-statistic):           4.35e-19
Time:                        14:00:24   Log-Likelihood:                -573.34
No. Observations:                 200   AIC:                             1151.
Df Residuals:                     198   BIC:                             1157.
Df Model:                           1
Covariance Type:            nonrobust
==============================================================================
```

```
R-squared      : 0.3320
Adj. R-squared : 0.3287
```

Interpretation

The threshold for an acceptable R^2 value depends on the domain. Therefore, it is most useful as a tool for comparing different models with each other and selecting the most appropriate one.

28.2 Part II: Multiple Linear Regression using statsmodels

Simple linear regression can easily be extended to include multiple features simultaneously, resulting in models for

Multiple Linear regression:

$$\hat{y} = \beta_0 + \beta_1 \cdot x_1 + ... + \beta_n \cdot x_n + \epsilon$$

Each x_i represents a different feature, and each feature has its coefficient β_i. In this case, the

regression formula becomes:

$$y = \beta_0 + \beta_1 \cdot TV + \beta_2 \cdot Radio \\ + \beta_3 \cdot Newspaper + \epsilon$$

The statsmodels package is used to estimate the coefficients β_0, β_1 and β_2.

```
import statsmodels.formula.api as smf

# inspect
print(data.head())
```

```
      TV  Radio  Newspaper  Sales
0  230.1   37.8       69.2   22.1
1   44.5   39.3       45.1   10.4
2   17.2   45.9       69.3    9.3
3  151.5   41.3       58.5   18.5
4  180.8   10.8       58.4   12.9
```

We implement a multiple linear regression model by using the `ols()` method from the statsmodels library, which has this signature:

```
model = smf.ols(formula='Sales ~ TV + Radio + Newspaper',
                data=data).fit()
```

In the following Python code segment, the model is implemented, by using the very convenient formula syntax to describe the regression model.

```
# fit model
model = smf.ols(formula='Sales ~ TV + Radio + Newspaper',
                                             data=data).fit()
```

(continues on next page)

(continued from previous page)

```
# inspect
print_img(model.summary().tables[1])
print('coefficients:')
print(model.params,'\n')
print('std_err:')
print(model.bse,'\n')
print('t-values:')
print(model.tvalues,'\n')
print('p-values:')
print(model.pvalues)
```

```
==============================================================================
                 coef    std err          t      P>|t|      [0.025      0.975]
------------------------------------------------------------------------------
Intercept      2.9389      0.312      9.422      0.000       2.324       3.554
TV             0.0458      0.001     32.809      0.000       0.043       0.049
Radio          0.1885      0.009     21.893      0.000       0.172       0.206
Newspaper     -0.0010      0.006     -0.177      0.860      -0.013       0.011
==============================================================================
```

```
coefficients:
Intercept    2.938889
TV           0.045765
Radio        0.188530
Newspaper   -0.001037
dtype: float64

std_err:
Intercept    0.311908
TV           0.001395
Radio        0.008611
Newspaper    0.005871
dtype: float64

t-values:
Intercept     9.422288
TV           32.808624
Radio        21.893496
Newspaper    -0.176715
dtype: float64

p-values:
Intercept    1.267295e-17
TV           1.509960e-81
Radio        1.505339e-54
Newspaper    8.599151e-01
dtype: float64
```

Interpretation

For a given amount of TV spending, an increase of 1 thousand dollars in TV Ad spending is associated with an increase in Sales of 0.045765 units.

For a given amount of Radio spending, an increase of 1 thousand dollars in TV Ad spending is associated with an increase in Sales of 0.18853 units.

For a given amount of Newspaper spending, an increase of 1 thousand dollars in Newspaper Ad spending is associated with a decrease in Sales of 0.001037 units.

28.2.1 Summary table of key performance figures

We make use of the summary() method of the result object to list a tabular output of many key performance figures of the regression model.

```
print('summary:')
print('table 0:')
print_img(model.summary().tables[0])
print('table 1:')
print_img(model.summary().tables[1])
print('table 2:')
print_img(model.summary().tables[2])
```

```
summary:
table 0:
```

```
                            OLS Regression Results
==============================================================================
Dep. Variable:                  Sales   R-squared:                       0.897
Model:                            OLS   Adj. R-squared:                  0.896
Method:                 Least Squares   F-statistic:                     570.3
Date:                Tue, 02 Jul 2024   Prob (F-statistic):           1.58e-96
Time:                        14:00:26   Log-Likelihood:                -386.18
No. Observations:                 200   AIC:                             780.4
Df Residuals:                     196   BIC:                             793.6
Df Model:                           3
Covariance Type:            nonrobust
==============================================================================
```

```
table 1:
```

```
==============================================================================
                 coef    std err          t      P>|t|      [0.025      0.975]
------------------------------------------------------------------------------
Intercept      2.9389      0.312      9.422      0.000       2.324       3.554
TV             0.0458      0.001     32.809      0.000       0.043       0.049
Radio          0.1885      0.009     21.893      0.000       0.172       0.206
Newspaper     -0.0010      0.006     -0.177      0.860      -0.013       0.011
==============================================================================
```

```
table 2:
```

```
==============================================================================
Omnibus:                       60.414   Durbin-Watson:                   2.084
Prob(Omnibus):                  0.000   Jarque-Bera (JB):              151.241
Skew:                          -1.327   Prob(JB):                     1.44e-33
Kurtosis:                       6.332   Cond. No.                         454.
==============================================================================
```

Interpretation

The TV and Radio parameters have significant p_{values}, whereas the Newspaper coefficient does not. Thus we reject the null hypothesis for TV and Radio, that there is no association between those feature variables and Sales, and fail to reject the null hypothesis H_0 for Newspapers.

TV and Radio Ad spending are both positively associated with Sales, whereas Newspaper ad spending is slightly negatively associated with Sales. However, this is irrelevant since we have failed to reject the null hypothesis H_0 for Newspaper Ads.

In comparison to the model computed from the previous section, this model reports a R^2 measure of 0.897, which means that this model performs significantly better in explaining the variance in the sample, than the model that includes only the TV Ads feature variable, reporting an $R^2 = 0.612$.

28.2.2 Feature Selection

How to decide which features to include in the linear regression model?

- try different models, and only keep predictor variables in the model if they have significant p_{values}
- assess the improvement in the R^2 and the $adjustedR^2$ measures, when successively adding predictor variables

However, linear regression models rely on several assumptions, such as the feature variables being independent, the normal distribution of the error variance, etc, and if one or more of those assumptions are violated R^2 and p_{values} become unreliable or biased, and we cannot expect the model to make valid predictions.

The coefficient of determination or R^2 measure is susceptible to overfitting, and thus there is no guarantee that a model with a high R^2 measure will generalize well when subjected to new data items.

For example, if we are using $\alpha = 0.05$ which means that if we add 100 predictors to a model which are are "pure noise", at least 5 of those will still be identified as significant. To compensate for this issue the $adjustedR^2$ measure is used, which introduces a penalty for adding new predictor variables to the model.

```
# TV and Radio included in the model
model = smf.ols(formula='Sales ~ TV + Radio',
                data=data).fit()
# results
print("model equation      : Sales ~ TV + Radio")
print(f"R-squared            : {model.rsquared:.4f}")
print(f"adjusted R2-squared : {model.rsquared_adj:.4f}")
```

```
model equation      : Sales ~ TV + Radio
R-squared           : 0.8972
adjusted R2-squared : 0.8962
```

```
# Add newspaper to the model
model = smf.ols(formula='Sales ~ TV + Radio + Newspaper',
                data=data).fit()
# results
print("model equation      : Sales ~ TV + Radio + Newspaper")
print(f"R-squared            : {model.rsquared:.4f}")
print(f"adjusted R2-squared : {model.rsquared_adj:.4f}")
```

```
model equation      : Sales ~ TV + Radio + Newspaper
R-squared           : 0.8972
adjusted R2-squared : 0.8956
```

28.2.3 The coefficient of determination

The coefficient of determination or R^2 measure will always increase as we add more feature variables to the model. This is even true if they are not related to the response variable. Meaning, that the model with the highest R^2 measure, is not always the best.

The $adjusted R^2$ measure penalizes model complexity and is generally considered a better indicator of model competence in fitting the sample data.

28.2.4 Cross-validation of the model

The cross-validation procedure provides a more reliable estimate of the out-of-sample error and thus is a better way to choose which models will best generalize the data.

There is extensive functionality for cross-validation in the scikit-learn package, including automated methods for searching different sets of parameters. Importantly, cross-validation can be applied to any model.

28.2.5 Prediction with new data item

A set of new input data is given, which is used to make a prediction, using the fitted model. For example, the next month's advertising budget consists of TV=100, Radio=25, and Newspaper=25 thousand dollars. Given this new budget, in each Ad category, what is the best estimate of the resulting Sales volume?

In the following Python code segment, we make such a prediction and show the result.

```
# new data item
X_new = pd.DataFrame({'TV':[100],
                      'Radio':[25],
                      'Newspaper':[25]})
# prediction
pred= model.predict(X_new)
# results
print(f"Forecast Sales(TV=100, Radio=25, Newspaper=25) = {pred[0]:.3f}
 ↪")
```

```
Forecast Sales(TV=100, Radio=25, Newspaper=25) = 12.203
```

28.3 Part III: Multiple Linear Regression with the scikit-learn package

We apply the linear regression method provided by the scikit-learn library, to perform the analysis. In this model, we use all 3 feature variables to fit the model and arrive at the following model specification.

Multiple linear regression model:

$$\hat{y} = \beta_0 + \beta_1 \cdot TV + \beta_2 \cdot Radio \\ + \beta_3 \cdot Newspaper + \epsilon$$

We estimate the coefficients using the `linear_model()` method of the sklearn package, which has this signature:

```
model = LinearRegression().fit(X, y)
```

where

- X: is the feature vector
- y: is the response variable

In Python, this regression model is implemented and the results are presented.

Unfortunately, the LinearRegression()` function does not compute the p_{values}, so we compute those values using the statsmodels package, like so:

```
from sklearn.linear_model import LinearRegression
import statsmodels.api as sm

feature_cols = ['TV', 'Radio', 'Newspaper']
X = data[feature_cols]
y = data.Sales
X2 = sm.add_constant(X)
# model
model_sm = sm.OLS(y, X2).fit()
# results
print_img(model_sm._results.summary().tables[1])
print('coefficients:')
print(model_sm._results.params)
print('p-values:')
print(model_sm._results.pvalues)
```

	coef	std err	t	P>|t|	[0.025	0.975]
const	2.9389	0.312	9.422	0.000	2.324	3.554
TV	0.0458	0.001	32.809	0.000	0.043	0.049
Radio	0.1885	0.009	21.893	0.000	0.172	0.206
Newspaper	-0.0010	0.006	-0.177	0.860	-0.013	0.011

```
coefficients:
[ 2.93888937e+00  4.57646455e-02  1.88530017e-01 -1.03749304e-03]
p-values:
[1.26729451e-17 1.50995995e-81 1.50533892e-54 8.59915050e-01]
```

```
from sklearn.linear_model import LinearRegression

# features X and target y
feature_cols = ['TV', 'Radio', 'Newspaper']
X = data[feature_cols]
y = data.Sales
# fit model
model = LinearRegression().fit(X, y)
# results
print("results:")
print(f"intercept      : {model.intercept_ :.8f}")
print(f"p-value        : {model_sm._results.pvalues[0]:.8f}")
print(f"feature names  : {model.feature_names_in_}")
print(f"coefficients   : {model.coef_}")
print(f'p-values       : {model_sm._results.pvalues[1:]}')
```

```
results:
intercept     : 2.93888937
p-value       : 0.00000000
feature names : ['TV' 'Radio' 'Newspaper']
coefficients  : [ 0.04576465  0.18853002 -0.00103749]
p-values      : [1.50995995e-81 1.50533892e-54 8.59915050e-01]
```

28.3.1 Evaluate the regression results

```
# pair the feature names with the coefficients
feature_cols = ['TV', 'Radio', 'Newspaper']
zip(feature_cols, model.coef_)
# results
print("coefficients:")
print("Intercept       : {:.8f}".format(model.intercept_))
for i, (f,c) in enumerate( zip(feature_cols, model.coef_)):
    print(f.ljust(14),': {:.8f}'.format(c))
```

```
coefficients:
Intercept      : 2.93888937
TV             : 0.04576465
Radio          : 0.18853002
Newspaper      : -0.00103749
```

28.3.2 Prediction with new data items

We have next month's advertising budget of TV=100, Radio=25, Newspaper=25 dollars. Now we would like to predict the expected Sales volume. For this, we employ the `predict()` method of the model, which has the following signature:

```
r = model.predict( [[100,25,25]] )
```

where we pass in a list of parameters, corresponding to the feature variables of the model.

In Python code, this can be accomplished, like so.

```
import warnings
warnings.filterwarnings('ignore')

# prediction
r = model.predict([[100,25,25]]) # list of list
# results
```

(continues on next page)

(continued from previous page)

```
print("prediction:")
print("Sales(TV=100, Radio=25, Newspaper=25) = {:.3f}".format(r[0]))
```

```
prediction:
Sales(TV=100, Radio=25, Newspaper=25) = 12.203
```

28.3.3 The coefficient of determination

As documented in ScikitDocs [2023], we assess the quality of the model as a whole, by evaluating the R^2 and the $adjustedR^2$ measure. We make use of the `rs_score()` method of the model, which has this signature:

```
r = r2_score(y, y_pred)
```

where

- `y`: are the true y values
- `y_pred`: are the predicted y values by the model

The computation yields the expected coefficient of determination or R^2 measure.

```
from sklearn.metrics import r2_score

# calculate R-squared
r2 = model.score(X, y)
# prediction
y_pred = model.predict(X)
r = r2_score(y, y_pred)
# report
print(f"R-squared lm.score           : {r2:.4f}")
print(f"R-squared sklearn r2_score : {r:.4f}")
```

```
R-squared lm.score           : 0.8972
R-squared sklearn r2_score : 0.8972
```

28.4 Part IV: Categorical predictors

28.4.1 Predictors with two categories

Up til now, all of the predictors have been numeric, and now we are introducing categorical predictors. For that, we introduce an additional feature called `Market` and assign randomly a value of `consumer` or `professional` to it. The Market variable can be modeled as so-called dummy variables.

Market dummy variable:

- `Market=1`: denotes professional market
- `Market=0`: denotes consumer market

A categorical variable with two categories can be modeled by one dummy variable. For the newly introduced `MarketType` variable we distinguish between the `professional` and the `consumer` market, hence we encode professional=1 and the consumer market is considered the baseline case, to which we compare the results.

In the following Python code segment, this approach is implemented and its results are presented.

```
import numpy as np

# baseline cases
data['MarketType'] = 'consumer'

np.random.seed(1) # reproducibility
for index, row in data.iterrows():
    # dummy variable MarketType
    data['MarketType'].iat[index] = np.random.choice([
                                'consumer', 'professional'])
# inspect
print(data.head(10))
```

```
      TV  Radio  Newspaper  Sales    MarketType
0  230.1   37.8       69.2   22.1  professional
1   44.5   39.3       45.1   10.4  professional
2   17.2   45.9       69.3    9.3      consumer
3  151.5   41.3       58.5   18.5      consumer
4  180.8   10.8       58.4   12.9  professional
5    8.7   48.9       75.0    7.2  professional
6   57.5   32.8       23.5   11.8  professional
7  120.2   19.6       11.6   13.2  professional
8    8.6    2.1        1.0    4.8  professional
9  199.8    2.6       21.2   10.6      consumer
```

The scikit-learn package requires that all feature variables be numeric. So we have to encode our categorical data (consumer, professional) numerically, like (consumer=0, professional=1). If the given categorical feature only has two categories, we can simply create a dummy variable that represents the categories as a binary value.

For the following example, we create a dummy variable Market and employ the following mapping to it.

```
data['Market'] = data.MarketType.map({'consumer':0,
                                      'professional':1})
```

```
# dummy variable encoding
data['Market'] = data.MarketType.map({'consumer':0,
                                      'professional':1})
# inspect
print(data.head(10))
```

```
      TV  Radio  Newspaper  Sales    MarketType  Market
0  230.1   37.8       69.2   22.1  professional       1
1   44.5   39.3       45.1   10.4  professional       1
2   17.2   45.9       69.3    9.3      consumer       0
3  151.5   41.3       58.5   18.5      consumer       0
4  180.8   10.8       58.4   12.9  professional       1
5    8.7   48.9       75.0    7.2  professional       1
6   57.5   32.8       23.5   11.8  professional       1
7  120.2   19.6       11.6   13.2  professional       1
8    8.6    2.1        1.0    4.8  professional       1
9  199.8    2.6       21.2   10.6      consumer       0
```

As we have extended the regression model, it now looks like this:

Multiple linear regression model:

$$\begin{aligned}\hat{y} = \beta_0 &+ \beta_1 \cdot TV + \beta_2 \cdot Radio \\ &+ \beta_3 \cdot Newspaper \\ &+ \beta_4 \cdot Market + \epsilon\end{aligned}$$

where:

- Market: is the category (coding: consumer=0, professional=1)

Next, we perform the regression analysis with this enhanced model, including the Market predictor, which was modeled as a dummy variable.

```
features = ['TV', 'Radio', 'Newspaper', 'Market']
X = data[features]
y = data.Sales
# instantiate and fit
model = LinearRegression().fit(X, y)
```

(continues on next page)

(continued from previous page)

```
# results
print('features:'); print(features)
print('lm.coef_:'); print(model.coef_)
print('feature     coefficient:')
for i, (f,c) in enumerate(zip(features,model.coef_)):
    print(f.ljust(9),': {:.6f}'.format(c))
```

```
features:
['TV', 'Radio', 'Newspaper', 'Market']
lm.coef_:
[ 0.04579724  0.18862733 -0.00113329 -0.07310305]
feature     coefficient:
TV        : 0.045797
Radio     : 0.188627
Newspaper : -0.001133
Market    : -0.073103
```

Interpretation

For a given amount of TV, Radio, and Newspaper Ads spending, targeting the professional market segment (Market=1) is associated with an average decrease in Sales of -0.0731 units, which is compared to a consumer market segment (Market=0), called the baseline level.

As such, the choice of category for the baseline case does not matter, all that changes the interpretation of the coefficients.

Of course, we have to evaluate the model further, to test the significance of all feature variables, and assess the model's performance as a whole by evaluating the R^2 and the $adjustedR^2$ measures, and convince ourselves that the regression model is competent in performing high-quality predictions.

28.4.2 Predictors with more than two categories

We create a new feature variable called Season and randomly assign observations to be: summer, winter, autumn, and spring. The Season dummy variable is encoded, like so:

```
data['Season'] = data.SeasonType.map(
    {'summer':0, 'autumn':1, 'winter':2, 'spring':3})
```

The summer is defined as the baseline case. In the following code segment, this is implemented and the results are presented.

```
# baseline case
data['SeasonType'] = 'autumn'
```

(continues on next page)

(continued from previous page)

```
# dummy variable SeasonType
np.random.seed(1) # reproducibility
for index, row in data.iterrows():
    data['SeasonType'].iat[index] = np.random.choice([
                'autumn', 'winter', 'spring', 'summer'])
# inspect
print('dataset:')
print(data.head(10))
```

```
dataset:
      TV  Radio  Newspaper  Sales    MarketType  Market SeasonType
0  230.1   37.8       69.2   22.1  professional       1     winter
1   44.5   39.3       45.1   10.4  professional       1     summer
2   17.2   45.9       69.3    9.3      consumer       0     autumn
3  151.5   41.3       58.5   18.5      consumer       0     autumn
4  180.8   10.8       58.4   12.9  professional       1     summer
5    8.7   48.9       75.0    7.2  professional       1     winter
6   57.5   32.8       23.5   11.8  professional       1     summer
7  120.2   19.6       11.6   13.2  professional       1     winter
8    8.6    2.1        1.0    4.8  professional       1     summer
9  199.8    2.6       21.2   10.6      consumer       0     autumn
```

28.4.3 Modeling with dummy variables

We have to represent Season numerically, but we can not simply code it as (summer=0, autumn=1, winter=2, and spring=4) because that would imply an ordered relationship, which is not there. Instead, we have to create k-1 dummy variables to encode such a Season variable, like so.

```
Season    season_summer season_winter season_spring
Summer    1             0             0
Winter    0             1             0
Spring    0             0             1
Autumn    baseline case
```

This leaves autumn not encoded, which represents the baseline case, to compare the results against.

To generate the appropriate set of dummy variables, we make use of the `get_dummies()` method of the pandas package, which has this signature:

```
season_dummies = pd.get_dummies(
    data.SeasonType, prefix='Season').iloc[:,1:]
```

```
# dummy variables
season_dummies = pd.get_dummies(
        data.SeasonType, prefix='Season').iloc[:,1:]
# DataFrame, column
data = pd.concat([data, season_dummies], axis=1)
# inspect
print('dataset:')
print(data[['TV', 'Radio', 'Newspaper', 'Sales']].head(10))
print(); print(data[['MarketType', 'Market']].head(10))
print()
print(data[['SeasonType', 'Season_spring',
            'Season_summer','Season_winter']].head(10))
```

```
dataset:
      TV  Radio  Newspaper  Sales
0  230.1   37.8       69.2   22.1
1   44.5   39.3       45.1   10.4
2   17.2   45.9       69.3    9.3
3  151.5   41.3       58.5   18.5
4  180.8   10.8       58.4   12.9
5    8.7   48.9       75.0    7.2
6   57.5   32.8       23.5   11.8
7  120.2   19.6       11.6   13.2
8    8.6    2.1        1.0    4.8
9  199.8    2.6       21.2   10.6

     MarketType  Market
0  professional       1
1  professional       1
2      consumer       0
3      consumer       0
4  professional       1
5  professional       1
6  professional       1
7  professional       1
8  professional       1
9      consumer       0

  SeasonType  Season_spring  Season_summer  Season_winter
0     winter              0              0              1
1     summer              0              1              0
2     autumn              0              0              0
3     autumn              0              0              0
4     summer              0              1              0
5     winter              0              0              1
6     summer              0              1              0
7     winter              0              0              1
8     summer              0              1              0
9     autumn              0              0              0
```

Dummy encoding for the Season category

Here is the specification of the dummy encoding for the Season category.

- `Summer`: is encoded as Season_summer=1 and Season_winter=0 and Season_spring=0
- `Winter`: is encoded as Season_summer=0 and Season_winter=1 and Season_spring=0
- `Spring`: is encoded as Season_summer=0 and Season_winter=0 and Season_spring=1
- `Autumn`: is not encoded and serves as a baseline case

The category `autumn` is not encoded and represents the baseline case, to compare against.

For a category that can have 3 representations, we only need 2 dummy variables, to capture all 3 possibilities. In general, if we have a categorical feature with k levels, we require only $k-1$ dummy variables. To demonstrate this approach, we include the `Season` feature, encoded as 3 dummy variables into the regression model, resulting in this enhanced regression model:

$$
\begin{aligned}
\hat{y} = \beta_0 &+ \beta_1 \cdot TV + \beta_2 \cdot Radio \\
&+ \beta_3 \cdot Newsp. + \beta_4 \cdot Market \\
&+ \beta_5 \cdot summer + \beta_6 \cdot spring \\
&+ \beta_7 \cdot winter + \epsilon
\end{aligned}
$$

where:

- `Market`: is a dummy variable encoding the Market feature professional=1, consumer=0
- `season_summer`: is a dummy variable encoding the Season features

A summary of the encoding scheme is presented below:

Market dummy encoding:

```
Market         Market
professional   1
consumer       baseline case
```

Season dummy encoding:

```
Season    season_summer season_winter season_spring
Summer    1             0             0
Winter    0             1             0
Spring    0             0             1
Autumn     baseline case
```

The Python code, the implementation becomes:

```
# features X, target y
features = ['TV', 'Radio', 'Newspaper',
            'Market', 'Season_summer',
            'Season_winter','Season_spring']
X = data[features]
y = data.Sales
# fit model
model = LinearRegression().fit(X, y)
# coefficients
zip(features, model.coef_)
print('features:')
print(features[0:4])
print(features[4:])
print('lm.coef_:')
# print(model.coef_)
print('[', end='')
for i, c in enumerate(model.coef_):
    print('{:.5f} '.format(c), end='')
print(']')
print('feature          coefficient')
for i, (f,c) in enumerate( zip(features, model.coef_)):
    print(i, f.ljust(14),': {:.3f}'.format(c))
```

```
features:
['TV', 'Radio', 'Newspaper', 'Market']
['Season_summer', 'Season_winter', 'Season_spring']
lm.coef_:
[0.04617 0.18968 -0.00152 0.10841 0.26081 -0.15240 0.53978 ]
feature          coefficient
0 TV             : 0.046
1 Radio          : 0.190
2 Newspaper      : -0.002
3 Market         : 0.108
4 Season_summer  : 0.261
5 Season_winter  : -0.152
6 Season_spring  : 0.540
```

Interpretation

A spring season campaign is associated with an average increase in Sales volume of 0.5398 units per 1 dollar spent on Ads, as compared to the baseline level, which is autumn.

A winter campaign is associated with an average decrease in Sales of -0.1524 units per 1 dollar spent on Ads, as compared to the baseline autumn season.

A summer campaign is associated with an average increase in Sales of 0.2608 units per 1 dollar spent on Ads, as compared to the baseline autumn season.

Targeting the professional market is associated with a decrease in Sales of

0.1084 per 1 dollar spent, as compared with the baseline, which is the consumer market.

Note: If we have categories which can be ranked (strongly disagree, disagree, neutral, agree, strongly agree), we can potentially use a single dummy variable and represent the categories numerically (such as 1, 2, 3, 4, 5), thereby capturing the ordering or ranking.

Prediction with new data items

For next month's marketing campaign, we would like to use the fitted regression model, to make a prediction, and decide where to best spend the advertising dollars. We have the advertising budget given as:

```
TV=100, Radio=25, Newspaper=25,
Market=professional, Season=summer
```

Remember, the Market=professional is encoded as (1), and Season=summer is encoded as (0,1,0).

Now we would like to predict the expected Sales volume, by using the `predict()` method of the model object, which signature becomes:

```
r = model.predict([[100,25,25, 1, 0, 1, 0]])
```

where the input data items are provided as list-of-list $[[100, 25, 25, 1, 0, 1, 0]]$, corresponding to the encoding of the features variables. The returned `r` variable contains the one-step ahead predicted value.

```
import warnings
warnings.filterwarnings('ignore')

# campaign 1
# Market=professional, Season=winter
r = model.predict([[100,25,25, 1, 0, 1, 0]]) # list
# results
print("Budget for campaign 1:")
print("TV=100", "Radio=25", "Newspaper=25",
      "Market=professional",
      "Season=winter")
print('Forecasted Sales = {:.3f}'.format(r[0]))
print()
# campaign 2
# Market=professional, Season=autumn
r = model.predict([[100,25,25, 1, 0, 0, 0]]) # list
print("Budget for campaign 2:")
```

(continues on next page)

(continued from previous page)

```
print("TV=100","Radio=25","Newspaper=25",
      "Market=professional",
      "Season=autumn")
print('Forecasted Sales = {:.3f}'.format(r[0]))
```

```
Budget for campaign 1:
TV=100 Radio=25 Newspaper=25 Market=professional Season=winter
Forecasted Sales = 11.944

Budget for campaign 2:
TV=100 Radio=25 Newspaper=25 Market=professional Season=autumn
Forecasted Sales = 12.097
```

Interpretation

In the first marketing campaign, we allocate the upcoming advertising budget as so: TV = 100, Radio = 25, Newspaper = 25, Market = professional, Season = `summer`. The predicted Sales volume is 11.944.

In the second marketing campaign, we allocate the advertising budget, like so: TV = 100, Radio = 25, Newspaper = 25, Market = `professional`, Season = `autumn`. The predicted Sales volume is 12.097.

We might conclude that the second campaign is slightly more beneficial to the firm since it yields a higher Sales volume with the same advertising budget.

28.5 Limitation of linear regression

The knowledge of linear regression analysis is crucial for building a solid understanding of the regression methods, however, these types of models are limited by the fact that they rely on several underlying assumptions to be met. In particular, the relationship between the features and response variables is to be linear. These underlying assumptions must be satisfied before valid predictions can be made with such models.

More complex methods often outperform linear regression models, therefore we want to learn the fundamentals of linear regression and understand its strengths and weaknesses as a foundation for tackling more complex models and techniques.

CHAPTER 29

LINEAR REGRESSION WITH FORECASTS

The linear regression method attempts to draw a straight line that minimizes the residual sum of squares between the observed responses in the dataset, and the responses predicted by the linear regression model.

We use the first feature variable of the diabetes dataset, to visualize a two-dimensional plot of this regression technique. Visualizing the data in a scatter plot along with the regression line, gives an intuitive view of how the linear regression model attempts to minimize the sum of squared errors.

```
import matplotlib as mpl
import numpy as np
import matplotlib.pyplot as plt
import sklearn
from sklearn import datasets, linear_model
from sklearn.metrics import mean_squared_error, r2_score

print('version matplotlib :', mpl.__version__)
print('version numpy      :', np.__version__)
print('version sklearn    :', sklearn.__version__)
```

```
version matplotlib : 3.6.2
version numpy      : 1.22.4
version sklearn    : 1.1.3
```

29.1 Loading dataset from an online resource

The dataset consists of 8 feature variable and one binary class as target variable. The Diabetes dataset is available from the sklean data repository, and it has 768 records, 8 features and 1 target.

It can be obtained from the online repository, like so:

```
diabetes = datasets.load_diabetes()
```

```
# Load the diabetes dataset
diabetes = datasets.load_diabetes()
# features
diabetes_X = diabetes.data[:, np.newaxis, 2]
y = diabetes.target
# inspect
print('feature X:')
print(diabetes_X[0:10])
print('X.shape:', diabetes_X.shape)
print('target  y:', diabetes.target[0:10])
print('y.shape:', y.shape)
```

```
feature X:
[[ 0.06169621]
 [-0.05147406]
 [ 0.04445121]
 [-0.01159501]
 [-0.03638469]
 [-0.04069594]
 [-0.04716281]
 [-0.00189471]
 [ 0.06169621]
 [ 0.03906215]]
X.shape: (442, 1)
target  y: [151.  75. 141. 206. 135.  97. 138.  63. 110. 310.]
y.shape: (442,)
```

29.2 Split dataset into training and testing dataset

We can make use of the slice operator [ ] to split the dataset into two partitions, the training set and the testing set, for that we use the slice operator, like so:

```
diabetes_X_train = diabetes_X[:-20]
diabetes_X_test = diabetes_X[-20:]
```

We do the equivalent with the target variable. This split of the dataset helps in the data analysis and allows for subsequent performance evaluation.

```
# parameters
N = 20
# slice operator
diabetes_X_train = diabetes_X[:-N]
diabetes_X_test = diabetes_X[-N:]
# split into training and testing sets
diabetes_y_train = diabetes.target[:-N]
diabetes_y_test = diabetes.target[-N:]
# inspect
print('training-dataset:')
print('features X:', diabetes_X_train.shape)
print('target   y:', diabetes_y_train.shape)
print()
print('testing-dataset:')
print('feature X:', diabetes_X_test.shape)
print('target  y:', diabetes_y_test.shape)
```

```
training-dataset:
features X: (422, 1)
target   y: (422,)

testing-dataset:
feature X: (20, 1)
target  y: (20,)
```

29.3 Simple Linear Regression

Linear regression model:

$$\hat{y} = \beta_0 + \beta_1 1 \cdot x1 + \epsilon$$

where

- $\hat{y}$: the dependent, or target variable
- x_1: independent or feature variables
- ϵ: residual or error term

In the following Python code segment, this approach is implemented and the results are presented.

```
# linear regression object
regr = linear_model.LinearRegression()
# model fit
```

(continues on next page)

(continued from previous page)

```
regr.fit(diabetes_X_train, diabetes_y_train)
# prediction
diabetes_y_pred = regr.predict(diabetes_X_test)
print('predictions:')
print('  x              y            y-pred')
for i in range(len(diabetes_y_pred)):
    print('{:8.4f}      {:8.4f}    {:8.4f}'.format(
            diabetes_X_test[i][0], diabetes_y_test[i],
                                    diabetes_y_pred[i]))
```

```
predictions:
  x              y            y-pred
  0.0779      233.0000      225.9732
 -0.0396       91.0000      115.7476
  0.0110      111.0000      163.2761
 -0.0407      152.0000      114.7364
 -0.0342      120.0000      120.8039
  0.0056       67.0000      158.2199
  0.0886      310.0000      236.0857
 -0.0332       94.0000      121.8151
 -0.0569      183.0000       99.5677
 -0.0310       66.0000      123.8376
  0.0552      173.0000      204.7371
 -0.0601       72.0000       96.5340
  0.0013       49.0000      154.1749
 -0.0235       64.0000      130.9163
 -0.0741       48.0000       83.3878
  0.0197      178.0000      171.3661
 -0.0159      104.0000      137.9950
 -0.0159      132.0000      137.9950
  0.0391      220.0000      189.5685
 -0.0730       57.0000       84.3991
```

29.3.1 Visualize as a scatter diagram with a regression line

```
# plot
fig, ax = plt.subplots(1, figsize=(6,4))
ax.scatter(diabetes_X_test,
           diabetes_y_test,
           color='blue')
ax.plot(diabetes_X_test,
        diabetes_y_pred,
        color='blue', linewidth=1,
        linestyle='dotted')
txt='$\\hat y =\\beta_0 +\\beta_1\\cdot x +\\epsilon$'
ax.title.set_text('Regress: '+txt)
ax.grid(True)
```

(continues on next page)

(continued from previous page)

```
ax.set_xlabel('x')
ax.set_ylabel('y')
plt.show()
```

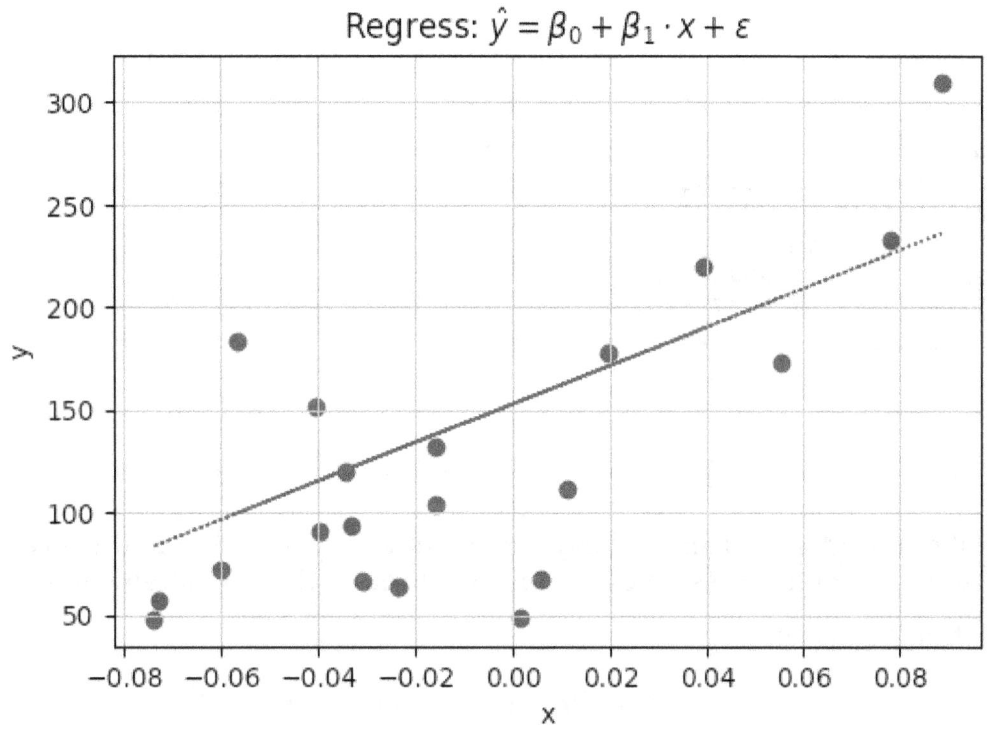

29.3.2 Make predictions using the testing dataset

In the first attempt, a prediction is made, using this fitted model, by using the previously sliced testing dataset diabetes_X_test.

```
import sklearn.metrics as metr

# predictions
diabetes_y_pred = regr.predict(diabetes_X_test)
# report
print('results:')
print(f'Equation    y = {regr.intercept_:.2f} + \
{regr.coef_[0]:.2f} * x + eps')
print(f'intercept     : {regr.intercept_:.2f}')
print(f'coefficients : {regr.coef_[0]:.2f}')
mse =  metr.mean_squared_error(diabetes_y_test,
                               diabetes_y_pred)
test1_r2 = metr.r2_score(diabetes_y_test,
                         diabetes_y_pred)
```

(continues on next page)

(continued from previous page)

```
test2_r2 = regr.score(diabetes_X_test,
                      diabetes_y_test)
print('performance metrics:')
print(f'MSE           : {mse:.6f}')
print(f'R2 test 1     : {test1_r2:.6f}')
print(f'R2 test 2     : {test2_r2:.6f}')
```

```
results:
Equation    y = 152.92 + 938.24 * x + eps
intercept    : 152.92
coefficients : 938.24
performance metrics:
MSE          : 2548.072399
R2 test 1    : 0.472575
R2 test 2    : 0.472575
```

29.3.3 Make predictions with out-of-sample data items

We make a prediction using a single new data item for the x feature variable and use the fitted regression equation, resulting in the predicted value.

Prediction equation:

$$\hat{y}(0.11) = 152.92 + 938.24 * 0.11 = 256.13$$

In Python, the `predict()`` method, available on the LinearRegression package is used, which has the following signature:

```
y_pred_1 = regr.predict(x_new_1)
```

where

- x_new_1 : is the new value for the x feature variable.

Observe that the data is to be passed in as a list-of-list `[[0.11]]`, and in Python code, this is implemented and the predicted value is presented.

```
# new out of sample data item (x=0.11)
x_new_1 = [[0.11]]
y_pred_1 = regr.predict(x_new_1)
# results
print('prediction:')
print('x_new_1 value : {:.2f}'.format(x_new_1[0][0]))
print('y-predicted   : {:.4f}'.format(y_pred_1[0]))
```

```
prediction:
x_new_1 value : 0.11
y-predicted   : 256.1250
```

It is encouraging, that the result matches the manual calculation made previously.

29.3.4 A two-step ahead prediction with new data items

We attempt to make a two-period forecast, therefore we supply 2 input values, in the required list-of-lists format, to the `predict()` function like so:

```
y_pred_2 = regr.predict([ [0.1], [0.11] ])
```

the function returns 2 predictions, corresponding to both input values provided.

In the following Python code segment, the two-step ahead prediction is implemented and its results are presented.

```
# prediction
x_new_2 = [[0.10], [0.11]]
y_pred_2 = regr.predict(x_new_2)
# results
print('predictions:')
print('feature   x :', x_new_2)
print('predicted y :', y_pred_2)
```

```
predictions:
feature   x : [[0.1], [0.11]]
predicted y : [246.74264795 256.12502656]
```

29.3.5 Visualize regression line with forecast values

We made the two-step ahead prediction, and now we visualize the obtained results in a scatter plot. The forecasted values are highlighted as "red crosses".

```
# plot
fig,ax = plt.subplots(1, figsize=(6,4))
ax.scatter(diabetes_X_test, diabetes_y_test,
           color='blue', label='actual')
ax.scatter(x_new_2, y_pred_2, marker='x',
        color='r', s=80, label='forecast')
ax.plot(diabetes_X_test, diabetes_y_pred,
        color='blue', linewidth=2, linestyle='dotted')
```

(continues on next page)

(continued from previous page)

```
txt = 'Regress: $\\hat y = b_0 + b_1 \cdot x + \\epsilon$'
ax.title.set_text(txt)
ax.legend(loc='best')
ax.grid(True)
ax.set_xlabel('x')
ax.set_ylabel('$\\hat y$')
plt.show()
```

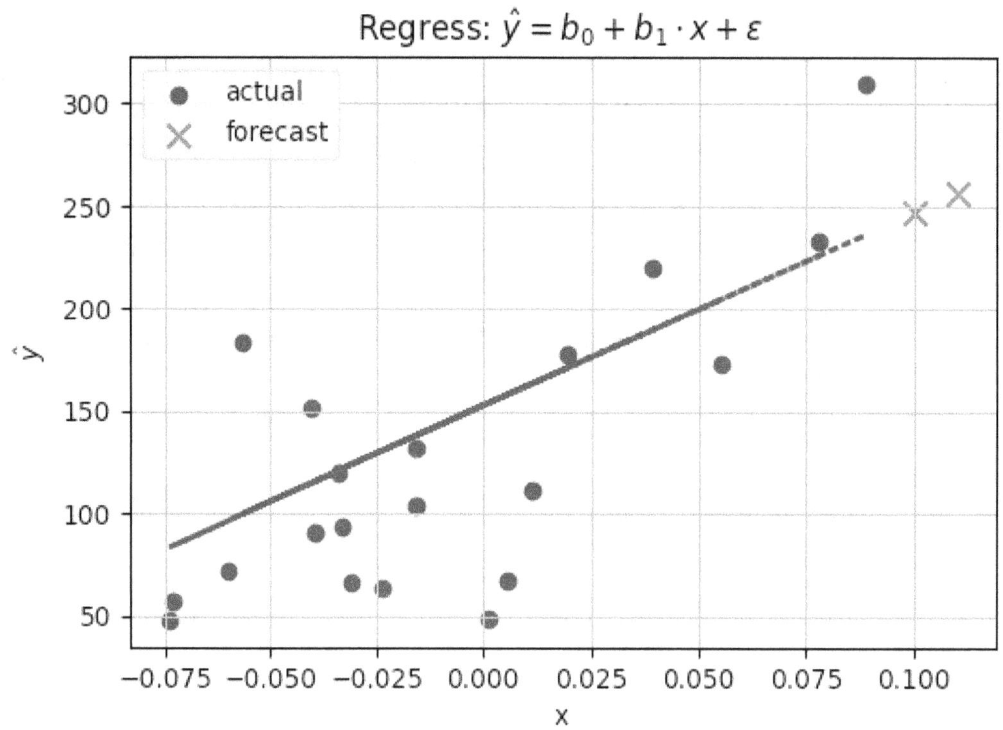

CHAPTER 30

THE REGRESSION SUMMARY REPORT

Linear Regression Analysis is the workhorse of the quantitative discipline. It provides tools to assess the strength of a linear relationship among one or several independent variables and a dependent or target variable.

In this example, we will perform a small multiple linear regression analysis to arrive at a `summary()` report generated by the model. We discuss this summary report item by item and demonstrate how to extract specific values from the results object.

> We create a small sample dataset, and make use of statsmodels regression module to perform the regression analysis by using the `ols()` method.

```
import matplotlib.pyplot as plt
import pandas as pd
%matplotlib inline

# DataFrame
df = pd.DataFrame({
    "Study_Hours": [3, 7, 16, 14, 12, 7, 4, 19, 4, 8, 8, 3],
    "Prep_Exams": [2, 6, 5, 2, 7, 4, 4, 2, 8, 4, 1, 3],
    "Exam_Score": [76, 88, 96, 90, 98, 80, 86, 89, 90,
                   75, 72, 76],})
# required by statsmodels
df["Const"] = 1
# inspect
```

(continues on next page)

(continued from previous page)

```
print('dataset:')
print(df)
print()
print('describe:')
print(df.describe())
```

```
dataset:
    Study_Hours  Prep_Exams  Exam_Score  Const
0             3           2          76      1
1             7           6          88      1
2            16           5          96      1
3            14           2          90      1
4            12           7          98      1
5             7           4          80      1
6             4           4          86      1
7            19           2          89      1
8             4           8          90      1
9             8           4          75      1
10            8           1          72      1
11            3           3          76      1

describe:
       Study_Hours  Prep_Exams  Exam_Score  Const
count    12.000000   12.000000   12.000000   12.0
mean      8.750000    4.000000   84.666667    1.0
std       5.344921    2.174229    8.637480    0.0
min       3.000000    1.000000   72.000000    1.0
25%       4.000000    2.000000   76.000000    1.0
50%       7.500000    4.000000   87.000000    1.0
75%      12.500000    5.250000   90.000000    1.0
max      19.000000    8.000000   98.000000    1.0
```

30.1 Visualizing the dataset

The first step is to visualize the data in a scatter plot, to gain an intuition on how the data is distributed.

```
# plot
fig, axs = plt.subplots(1, 2, sharey=True, figsize=(10,3))
df.plot(kind="scatter", x="Study_Hours",
        y="Exam_Score",
        color="r", ax=axs[0])
df.plot(kind="scatter", x="Prep_Exams",
        y="Exam_Score",
        color="g", ax=axs[1])
axs[0].grid(True)
```

(continues on next page)

(continued from previous page)

```
axs[1].grid(True)
plt.suptitle("Visualization of features vs. target variable")
plt.show()
```

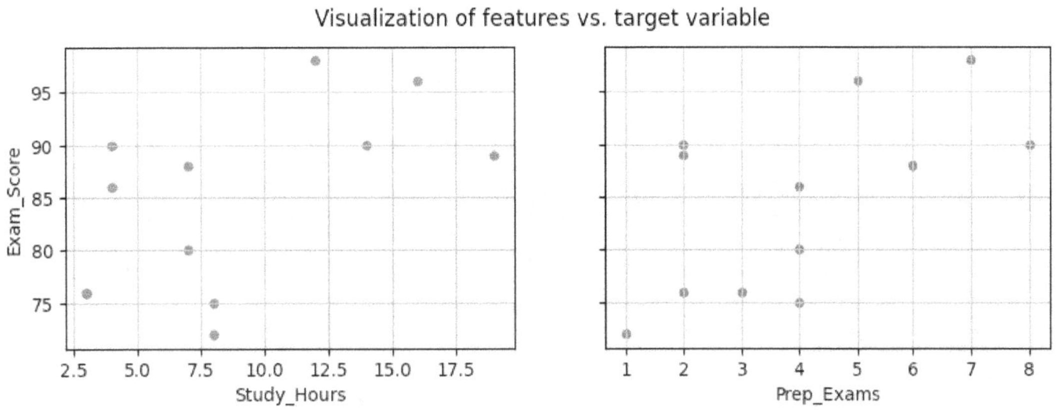

30.2 Typical model summary report

```
import warnings
import statsmodels.api as sm
from quantlib import print_img
from statsmodels.formula.api import ols
warnings.filterwarnings("ignore")

# model in formula notation
model = ols("Exam_Score ~  Study_Hours + Prep_Exams",
            data=df)
# fit
results = model.fit()
# inspect
print_img(results.summary())
```

```
                            OLS Regression Results
==============================================================================
Dep. Variable:             Exam_Score   R-squared:                       0.779
Model:                            OLS   Adj. R-squared:                  0.729
Method:                 Least Squares   F-statistic:                     15.83
Date:                Thu, 02 May 2024   Prob (F-statistic):            0.00113
Time:                        18:41:16   Log-Likelihood:                -33.331
No. Observations:                  12   AIC:                             72.66
Df Residuals:                       9   BIC:                             74.12
Df Model:                           2
Covariance Type:            nonrobust
===============================================================================
                  coef    std err          t      P>|t|      [0.025      0.975]
-------------------------------------------------------------------------------
Intercept      64.5216      3.809     16.940      0.000      55.905      73.138
Study_Hours     1.0546      0.256      4.124      0.003       0.476       1.633
Prep_Exams      2.7294      0.629      4.342      0.002       1.307       4.151
==============================================================================
Omnibus:                        1.874   Durbin-Watson:                   1.715
Prob(Omnibus):                  0.392   Jarque-Bera (JB):                0.501
Skew:                          -0.486   Prob(JB):                        0.778
Kurtosis:                       3.241   Cond. No.                         31.8
==============================================================================

Notes:
[1] Standard Errors assume that the covariance matrix of the errors is correctly specified.
```

30.3 Explain the summary report table-by-table

The `summary()` method of the regression object provides and stores a summary table of statistical metrics, parameters, and performance measures. We can report these items table-by-table, like so:

```
print(model.summary().tables[0])
```

The output gives us an abbreviated report of the first section of the total summary report. Statsmodels [2023]. Then we demonstrate how to extract individual values from the report objects.

30.4 Summary report values in table 0

```
print_img(results.summary().tables[0])
```

```
                            OLS Regression Results
==============================================================================
Dep. Variable:             Exam_Score   R-squared:                       0.779
Model:                            OLS   Adj. R-squared:                  0.729
Method:                 Least Squares   F-statistic:                     15.83
Date:                Thu, 02 May 2024   Prob (F-statistic):            0.00113
Time:                        18:41:16   Log-Likelihood:                -33.331
No. Observations:                  12   AIC:                             72.66
Df Residuals:                       9   BIC:                             74.12
Df Model:                           2
Covariance Type:            nonrobust
==============================================================================
```

30.4.1 Extracting individual values from table 0

```
print("left-side:")
print(f"Dep.Variable        : {results.model.endog_names}")
print("Model              :")
print("Method             :")
print(f"No. Observations   : {model.nobs:.0f}")
print(f"Df Residuals        : {model.df_resid:.0f}")
print(f"Df Model            : {model.df_model:.0f}")
print(f"Covariance Type     : {results.cov_type}")
print()
print("right-side:")
print(f"R-squared           : {results.rsquared:.4f}")
print(f"Adj. R-squared      : {results.rsquared_adj:.4f}")
print(f"F-statistic         : {results.fvalue:.4f}")
print(f"Prob(F-statistic)   : {results.f_pvalue:.4f}")
print(f"Log-Likelihood      : {results.llf:.4f}")
print(f"AIC                 : {results.aic:.4f}")
print(f"BIC                 : {results.bic:.4f}")
```

```
left-side:
Dep.Variable        : Exam_Score
Model               :
Method              :
No. Observations    : 12
Df Residuals        : 9
Df Model            : 2
Covariance Type     : nonrobust

right-side:
R-squared           : 0.7786
```

(continues on next page)

(continued from previous page)

```
Adj. R-squared      : 0.7294
F-statistic         : 15.8280
Prob(F-statistic) : 0.0011
Log-Likelihood      : -33.3310
AIC                 : 72.6620
BIC                 : 74.1167
```

30.4.2 Explaining the reported metrics in Table 0

Dep. Variable

The Exam_Score variable is the dependent or target variable.

Model and Method

ordinary least square `ols()` method. The least squares procedure attempts to minimize the sum of squared residuals.

No Observations

The number of observations in the dataset

- nobs: 12

DF Residual

We have a total of 12 observations (n=12), and we have 2 independent feature variables (k=2). The degree of freedom for the residuals is:

- `DF-Residual`: (n-k-1) (12-2-1) = 9

DF model

We have a total of 12 observations (n=12), and we have 2 independent feature variables (k=2). The degree of freedom for the model is:

- `DF-Model`: (k)

where

- `DF-Model`: 3
- `DF-Residual`: (10-2-1) = 9

Covariance type

The covariance type is typically `nonrobust` which means there is no elimination of data to calculate the covariance between the feature variables.

If desired, heteroscedasticity robust covariance can be configured, by setting the `cov_type` to either (HC0, HC1, HC2, HC3), as explained in Statsmodels-Docs [2023].

R-squared

The coefficient of determination or R^2 measures the portion of total error variation explained by the regression model. According to Statsmodels [2023] it is defined as:

(a) if the constant is included in the model:

$$R^2 = 1 - \frac{SSR}{TSS_{centered}}$$

(b) if the constant is omitted:

$$R^2 = 1 - \frac{SSR}{TSS_{uncentered}}$$

where

- SSR: the sum of squared residuals
- $TSS_{uncentered}$: is the total sum of squared

Adjusted R-Square

By adding more independent variables to the regression model, the measure for R^2 will always improve, this is because we are mapping a larger input space onto a single scalar target value.

The $AdjustedR^2$ takes into account the number of predictor variables, the degrees of freedom and the number of observations and controls for the increased number of regressor variables.

$AdjustedR^2$

$$Adj.\ R^2 = 1 - (1 - R^2)\frac{N-1}{N-P-1}$$

where

- N: the number of observations
- P: the number of predictor variables

Note: This formula introduces some sort of penalty for adding more independent variables to the model, resulting in a more reliable measure of the models's performance. However for a single independent variable, R-square measure, Adjusted R-square measure are equal.

F-statistic

The F-test assesses the significance of the model as a whole and produces the F-statistic and the Prob(F-statistic) or p_{value} as output.

Hypothesis

- H_0: all regressor coefficients are equal to zero
- H_1: at least one of the regressor coefficients is different from zero

level of significance

- $\alpha = 0.05$
- two-tailed test

Since the F-Test is a two-tailed test, we allocate $\frac{\alpha}{2}$ in either tail of the distribution.

It measures how well the model performs compared with the intercept-only model, in which all coefficients are simultaneously zero. The statistic is computed as:

F-statistic

$$F = \frac{\frac{SSM/\sigma^2}{P}}{\frac{SSE/\sigma^2}{N-P-1}} = \frac{MSM}{MSE}$$

where

- MSE: is the mean squared error
- MSM: is the mean squared model

Prop(F-statistic) or p_{value}

Assuming the level of significance (α) is set to be 0.05, then the interpretation becomes:

If Prob(F-statistic) is less than the chosen level of significance $\alpha = \frac{0.05}{2}$, we reject the null hypothesis H_0 in favor of the alternative hypothesis H_1, and we conclude that at least one regression coefficient is significantly different from zero.

If, on the other hand, Prob(F-statistic) is greater than the chosen level of significance $\alpha = \frac{0.05}{2}$, we fail to reject H_0 and conclude that all regression coefficients are zero.

Log-likelihood

The Log-likelihood value is a measure of how well the model fits the given data. It is useful in comparing several model alternatives, and models with higher log-likelihood are preferred.

Akaike's Information Criterion (AIC)

The goal is to minimize these values and to select a better model.

Bayesian Information Criterion (BIC)

The goal is to minimize these values and to select a better model.

30.5 Summary report om Table 1

```
print_img(results.summary().tables[1])
```

```
================================================================================
                 coef    std err          t      P>|t|      [0.025      0.975]
--------------------------------------------------------------------------------
Intercept     64.5216      3.809     16.940      0.000      55.905      73.138
Study_Hours    1.0546      0.256      4.124      0.003       0.476       1.633
Prep_Exams     2.7294      0.629      4.342      0.002       1.307       4.151
================================================================================
```

30.5.1 Extracting individual values from Table 1

```
print("Parameters:", results.params,"",
    "Std. error:", results.bse, "",
    "t:", results.tvalues, "",
    "P > |t|:", results.pvalues, "",
    "CI [0.025 0.095]:",
    results.conf_int().to_string(header=False),
    "", sep="\n",)
```

```
Parameters:
Intercept      64.521638
Study_Hours     1.054573
Prep_Exams      2.729380
dtype: float64

Std. error:
Intercept      3.808914
Study_Hours    0.255716
Prep_Exams     0.628628
dtype: float64

t:
Intercept      16.939643
Study_Hours     4.123999
Prep_Exams      4.341802
dtype: float64

P > |t|:
Intercept      3.907089e-08
Study_Hours    2.582491e-03
Prep_Exams     1.872530e-03
dtype: float64

CI [0.025 0.095]:
Intercept    55.905276  73.138000
Study_Hours   0.476103   1.633042
Prep_Exams    1.307324   4.151435
```

30.5.2 Explaining reported metrics line-items in Table 1

coef

The `coef` column represents the coefficients for each independent variable along with the intercept value.

std err

`std err` is the standard deviation of the corresponding variable's coefficient across all the data points. When using only one predicting variable, the standard error can be obtained from this two-dimensional space as shown below

t

The `t` column provides the t-statistic corresponding to each independent variable. The Student-t statistic is used to calculate the p_{values}.

P > |t|

When the p_{value} is less than the chosen level of significance of $\frac{\alpha}{2} = 0.025$, it indicates that the corresponding parameter estimate is significantly different from zero.

Confidence Interval

The `[0.025 0.975]` column, gives the confidence interval for the parameter estimate at the level of significance $\alpha = 0.05$. This means, that we are 95% confident, that the "true" parameter estimate for the regressor variable (const, x1, x2) lies within the reported interval.

30.5.3 Renaming coefficients

Sometimes it is desirable to rename the coefficients. This can be achieved by using the `xname` parameter to the report `summary()` function, as described in StatsmodelsDocs [2023], the function call becomes:

```
results.summary(xname=['const','x1','x2'])
```

```
print('Before:')
print_img(results.summary().tables[1])
print('After:')
# change variable names
print_img(results.summary(
    xname=["const", "x1", "x2"]).tables[1])
```

```
Before:
```

```
===============================================================================
                  coef    std err          t      P>|t|      [0.025      0.975]
-------------------------------------------------------------------------------
Intercept      64.5216      3.809     16.940      0.000      55.905      73.138
Study_Hours     1.0546      0.256      4.124      0.003       0.476       1.633
Prep_Exams      2.7294      0.629      4.342      0.002       1.307       4.151
===============================================================================
```

After:

```
===============================================================================
                 coef    std err          t      P>|t|      [0.025      0.975]
-------------------------------------------------------------------------------
const         64.5216      3.809     16.940      0.000      55.905      73.138
x1             1.0546      0.256      4.124      0.003       0.476       1.633
x2             2.7294      0.629      4.342      0.002       1.307       4.151
===============================================================================
```

The variable names have changed, as desired.

30.6 Summary report in Table 2

```
# inspect
print_img(results.summary().tables[2])
```

```
==============================================================================
Omnibus:                        1.874   Durbin-Watson:                   1.715
Prob(Omnibus):                  0.392   Jarque-Bera (JB):                0.501
Skew:                          -0.486   Prob(JB):                        0.778
Kurtosis:                       3.241   Cond. No.                         31.8
==============================================================================
```

30.6.1 Extract specific values in Table 2

We can extract the corresponding values from the diagnostics object `diagn`, which has the following signature:

```
results.diagn
```

and it reports an object with the required values. Unfortunately, the `diagn` object does not provide a value for the Durbin-Watson statistic. However, the DW-statistic can be computed by applying the `durbin_watson()` method from the statsmodels package, like so:

```
dw = durbin_watson(result.resid)
```

```
from statsmodels.stats.stattools import durbin_watson

print("extracted:")
print(f"Omnibus             : {results.diagn['omni']:.4f}")
print(f"Prob. (Omnibus)     : {results.diagn['omnipv']:.4f}")
print(f"Skewness            : {results.diagn['skew']:.4f}")
print(f"Kurtosis            : {results.diagn['kurtosis']:.4f}")
print()
print(f"Durbin-Watson       : {durbin_watson(results.resid):.4f}")
print(f"Jarque-Bera (JB)    : {results.diagn['jbpv']:.4f}")
print(f"Prob. (JB)          : {results.diagn['jb']:.4f}")
print(f"Condition No.       : {results.diagn['condno']:.4f}")
```

```
extracted:
Omnibus          : 1.8739
Prob. (Omnibus)  : 0.3918
Skewness         : -0.4860
Kurtosis         : 3.2406

Durbin-Watson    : 1.7155
Jarque-Bera (JB) : 0.7783
Prob. (JB)       : 0.5013
Condition No.    : 31.8302
```

30.6.2 Explain the reported metrics in Table 2

Omnibus

One of the underlying assumptions of linear regression models is that the residuals are normally distributed. The Omnibus Test allows us to confirm that the residuals are indeed normally distributed.

Prob (Omnibus)

If the probability Prob(Omnibus) is less than the chosen level of significance α = 0.05, we can reject the Null Hypothesis of normality, and conclude that the residuals are normally distributed, meaning that the aforementioned underlying assumption is met.

Skewness

The Skew metric represents the skewness of the residual distribution. Skewness refers to the notion that the distribution is either tilted to the left or right. A fully normally distributed variable has a skew of 0.

As a general guideline, a skewness value between -1 and +1 is considered excellent, but a value between -2 and +2 is generally considered acceptable. Values beyond -2 and +2 are considered indicative of substantial non-normality. Joseph F. Hair Jr [2022]

Kurtosis

The Kurtosis is a measure of the thickness of the tails or heavy-tailed distribution compared to normal distribution. High kurtosis indicates the distribution is peaked, or narrow, whereas low kurtosis on the other hand indicates fat-tails. A kurtosis of 3 indicates a normal distribution.

Analogous to the skewness, the general guideline is that if the kurtosis is greater than +2, the distribution is too peaked. Likewise, a kurtosis of less than -2 indicates a distribution that is too flat. When both skewness and kurtosis are close to zero, the pattern of responses is considered a normal distribution. George [2023], Joseph F. Hair Jr [2022]

Note: Sometimes the kurtosis measure is given as access kurtosis which means a reported value of 0 access kurtosis is equivalent to a reported kurtosis of 3, which is just an offset of 3, and both are indicative of a normal distribution.

Durbin-Watson (DW)

The Durbin-Watson statistic quantifies autocorrelation in the residuals. If the residuals suffer from autocorrelation, the model and the coefficient estimates become biased, rendering the regression model invalid.

The interpretation of the DW-statistic relies on two critical values (DL and DU), which are to be looked up in specific critical value tables.

Jarque-Bera (JB)

The Jarque-Bera (JB) Test is somewhat similar to the Omnibus Test, asserting the normality of the residual terms distribution.

Prob (JB)

If the computed Prob (JB) probability is less than the desired level of significance $\alpha = 0.05$ we can reject the null hypothesis H_0, and conclude that the residuals are not normally distributed.

Condition Number

The condition number measures the presence of multicollinearity among the independent feature variables in the dataset. A measure of above 30 is deemed to be significant, and measures should be taken to correct for the presence of multicollinearity, by for example eliminating one or more of the feature variables from the analysis.

Note: In simple linear regression, with only one predictor variable, the problem of multicollinearity rarely occurs, resulting in a fairly low condition number.

CHAPTER 31

DATA FITTING

We compare two regression libraries, first the NumPy library, and second the Scikit-learn library.

- Part 1: Data Fitting using the `polyfit()` method from the NumPy library
- Part 2: Data Fitting using the `LinearRegression()` method from the Scikit-learn library

Additional information on the background of curve fitting can be found at Wikipedia [2023], and on polynomial interpolation at Wikipedia [2023].

31.1 Generate dataset and visually inspect

```
import math
import numpy as np
import scipy as sp
import matplotlib.pyplot as plt
%matplotlib inline

# generate data
nsamples = 100
x = np.linspace(0, 1, nsamples)
y = 0.05*x + 0.05*x**2 + 0.1*x**3 + 0.05*np.sin(3.5*np.pi*x)
# plot
fig = plt.figure(figsize=(5,3))
plt.scatter(x, y)
plt.title("observations (x,y)")
```

(continues on next page)

(continued from previous page)

```
plt.xlabel('x')
plt.ylabel('y')
plt.grid()
plt.show()
```

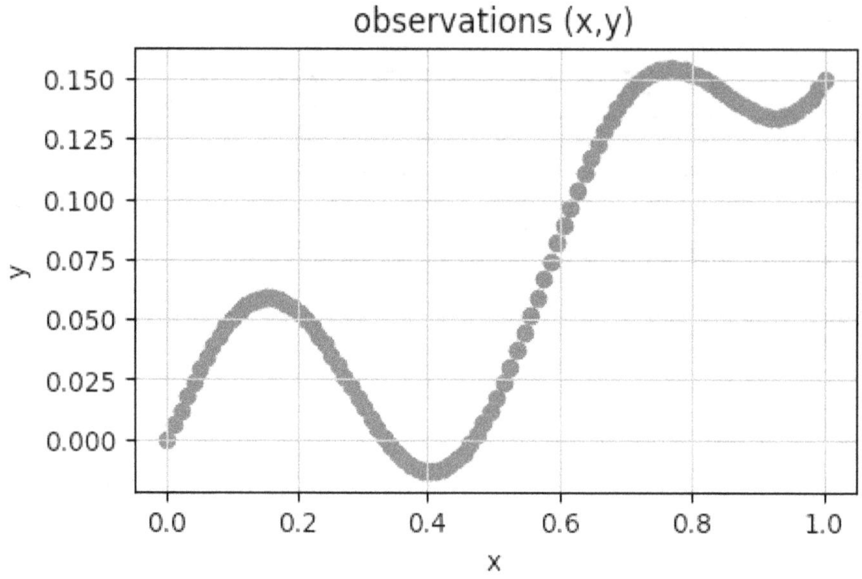


```
# helper function
def error(f, x, y):
    """ return sp.sum((f(x)-y)**2) """
    return np.sum((f(x)-y)**2)
```

31.2 Part 1: Data Fitting using NumPy

The NumPy library has this `polyfit()` method, which we are going to explore, by creating the following set of models:

- Linear relationship
- Quadratic relationship
- 3rd order polynomial regression
- 4th order polynomial regression

The polynomial regression uses least squares minimization for computation and it can model the expected dependent variables y as an nth order polynomial, resulting in a general polynomial regression model. The expression linear in this context means, that the regression function is linear to estimate the unknown parameters.

The computation and inference part of polynomial regression relies on multiple linear regression by treating $x, x2, x3, x4, ...xn$ as being distinct independent variables. According to NumpyDocs [2023], the fitting algorithm attempts to minimize the following

Error equation:

$$\text{minimize E} = \sum_{j=0}^{k} |p(x_j) - y_j|^2$$

where

- k: is the number of observations
- $p(x_j)$: is the predicted value at x_j
- y_j: is the true value y at x_j

In the following code example, we demonstrate this and implement:

31.2.1 Linear relationship

1st order polynomial, linear

```
# polyfit and poly1d method
coefs = np.polyfit(x, y, 1)
fitted_curve = np.poly1d(coefs)(x) # Linear
f = np.poly1d(coefs) # formula
# plot
fig = plt.figure(figsize=(5,3))
plt.scatter(x, y,
            label="observed")
plt.plot(x, fitted_curve,
         c="red", label="fitted")
plt.title('linear')
plt.xlabel('x')
plt.ylabel('y')
plt.grid()
plt.legend()
plt.show()
# report
print('coefficients:')
print(f'coefficients : {coefs[:-1]}')
print(f'intercept    : {coefs[-1]:.5f}')
print(f'error        : {error(f, x, y):.5f}')
# print('function:', f)
```

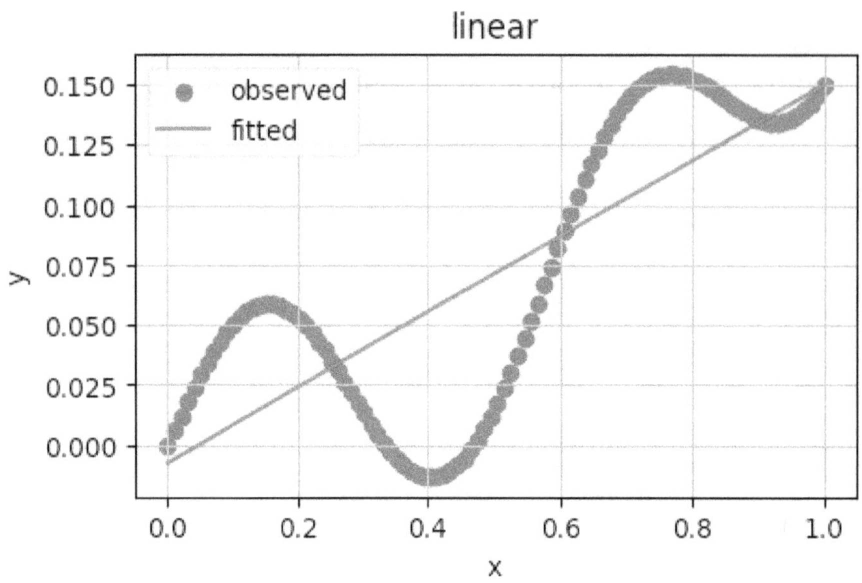


```
coefficients:
coefficients : [0.15756121]
intercept    : -0.00753
error        : 0.13938
```

Interpretation

Observe, that the linear regression line, makes it obvious, that a non-linear relationship exists between the independent variable x and the dependent variable y. The linear regression model is not able to capture such a non-linear function very well.

31.2.2 Quadratic relationship

2nd order polynomial, quadratic

```
# polyfit and poly1d method
coefs = np.polyfit(x, y, 2)
fitted_curve = np.poly1d(coefs)(x)
f = np.poly1d(coefs) # formula
# plot
fig = plt.figure(figsize=(5,3))
plt.scatter(x, y,
            label="observed")
plt.plot(x, fitted_curve,
         c="red", label="fitted")
plt.title('quadratic')
plt.xlabel('x')
plt.ylabel('y')
```

(continues on next page)

(continued from previous page)

```
plt.grid()
plt.legend()
plt.show()
# report
print(f'Coefficients : {coefs[:-1]}')
print(f'Intercept    : {coefs[-1]:.5f}')
print(f'Error        : {error(f, x, y):.5f}')
# print('function:', f)
```

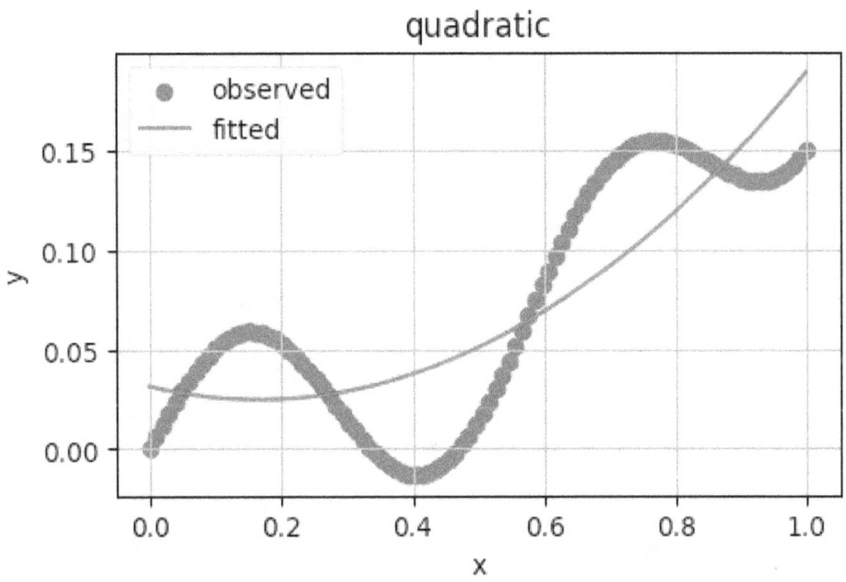


```
Coefficients : [ 0.23743624 -0.07987503]
Intercept    : 0.03164
Error        : 0.10679
```

Interpretation

Observe, that the non-linear relationship is also not captured well by a quadratic regression model.

31.2.3 3rd order polynomial

3rd order polynomial, cubic

```
# polyfit and poly1d method
coefs = np.polyfit(x, y, 3)
fitted_curve = np.poly1d(coefs)(x)
f = np.poly1d(coefs) # formula
# plot
fig = plt.figure(figsize=(5,3))
```

(continues on next page)

(continued from previous page)

```
plt.scatter(x, y,
            label="observed")
plt.plot(x, fitted_curve, c="red", label="fitted")
plt.title('3rd order polynomial')
plt.xlabel('x')
plt.ylabel('y')
plt.grid()
plt.legend()
plt.show()
# report
print(f'Coefficients : {coefs[:-1]}')
print(f'Intercept    : {coefs[-1]:.5f}')
print(f'Error        : {error(f, x, y):.5f}')
# print('function', f)
```

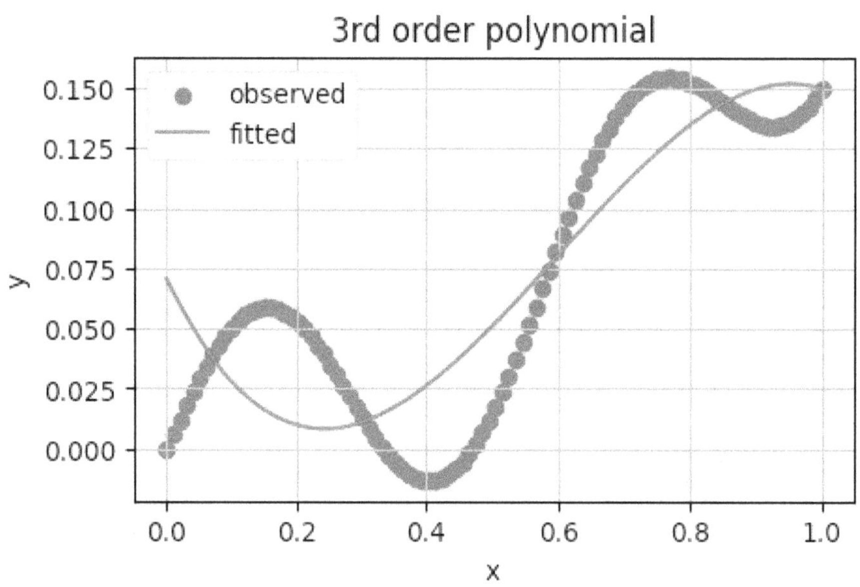


```
Coefficients : [-0.80510309  1.44509087 -0.56051361]
Intercept    : 0.07069
Error        : 0.08224
```

Interpretation

Even a cubic or $3rd$ order polynomial model is not able to capture this type of non-linear behavior.

31.2.4 4th order polynomial

4th order polynomial, higher order

```
# poly1d and poly1d method
coefs = np.polyfit(x, y, 4)
fitted_curve = np.poly1d(coefs)(x)
f = np.poly1d(coefs) # formula
# plot
fig = plt.figure(figsize=(5,3))
plt.scatter(x, y,
            label="observed")
plt.plot(x, fitted_curve,
         c="red",
         label="fitted")
plt.title('4th order polynomial')
plt.xlabel('x')
plt.ylabel('y')
plt.grid()
plt.legend()
plt.show()
# report
print(f'Coefficients : {coefs[:-1]}')
print(f'Intercept    : {coefs[-1]:.5f}')
print(f'Error        : {error(f, x, y):.5f}')
# print('function:', f)
```

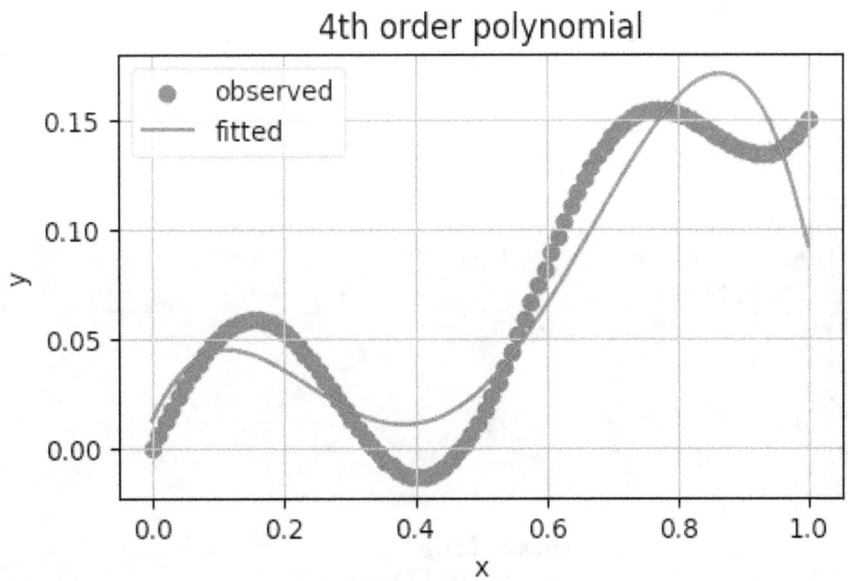


```
Coefficients : [-4.31381994  7.82253679 -4.08288889  0.65364622]
Intercept    : 0.01273
Error        : 0.03665
```

Interpretation

The *4th* order model does capture the non-linear relationship quite well. However, higher polynomial models are prone to wide swings. We estimated the coefficients using the ordinary least squares `ols()` method.

31.3 Part 2: Data Fitting using Scikit-learn

We make use of the `LinearRegression()` method, provided by the scikit-learn library, which uses the ordinary least squares minimization to estimate the coefficients and intercept terms. In this section, we investigate variations of this model, like:

- Linear relationship
- Quadratic relationship
- 3rd order polynomial
- 4th order polynomial

We defined a helper function for drawing and pass-in the parameters for the different models.

```
def regression_line(model, coefs, intercept,
                          X_, title_text=None):
    """ helper function """

    # plot
    fig = plt.figure(figsize=(5,3))
    plt.scatter(x, y,
                label="observed")
    plt.plot(x,
             model.predict(X_), c='green',
             label="fitted", linewidth=3)
    plt.title(title_text)
    plt.xlabel('x')
    plt.ylabel('y')
    plt.grid()
    plt.legend()
    plt.show()
    # results
    print('results:')
    print('Coefficients : {}'.format(coefs))
    print('Intercept    : {:.5f}'.format(intercept))
    a = np.linalg.norm(y - model.predict(X_)) ** 2
    print(f'Error        : {a:.5f}')

    return
```

31.3.1 Linear relationship

The linear regression model, from the scikit.learn library has the following signature:

```
linear_reg_1d = LinearRegression()
linear_reg_1d.fit(X1, y)
```

The polynomial regression model, from the scikit.learn library has the following signature:

```
poly1d = PolynomialFeatures(degree=1)
X1 = poly1d.fit_transform(np.array(x).reshape(-1, 1))
```

```
from sklearn.preprocessing import PolynomialFeatures
from sklearn.linear_model import LinearRegression
from sklearn.pipeline import Pipeline

# polynomial features
poly1d = PolynomialFeatures(degree=1)
X1 = poly1d.fit_transform(np.array(x).reshape(-1, 1))
# linear regression
linear_reg_1d = LinearRegression()
linear_reg_1d.fit(X1, y)
# plot
regression_line(linear_reg_1d,
                linear_reg_1d.coef_[1:],
                linear_reg_1d.intercept_, X1,
                title_text='linear')
plt.show()
```

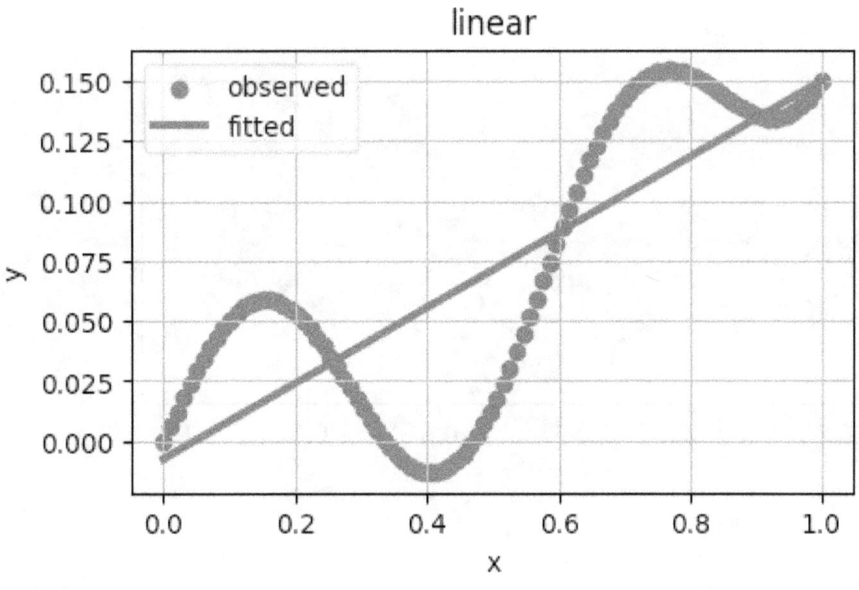

```
results:
Coefficients : [0.15756121]
Intercept    : -0.00753
Error        : 0.13938
```

31.3.2 Quadratic relationship

We make use of the PolynomialFeatures(degree=2) method, to build the quadratic regression model. The method signature becomes:

```
poly2d = PolynomialFeatures(degree=2)
X2 = poly2d.fit_transform(np.array(x).reshape(-1, 1))
```

```
# polynomial features
poly2d = PolynomialFeatures(degree=2)
X2 = poly2d.fit_transform(np.array(x).reshape(-1, 1))
# linear regression
linear_reg_2d = LinearRegression()
linear_reg_2d.fit(X2, y)
# plot
regression_line(linear_reg_2d,
                linear_reg_2d.coef_[1:],
                linear_reg_2d.intercept_, X2,
                title_text='quadratic')
plt.show()
```

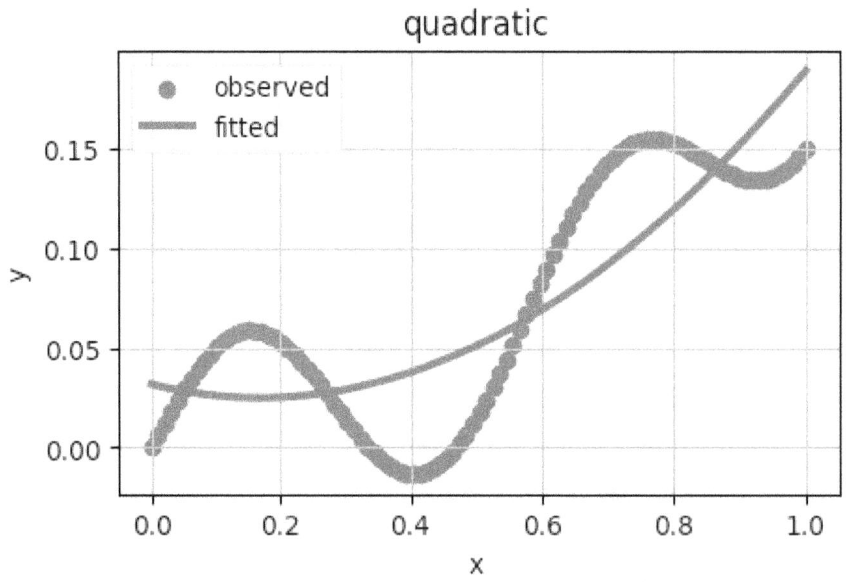

```
results:
Coefficients : [-0.07987503  0.23743624]
Intercept    : 0.03164
Error        : 0.10679
```

31.3.3 3rd order polynomial

We make use of the `PolynomialFeatures(degree=3)` method, to build the quadratic regression model. The method signature becomes:

```
poly3d = PolynomialFeatures(degree=3)
X3 = poly3d.fit_transform(np.array(x).reshape(-1, 1))
```

```
# polynomial features
poly3d = PolynomialFeatures(degree=3)
X3 = poly3d.fit_transform(np.array(x).reshape(-1, 1))
# linear regression
linear_reg_3d = LinearRegression()
linear_reg_3d.fit(X3, y)
# plot
regression_line(linear_reg_3d,
                linear_reg_3d.coef_[1:],
                linear_reg_3d.intercept_, X3,
                title_text='3rd order polynomial')
plt.show()
```

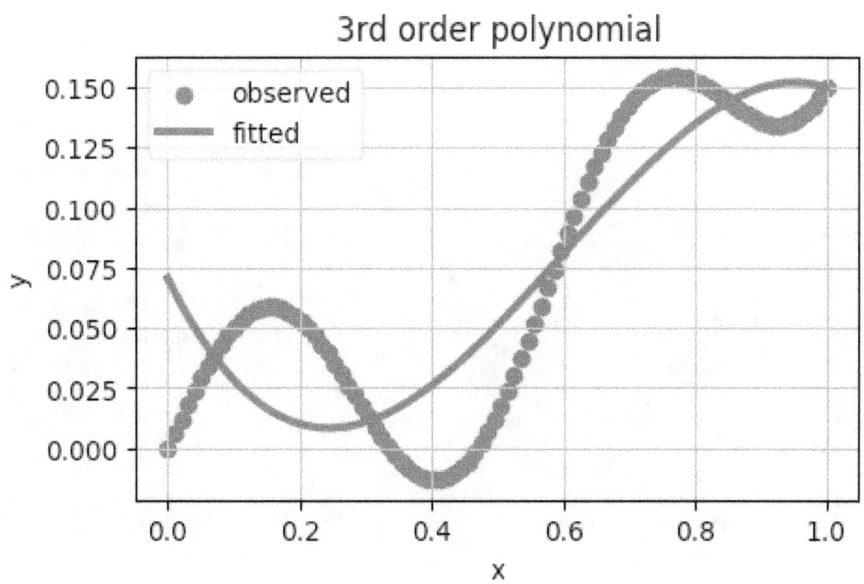

```
results:
Coefficients : [-0.56051361  1.44509087 -0.80510309]
Intercept    : 0.07069
Error        : 0.08224
```

31.3.4 4th order polynomial

We make use of the PolynomialFeatures(degree=4) method, to build the quadratic regression model. The method signature becomes:

```
poly4d = PolynomialFeatures(degree=4)
X4 = poly4d.fit_transform(np.array(x).reshape(-1, 1))
```

```
# polynomial features
poly4d = PolynomialFeatures(degree=4)
X4 = poly4d.fit_transform(np.array(x).reshape(-1, 1))
# linear regression
linear_reg_4d = LinearRegression()
linear_reg_4d.fit(X4, y)
# plot
regression_line(linear_reg_4d,
                linear_reg_4d.coef_[1:],
                linear_reg_4d.intercept_, X4,
                title_text='4th order polynomial')
plt.show()
```

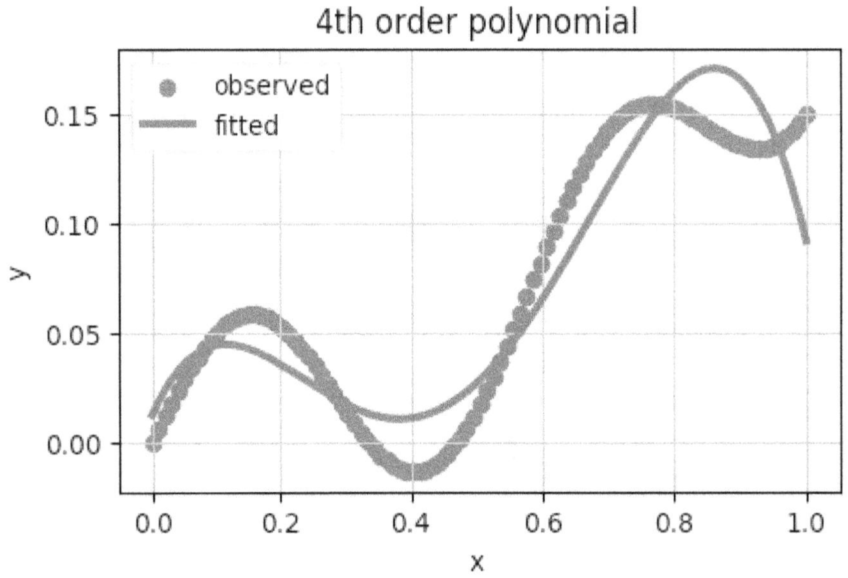

```
results:
Coefficients : [ 0.65364622 -4.08288889  7.82253679 -4.31381994]
Intercept    : 0.01273
Error        : 0.03665
```

Interpretation

The `polyfit()` function of the NumPy package, and the `LinearRegression()` function from the scikit-learn package, produce similar results, which is expected.

CHAPTER 32

ORDINARY LEAST SQUARE REGRESSION

Ordinary Least Square Regression attempts to minimize the squared error term, that is the difference between the target observations and the values produced by the regression equation.

- Part 1: Multiple Linear Regression
- Part 2: Fit model and report summary table
- Part 3: Modeling categorical features as dummy variables
- Part 4: Study the impact of multicollinear data

```
import matplotlib.pyplot as plt
import pandas as pd
import numpy as np
import statsmodels.api as sm
import warnings
warnings.filterwarnings('ignore')
# no scientific notation
np.set_printoptions(suppress=True)
%matplotlib inline
```

32.1 Part 1: Multiple linear regression model

> A set of data is generated, with known parameters and target values. In this way we can study the competence of any regression model estimating the target coefficients and recovering the original parameters used to create the dataset.

Keep in mind, that the model needs an intercept term, and so we have to add a column with 1s to the dataset, as we perform the regression analysis. Then we assess the model and the summary report.

In the following Python code segment, we implement this approach and present the computed results.

```
# parameters
nsample = 100
sigma = 0.7
noise_level = 650
# features
x = np.linspace(0, 20, nsample)
f_x1 = -100 * np.cos(x)
f_x2 = 5 * np.tanh(x)
f_x3 = -2.4*x**2
ones = np.ones(nsample) # required by model
X = np.column_stack((ones, f_x1, f_x2, f_x3))
b_vector = [20, 2.5, -0.5, 3.0] # const, x1, x2, x3
y_true = np.dot(X, b_vector)
np.random.seed(1) # reproducibility
y = y_true + sigma * np.random.normal(size=nsample) * noise_level
X = pd.DataFrame(X, columns=['const', 'x1', 'x2', 'x3'])
# target with added noise
y_noisy = y
# inspect
print('dataset:')
print(X.head())
print('X.shape       : ', X.shape)
print('x.shape       : ', x.shape)
print('y_noisy.shape : ', y_noisy.shape)
print('y_true.shape  : ', y_true.shape)
```

```
dataset:
   const          x1        x2        x3
0    1.0 -100.000000  0.000000 -0.000000
1    1.0  -97.966323  0.996580 -0.097949
2    1.0  -91.948007  1.917004 -0.391797
3    1.0  -82.189840  2.706741 -0.881543
4    1.0  -69.088721  3.342651 -1.567187
X.shape       :  (100, 4)
x.shape       :  (100,)
```

(continues on next page)

(continued from previous page)

```
y_noisy.shape :  (100,)
y_true.shape  :  (100,)
```

Observe the added `const` column in the dataset.

32.1.1 Fitting the regression model

We make use of the `ols()` method from the statsmodels package, to fit the model, which has the following signature:

```
model = sm.OLS(y_noisy, X)
result = model.fit()
```

it returns a model object and a result object.

In the following code section, both the model object and the result object are examined and the computed regression result table is shown.

```
from quantlib import print_img

# fit ols model
model = sm.OLS(y_noisy, X)
results = model.fit()
# inspect
print_img(results.summary().tables[0])
print_img(results.summary().tables[1])
print_img(results.summary().tables[2])
```

```
                            OLS Regression Results
==============================================================================
Dep. Variable:                      y   R-squared:                       0.827
Model:                            OLS   Adj. R-squared:                  0.822
Method:                 Least Squares   F-statistic:                     153.1
Date:                Tue, 02 Jul 2024   Prob (F-statistic):           1.87e-36
Time:                        14:01:04   Log-Likelihood:                -741.28
No. Observations:                 100   AIC:                             1491.
Df Residuals:                      96   BIC:                             1501.
Df Model:                           3
Covariance Type:            nonrobust
==============================================================================

==============================================================================
                 coef    std err          t      P>|t|      [0.025      0.975]
------------------------------------------------------------------------------
const         93.7425    277.996      0.337      0.737    -458.075     645.560
x1             2.5890      0.614      4.214      0.000       1.370       3.808
x2           -19.3828     59.748     -0.324      0.746    -137.982      99.216
x3             2.8602      0.152     18.780      0.000       2.558       3.162
==============================================================================
```

```
==============================================================================
Omnibus:                        0.189   Durbin-Watson:                   2.058
Prob(Omnibus):                  0.910   Jarque-Bera (JB):                0.046
Skew:                           0.051   Prob(JB):                        0.977
Kurtosis:                       3.025   Cond. No.                     3.00e+03
==============================================================================
```

32.1.2 Extract specific values from the result object

To further process any reported results, we need to extract specific values from the result object. In the following Python code segment, this is demonstrated and the results are presented.

```python
print('parameters:')
for i in range(len(results.params)):
    index = results.params.index[i].ljust(11)
    param = results.params[i]
    print(f"{index}: {param:.4f}")
print('metrics:')
print(f"R2          : {results.rsquared:.4f}")
print(f'aic         : {results.aic:.4f}')
print(f'bic         : {results.bic:.4f}')
print(f'ess         : {results.ess:.4f}')
print(f'ssr         : {results.ssr:.4f}')
print(f'mse_model   : {results.mse_model:.4f}')
print(f'mse_resid   : {results.mse_resid:.4f}')
print(f'mse_total   : {results.mse_total:.4f}')
print(f'fvalue      : {results.fvalue:.4f}')
print(f'f_pvalue    : {results.f_pvalue:.4f}')
cn1 = np.linalg.cond(X)
print(f'condition number by linalg.cond : {cn1:.4f}')
cn2 = np.linalg.cond(model.exog)
print(f'condition number by model.exog  : {cn2:.4f}')
```

```
parameters:
const      : 93.7425
x1         : 2.5890
x2         : -19.3828
x3         : 2.8602
metrics:
R2         : 0.8271
aic        : 1490.5675
bic        : 1500.9882
ess        : 76901076.7217
ssr        : 16078098.4725
mse_model  : 25633692.2406
mse_resid  : 167480.1924
mse_total  : 939183.5878
fvalue     : 153.0551
```

(continues on next page)

(continued from previous page)

```
f_pvalue    : 0.0000
condition number by linalg.cond : 3003.5008
condition number by model.exog  : 3003.5008
```

We use the get_prediction() method from the statsmodels library, to obtain the prediction values. The method has the following signature:

```
pred_ols = results.get_prediction()
```

As described in StatsmodelsDocs [2023], we compute the confidence interval around those predictions, therefore we extract the appropriate values from the model object by using the summary_frame() method, like so:

```
iv_l = pred_ols.summary_frame()["obs_ci_lower"]
iv_u = pred_ols.summary_frame()["obs_ci_upper"]
```

```
# predictions
pred = results.get_prediction()
# inspect
print('pred_ols summary frame:')
print(pred.summary_frame()[['obs_ci_lower',
                            'obs_ci_upper']])
```

```
pred_ols summary frame:
    obs_ci_lower  obs_ci_upper
0   -1133.787511    803.475429
1   -1092.950702    733.975513
2   -1055.969444    690.795143
3   -1022.054868    673.991861
4    -988.220975    679.421552
..           ...           ...
95  -3610.700806  -1940.112763
96  -3641.884957  -1971.147930
97  -3664.589104  -1993.767447
98  -3680.358387  -2008.981067
99  -3691.049216  -2018.116141

[100 rows x 2 columns]
```

We extract the values for the confidence interval and the degree of freedom df from the model object, like so:

```
# Extract values from the model object
print('degree of freedom df: {:.0f}'.format(pred.df))
print('row_labels:', pred.row_labels)
# last 5 only
```

(continues on next page)

(continued from previous page)

```
print('conf_int:\n', pred.conf_int(obs=True,
                                  alpha=0.05)[-5:])
```

```
degree of freedom df: 96
row_labels: RangeIndex(start=0, stop=100, step=1)
conf_int:
 [[-3610.70080616 -1940.11276307]
 [-3641.88495706 -1971.14793004]
 [-3664.58910442 -1993.76744705]
 [-3680.35838727 -2008.98106715]
 [-3691.04921572 -2018.11614094]]
```

32.1.3 Visualize the data in a scatter plot with confidence interval

We make use of the `summary_frame()` method of the prediction object, to extract the upper and lower band representing the confidence interval. The signatures of these methods are:

```
pred_ols = results.get_prediction()
ci_upper = pred_ols.summary_frame()["obs_ci_lower"]
ci_lower = pred_ols.summary_frame()["obs_ci_upper"]
```

In the following Python code segment, this approach is implemented and the resulting plot is presented.

```
# obtain predictions
pred = results.get_prediction()
# confidence interval
iv_l = pred.summary_frame()["obs_ci_lower"]
iv_u = pred.summary_frame()["obs_ci_upper"]
# plot
fig, ax = plt.subplots(figsize=(6,3.5))
ax.plot(x, y_noisy, "o",
        label="data")
ax.plot(x, y_true, color="green",
        linestyle="solid", linewidth=4,
        alpha=0.7, label="True")
ax.plot(x, results.fittedvalues,
        color='red', linestyle="--",
        linewidth=5, alpha=0.9, label="OLS")
ax.plot(x, iv_u,
        color="grey", linestyle="--")
ax.plot(x, iv_l,
        color="grey", linestyle="--")
ax.set_title('Regression with Confidence Envelope',
```

(continues on next page)

(continued from previous page)

```
                fontsize=10)
ax.legend(loc="best")
ax.set_xlabel('x')
plt.grid(True)
plt.show()
```

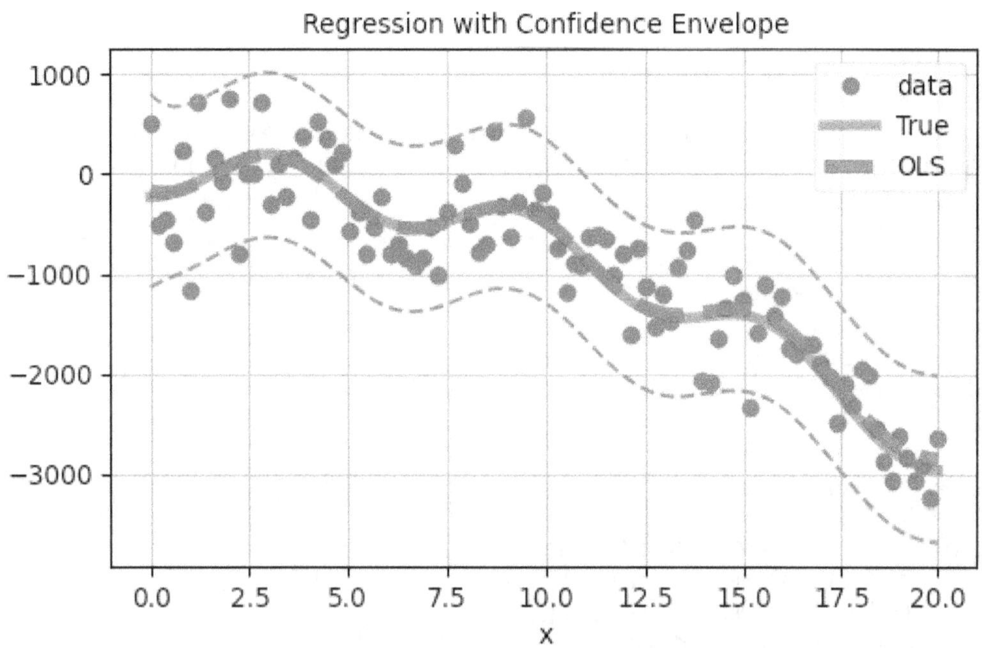

32.1.4 Investigate the impact of added noise on the data

To further study the impact of the noise level on the ability of the model to recover the equation used to generate the sample data. The `b_vector` is set to values for ($x1$=0.5, and $x2$=9), and we set the noise level to zero, and we attempt to recover these values used to create the dataset.

```
b_vector = np.array([1.0, 0.5, 9])
```

Try this out by setting the noise level to zero. In the following Python example, we implement this approach.

```
from quantlib import print_img

# parameters
nsample = 100
sigma = 0.7
noise_level = 0
# features
```

(continues on next page)

(continued from previous page)

```
x = np.linspace(0, 20, nsample)
f_x1 = -100 * np.cos(x)
f_x2 = 5 * np.tanh(x)
f_x3 = -2.4*x**2
ones = np.ones(nsample) # required by model
X = np.column_stack((ones, f_x1, f_x2, f_x3))
# target
b_vector = [20, 2.5, -0.5, 3.0] # const, x1, x2, x3
y_true = np.dot(X, b_vector)
np.random.seed(1) # reproducibility
y = y_true + sigma * np.random.normal(size=nsample) * noise_level
X = pd.DataFrame(X, columns=['const', 'x1', 'x2', 'x3'])
# target
y_noisy = y
# fit the OLS model
model = sm.OLS(y_noisy, X)
results = model.fit()
print_img(results.summary().tables[0])
print_img(results.summary().tables[1])
# inspect
print('dataset:')
print(X.head())
# plot
pred_ols = results.get_prediction()
iv_l = pred_ols.summary_frame()["obs_ci_lower"]
iv_u = pred_ols.summary_frame()["obs_ci_upper"]
fig, ax = plt.subplots(figsize=(6,3.5))
ax.plot(x, y_noisy, "o",
        label="data")
ax.plot(x, y_true,
        color="green", linestyle="solid",
        linewidth=4, alpha=0.7,
        label="True")
ax.plot(x, results.fittedvalues,
        color='red', linestyle="--",
        linewidth=5, alpha=0.9,
        label="OLS")
ax.plot(x, iv_u,
        color="grey",
        linestyle="--")
ax.plot(x, iv_l,
        color="grey",
        linestyle="--")
ax.set_title('Regression with Confidence Envelope',
             fontsize=14)
ax.legend(loc="best")
plt.grid(True)
plt.show()
# inspect
print('parameters estimated:')
```

(continues on next page)

(continued from previous page)

```
print(results.params)
```

```
                            OLS Regression Results
==============================================================================
Dep. Variable:                      y   R-squared:                       1.000
Model:                            OLS   Adj. R-squared:                  1.000
Method:                 Least Squares   F-statistic:                 3.864e+31
Date:                Tue, 02 Jul 2024   Prob (F-statistic):               0.00
Time:                        14:01:07   Log-Likelihood:                 2639.9
No. Observations:                 100   AIC:                            -5272.
Df Residuals:                      96   BIC:                            -5261.
Df Model:                           3
Covariance Type:            nonrobust
==============================================================================

==============================================================================
                 coef    std err          t      P>|t|      [0.025      0.975]
------------------------------------------------------------------------------
const         20.0000   5.75e-13   3.48e+13      0.000      20.000      20.000
x1             2.5000   1.27e-15   1.97e+15      0.000       2.500       2.500
x2            -0.5000   1.24e-13  -4.05e+12      0.000      -0.500      -0.500
x3             3.0000   3.15e-16   9.53e+15      0.000       3.000       3.000
==============================================================================
```

```
dataset:
   const          x1        x2        x3
0    1.0 -100.000000  0.000000 -0.000000
1    1.0  -97.966323  0.996580 -0.097949
2    1.0  -91.948007  1.917004 -0.391797
3    1.0  -82.189840  2.706741 -0.881543
4    1.0  -69.088721  3.342651 -1.567187
```

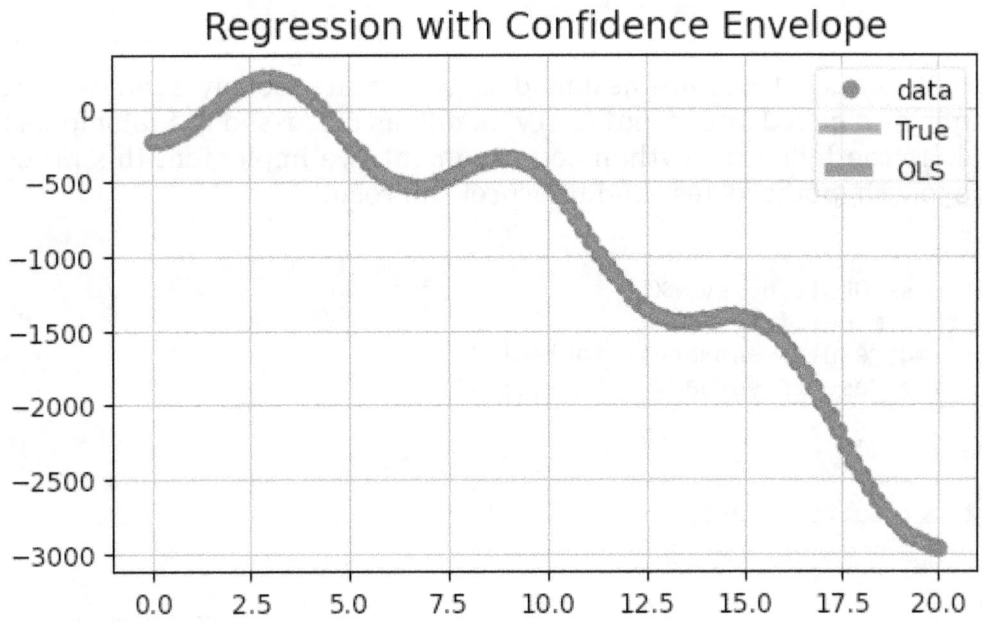

```
parameters estimated:
const    20.0
x1        2.5
x2       -0.5
x3        3.0
dtype: float64
```

We used the `b_vector` of `[20,2.5,-0.5,3.0]` to generate the sample data, and we can observe that the above regression model was able to fully recover such values.

32.1.5 F-Test for joint hypothesis testing

To set up the statistical procedure, we formulate:

Hypothesis

- H_0: all independent variables are jointly zero
- H_1: at least one of the variables is different from zero

level of significance

- $\alpha = 0.05$
- two-sided test

To compute the F-Test for a joint linear hypothesis, which is a special case of `wald_test` that uses the F-distribution. To perform the F-Test, we make use of the formula notation, which has the following signature:

```
result.f_test("x1=0, x2=0")
```

The coefficients ($x1$, $x2$) are assumed to be simultaneously equal to zero, resulting in a so-called `intercept-only` model, as discussed in StatsmodelsDocs [2023]. In the following Python code segment, we implement this procedure for the joint hypothesis test and interpret the results.

```
# refit the model
model = sm.OLS(y_noisy, X[['x1','x2','const']])
results = model.fit()
print_img(results.summary().tables[0])
print_img(results.summary().tables[1])
# parameters
alpha = 0.05
# F-Test as a joint hypothesis test
ftest = results.f_test("x1=0, x2=0") # both zero
# hypothesis test
print('F-Test:')
```

(continues on next page)

(continued from previous page)

```
print(f'F-statistic              : {ftest.fvalue:.4f}')
print(f'P(F-statistic )          : {ftest.pvalue:.4E}')
print(f'level of significance : {alpha:.2f}')
print('two-sided test')
print('Hypothesis')
print('H0: coefficients for (x1,x2) are both zero')
print('H1: at least one coefficient is not zero')
if (ftest.pvalue < alpha/2):
    print('jointly Significant')
else:
    print('jointly Not Significant')
```

```
                            OLS Regression Results
==============================================================================
Dep. Variable:                      y   R-squared:                       0.217
Model:                            OLS   Adj. R-squared:                  0.201
Method:                 Least Squares   F-statistic:                     13.46
Date:                Tue, 02 Jul 2024   Prob (F-statistic):           6.94e-06
Time:                        14:01:08   Log-Likelihood:                -811.12
No. Observations:                 100   AIC:                             1628.
Df Residuals:                      97   BIC:                             1636.
Df Model:                           2
Covariance Type:            nonrobust
==============================================================================

==============================================================================
                 coef    std err          t      P>|t|      [0.025      0.975]
------------------------------------------------------------------------------
x1             5.4277      1.192      4.553      0.000       3.061       7.794
x2          -405.0585    112.220     -3.610      0.000    -627.784    -182.333
const       1013.3324    546.793      1.853      0.067     -71.900    2098.565
==============================================================================
```

```
F-Test:
F-statistic              : 13.4590
P(F-statistic )          : 6.9408E-06
level of significance : 0.05
two-sided test
Hypothesis
H0: coefficients for (x1,x2) are both zero
H1: at least one coefficient is not zero
jointly Significant
```

Interpretation

The reported F-statistic is 13.459 with the corresponding P(F-statistic) or p_{value} of 6.94E-6, almost zero.

Since the F-Test is set up to be a two-tailed test, we allocate $\frac{\alpha}{2}$ in either tail of the distribution.

Observe that the coefficients $x1$ and $x2$ are in reality both statistically significant at the chosen level of significance α = 0.05, therefore the null hypothesis H_0, that both coefficients are jointly zero, is rejected, in favor of the alternative hypothesis H_1, which states that at least one of the coefficients is statistically significantly different from zero.

The reported coefficient estimates and the corresponding $P > |t|$ values are in full agreement with our expectations, which is a very encouraging result.

32.2 Part 2: Ordinary Least Squares regression on non-linear curve

> We simulate artificial data with a non-linear relationship between x and y, however the regress is linear in its parameters.

In the following Python code segment, this is implemented and the results are presented.

```
# parameters
nsample = 100
sigma = 0.5
x = np.linspace(0, 20, nsample)
# features
f_x1 = 1.5 * np.sin(x)
f_x2 = (x-2)**2
ones = np.ones(nsample) # required by model
X = np.column_stack((x, f_x1, f_x2, ones))
b_vector = [0.5, 0.5, -0.02, 5.0]
# target
y_true = np.dot(X, b_vector)
np.random.seed(1) # reproducibility
y = y_true + sigma * np.random.normal(size=nsample)
```

32.2.1 Fit the model and report the summary table

```
# fit model
model = sm.OLS(y, X)
results = model.fit()
# inspect
print_img(results.summary())
```

```
                            OLS Regression Results
==============================================================================
Dep. Variable:                      y   R-squared:                       0.892
Model:                            OLS   Adj. R-squared:                  0.889
Method:                 Least Squares   F-statistic:                     265.6
Date:                Tue, 02 Jul 2024   Prob (F-statistic):           2.41e-46
Time:                        14:01:09   Log-Likelihood:                -59.299
No. Observations:                 100   AIC:                             126.6
Df Residuals:                      96   BIC:                             137.0
Df Model:                           3
Covariance Type:            nonrobust
==============================================================================
                 coef    std err          t      P>|t|      [0.025      0.975]
------------------------------------------------------------------------------
x1             0.5213      0.025     20.724      0.000       0.471       0.571
x2             0.4705      0.044     10.805      0.000       0.384       0.557
x3            -0.0209      0.001    -14.049      0.000      -0.024      -0.018
const          4.9032      0.130     37.707      0.000       4.645       5.161
==============================================================================
Omnibus:                        0.810   Durbin-Watson:                   2.086
Prob(Omnibus):                  0.667   Jarque-Bera (JB):                0.595
Skew:                           0.188   Prob(JB):                        0.743
Kurtosis:                       3.030   Cond. No.                         412.
==============================================================================

Notes:
[1] Standard Errors assume that the covariance matrix of the errors is correctly specified.
```

Extract specific values from the results and model objects.

```
from quantlib import print_img

# results
cn1 = results.condition_number
print(f'Condition number result : {cn1:.0f}')
cn2 = np.linalg.cond(model.exog)
print(f'Condition number linalg : {cn2:.0f}')
print()
print("parameters:")
print(results.params)
print()
print("std errors:")
print(results.bse)
print()
np.set_printoptions(formatter={
    'float':lambda x: "{0:.3f}".format(x)})
print("predicted values")
print_img(results.predict())
```

```
Condition number result : 412
Condition number linalg : 412

parameters:
[ 0.52134924  0.4705344  -0.02086642  4.90320604]

std errors:
[0.02515707 0.04354634 0.00148529 0.13003384]
```

(continues on next page)

(continued from previous page)

```
predicted values

 [4.820 5.083 5.338 5.581 5.805 6.007 6.183 6.330 6.448 6.535 6.592 6.622
  6.627 6.612 6.581 6.539 6.493 6.447 6.408 6.381 6.370 6.381 6.415 6.475
  6.562 6.676 6.816 6.978 7.159 7.356 7.563 7.775 7.985 8.189 8.380 8.553
  8.705 8.830 8.928 8.995 9.032 9.040 9.019 8.974 8.908 8.825 8.731 8.632
  8.533 8.440 8.358 8.293 8.248 8.227 8.231 8.263 8.321 8.405 8.512 8.639
  8.781 8.934 9.093 9.250 9.402 9.542 9.664 9.765 9.841 9.888 9.906 9.893
  9.850 9.779 9.683 9.566 9.432 9.286 9.134 8.982 8.835 8.699 8.579 8.479
  8.402 8.351 8.327 8.329 8.357 8.409 8.481 8.569 8.669 8.774 8.879 8.979
  9.067 9.138 9.189 9.214]
```

32.2.2 Visualize the data in a plot with a confidence interval

We draw a plot to compare the "true" values versus the OLS predictions, along with the confidence interval values which are extracted from the `summary_frame()` method result object.

```python
# obtain predictions
pred = results.get_prediction()
iv_l = pred.summary_frame()["obs_ci_lower"]
iv_u = pred.summary_frame()["obs_ci_upper"]
# plot
fig, ax = plt.subplots(figsize=(6,3.5))
txt = 'True vs. Regression with Confidence Envelope'
ax.set_title(txt)
ax.plot(x, y,
        "o", label="data")
ax.plot(x, y_true,
        "b-", label="true")
ax.plot(x, results.fittedvalues,
        "r--.", label="OLS")
ax.plot(x, iv_u, color='grey',
        linestyle=":", alpha=0.8)
ax.plot(x, iv_l, color='grey',
        linestyle=":", alpha=0.8)
ax.set_xlabel('x')
ax.set_ylabel('y')
ax.grid(True)
ax.legend(loc="best")
plt.show()
```

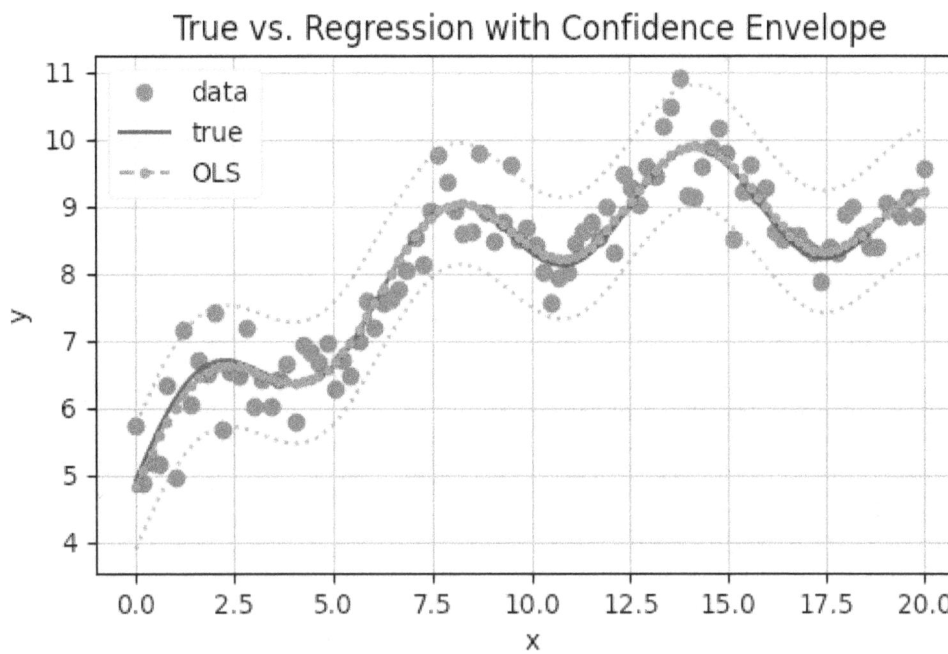

32.3 Part 3: Modeling categorical features as dummy variables

32.3.1 Dataset without dummy variables

> We built a generic dataset, for that we generate 100 rows of features ($x1$,$x2$,$x2$) and target or y_{true} values. Then we add noise to the y_{true} values to arrive at the y target values, which we use in the regression analysis.

The idea behind using artificial data is that the researcher knows the true outcomes. In this way, we can evaluate the performance of the regression analysis, while attempting to recover the original parameters used in generating the data.

```
# parameters
nsample = 100
sigma = 0.7
noise_level = 650
# features
x = np.linspace(0, 20, nsample)
f_x1 = -100 * np.cos(x)
f_x2 = 5 * np.tanh(x)
f_x3 = -2.4*x**2
ones = np.ones(nsample) # required by model
```

(continues on next page)

(continued from previous page)

```
X = np.column_stack((ones, f_x1, f_x2, f_x3))
# const, x1, x2, x3
b_vector = [20, 2.5, -0.5, 3.0]
y_true = np.dot(X, b_vector)
np.random.seed(1) # reproducibility
y = y_true + sigma * np.random.normal(
    size=nsample) * noise_level
X = pd.DataFrame(X, columns=['const','x1','x2','x3'])
# model
model = sm.OLS(y, X)
results = model.fit()
print_img(results.summary())
# inspect
print('dataset:')
print(X.head())
```

```
                            OLS Regression Results
==============================================================================
Dep. Variable:                      y   R-squared:                       0.827
Model:                            OLS   Adj. R-squared:                  0.822
Method:                 Least Squares   F-statistic:                     153.1
Date:                Tue, 02 Jul 2024   Prob (F-statistic):           1.87e-36
Time:                        14:01:12   Log-Likelihood:                -741.28
No. Observations:                 100   AIC:                             1491.
Df Residuals:                      96   BIC:                             1501.
Df Model:                           3
Covariance Type:            nonrobust
==============================================================================
                 coef    std err          t      P>|t|      [0.025      0.975]
------------------------------------------------------------------------------
const         93.7425    277.996      0.337      0.737    -458.075     645.560
x1             2.5890      0.614      4.214      0.000       1.370       3.808
x2           -19.3828     59.748     -0.324      0.746    -137.982      99.216
x3             2.8602      0.152     18.780      0.000       2.558       3.162
==============================================================================
Omnibus:                        0.189   Durbin-Watson:                   2.058
Prob(Omnibus):                  0.910   Jarque-Bera (JB):                0.046
Skew:                           0.051   Prob(JB):                        0.977
Kurtosis:                       3.025   Cond. No.                     3.00e+03
==============================================================================

Notes:
[1] Standard Errors assume that the covariance matrix of the errors is correctly specified.
[2] The condition number is large,  3e+03. This might indicate that there are
strong multicollinearity or other numerical problems.
```

```
dataset:
   const          x1        x2        x3
0    1.0 -100.000000  0.000000 -0.000000
1    1.0  -97.966323  0.996580 -0.097949
2    1.0  -91.948007  1.917004 -0.391797
3    1.0  -82.189840  2.706741 -0.881543
4    1.0  -69.088721  3.342651 -1.567187
```

32.3.2 Visualize the data in a plot with a confidence interval

We draw a plot to compare the "true" values with the predicted values, along with the confidence interval.

```
# prediction
pred = results.get_prediction()
iv_l = pred.summary_frame()["obs_ci_lower"]
iv_u = pred.summary_frame()["obs_ci_upper"]
# plot
fig, ax = plt.subplots(figsize=(6,3.5))
txt = 'True vs. Predicted with confidence Envelope'
ax.set_title(txt, fontsize=11)
ax.plot(x, y,
        "o", label="Data")
ax.plot(x, y_true,
        "b-", label="true")
ax.plot(x, results.fittedvalues,
        "r--.", label="predicted")
ax.plot(x, iv_u, "y--")
ax.plot(x, iv_l, "y--")
ax.set_xlabel('x')
ax.set_ylabel('y')
ax.grid(True)
ax.legend(loc="best")
plt.show()
```

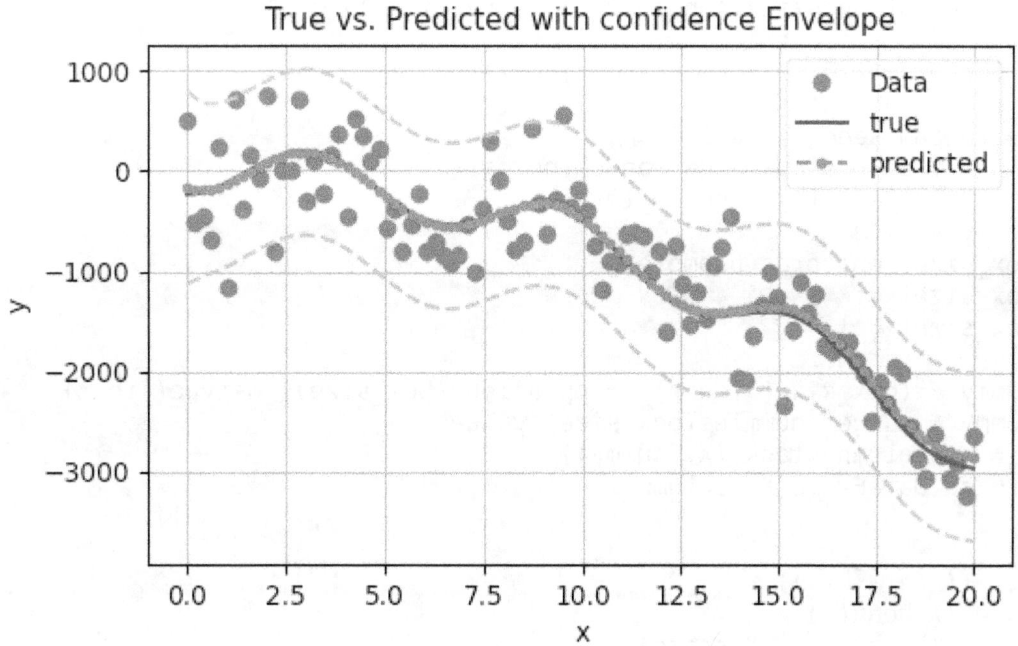

32.3.3 Dataset with 3 dummy variables

> We build a dataset, like in the previous example, however, now we add the categorical variable box_size which can take on three values (small=0, medium=1, large=2).

We apply the `get_dummy()` method from the Numpy library, which has the following signature:

```
dummy = pd.get_dummies(box_size).values
```

then we stack the newly created dummy variables onto previously created features matrix X, like so.

```
X = np.column_stack((X, dummy))
```

```
# parameters
nsample = 100
sigma = 0.7
noise_level = 650
# features
x = np.linspace(0, 20, nsample)
f_x1 = -100 * np.cos(x)
f_x2 = 5 * np.tanh(x)
f_x3 = -2.4*x**2
ones = np.ones(nsample) # required by model
X = np.column_stack((ones, f_x1, f_x2, f_x3))
# target variable
b_vector = [20, 2.5, -0.5, 3.0]
y_true = np.dot(X, b_vector)
np.random.seed(1) # reproducibility
y = y_true + sigma * np.random.normal(
    size=nsample) * noise_level
# categorical variable
box_size= np.zeros(nsample, int) # 0 is small
box_size[20:40] = 1 # 1 is medium
box_size[40:] = 2 # 2 is large
# dummy variables
dummy = (box_size[:,None] == np.unique(box_size)).astype(float)
dummy = pd.get_dummies(box_size).values
X = np.column_stack((X, dummy))
X = pd.DataFrame(X, columns=['const','x1','x2','x3',
                             'dummy1','dummy2','dummy3'])
# inspect
print('dataset:')
print(X.head())
print('X.shape:', X.shape)
print('y.shape:', y.shape)
```

```
dataset:
   const          x1        x2        x3  dummy1  dummy2  dummy3
0    1.0 -100.000000  0.000000 -0.000000     1.0     0.0     0.0
1    1.0  -97.966323  0.996580 -0.097949     1.0     0.0     0.0
2    1.0  -91.948007  1.917004 -0.391797     1.0     0.0     0.0
3    1.0  -82.189840  2.706741 -0.881543     1.0     0.0     0.0
4    1.0  -69.088721  3.342651 -1.567187     1.0     0.0     0.0
X.shape: (100, 7)
y.shape: (100,)
```

In the next step, we fit the regression model and visualize the result in the following section.

```
# fit model
model = sm.OLS(y, X)
results = model.fit()
# inspect
print_img(results.summary().tables[0])
print_img(results.summary().tables[1])
```

```
                            OLS Regression Results
==============================================================================
Dep. Variable:                      y   R-squared:                       0.830
Model:                            OLS   Adj. R-squared:                  0.821
Method:                 Least Squares   F-statistic:                     91.85
Date:                Tue, 02 Jul 2024   Prob (F-statistic):           1.27e-34
Time:                        14:01:14   Log-Likelihood:                -740.41
No. Observations:                 100   AIC:                             1493.
Df Residuals:                      94   BIC:                             1508.
Df Model:                           5
Covariance Type:            nonrobust
==============================================================================
```

```
==============================================================================
                 coef    std err          t      P>|t|      [0.025      0.975]
------------------------------------------------------------------------------
const        179.3517    249.035      0.720      0.473    -315.113     673.816
x1             2.5354      0.706      3.591      0.001       1.134       3.937
x2           -45.1820     70.912     -0.637      0.526    -185.980      95.616
x3             3.0642      0.239     12.840      0.000       2.590       3.538
dummy1       -40.4652     87.310     -0.463      0.644    -213.822     132.891
dummy2        50.3688    144.035      0.350      0.727    -235.616     336.353
dummy3       169.4481    132.843      1.276      0.205     -94.315     433.211
==============================================================================
```

Interpretation

The R^2 measure is reported as 0.83 with the corresponding Prob(F-statistic) of 1.22E-34, almost zero.

This means that the regression model explains 83% of the variation in the data, and the model as a whole is statistically significant, at the chosen level of significance $\alpha = 0.05$.

Observe, that the 3 dummy variables are all not-significant. A further study into the parameter significance on a one-by-one basis is required, to arrive at a valid model specification. As for now, the dummy variables help the regression model only insignificantly in explaining the variation in the data.

32.3.4 F-Test to assess the model significance

The F-test assesses the significance of the regression model as a whole. To set up the statistical test, we formulate:

Hypothesis

- H_0: both regressor variables x_0 and x_1 are equal to zero
- H_1: at least one regressor is significantly different from zero

level of significance

- $\alpha = 0.05$

F-statistic

$$F_{statistic} = \frac{MSR}{MSE}$$

where

- MSR = is the mean square regression
- MSE = is the mean square residual

level of significance

- α = 0.05
- two-sided test

In the following Python code segment, a full F-Test is implemented and its results are reported.

```
MSR = results.mse_model
MST = results.mse_total
MSE = results.mse_resid
F = MSR / MSE
fpvalue = results.f_pvalue
# parameters
alpha = 0.05
print('F-Test:')
print(f'F-statistic             : {F:.4f}')
print(f'Prob(F-statistic)       : {results.f_pvalue:.4E}')
print(f'level of significance : {alpha:.2f}')
print('two-sided test')
print('Hypothesis')
```

(continues on next page)

(continued from previous page)

```
print('H0: all regressor variables are equal to zero')
print('H1: at least one regressor is different from zero')
if fpvalue < alpha/2:
    print('reject H0')
    print('jointly Significant')
else:
    print('fail to reject H0')
    print("jointly Not Significant")
```

```
F-Test:
F-statistic            : 91.8462
Prob(F-statistic)      : 1.2690E-34
level of significance : 0.05
two-sided test
Hypothesis
H0: all regressor variables are equal to zero
H1: at least one regressor is different from zero
reject H0
jointly Significant
```

Interpretation

The F-statistic is reported as 91.85 and the Prob(F-statistic) as 1.269E-34, almost zero.

Since the Prob(F-statistic) value is less than $\frac{\alpha}{2} = 0.025$, we reject H_0 and conclude that at least one of the regression coefficients is significantly different from zero.

To further study the impact of setting all regression variables to zero, we can employ the formula-like syntax of the `f_test()` method, which is available on the result object. We demonstrate this approach in the following section, and we implement:

32.3.5 F-Test for joint hypothesis testing

To set up the statistical test we formulate:

Hypothesis

- H_0: all independent variables are jointly zero
- H_1: at least one of the variables is different from zero

level of significance

- $alpha = 0.05$
- two-sided test

To compute the F-test for the joint linear hypothesis. We make use of the convenient formula notation, of this test like so:

```
result.f_test("x1=0, x2=0, x3=0")
```

The coefficients ($x1$, $x2$, $x2$) are assumed to be simultaneously equal to zero, resulting in a so-called intercept-only model, as pointed out in StatsmodelsDocs [2023].

```
print_img(results.summary().tables[1])
# F-test testing the joint hypothesis
fstr = "x1=0, x2=0, x3=0, dummy1=0, dummy2=0, dummy3=0"
ftest = results.f_test(fstr)
# parameters
alpha = 0.05
print('F-Test:')
print(f'F-statistic            : {ftest.fvalue:.4f}')
print(f'P(F-statistic)         : {ftest.pvalue:.4E}')
print(f'level of significance : {alpha:.2f}')
print('two-sided test')
print('Hypothesis')
print('H0: all independent variables are jointly zero')
print('H1: at least one variable is different from zero')
print('result:')
if (ftest.pvalue < alpha/2):
    print('reject H0')
    print('jointly Significant')
else:
    print('fail to reject H0')
    print('jointly Not Significant')
```

	coef	std err	t	P>|t|	[0.025	0.975]
const	179.3517	249.035	0.720	0.473	-315.113	673.816
x1	2.5354	0.706	3.591	0.001	1.134	3.937
x2	-45.1820	70.912	-0.637	0.526	-185.980	95.616
x3	3.0642	0.239	12.840	0.000	2.590	3.538
dummy1	-40.4652	87.310	-0.463	0.644	-213.822	132.891
dummy2	50.3688	144.035	0.350	0.727	-235.616	336.353
dummy3	169.4481	132.843	1.276	0.205	-94.315	433.211

```
F-Test:
F-statistic            : 162.8080
P(F-statistic)         : 2.1485E-47
level of significance : 0.05
two-sided test
Hypothesis
H0: all independent variables are jointly zero
H1: at least one variable is different from zero
```

(continues on next page)

(continued from previous page)

```
result:
reject H0
jointly Significant
```

Interpretation

The F-statistic is reported as 162.81, and the corresponding Prob(F-statistic) as 2.14e-47, almost zero.

Since the Prob(F-statistic) is far smaller than $\frac{\alpha}{2}$ of 0.025, we reject the null hypothesis H_0 in favor of the alternative hypothesis H_1, at a level of significance of $\alpha = 0.05$.

We can conclude that the model fits the data significantly better than an `intercept-only` model, in which all regressor variables are simultaneously zero, which is not the case here.

Observe, that the $x1$ and $x3$ parameters are statistically significant with p_{values} of 0.001 and 0.000 respectively, however, all other parameters (`const`, `x2`, `dummy1`, `dummy2`, `dummy3`) are not significant, meaning that the model is not suitable to make important predictions and therefore is to be revised.

32.4 Part 4: Study the impact of multicollinearity

> We make use of the build-in Longley dataset, which contains various US macroeconomic variables that are known to be highly collinear, according to Longley [1967]. The dataset consists of 16 observations, and we use this dataset to further investigate multicollinearity.

The chosen dataset is known to exhibit high multicollinearity. That is, the dependent or predictor variables are highly correlated with each other, or even an external variable which is not included in the model. This is problematic because it can affect the stability of regression models and render the estimated coefficients unreliable.

```
from statsmodels.datasets.longley import load_pandas

# prepare the dataset
y = load_pandas().endog
X = load_pandas().exog
X = sm.add_constant(X)
# dataset
data = load_pandas()
# inspect
# print(type(data))
print('dataset:')
```

(continues on next page)

(continued from previous page)

```
print(data.raw_data[0:5])
print()
print("feature variables (exog):")
print(X.head())
print()
print('target variable (endog):')
print(y.to_list()[0:5])
```

```
dataset:
    TOTEMP  GNPDEFL       GNP   UNEMP   ARMED       POP    YEAR
0  60323.0     83.0  234289.0  2356.0  1590.0  107608.0  1947.0
1  61122.0     88.5  259426.0  2325.0  1456.0  108632.0  1948.0
2  60171.0     88.2  258054.0  3682.0  1616.0  109773.0  1949.0
3  61187.0     89.5  284599.0  3351.0  1650.0  110929.0  1950.0
4  63221.0     96.2  328975.0  2099.0  3099.0  112075.0  1951.0

feature variables (exog):
   const  GNPDEFL       GNP   UNEMP   ARMED       POP    YEAR
0    1.0     83.0  234289.0  2356.0  1590.0  107608.0  1947.0
1    1.0     88.5  259426.0  2325.0  1456.0  108632.0  1948.0
2    1.0     88.2  258054.0  3682.0  1616.0  109773.0  1949.0
3    1.0     89.5  284599.0  3351.0  1650.0  110929.0  1950.0
4    1.0     96.2  328975.0  2099.0  3099.0  112075.0  1951.0

target variable (endog):
[60323.0, 61122.0, 60171.0, 61187.0, 63221.0]
```

Fit the model and report the `ols()` regression results.

```
# fit model
model = sm.OLS(y, X)
results = model.fit()
# inspect
print_img(results.summary())
```

```
                            OLS Regression Results
==============================================================================
Dep. Variable:                 TOTEMP   R-squared:                       0.995
Model:                            OLS   Adj. R-squared:                  0.992
Method:                 Least Squares   F-statistic:                     330.3
Date:                Tue, 02 Jul 2024   Prob (F-statistic):           4.98e-10
Time:                        14:01:16   Log-Likelihood:                -109.62
No. Observations:                  16   AIC:                             233.2
Df Residuals:                       9   BIC:                             238.6
Df Model:                           6
Covariance Type:            nonrobust
==============================================================================
                 coef    std err          t      P>|t|      [0.025      0.975]
------------------------------------------------------------------------------
const      -3.482e+06    8.9e+05     -3.911      0.004    -5.5e+06   -1.47e+06
GNPDEFL       15.0619     84.915      0.177      0.863    -177.029     207.153
GNP           -0.0358      0.033     -1.070      0.313      -0.112       0.040
UNEMP         -2.0202      0.488     -4.136      0.003      -3.125      -0.915
ARMED         -1.0332      0.214     -4.822      0.001      -1.518      -0.549
POP           -0.0511      0.226     -0.226      0.826      -0.563       0.460
YEAR        1829.1515    455.478      4.016      0.003     798.788    2859.515
==============================================================================
Omnibus:                        0.749   Durbin-Watson:                   2.559
Prob(Omnibus):                  0.688   Jarque-Bera (JB):                0.684
Skew:                           0.420   Prob(JB):                        0.710
Kurtosis:                       2.434   Cond. No.                     4.86e+09
==============================================================================

Notes:
[1] Standard Errors assume that the covariance matrix of the errors is correctly specified.
[2] The condition number is large, 4.86e+09. This might indicate that there are
strong multicollinearity or other numerical problems.
```

32.4.1 Condition number

One way to assess multicollinearity is to compute the condition number. There is no strict way how the condition number to be interpreted, however, values over 30 indicate the presence of multicollinearity.

```
# condition numbers
cn1 = np.linalg.cond(model.exog)
print('condition_number         : {:.4f}'.format(cn1))
cn2 = results.condition_number
print('condition_number results : {:.4f}'.format(cn2))
# inspect
print('results:')
if (results.condition_number < 30 ):
    print('Multicollinearity Not present')
else:
    print('Multicollinearity present')
```

```
condition_number         : 4859257015.4549
condition_number results : 4859257015.4549
results:
Multicollinearity present
```

32.4.2 Dropping feature or outlier observations to remedy multicollinearity

To correct for multicollinearity, we can drop feature variables, successively and recompute the condition number to assess if the multicollinearity issue persists.

Additionally, as Greene [2003] noted dropping a single outlier observation can have a drastic impact on the results of the regression model, and in particular on the coefficient estimates. Please note that even the elimination of a single outlier observation might eliminate the multicollinearity condition in a given model. However, great care must be taken before eliminating outliers automatically from the analysis.

In the following Python code segment, we study the elimination of feature variables and compare and contrast the results.

```
print('Before:')
model_all = sm.OLS(y, X)
results_all = model_all.fit()
print('X-shape:', X.shape)
print('features:', results_all.params.index.values)
print_img(results_all.summary().tables[1])
print_img(results_all.summary().tables[2])
print(f'condition number : {results_all.condition_number:.4f}')
print()
print('After:')
N = 4 # first N independent feature variables
X_drop = X.iloc[0:,:N]
model_drop = sm.OLS(y,X_drop )
results_drop = model_drop.fit()
print('X-shape:', X_drop.shape)
print('features:', results_drop.params.index.values)
print_img(results_drop.summary().tables[1])
print_img(results_drop.summary().tables[2])
print(f'condition number : {results_drop.condition_number:.4f}')
```

```
Before:
X-shape: (16, 7)
features: ['const' 'GNPDEFL' 'GNP' 'UNEMP' 'ARMED' 'POP' 'YEAR']
```

```
==============================================================================
                 coef    std err          t      P>|t|      [0.025      0.975]
------------------------------------------------------------------------------
const      -3.482e+06    8.9e+05     -3.911      0.004    -5.5e+06   -1.47e+06
GNPDEFL       15.0619     84.915      0.177      0.863    -177.029     207.153
GNP           -0.0358      0.033     -1.070      0.313      -0.112       0.040
UNEMP         -2.0202      0.488     -4.136      0.003      -3.125      -0.915
ARMED         -1.0332      0.214     -4.822      0.001      -1.518      -0.549
POP           -0.0511      0.226     -0.226      0.826      -0.563       0.460
YEAR        1829.1515    455.478      4.016      0.003     798.788    2859.515
==============================================================================

==============================================================================
Omnibus:                        0.749   Durbin-Watson:                   2.559
Prob(Omnibus):                  0.688   Jarque-Bera (JB):                0.684
Skew:                           0.420   Prob(JB):                        0.710
Kurtosis:                       2.434   Cond. No.                     4.86e+09
==============================================================================

condition number : 4859257015.4549

After:
X-shape: (16, 4)
features: ['const' 'GNPDEFL' 'GNP' 'UNEMP']

==============================================================================
                 coef    std err          t      P>|t|      [0.025      0.975]
------------------------------------------------------------------------------
const       5.393e+04   6159.792      8.755      0.000    4.05e+04    6.73e+04
GNPDEFL      -25.9424    102.946     -0.252      0.805    -250.242     198.357
GNP            0.0406      0.011      3.689      0.003       0.017       0.065
UNEMP         -0.5334      0.193     -2.762      0.017      -0.954      -0.113
==============================================================================

==============================================================================
Omnibus:                        1.930   Durbin-Watson:                   0.949
Prob(Omnibus):                  0.381   Jarque-Bera (JB):                0.663
Skew:                           0.474   Prob(JB):                        0.718
Kurtosis:                       3.310   Cond. No.                     1.81e+07
==============================================================================

condition number : 18073015.3281
```

Observe the significant reduction in the reported condition number from 4859257015.46 to 18073015.33, by dropping 3 ('ARMED' 'POP' 'YEAR') of the possible 6 independent feature variables.

However, this demonstration was not able to remove the issue of multi-collinearity in the dataset, and further changes to the regression model are required, to arrive at a valid and competent model.

Checking for multicollinearity.

```
# confirmation
print_img(results_drop.summary().tables[2])
# condition number
cn1 = np.linalg.cond(model_drop.exog)
print(f'condition_number exog   : {cn1:.4f}')
cn2 = results_drop.condition_number
print(f'condition_number result : {cn2:.4f}')
print('results:')
if (results_drop.condition_number < 30 ):
    print('Multicollinearity Not present')
else:
    print('Multicollinearity present')
```

```
==============================================================================
Omnibus:                        1.930   Durbin-Watson:                   0.949
Prob(Omnibus):                  0.381   Jarque-Bera (JB):                0.663
Skew:                           0.474   Prob(JB):                        0.718
Kurtosis:                       3.310   Cond. No.                     1.81e+07
==============================================================================
```

```
condition_number exog   : 18073015.3281
condition_number result : 18073015.3281
results:
Multicollinearity present
```

32.4.3 Influencing factors

To investigate the most influential features, we can analyze the DFBETAS, which is a standardized measure of how much each coefficient changes when that outlier observation is left out. For this analysis, we apply the `get_influence()` method available on the results object, which has this signature:

```
infl = results.get_influence()
```

it returns an `OLSInfluence` object containing the influence value for all observations.

We consider influence values, in absolute terms, greater than $\frac{2}{\sqrt(N)}$ to be an influential observation.

In the following Python code section, the usage is demonstrated and the results are reported.

```
# influential values
infl = results.get_influence()
# parameters
N = 5
```

(continues on next page)

(continued from previous page)

```
# inspect
print(type(infl))
print('influencing factors:')
print(results.params.index.values)
print(infl.dfbetas[0:5]) # first N only
print('first', N, 'observations')
```

```
<class 'statsmodels.stats.outliers_influence.OLSInfluence'>
influencing factors:
['const' 'GNPDEFL' 'GNP' 'UNEMP' 'ARMED' 'POP' 'YEAR']
[[-0.016 -0.235 -0.045 -0.122 -0.149 0.211 0.013]
 [-0.021 -0.289 0.124 0.157 0.288 -0.162 0.026]
 [-0.008 0.007 -0.017 0.010 0.002 0.015 0.008]
 [0.018 0.908 -0.500 -0.496 0.090 0.711 -0.040]
 [1.871 -0.219 1.611 1.562 1.169 -1.082 -1.864]]
first 5 observations
```

Interpretation

By applying the formula $\frac{2}{\sqrt{(N)}}$ we arrive at a threshold of 0.5 to indicate influential observations.

```
from quantlib import print_img

threshold = 2.0 / len(X) ** 0.5
print('N               :', len(X))
print('influential_at :', threshold)
print('summary_frame:')
print_img(infl.summary_frame().applymap(
        lambda x: f"{x:.4f}").filter(regex="dfb"))
```

```
N               : 16
influential_at : 0.5
summary_frame:
```

	dfb_const	dfb_GNPDEFL	dfb_GNP	dfb_UNEMP	dfb_ARMED	dfb_POP	dfb_YEAR
0	-0.0164	-0.2346	-0.0451	-0.1215	-0.1490	0.2111	0.0134
1	-0.0206	-0.2891	0.1245	0.1570	0.2877	-0.1619	0.0260
2	-0.0084	0.0072	-0.0168	0.0096	0.0022	0.0149	0.0081
3	0.0181	0.9080	-0.5000	-0.4960	0.0900	0.7111	-0.0401
4	1.8713	-0.2194	1.6114	1.5615	1.1693	-1.0815	-1.8642
5	-0.3214	-0.0770	-0.1981	-0.1930	-0.4306	0.0799	0.3233
6	0.3159	-0.2420	0.4381	0.4718	-0.0195	-0.4485	-0.3075
7	0.0158	-0.0027	0.0186	0.0051	-0.0313	-0.0158	-0.0156
8	-0.0040	-0.0457	0.0237	0.0181	0.0137	-0.0348	0.0051
9	-1.0182	-0.2821	-0.4126	-0.6639	-0.7150	-0.2295	1.0357
10	0.0309	-0.0248	0.0295	0.0354	0.0345	-0.0142	-0.0308
11	0.0060	-0.0797	0.0303	-0.0089	-0.0069	-0.0107	-0.0053
12	-0.1359	0.0923	-0.2530	-0.2115	0.0947	0.3314	0.1291
13	0.0327	-0.0242	0.0175	0.0332	0.0907	0.0076	-0.0331
14	0.3059	0.1481	0.0014	0.1693	0.2534	0.3430	-0.3180
15	-0.5383	0.4320	-0.2613	-0.1434	-0.3609	-0.4673	0.5524

CHAPTER 33

MULTIPLE LINEAR REGRESSION

We perform multiple linear regression in Python using both the sklearn and the statsmodels library packages.

- Multiple linear regression
- Checking for Linearity
- Part 1: Linear regression analysis using the sklearn package
- Part 2: Linear regression analysis using the statsmodels package
- Making predictions using the fitted model

We define our multiple linear regression model as follows:

Multiple linear regression model:

$$\hat{y} = \beta_0 + \beta_1 \cdot x1 + \beta_2 \cdot x2 + \epsilon$$

where:

- $x1$: independent variable interest_rate
- $x2$: independent variable unemployment_rate
- $\hat{y}$: dependent/target variable index_price
- ϵ: random error term ϵ

We have to make sure that the assumptions that underlay the linear regression models are met. Most notably, a linear relationship exists between the dependent and the independent variables.

33.1 Dataset: unemployment rate versus interest rate

The dataset for unemployment rate and long-term interest rate is compiled from the Oecd [2023] site. The rates for the European zone of 19 countries, covering the year 2022, are subsequently merged with index price values for a fictitious economy.

Independent of features variables:

- `unemployment_rate`: denotes the unemployment rate for the Eurozone
- `interest_rate`: denotes the long-term interest rates for Germany

Dependent or target variable:

- `index_price`: the index price levels for a fictitious economy

```
import pandas as pd

df = pd.DataFrame({
    'year':[2022, 2022, 2022, 2022, 2022, 2022,
            2022, 2022, 2022, 2022, 2022, 2022],
    'month':[12, 11, 10, 9, 8, 7, 6, 5, 4, 3, 2,1],
    'interest_rate': reversed([2.085, 2.066, 2.187,
            1.795, 1.034, 1.083, 1.445, 0.953, 0.746,
            0.282, 0.150, -0.115]),
    'unemployment_rate': [6.70, 6.75, 6.60, 6.70, 6.73,
                          6.70, 6.72, 6.68, 6.80,
                          6.90, 7.00, 7.10],
    'index_price':[1149, 1139, 1130, 1075, 1047, 965,
                   943, 958, 971, 949, 884, 866]})
df = df.sort_values(by=['year','index_price'],
                               ascending=False)
# inspect
print('dataset:')
print(df[['interest_rate', 'unemployment_rate',
        'index_price']])
print(df.shape)
```

```
dataset:
    interest_rate  unemployment_rate  index_price
0          -0.115               6.70         1149
1           0.150               6.75         1139
2           0.282               6.60         1130
3           0.746               6.70         1075
4           0.953               6.73         1047
8           1.795               6.80          971
5           1.445               6.70          965
7           1.034               6.68          958
```

(continues on next page)

(continued from previous page)

```
9           2.187           6.90        949
6           1.083           6.72        943
10          2.066           7.00        884
11          2.085           7.10        866
(12, 5)
```

33.2 Checking for Linearity

One of the regression model's underlying assumptions is concerned with the linearity of the relationship between the dependent variable and the independent variables.

We make use of a scatter plot, to visually inspect the dataset and gain an intuition on how the data looks like and assert that a linear relationship indeed exists between the index_price and the interest_rate, and unemployment_rate, respectively.

In the following Python code segment, the dataset is plotted and the resulting diagrams are interpreted.

```
import matplotlib.pyplot as plt
%matplotlib inline

# plot
fig, (ax1,ax2) = plt.subplots(1,2, sharey=False,
                figsize=(8,4), tight_layout=False)
fig.suptitle('Checking for Linearity', fontsize=12)
# left plot
ax1.scatter(df['interest_rate'],
            df['index_price'],
            color='green')
ax1.set_xlabel('Interest Rate')
ax1.set_ylabel('Index Price')
ax1.grid(True)
# right plot
ax2.scatter(df['unemployment_rate'],
            df['index_price'],
            color='brown')
ax2.set_xlabel('Unemployment Rate')
ax2.set_ylabel('Index Price')
ax2.grid(True)
plt.show()
```

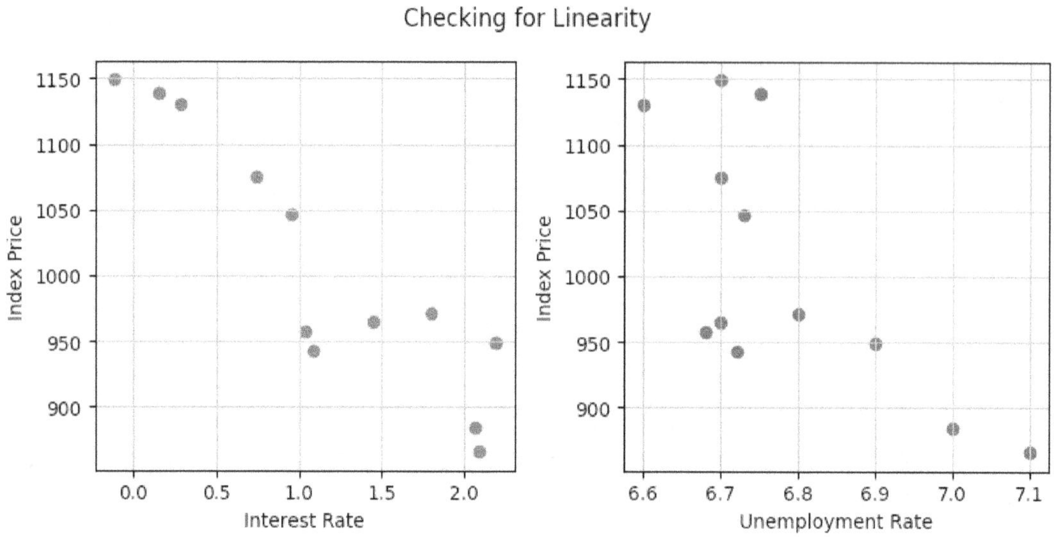

Interpretation

Please observe, that when the `interest_rate` goes up, the `index_price` goes down. By visual inspection, we can confirm that a somewhat linear relationship does exist between the `index_price` and the `interest_rate` feature variables.

Please observe, when the `unemployment_rate` rates go up, the `index_price` goes down. By visual inspection, we can confirm that a somewhat linear relationship does exist between the `index_price` and the `unemployment_rate`.

It can be concluded that the linearity assumption underlying the linear regression analysis is met. We can go ahead and create the multiple linear regression model. Of course, a more quantitative assessment of linearity is required, and we discuss suitable statistical tests for this purpose further below.

33.3 Part 1: Multiple Linear Regression using the sklearn

Before using the `LinearRegression()` method from the sklearn package, we might want to consult the documentation, its parameters, return values, and any restrictions or limitations.

```
from sklearn import linear_model
# print(help(linear_model.LinearRegression()))
# print(help(linear_model))
```

We need to add a `const` term to the dataset, since this is required by the statsmodels package to function properly. This can be accomplished like so:

```
df['const'] = 1
```

```
# add a column with ones, as required by statsmodels
df['const'] = 1
# inspect
print('dataset:')
print(df.to_string(index=False))
```

```
dataset:
 year  month  interest_rate  unemployment_rate  index_price  const
 2022     12         -0.115               6.70         1149      1
 2022     11          0.150               6.75         1139      1
 2022     10          0.282               6.60         1130      1
 2022      9          0.746               6.70         1075      1
 2022      8          0.953               6.73         1047      1
 2022      4          1.795               6.80          971      1
 2022      7          1.445               6.70          965      1
 2022      5          1.034               6.68          958      1
 2022      3          2.187               6.90          949      1
 2022      6          1.083               6.72          943      1
 2022      2          2.066               7.00          884      1
 2022      1          2.085               7.10          866      1
```

In Python, we implement:

```
import statsmodels.api as sm
import numpy as np
import warnings
warnings.filterwarnings('ignore')
from sklearn import linear_model

# DataFrame
x = df[['interest_rate','unemployment_rate', 'const']]
y = df['index_price']
# model
regr = linear_model.LinearRegression().fit(x.values, y)
print(type(regr))
# results
print('intercept    : {:.5f}'.format(regr.intercept_))
print('coefficients :', regr.coef_)
print('R-squared    : {:.5f}'.format(regr.score(x, y)))
```

```
<class 'sklearn.linear_model._base.LinearRegression'>
intercept    : 1336.40080
coefficients : [-110.00784854  -30.13629896    0.        ]
R-squared    : 0.83891
```

33.3.1 Make predictions with new data items

To make a prediction the `predict()` function from the model object is used. It has the following signature:

```
y_pred = regr.predict([[2.20, 7.15, 1]])
```

Observe that we pass in the new values as a list-of-list or 2D array.

```
# prediction
print('prediction:')
v = regr.predict([[2.20, 7.15, 1]])[0]
print(f'y(x1=2.20, x2=7.15, const=1) = {v:.2f}')
```

```
prediction:
y(x1=2.20, x2=7.15, const=1) = 878.91
```

Given the two input variables: $x1 = 2.20$ and $x2 = 7.15$ for the upcoming period. We can use these inputs and the fitted model to make a prediction, by inserting the values into the derived regression equation:

$$y = 1336.4 + (-110.01 * 2.15) + (-30.136 * 7.15) = 878.91$$

This confirms the value for the prediction we have computed earlier.

33.3.2 Extract specific values from the regression result object

It is often helpful to be able to extract specific values from the result object to be used in subsequent analytics. In this code segment, we demonstrate how the values can be accessed.

```
# results
print('extracted values:')
print('coef_             :', regr.coef_)
print('intercept_        :', regr.intercept_)
print('score             :', regr.score(x,y))
print('rank              :', regr.rank_)
print('predict           :', regr.predict( [[2.20, 7.15, 1]] ))
print('fit_intercept     :', regr.fit_intercept)
print('n_features_in     :', regr.n_features_in_)
print('positive          :', regr.positive)
print('singular          :', regr.singular_)
```

```
extracted values:
coef_          : [-110.00784854  -30.13629896    0.        ]
intercept_     : 1336.4008016986504
```

(continues on next page)

(continued from previous page)

```
score            : 0.8389057791793988
rank             : 2
predict          : [878.90899738]
fit_intercept    : True
n_features_in    : 3
positive         : False
singular         : [2.64590449 0.31307352 0.        ]
```

33.3.3 Report performance metrics for the metrics object

We compute performance metrics, by using the `metrics` object, provided by the sklearn.metrics library, which has the following signature:

```
explained_variance = metrics.explained_variance_score(y_true,y_pred)
```

In the following Python code segment, we demonstrate the computation of a set of performance metrics.

```
import sklearn.metrics as m

#
# helper function
def regression_results(y_true, y_pred):
    """ report regression results """
    exp_variance = m.explained_variance_score(y_true, y_pred)
    mean_abs_error = m.mean_absolute_error(y_true, y_pred)
    mse = m.mean_squared_error(y_true, y_pred)
    mean_sq_log_err = m.mean_squared_log_error(y_true, y_pred)
    median_abs_err = m.median_absolute_error(y_true, y_pred)
    r2 = m.r2_score(y_true, y_pred)
    # reports
    print(f'explained_variance      : {exp_variance:.4f}')
    print(f'mean_absolute_error     : {mean_abs_error:.4f}')
    print(f'mean_squared_log_error : {mean_sq_log_err:.4f}')
    print(f'median_absolute_error   : {median_abs_err:.4f}')
    print(f'R2                      : {r2:.4f}')
    print(f'MAE                     : {mean_abs_error:.4f}')
    print(f'MSE                     : {mse:.4f}')
    print(f'RMSE                    : {np.sqrt(mse):.4f}')

# prediction
y_pred = regr.predict(x.values)
# results
print('results:')
regression_results(y, y_pred)
```

```
results:
explained_variance     : 0.8389
mean_absolute_error    : 31.1420
mean_squared_log_error : 0.0015
median_absolute_error  : 23.0496
R2                     : 0.8389
MAE                    : 31.1420
MSE                    : 1434.6335
RMSE                   : 37.8766
```

33.4 Part 2: Multiple Linear Regression using statsmodels

This analysis produces a comprehensive table with statistical metrics. This report table provides additional insights into the model, its performance and usability.

Before using the `ols()` method from the statsmodels packages, we might want to consult the documentation on the function, its parameters, return values, and any restrictions or limitations.

```
import statsmodels.api as sm
# help(sm.OLS)
# print(sm.OLS.__doc__[:1380])
```

33.4.1 Ordinary Least Square regression

As described in StatsmodelsDocs [2023] the regression model provides a result object, with performance metrics.

Observe that we renamed the features variables, to better suit our needs. For that, we make use of the `xname` parameter of the `summary()` method, like so:

```
from quantlib import print_img

# fit model
model = sm.OLS(y, x).fit()
# prediction
predictions = model.predict(x)
# inspect
print_img(model.summary(xname=['const', 'interest',
                               'unemployment']))
```

```
                            OLS Regression Results
==============================================================================
Dep. Variable:            index_price   R-squared:                       0.839
Model:                            OLS   Adj. R-squared:                  0.803
Method:                 Least Squares   F-statistic:                     23.43
Date:                Tue, 02 Jul 2024   Prob (F-statistic):           0.000270
Time:                        14:01:35   Log-Likelihood:                -60.639
No. Observations:                  12   AIC:                             127.3
Df Residuals:                       9   BIC:                             128.7
Df Model:                           2
Covariance Type:            nonrobust
================================================================================
                   coef    std err          t      P>|t|      [0.025      0.975]
--------------------------------------------------------------------------------
const         -110.0078     25.549     -4.306      0.002    -167.805     -52.211
interest       -30.1363    138.334     -0.218      0.832    -343.069     282.797
unemployment  1336.4008    916.320      1.458      0.179    -736.460    3409.261
==============================================================================
Omnibus:                        0.874   Durbin-Watson:                   2.467
Prob(Omnibus):                  0.646   Jarque-Bera (JB):                0.665
Skew:                          -0.500   Prob(JB):                        0.717
Kurtosis:                       2.427   Cond. No.                         511.
==============================================================================

Notes:
[1] Standard Errors assume that the covariance matrix of the errors is correctly specified.
```

We arrived at consistent results by applying both the sklearn and statsmodels packages. Notice that the coefficients captured in this table match with the coefficients computed by the sklearn library.

33.4.2 Report specific values from the result object

The `ols()` regression model produces a summary results table by invoking the `summary()` function, which is available on the model object. It has the following signature.

```
t = model.summary()
```

it returns a comprehensive table with relevant model statistics.

Additionally, the summary report table can be used individually, by specifying a specific table by number, like so:

```
model.summary().tables[0]
```

In the following code section, it is demonstrated how to extract specific values from that summary table.

```
from statsmodels.stats.stattools import durbin_watson

# confirmation
print_img(model.summary().tables[0])
# extract values
print('extracted:')
```

(continues on next page)

(continued from previous page)

```
print('cov_type            :', model.cov_type)
print('nobs                :', int(model.nobs))
print(f'R-squared           : {model.rsquared:.4f}')
print(f'R-squared Adj       : {model.rsquared_adj:.4f}')
print(f'F-Statistic         : {model.fvalue:.4f}')
print(f'Prob(F-Statistic)   : {model.f_pvalue:.2E}')
print(f'Log-Likelihood      : {model.llf:.4f}')
print(f'aic                 : {model.aic:.4f}')
print(f'bic                 : {model.bic:.4f}')
print(f'condition_number    : {model.condition_number:.4f}')
```

```
                            OLS Regression Results
==============================================================================
Dep. Variable:            index_price   R-squared:                       0.839
Model:                            OLS   Adj. R-squared:                  0.803
Method:                 Least Squares   F-statistic:                     23.43
Date:                Tue, 02 Jul 2024   Prob (F-statistic):           0.000270
Time:                        14:01:36   Log-Likelihood:                -60.639
No. Observations:                  12   AIC:                             127.3
Df Residuals:                       9   BIC:                             128.7
Df Model:                           2
Covariance Type:            nonrobust
==============================================================================
```

```
extracted:
cov_type             : nonrobust
nobs                 : 12
R-squared            : 0.8389
R-squared Adj        : 0.8031
F-Statistic          : 23.4340
Prob(F-Statistic)    : 2.70E-04
Log-Likelihood       : -60.6393
aic                  : 127.2785
bic                  : 128.7332
condition_number     : 510.5149
```

33.4.3 The Durbin-Watson (DW) statistic

We compute the DW-statistic, by extracting the appropriate values from the results object, like so:

```
DW = np.sum(np.diff(model.resid.values)**2) / model.ssr
```

Additional information on the Durbin-Watson statistic can be found in Kenton [2023].

```
# confirmation
print_img(model.summary().tables[2])
```

(continues on next page)

(continued from previous page)

```
print('DW-statistic:')
# DW-statistic computed manually
DWa = np.sum(np.diff(model.resid.values)**2) / model.ssr
print(f'DW-statistic (computed)    : {DWa:.4f}')
# DW-statistics from stattools library
DWb = durbin_watson(model.resid)
print(f"DW-statistic (from model) : {DWb:.4f}")
```

```
==============================================================================
Omnibus:                        0.874   Durbin-Watson:                   2.467
Prob(Omnibus):                  0.646   Jarque-Bera (JB):                0.665
Skew:                          -0.500   Prob(JB):                        0.717
Kurtosis:                       2.427   Cond. No.                         511.
==============================================================================
```

```
DW-statistic:
DW-statistic (computed)    : 2.4672
DW-statistic (from model) : 2.4672
```

33.4.4 Renaming regressor variables

```
print('Before:')
print_img(model.summary().tables[1])
print('After:')
print_img(model.summary(
    xname=['const', 'interest',
           'unemployment']).tables[1])
```

```
Before:
```

```
=====================================================================================
                        coef    std err          t      P>|t|      [0.025      0.975]
-------------------------------------------------------------------------------------
interest_rate      -110.0078     25.549     -4.306      0.002    -167.805     -52.211
unemployment_rate   -30.1363    138.334     -0.218      0.832    -343.069     282.797
const              1336.4008    916.320      1.458      0.179    -736.460    3409.261
=====================================================================================
```

```
After:
```

```
================================================================================
                   coef    std err          t      P>|t|      [0.025      0.975]
--------------------------------------------------------------------------------
const         -110.0078     25.549     -4.306      0.002    -167.805     -52.211
interest       -30.1363    138.334     -0.218      0.832    -343.069     282.797
unemployment  1336.4008    916.320      1.458      0.179    -736.460    3409.261
================================================================================
```

Observe the changed names on the regressor variables.

33.4.5 Extract specific values from the model object

To facilitate additional research and investigation, it is helpful to be able to extract specific values from the model object. Here we provide a few examples, like so:

```
# confirmation
print_img(model.summary().tables[1])
# extracted values
print('extracted:')
print('coefficients:'); print(model.params)
print()
print('standard error:'); print(model.bse)
print()
print('tvalues:');print(model.tvalues)
print()
print('pvalues:');print(model.pvalues)
# others
# print('HC0_se:\n', model.HC0_se,'\n')
# print('HC1_se:\n', model.HC1_se,'\n')
# print('HC2_se:\n', model.HC2_se,'\n')
# print('HC3_se:\n', model.HC3_se,'\n')
```

	coef	std err	t	P>|t|	[0.025	0.975]
interest_rate	-110.0078	25.549	-4.306	0.002	-167.805	-52.211
unemployment_rate	-30.1363	138.334	-0.218	0.832	-343.069	282.797
const	1336.4008	916.320	1.458	0.179	-736.460	3409.261

```
extracted:
coefficients:
interest_rate        -110.007849
unemployment_rate     -30.136299
const                1336.400802
dtype: float64

standard error:
interest_rate         25.549470
unemployment_rate    138.333968
const                916.320199
dtype: float64

tvalues:
interest_rate       -4.305680
unemployment_rate   -0.217852
const                1.458443
```

(continues on next page)

(continued from previous page)

```
dtype: float64

pvalues:
interest_rate         0.001974
unemployment_rate     0.832404
const                 0.178715
dtype: float64
```

33.4.6 Statistical evaluation of the model

Evaluating coefficient significance

In the following section, the regressor variables are tested for statistical significance. For that purpose, a Student-t Test is employed.

```
from statsmodels.stats.stattools import durbin_watson
import statsmodels.stats.api as sms

# confirmation
print_img(model.summary().tables[1])
# parameters
alpha = 0.05
# Student-t Test
print('Student-t Test:')
print('level of significance :', alpha)
print('two-tailed test')
print('Hypothesis')
print('H0: parameter is zero')
print('H1: parameter is significantly differs from zero')
df = pd.DataFrame(model.pvalues)
print('results:')
for i, row in df.iterrows():
    if row[0] < alpha/2: # two-tailed test
        print( str(i).ljust(18,' '), ':',
               'reject H0'.ljust(18), 'Significant')
    else:
        print( str(i).ljust(18,' '),':',
               'fail to reject H0'.ljust(18),
               'Not Significant')
```

	coef	std err	t	P>|t|	[0.025	0.975]
interest_rate	-110.0078	25.549	-4.306	0.002	-167.805	-52.211
unemployment_rate	-30.1363	138.334	-0.218	0.832	-343.069	282.797
const	1336.4008	916.320	1.458	0.179	-736.460	3409.261

```
Student-t Test:
level of significance : 0.05
two-tailed test
Hypothesis
H0: parameter is zero
H1: parameter is significantly differs from zero
results:
interest_rate      : reject H0          Significant
unemployment_rate  : fail to reject H0  Not Significant
const              : fail to reject H0  Not Significant
```

Interpretation

The Student-t Test is set up to be a two-tailed test, so we allocate $\frac{\alpha}{2}$ in either fail of the distribution.

Observe that only the `interest_rate` coefficient is reported as statistically significant, at the chosen level of significance $\alpha = 0.05$. The other coefficients are both not significant, which means, that the model is to be revised, to arrive at a more competent regression model to make important predictions with it.

The coefficient of determination

The coefficient of determination is denoted as R^2 and quantifies how well the regression model fits the given data.

```python
import statsmodels.stats.api as sms

# confirmation
print_img(model.summary().tables[0])
# coefficient of determination
print('extracted:')
print(f'R-squared     : {model.rsquared:.4f}')
print(f'R-squared Adj : {model.rsquared_adj:.4f}')
```

```
                            OLS Regression Results
==============================================================================
Dep. Variable:            index_price   R-squared:                       0.839
Model:                            OLS   Adj. R-squared:                  0.803
Method:                 Least Squares   F-statistic:                     23.43
Date:                Tue, 02 Jul 2024   Prob (F-statistic):           0.000270
Time:                        14:01:39   Log-Likelihood:                -60.639
No. Observations:                  12   AIC:                             127.3
Df Residuals:                       9   BIC:                             128.7
Df Model:                           2
Covariance Type:            nonrobust
==============================================================================
```

```
extracted:
R-squared     : 0.8389
R-squared Adj : 0.8031
```

Significance of the regression model as a whole

```
# parameters
alpha = 0.05
# assess the model significance as a whole
print('F-Test:')
print(f'F-Statistic            : {model.fvalue:.6f}')
print(f'Prob(F-Statistic )     : {model.f_pvalue:.6f}')
print(f'level of significance : {alpha:.2f}')
print('two-sided test')
print('Hypothesis')
print('H0: all regressor variables are simultaneously zero')
print('H1: at least on regressor is different from zero')
print('the model as a whole is considered ')
if model.f_pvalue < alpha/2:
    print('Significant')
else:
    print('Not Significant')
```

```
F-Test:
F-Statistic            : 23.433963
Prob(F-Statistic )     : 0.000270
level of significance : 0.05
two-sided test
Hypothesis
H0: all regressor variables are simultaneously zero
H1: at least on regressor is different from zero
the model as a whole is considered
Significant
```

Multicollinearity

A reported condition number of above 30 is considered to indicate the presence of multicollinearity. However, there is no strict cutoff point for this detection, as it depends on the type of data.

```
import statsmodels.stats.api as sms

# check for multicollinearity
print(f'Condition Number : {model.condition_number:.4f}')
print('results:')
```

(continues on next page)

(continued from previous page)

```
if model.condition_number < 30:
    print('No Multicollinearity present')
else:
    print('Multicollinearity present')
```

```
Condition Number : 510.5149
results:
Multicollinearity present
```

Durbin-Watson (DW) Test for Autocorrelation

To check for autocorrelation, we employ the Durbin-Watson Test Kenton [2021].

The Durbin-Watson Test required two cutoff points (DU, DL) to distinguish between positive and negative autocorrelation, there is also an undetermined region in between.

The critical values DL and DU are to be looked up in a critical value table, however in this case we set DL = 2, and DU = 4 and in the following Python code segment, we demonstrate the usage.

```
from statsmodels.stats.stattools import durbin_watson
import statsmodels.stats.api as sms

# autocorrelation
print('Durbin-Watson Test for autocorrelation:')
dw = durbin_watson(model.resid)
print(f'DW-statistic    : {dw:.4f}')
print('DU               :', 4) # fixed values
print('DL               :', 2) # fixed values
print('results:')
if  2 < dw < 4:
    print('Negative autocorrelation')
elif 0 < dw < 2:
    print('Positive autocorrelation')
else:
    print('No autocorrelation')
```

```
Durbin-Watson Test for autocorrelation:
DW-statistic   : 2.4672
DU             : 4
DL             : 2
results:
Negative autocorrelation
```

Jarque-Bera (JB) Test for Normality

To verify the normality of the sample distribution, we make use of the `jarque_bera()` function, which is available from the statsmodels library. It has the following signature:

```
jb_test = sms.jarque_bera(model.resid)
```

where

- `model.resid`: are the residuals from the fitted model

it returns the JB-statistic and the corresponding p_{value}.

To set up the statistical procedure, we formulate:

Hypothesis

- H_0: the data sample is normally distributed
- H_1: the data sample is not normally distributed

level of significance

- $\alpha = 0.05$

The Jarque-Bera Test is set up to be a two-tailed test, so we allocate $\frac{\alpha}{2}$ in either fail of the distribution.

```
import statsmodels.stats.api as sms

# parameters
alpha = 0.05
# check for normality
print('Jarque-Bera Test:')
jb_test = sms.jarque_bera(model.resid)
print(f'JB-statistic          : {jb_test[0]:.4f}')
print(f'JB p-value            : {jb_test[1]:.4f}')
print(f'level of significance : {alpha:.2f}')
print('two-sided test')
print('Hypothesis')
print('H0: data distribution is Normal')
print('H1: data distribution is Not Normal')
if jb_test[1] < alpha/2:
    print('reject H0')
    print('Not Normal')
else:
    print('fail to reject H0')
    print('Normal')
```

```
Jarque-Bera Test:
JB-statistic          : 0.6646
```

(continues on next page)

(continued from previous page)

```
JB p-value              : 0.7173
level of significance : 0.05
two-sided test
Hypothesis
H0: data distribution is Normal
H1: data distribution is Not Normal
fail to reject H0
Normal
```

Interpretation

The JB-statistic is reported as 0.6646 and the corresponding p_{value} is 0.7173.

Since the $p_{value} > \frac{\alpha}{2} = 0.025$, we fail to reject the null hypothesis H_0. The data provides sufficient evidence to conclude that indeed the distribution of the sample is normal. We can make this claim with (1-α) or 95% confidence.

33.4.7 Make predictions using the fitted model

Given are the two input variables $x1 = 2.20$ and $x2 = 7.15$ for the upcoming period. We can use these inputs, and use the fitted model to make a prediction, like so:

$$y(x1, x2) = \beta_0 + \beta_1 \cdot x1 + \beta_2 \cdot x2$$

now we insert the values.

$$y = 1336.4 + (-110.01 \cdot 2.15) + (-30.136 \cdot 7.15) = 878.91$$

In Python we have.

```
print_img(model.summary().tables[1])
# results
print('prediction:')
p = model.predict([2.20, 7.15, 1])[0] # 1 for the const
print(f'y(x=2.20, x2=7.15, const=1.00) = {p:.2f}')
```

	coef	std err	t	P>|t|	[0.025	0.975]
interest_rate	-110.0078	25.549	-4.306	0.002	-167.805	-52.211
unemployment_rate	-30.1363	138.334	-0.218	0.832	-343.069	282.797
const	1336.4008	916.320	1.458	0.179	-736.460	3409.261

```
prediction:
y(x=2.20, x2=7.15, const=1.00) = 878.91
```

Interpretation

We applied both the sklearn and statsmodels library methods to perform linear regression analysis and arrived at similar results.

Please note that, before applying any type of linear regression model, we must make sure that a linear relationship indeed exists between the independent features and the dependent variable. This is one of the underlying assumptions of linear regression. If the assumptions are not met, the computed results might be biased and therefore unreliable in making predictions.

CHAPTER 34

COOK'S DISTANCE

Cook's distance quantifies the level of influence each individual data observation has on the regression model, by measuring how much all fitted values of the model vary when the ith observation is omitted. This is much like sensitivity analysis.

- Cook's Distance
- Calculate Critical Value
- Visualize: Example without outliers
- Visualize: Example with outliers
- Inspect the summary_frame report
- Read summary_table and report as an image
- Convert summary_table report into Pandas DataFrame
- Extract specific values from the OLSInfluence object
- Inspect highly influential and outlier observations

Cook's distance D_i can be used in regression analysis to identify potential outliers in a set of observations. It can identify data points that have a significant impact on the regression model and its estimates.

Cook's measure is a combination of each observation's leverage and residuals, forming the Cook's distance value, as discussed in Cook [1977].

The procedure to calculate each Cook's D_i is by temporarily removing the ith data point from the dataset and recomputing the regression model. It summarizes how much all values in the regression model change when the ith observation is removed. More precisely, Cook's distance D_i measures how much the remaining fitted values in the model vary, when the ith observation is omitted. It can be computed using this formula.

Cook's distance equation:

$$D_i = \frac{\sum_{j=1}^{n}(\hat{Y}_j - \widehat{Y_{j(i)}})^2}{(p+1)\cdot\hat{\sigma}^2}$$

where

- $\hat{Y}$: is the jth estimate
- $\hat{Y}_{j(i)}$: is the fitted response value obtained while excluding i
- p: is the rank of the model
- $\hat{\sigma}^2$: is the mean squared error of the regression

In the following Python code section, this approach is implemented.

34.1 Fit the linear regression model

We fit a simple linear regression model on a small dataset, to arrive at a valid linear regression `model` object.

```
import statsmodels.api as sm
import pandas as pd

# DataFrame
df_normal = pd.DataFrame({
    'x': [8, 12, 12, 13, 14, 16, 17, 22, 24, 26, 29, 30],
    'y': [41, 42, 39, 37, 35, 39, 45, 46, 39, 49, 55, 54]})
# dataset
y = df_normal['y']
x = df_normal['x']
x = sm.add_constant(x) # required by statsmodels
# fit
model = sm.OLS(y, x).fit()
```

Before using the `get_influence()` method and the `cooks_distance` property, we might want to bring up the documentation.

```
# print(help(model.get_influence()))
```

34.2 Test Cook's distance for significance

To compute Cook's distance for each observation in the dataset, we make use of the `get_influence()` method of the regression model and extract the relevant values by supplying the `cooks_distance` property. In return, we receive an array of values for the Cook's distance of each observation, along with an array of corresponding p_{values}. To set up the statistical procedure, we formulate:

Hypothesis

- H_0: cooks value is significantly influential
- H_1: cooks value is not significantly influential

level of significance

- $\alpha = 0.05$
- one-sided test

We are using the `get_influence()` method from the statsmodels library, to extract the values by providing the `cooks_distance` property to it. The signature is:

```
res = model.get_influence().cooks_distance
```

It returns an array for the distances as well as an array of corresponding p values. The higher the Cook's distance D_i is, the higher its impact is the regression results. Any observation with a D_i above $D_{critical}$ is deemed highly influential.

In the following Python code segment, the cook's distances are computed and the results are presented.

```
import numpy as np

# Suppress scientific notation
np.set_printoptions(suppress=True)
# extract cooks values and pvalues
cooks = model.get_influence().cooks_distance
# parameters
alpha = 0.05
print('cooks distances:')
for i in range(len(cooks[0])):
    d = cooks[0][i]
    p = cooks[1][i]
    if (cooks[1][i] < alpha):
        print(f'dist.: {d:.4f} pvalue: {p:.3f} significant')
    else:
        print(f'dist.: {d:.4f} pvalue: {p:.3f} not significant')
```

```
cooks distances:
dist.: 0.3603 pvalue: 0.706 not significant
dist.: 0.0631 pvalue: 0.939 not significant
dist.: 0.0002 pvalue: 1.000 not significant
dist.: 0.0329 pvalue: 0.968 not significant
dist.: 0.1186 pvalue: 0.889 not significant
dist.: 0.0225 pvalue: 0.978 not significant
dist.: 0.0217 pvalue: 0.979 not significant
dist.: 0.0001 pvalue: 1.000 not significant
dist.: 0.3378 pvalue: 0.721 not significant
dist.: 0.0012 pvalue: 0.999 not significant
dist.: 0.2618 pvalue: 0.775 not significant
dist.: 0.1215 pvalue: 0.887 not significant
```

Interpretation

The test is set up to be a one-tailed test, so we allocate $\frac{\alpha}{2}$ in either tail of the distribution.

We make use of the returned p_{value} to determine if each observation is significantly greater than $\frac{\alpha}{2}$ of 0.025. According to the reported p_{values}, we conclude that none of the observations in our model are statistically significant.

A more visual approach to determining if an observation is to be further investigated is taken.

34.3 Calculate the D-critical value

The $D_{critical}$ value is used as a threshold, indicated by the red line in the following plots.

There are variations of the formulas to compute the critical value, although the differences are minor in particular with larger n, we use the one suggested by Algiers University [2020].

Compute the $D_{critical}$ value:

$$D_{critical} = \frac{4}{n - k - 1}$$

where

- n: number of observations
- k: number of predictor variables
- -1: for the intercept term

```
print('results:')
print(f'nobs (n)      : {model.nobs:.0f}')
print(f'df_model (k) : {model.df_model:.0f}')
print(f'df_resid      : {model.df_resid:.0f}')
d_critical = 4 / (model.nobs - model.df_model - 1)
print(f'd_critical    : {d_critical:.2f}')
```

```
results:
nobs (n)     : 12
df_model (k) : 1
df_resid     : 10
d_critical   : 0.40
```

34.4 Visualize an example dataset without outliers

We can create a scatter plot to visualize Cook's distance. The red line is set to be $D_{critical}$ and indicates the threshold at which an observation deserves further scrutiny. For additional examples see Wikipedia [2023].

```
import matplotlib.pyplot as plt

# plot
fig = plt.figure(figsize=(8,3.3))
markerline, stemlines, baseline = plt.stem(df_normal.x,
            cooks[0], markerfmt='D', linefmt='grey')
stemlines.set_linewidth(3)
baseline.set_ydata( [d_critical] ) # as list
plt.title('Cooks distance, no outliers',
          fontsize=12)
plt.xlabel('x-values')
plt.ylabel('distances')
plt.tight_layout = True
plt.ylim(0.0, 0.6)
plt.grid(True)
plt.show()
```

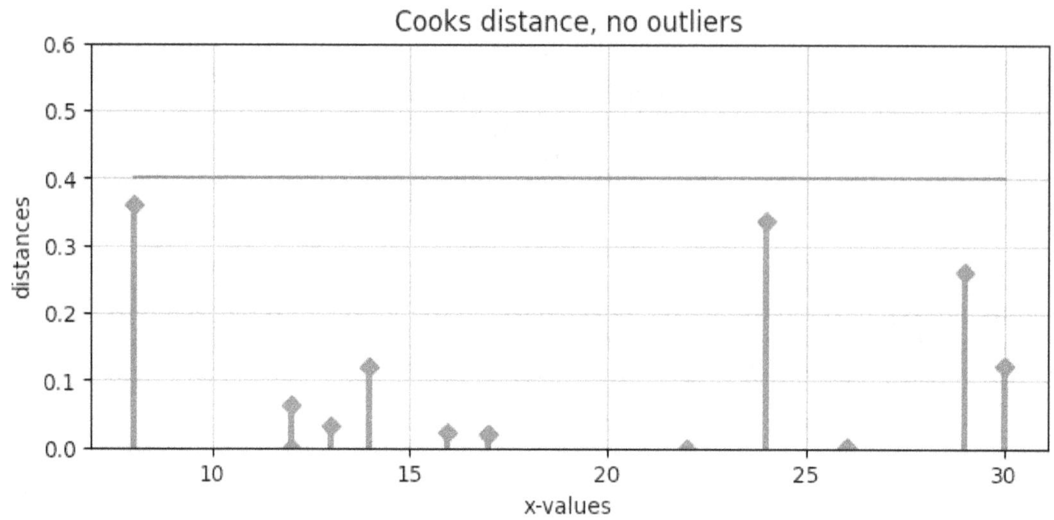

Interpretation

Any data point above $D_{critical}$ should be carefully scrutinized. Additionally, any value that significantly sticks out from the others is to be scrutinized as well.

If the current model reports many data points with abnormal D_i values, that could be an indication that the regression model is not correctly specified.

34.5 Visualize an example dataset with outliers

We altered the dataset and introduced a relatively large outlier observation. Observe the value 100, as the $8th$ y-value. In the following code example, we recompute and visualize the results, like so:

```
import statsmodels.api as sm
import pandas as pd
import numpy as np
import matplotlib.pyplot as plt
np.set_printoptions(suppress=True)

# DataFrame
df_outliers = pd.DataFrame({
    'x': [13, 12, 14, 16, 17, 18, 20, 21, 22, 15, 23, 19],
    'y': [48, 22, 39, 18, 35, 39, 40, 100, 31, 49, 50, 11]
    })
# fit model
y = df_outliers['y']
x = df_outliers['x']
x = sm.add_constant(x) # required by statsmodels
model = sm.OLS(y, x).fit()
# critical value
```

(continues on next page)

(continued from previous page)

```
d_critical = 4 / (model.nobs - model.df_model - 1)
# compute cooks' values
cooks = model.get_influence().cooks_distance
# plot
fig = plt.figure(figsize=(8,3.3))
markerline, stemlines, baseline = plt.stem(df_outliers.x,
                cooks[0], markerfmt='D', linefmt='grey')
stemlines.set_linewidth(3)
baseline.set_ydata( [d_critical] ) # as list
plt.title('Cooks distance with outliers',
          fontsize=12)
plt.xlabel('x-values')
plt.ylabel('distances')
plt.tight_layout = True
plt.grid(True)
plt.show()
```

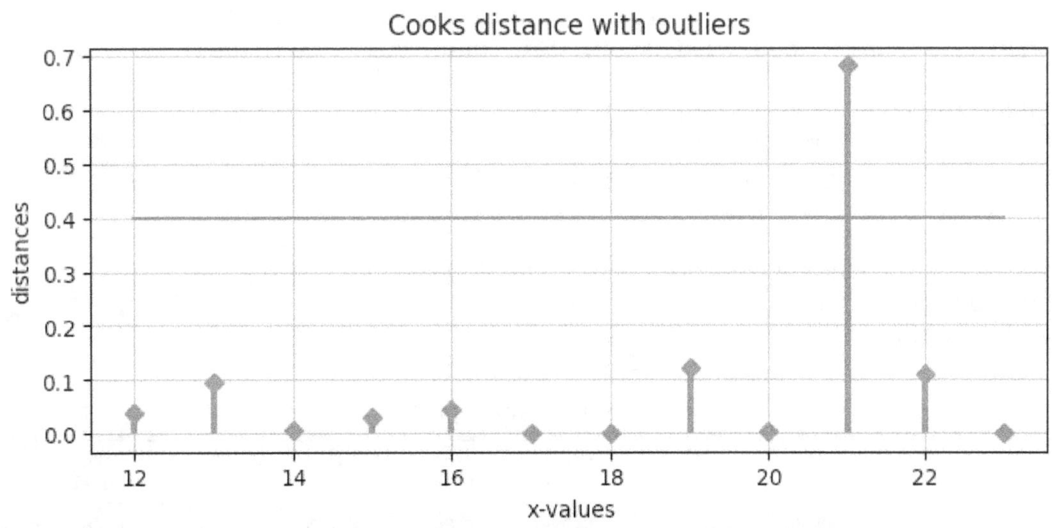

Interpretation

The single outstanding observation is to be investigated, to make sure that this is not an erroneous data point.

34.6 The summary_table report

In the following section we discuss the `summary_table`, reported by the `get_influence()` method, which has the following signature:

```
inf = model.get_influence().summary_table()
```

it returns a table of quantitative metrics to determine the level of influence a given data observation has on the regression estimates.

In the following Python code section, this analysis is implemented and the summary report is presented.

34.6.1 Read summary_table and save it as an image file

At times it is helpful to save the produced report as an image file, for further reporting and visualization.

```
import matplotlib.pyplot as plt

# plot
as_text = model.get_influence().summary_table().as_text()
fig = plt.figure(figsize=(6.4,3.2))
bbox = fig.get_window_extent().transformed(
                        fig.dpi_scale_trans.inverted())
width, height = bbox.width*fig.dpi, bbox.height*fig.dpi
# text
plt.figtext(0.6,0.87,'summary report',
            fontsize=14,
            horizontalalignment ="center")
plt.figtext(0.0, 0.0,
            str(as_text), {'fontsize':10},
            fontproperties='monospace')
plt.axis('off')
plt.show()
```

summary report

obs	endog	fitted value	Cook's d	student. residual	hat diag	dffits internal	ext.stud. residual	dffits
0	48.000	31.985	0.094	0.803	0.225	0.433	0.788	0.424
1	22.000	30.167	0.039	-0.429	0.295	-0.278	-0.411	-0.266
2	39.000	33.803	0.006	0.252	0.169	0.114	0.240	0.108
3	18.000	37.439	0.045	-0.904	0.099	-0.300	-0.895	-0.297
4	35.000	39.258	0.002	-0.197	0.085	-0.060	-0.187	-0.057
5	39.000	41.076	0.000	-0.096	0.085	-0.029	-0.091	-0.028
6	40.000	44.712	0.004	-0.223	0.127	-0.085	-0.212	-0.081
7	100.000	46.530	0.682	2.590	0.169	1.168	4.282	1.931
8	31.000	48.348	0.110	-0.870	0.225	-0.469	-0.859	-0.463
9	49.000	35.621	0.029	0.632	0.127	0.241	0.612	0.234
10	50.000	50.167	0.000	-0.009	0.295	-0.006	-0.008	-0.005
11	11.000	42.894	0.121	-1.484	0.099	-0.492	-1.594	-0.529

34.6.2 Load the summary_table report into a Pandas DataFrame

At times it is very convenient to have reports in DataFrame format, for further processing and analysis.

```
from pandas import read_csv
import os

# store output in a string variable
data_string = model.get_influence().summary_table().as_csv()
# write to temporary file
with open('summary_report.csv', 'w', encoding='utf-8') as f:
    f.write(data_string)
# read temp file into DataFrame
df = pd.read_csv('summary_report.csv',
                 index_col=None, header=0)
# remove temporary files
os.remove("summary_report.csv")
# inspect
print(df.info())
print(df.shape)
```

```
<class 'pandas.core.frame.DataFrame'>
RangeIndex: 13 entries, 0 to 12
Data columns (total 9 columns):
 #   Column                  Non-Null Count  Dtype
---  ------                  --------------  -----
 0   obs                     13 non-null     object
 1   endog                   13 non-null     object
 2         fitted            13 non-null     object
 3           Cook's          13 non-null     object
 4          student.         13 non-null     object
 5         hat diag          13 non-null     object
 6          dffits           13 non-null     object
 7         ext.stud.         13 non-null     object
 8           dffits          13 non-null     object
dtypes: object(9)
memory usage: 1.0+ KB
None
(13, 9)
```

34.6.3 Extract specific line items from the OLSInfluence object

It is at times beneficial to be able to extract specific values from the provided OLSInfluence object. Here we provide a few examples:

```
# OLSInfluence object
print(type(model.get_influence()))
# extracted values
print('extracted:')
print(f'nobs  : {model.get_influence().nobs:.0f}')
print(f'scale : {model.get_influence().scale:.4f}')
print('cooks distance:')
print(model.get_influence().cooks_distance[0])
print('cooks pvalues:')
print(model.get_influence().cooks_distance[1])
print('cov_ratio:')
print(model.get_influence().cov_ratio)
# others values
# print(model.get_influence().det_cov_params_not_obsi)
# print(model.get_influence().dfbeta)
# print(model.get_influence().dffits)
# print(model.get_influence().endog)
# print(model.get_influence().exog)
```

```
<class 'statsmodels.stats.outliers_influence.OLSInfluence'>
extracted:
nobs  : 12
scale : 512.8939
cooks distance:
[0.09362802 0.0385593  0.00644346 0.04496298 0.00179613 0.00042694
 0.00360849 0.68207811 0.10986689 0.02908882 0.00001606 0.12103361]
cooks pvalues:
[0.91141021 0.96231698 0.99358138 0.95622502 0.9982058  0.99957317
 0.99639931 0.52761122 0.89701991 0.97141206 0.99998394 0.88728245]
cov_ratio:
[1.39395526 1.68686122 1.46686837 1.15535787 1.33896996 1.34689796
 1.40023922 0.16101362 1.3608048  1.30341773 1.75081486 0.83340754]
```

34.7 The summary_frame report

34.7.1 Load the summary_frame report into a Pandas DataFrame

```
# DataFrame
df_summary_frame = model.get_influence().summary_frame()
# inspect
print(df_summary_frame.info())
```

```
<class 'pandas.core.frame.DataFrame'>
RangeIndex: 12 entries, 0 to 11
Data columns (total 8 columns):
 #   Column           Non-Null Count  Dtype
---  ------           --------------  -----
 0   dfb_const        12 non-null     float64
 1   dfb_x            12 non-null     float64
 2   cooks_d          12 non-null     float64
 3   standard_resid   12 non-null     float64
 4   hat_diag         12 non-null     float64
 5   dffits_internal  12 non-null     float64
 6   student_resid    12 non-null     float64
 7   dffits           12 non-null     float64
dtypes: float64(8)
memory usage: 896.0 bytes
None
```

34.7.2 Extract values from the OlSInfluence object

We can extract the values from the OLSInfluence object directly into a Pandas DataFrame, for further processing, it has the following signature:

```
df = model.get_influence().summary_frame()[['cooks_d',
                                            'standard_resid']]
```

Note that we can pass in a Python list of names we want to extract. In Python, we demonstrate this approach, like so:

```
# DataFrame
df = model.get_influence().summary_frame()[['cooks_d',
                                            'standard_resid']]
# inspect
print(type(df))
print('influence:')
print(df)
```

```
<class 'pandas.core.frame.DataFrame'>
influence:

    cooks_d  standard_resid
0  0.093628        0.803249
1  0.038559       -0.429435
2  0.006443        0.251730
3  0.044963       -0.904321
4  0.001796       -0.196543
5  0.000427       -0.095823
```

(continues on next page)

(continued from previous page)

```
6   0.003608        -0.222692
7   0.682078         2.589959
8   0.109867        -0.870123
9   0.029089         0.632275
10  0.000016        -0.008764
11  0.121034        -1.483707
```

34.8 Scrutinize outlier and highly influential observations

We advise against the automated deleting of highly influential observations since an in-depth analysis of such data points might reveal aspects previously overlooked.

The researcher should scrutinize such outlier observations and determine if they are valid data points, a result of data entry errors, or some other mistake. If it turns out to be a valid observation, we can either decide if it is appropriate to remove the data point, keep it, or replace it with for example the the mean or median value. Of course, such changes in the data set depend on the particular circumstances and the importance of the decisions to be made by the regression model.

Part IV

Appendix

CHAPTER 35

DATASETS USED

"Advertising_200rows.csv"

Description:

The Advertising budget for a fictitious company, launching Ads on TV, Radio and Newspapers. We want to statistically assess the level of advertising on the sales volume of the company.

Ref.: 730
Links: https://www.kaggle.com/datasets/ashydv/advertising-dataset

---

"Longley dataset"

Description:

The Longley dataset is available a the statsmodels repository. from statsmodels.datasets.longley import load_pandas. data = load_pandas().

Ref.: 760
Author: Longley
Bibliography: Longley [1967]

"unemployment_rate interest_rate index_price"

Description:

The dataset is compiled from OECD data and added random index prices.

Ref.: 760
Links:
https://data.oecd.org/unemp/unemployment-rate.htm#indicator-chart
https://data.oecd.org/interest/long-term-interest-rates.htm

"randomly generated dataset"

Description:

rv = random.normalvariate(mu,sigma), as random data set.

Ref.: 219

"randomly generated dataset"

temp = random.normalvariate(mu=m, sigma=s). The data is generated as random data set.

"random sample data"

Description:

We record 12 observation of students preparation for a final exam. The study hours, the number of preparation exams taken, and the final score is recorded. The data is crated as random data set.

Ref.: 264

"random sample data"

Description:

The dat set consists of 16 observations. The data is created as random data set.

Ref.: 272

"random sample data"

Description:

The data set consists of 10 observations in three categories (a, b, c). The data is created as random data set.

Ref.: 272

"sample data with missing data"

Description:

The data set consists of 10 observations in three categories (a, b). The data is created as random data set.

Ref.: 272

"random sample dataset"

Description:

A survey of 10 students and their grades in tree subjects (math, science, history) are records. The dataset is created as random data set.

Ref.: 276

"gender vs ice-cream flavor preference"

Description:

A survey of 250 customers at an ice-cream shop, with their choices (vanilla, chocolate, others) recorded, to study the data set for independence of such variables.

Ref.: 282

"quarter of residence versus occupation type"

Description:

A random sample of 150 residents of the large city is taken from each Quarter of the city. The occupation of each subject is recorded in one of the categories ("white collar", "blue collar", "no collar") and the quarter of residence in the categories ("North Quarter, East Quarter, South Quarter, West Quarter). The survey is adapted from the example given at Wikipedia.

Ref.: 282
Links: https://en.wikipedia.org/wiki/Chi-squared_test
Bibliography: Wikipedia [2023]

"Moore Car dataset"

Description:

The Moore data frame has 45 rows and 4 columns. The data are for subjects in a social-psychological experiment, who were faced with manipulated disagreement from a partner of either of low or high status. The subjects could either conform to the partner's judgment or stick with their own judgment.

Ref.: 286
Author: Fox, J. and Weisberg, S.
Bibliography: Fox and Weisberg [2019]

"Guerry.csv"

Description:

> The dataset is available as part of the rdataset repository of the statsmodels library. The Guerry dataset, a collection of historical data used in support of Andre-Michel Guerry's 1833 Essay on the Moral Statistics of France.

Ref.: 290
Author: Guerry
Links: https://raw.githubusercontent.com/vincentarelbundock/Rdatasets/master/csv/HistData/Guerry.csv
Bibliography:

"Sunspots dataset"

Description:

> The Sunspots dataset is provided by the statsmodels data repository. It contains annual data on sunspot activity for the years 1700 until 2008. The data is published by the National Geophysical Data Center. The data is available from the Statsmodels data library.

Ref.: 294
Links: https://ngdc.noaa.gov/stp/solar/ssndata.html
Bibliography: Center [2023]

"historical closing prices on SPY"

Description:

> We recorded historical trading data for the S&P500 index (SPY). It covers (data, open, high, low, close, volume) entries. Data recorded from Yahoo Finance.

Ref.: 410
Links: http://finance.yahoo.com
Bibliography: YahooFinance [2023]

"unemployment_rate vs index_price"

Description:

The dataset is compiled from OECD data, and random index prices are added. The dataset has 10 observation for unemployment_rate and index_price.

Ref.: 420
Author: Self
Links: https://data.oecd.org/unemp/unemployment-rate.htm#indicator-chart https://data.oecd.org/interest/long-term-interest-rates.htm
Bibliography: OECDTeam [2023]

"unemployment_rate vs index"

Description:

The dataset is compiled from OECD data, and random index prices are added. The dataset has 10 observations for unemployment_rate and index_price.

Ref.: 420
Links: https://data.oecd.org/unemp/unemployment-rate.htm#indicator-chart https://data.oecd.org/interest/long-term-interest-rates.htm
Bibliography: OECDTeam [2023]

"country vs gdp_per_capita dataset"

Description:

A small survey of gross domestic product per capita is conduction. It cover 8 countries and their respective GDP is recorded. The data is compiled from data provided be the Worldbank.

Ref.: 420
Links: https://data.worldbank.org/indicator/NY.GDP.PCAP.CD
Source: Worldbank [2023]

"random sample dataset"

Description:

Our job queue of jobs to be processed show the results in three states (pending, ongoing, completed). The total number of jobs is 647 jobs queue status data. The data created at random.

Ref.: 420

"SPY_20110701_20120630_Bollinger.csv"

Description:

We compiled historical trading data for the SPY symbol with Bollinger bands added. Data recorded from Yahoo Finance. It contains 252 daily bars.

Ref.: 440
Links: http://finance.yahoo.com

"SP500_NOV2019_IDay.csv"

1563 data rows in 5 columns.

Description:

Data recorded from Yahoo Finance.

Ref.: 440
Source: Yahoo Finance
Links: http://finance.yahoo.com

"yahoofinance-SPY-20080101-20180101.csv"

2519 Daily bars of SPY.

Description:

Data recorded from Yahoo Finance.

Ref.: 440
Source: Yahoo Finance
Links: http://finance.yahoo.com

"random sample dataset"

Description:

random data set.

Ref.: 470

"random three roc curves"

Description:

random data set.

Ref.: 470

"three random ROC curves"

Description:

A collection of specificity and sensitivity data of a logistic classifier application is recorded, in order to study the Receiver Operation Response (ROC) curve of each sample, we generated a random data set.

Ref.: 470

"Pima-Indians-Diabetes.data"

Description:

> The dataset consists of 8 feature variable and one binary class as target variable. The Diabetes dataset is available from the Sklean data repository. data = datasets.load_diabetes(), it has 768 records, 8 features and 1 target.

Ref.: 485, 740
Links:
https://raw.githubusercontent.com/jbrownlee/Datasets/master/pima-indians-diabetes.data.csv

BIBLIOGRAPHY

[1] Mohamed Nachid Boussiala Algiers University. Cooks distance. ():, 2020. URL: https://www.researchgate.net/publication/344522968_Cook's_Distance, doi:10.13140/RG.2.2.18888.55049.

[2] Ashish. Advertizing dataset. ():3, 2019. URL: https://www.kaggle.com/datasets/ashydv/advertising-dataset.

[3] National Geophysical Data Center. International sunspot number. ():8, 2023. URL: http://www.ngdc.noaa.gov/stp/solar/solarda3.html.

[4] Kku et al Chire, Wikipit. Roc-curve. ():8, 2023. URL: https://de.wikipedia.org/wiki/ROC-Kurve.

[5] R. Dennis Cook. *Detection of Influential Observations in Linear Regression*. American Statistical Association, 1977. ISBN.

[6] Gaäl de Mondragon. Human height. ():8, 2021. URL: https://distributionofthings.com/human-height/.

[7] Andreas Deak. How to get the data array from scatter_matrix. ():8, 2017. URL: https://stackoverflow.com/questions/47967734/how-to-get-the-data-array-from-scatter-matrix.

[8] Daniele Faraglia. Using the faker class. ():8, 2014. URL: https://faker.readthedocs.io/en/master/fakerclass.html.

[9] Tom Fawcett. *ROC Graphs: Notes and Practical Considerations for Data Mining Researchers*. In: Pattern Recognition Letters. 31. Jahrgang, Nr. 8. HP Laboratories, Palo Alto, 2003. ISBN. URL:.

[10] J. Fox. *Applied Regression Analysis and Generalized Linear Models, Third Ed*. Sage, 2016. ISBN.

[11] J. Fox and Weisberg. An r companion to applied, regression, third edition. ():, 2019. URL:.

[12] Jim Frost. *Regression Analysis: An Intuitive Guide for Using and Interpreting Linear Models*. StatisticsByJim.com, 2020. ISBN 978-1735431185. URL:.

[13] & Mallery George, D. Ibm spss statistics 23 step by step: a simple guide and reference. ():8, 2023. URL: https://doi.org/10.4324/9781315545899.

[14] W. Greene. *Econometric Analysis, 5th Edition*. 2003.

[15] Darren Dale et al John Hunter. Matplotlib.pyplot.subplot. ():8, 2012. URL: https://matplotlib.org/stable/api/_as_gen/matplotlib.pyplot.subplot.html.

[16] et.al. John Hunter, Darren Dale. Customizing matplotlib with style sheets and rcparams. ():8, 2012. URL: https://matplotlib.org/stable/tutorials/introductory/customizing.html.

[17] et.al. John Hunter, Darren Dale. Funcanimation. ():8, 2012. URL: https://matplotlib.org/stable/api/_as_gen/matplotlib.animation.FuncAnimation.html.

[18] William C. Black Joseph F. Hair Jr. *Multivariate Data Analysis 7th Edition*. Pearson, 2022. ISBN 978-0138132637. URL:.

[19] Will Kenton. Durbin watson test. ():, 2021. URL: https://www.investopedia.com/terms/d/durbin-watson-statistic.asp.

[20] Will Kenton. Durbin watson test. ():1, 2023. URL: https://www.investopedia.com/terms/d/durbin-watson-statistic.asp.

[21] J.W. Longley. *An Appraisal of Least Squares Programs for the Electronic Computer from the Point of View of the User.* Journal of the American Statistical Association, 1967. ISBN. URL: http://www.itl.nist.gov/div898/strd/lls/data/Longley.shtml.

[22] N.N. Matplotlib. Colormaps in matplotlib. ():8, 2023. URL: https://matplotlib.org/stable/tutorials/colors/colormaps.html.

[23] Jr. Moore, J. C. and E. Krupat. *Relationship between source status, authoritarianism and conformity in a social setting*. Sociometry 34, 1971. ISBN.

[24] N.N. Mplfinance. Plot examples with mplfinance. ():8, 2023. URL: https://github.com/matplotlib/mplfinance/tree/master/examples.

[25] NumpyDocs. Numpy.polyfit. ():3, 2023. URL: https://numpy.org/doc/stable/reference/generated/numpy.polyfit.html.

[26] Oecd. Unemployment rate data. ():1, 2023. URL: https://data.oecd.org/unemp/unemployment-rate.htm#indicator-chart.

[27] OECDTeam. Unemployment rate historical data. ():8, 2023. URL: https://data.oecd.org/unemp/unemployment-rate.htm#indicator-chart.

[28] PandasDocs. Kernel density estimate. ():3, 2023. URL: https://pandas.pydata.org/docs/reference/api/pandas.DataFrame.plot.kde.html.

[29] N.N. PandasDocs. Dataframe.plot.barh. ():8, 2023. URL: https://pandas.pydata.org/docs/reference/api/pandas.DataFrame.plot.barh.html#pandas.DataFrame.plot.barh.

[30] N.N. PandasDocs. Dataframe.plot.box. ():8, 2023. URL: https://pandas.pydata.org/docs/reference/api/pandas.DataFrame.plot.box.html.

[31] N.N. PandasDocs. Pandas.dataframe.plot.kde. ():8, 2023. URL: https://pandas.pydata.org/docs/reference/api/pandas.DataFrame.plot.kde.html.

[32] ScikitDocs. Sklearn.metrics.r2_score. ():3, 2023. URL: https://scikit-learn.org/stable/modules/generated/sklearn.metrics.r2_score.html.

[33] Scipy. Integrate quad. ():1, 2023. URL: https://docs.scipy.org/doc/scipy/reference/generated/scipy.integrate.quad.html.

[34] SciPyDocs. Norm function. ():1, 2023. URL: https://docs.scipy.org/doc/scipy/reference/generated/scipy.stats.norm.html.

[35] Everhart J.E. et al Smith J.W. Pima indians diabetes database. ():8, 1988. URL: https://www.kaggle.com/datasets/uciml/pima-indians-diabetes-database.

[36] Statista. Quantile. ():1, 2023. URL: https://de.statista.com/statistik/lexikon/definition/106/quantil/.

[37] Statsmodels. Regressionresults. ():5, 2023. URL: https://www.statsmodels.org/devel/generated/statsmodels.regression.linear_model.RegressionResults.html.

[38] Statsmodels. Rsquared. ():1, 2023. URL: https://www.statsmodels.org/stable/generated/statsmodels.regression.linear_model.OLSResults.rsquared.html.

[39] N.N. Statsmodels. Olsinfluence. ():6, 2023. URL: https://www.statsmodels.org/devel/generated/statsmodels.stats.outliers_influence.OLSInfluence.html.

[40] N.N. Statsmodels. Regression diagnostics and specification tests. ():8, 2023. URL: https://www.statsmodels.org/stable/diagnostic.html.

[41] N.N. Statsmodels. Graphics. ():8, 2023. URL: https://www.statsmodels.org/stable/graphics.html.

[42] StatsmodelsDocs. F-test. ():1, 2023. URL: https://www.statsmodels.org/dev/generated/statsmodels.regression.linear_model.OLSResults.f_test.html.

[43] StatsmodelsDocs. Get robust cov results. ():1, 2023. URL: https://www.statsmodels.org/devel/generated/statsmodels.regression.linear_model.OLSResults.get_robustcov_results.html.

[44] StatsmodelsDocs. Predictionresults.conf_int. ():1, 2023. URL: https://www.statsmodels.org/dev/generated/statsmodels.regression.linear_model.PredictionResults.conf_int.html#statsmodels.regression.linear_model.PredictionResults.conf_int.

[45] StatsmodelsDocs. Regressionresults. ():1, 2023. URL: https://www.statsmodels.org/devel/generated/statsmodels.regression.linear_model.RegressionResults.html.

[46] StatsmodelsDocs. Summary results. ():1, 2023. URL: https://www.statsmodels.org/dev/generated/statsmodels.regression.linear_model.OLSResults.summary.html.

[47] N.N. Study.com. Height of men have a bell shaped distribution with a mean of 178 cm and a standard deviation of 7. ():1, 2023. URL: https://homework.study.com/explanation/height-of-men-have-a-bell-shaped-distribution.html.

[48] Wikipedia. Cooks distance. ():, 2023. URL: https://en.wikipedia.org/wiki/Cook%27s_distance.

[49] Wikipedia. Curve fitting. (1):, 2023. URL: https://en.wikipedia.org/wiki/Curve_fitting.

[50] Wikipedia. Polynomial interpolation. ():1, 2023. URL: https://en.wikipedia.org/wiki/Polynomial_interpolation.

[51] N.N. Wikipedia. Example chi-squared test for categorical data. ():4, 2023. URL: https://en.wikipedia.org/wiki/Chi-squared_test.

[52] Worldbank. Gdp per capita, current us$, all countries and economies. ():8, 2023. URL: https://data.worldbank.org/indicator/NY.GDP.PCAP.CD?locations=AT.

[53] YahooFinance. Yahoo finance historical quotes. ():1, 2023. URL: https://finance.yahoo.com.

INDEX

D

Q

R

S

T

www.ingramcontent.com/pod-product-compliance
Lightning Source LLC
LaVergne TN
LVHW082027200926
848481LV00010B/2933
* 9 7 9 8 2 2 4 2 5 0 5 3 0 *